Publishing and Cultural Politics in Revolutionary Paris, 1789–1810

Studies on the History of Society and Culture
Victoria E. Bonnell and Lynn Hunt, Editors

Publishing and Cultural Politics in Revolutionary Paris, 1789–1810

CARLA HESSE

UNIVERSITY OF CALIFORNIA PRESS

Berkeley   Los Angeles   Oxford

University of California Press
Berkeley and Los Angeles, California

University of California Press, Ltd.
Oxford, England

Copyright ©1991 by
The Regents of the University of California

Library of Congress Cataloging-in-Publication Data
Hesse, Carla.
    Publishing and cultural politics in revolutionary Paris, 1789–1810
/ Carla Hesse.
        p.   cm. — (Studies on the history of society and culture)
    Includes bibliographical references and index.
    ISBN 0-520-07443-2 (alk. paper)
    1. Publishers and publishing—Political aspects—France—Paris—
History—18th century.   2. Publishers and publishing—Political
aspects—France—Paris—History—19th century.   3. Revolutionary
literature—Publishing—France—Paris—History.   4. France—History—
Revolution, 1789–1799—Literature and the revolution.   5. Paris
(France)—History—Consulate and Empire, 1799–1815.   6. Paris
(France)—History—Revolution, 1789–1799.   I. Title.   II. Series.
Z310.6.P37H47   1991
070.5′094436—dc20   90-26493
                                                                          CIP

Printed in the United States of America

1 2 3 4 5 6 7 8 9

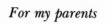

For my parents

In order to mobilize a general insurrection against absolutist governments, it was necessary to enlighten people continuously, not through voluminous and well reasoned books which they do not read, but through short works, . . . through a newspaper that would spread light in all directions. . . . [I] imagined that the project of spreading great political principles in France could be achieved easily if intrepid friends, enlightened by liberty, could unite, communicate their ideas to one another, and compose their works someplace where they could have them printed and circulated throughout the world.

JACQUES-PIERRE BRISSOT DE WARVILLE

CONTENTS

LIST OF ILLUSTRATIONS

Map

Plates

Figures

LIST OF TABLES

ACKNOWLEDGMENTS

The research for this book would not have been possible without generous financial support from the French government through the Bourse Châteaubriand, the Fulbright-Hayes Foundation, the Alliance Franco-Américain, and the Fribourg Foundation. Rutgers University, the history departments at Princeton University and the University of California, Berkeley, and the American Council of Learned Societies funded leave time from teaching duties for me to write and revise the manuscript. To these foundations and institutions I extend my gratitude.

I owe thanks as well to the many people who helped to make this book possible: first of all to Robert Darnton, Natalie Z. Davis, and Lawrence Stone, who have been continuous sources of guidance, dialogue, and criticism since this project began eight years ago as a graduate seminar paper at Princeton University. I doubt that there are finer mentors anywhere. I also owe a special debt to Lynn Hunt for her generous and challenging responses to my work over the years. Among the many others who have read part or all of this book and offered valuable comments, criticism, and advice I would like to thank in particular Keith Baker, Susanna Barrows, Jack Censer, Roger Chartier, Elizabeth Eisenstein, Leyla Ezdinli, Martin Jay, Thomas Laqueur, Kirstie McClure, Philip Nord, Jeremy Popkin, Robert Post, Daniel Roche, Peter Sahlins, Jerrold Seigel, Rachel Weil, and Isser Woloch. My gratitude also goes collectively to the members of the Berkshire Conference of Women Historians, the Early Modern History Colloquium at Rutgers University, the French History Group at the University of Maryland, and the participants of the French History Group at the University of California, Berkeley.

The research for this book could not have been accomplished without the enthusiastic and expert assistance of Mme Balayé and Mme Laffite, *conservatrices* at the Bibliothèque Nationale, M. Bouille, at the Archives Nationales, and Danielle Willemart, *bibliothécaire* at the Musée de la Révolution Française, Vizille. I would especially like to thank Jeanne Bornstein at The New York Public Library, who spent many hours with me searching for obscure pamphlets. Elizabeth Dudrow, Andrea Rusnock, and Joseph Zizek provided excellent research assistance in completing the project, and Peggy Reilly input the manuscript using WordPerfect. Sheila Levine, Rose Anne White, and Anne Geissman Canright at University of California Press saw this book into print, no small task, I know, and I thank them. Finally, a very special thanks to Laura Engelstein.

INTRODUCTION

In 1789, revolutionaries in France embarked on a cultural experiment that radically transformed the most basic elements of French literary civilization by liberating the printing and publishing world from the corporate institutions of the absolutist state and implementing a system of free-market exchange in the world of ideas. In so doing, they opened up unprecedented possibilities for French men and women to translate their thoughts and opinions into print, to circulate them among one another, and to spread them throughout the world. By reconstructing the new publishing world that emerged from the revolutionary struggles of the publishers and printers of Paris and the nation's new cultural legislators between 1789 and 1810, I hope with this book to open up a new view of the relationship between democratic revolution and modern cultural life.

Historians and literary critics have traditionally treated the literary culture of the French Revolution with total disregard if not utter contempt. Thus the literary critic Béatrice Didier recently observed that "most literary histories depict the revolutionary period as a catastrophic epoch for literary creativity."[1] But historians have lately begun to challenge this negative view of revolutionary cultural life. The work of François Furet, Mona Ozouf, and Lynn Hunt, in particular, has put the problem of culture squarely at the center of the history of the French

1. Béatrice Didier, *Ecrire la Révolution, 1789–1799* (Paris: PUF, 1989), 5 (my translation).

1

Revolution.[2] Instead of viewing the Revolution as a catastrophic inter-
ruption of the longer *durée* of French cultural progress, these historians
have asserted rather that it marked a beginning, indeed a founding
moment in the shaping of modern cultural life. Borrowing insights from
both symbolic anthropology and literary theory, these historians have
argued that revolutionary politics, by asserting the rule of "the people"
over the rule of the king, precipitated nothing less than a total reworking
of public modes of representation and systems of signification: the symbolic replaced the iconic; a utopian, "mythic present" replaced tradition;
and transparency replaced dissimulation. These historians have convinc-
ingly demonstrated that a distinctively modern political culture issued
forth from the revolutionary period.

However, the French Revolution did not simply produce new cultural
forms suited to the new regime; it reorganized the most basic mechanisms of cultural power, and in so doing it opened up cultural life to new
producers and instituted new, and sometimes contradictory, modes of
cultural production. In order to grasp the full magnitude and the significance of the cultural revolution that occurred in France between
1789 and 1799, we must look not only at the new systems of meaning
that the Revolution produced, but deeper still, at the new systems of
making meanings that the Revolution, both wittingly and unwittingly,
made possible. This calls for a shift of focus from symbolic and textual
interpretation to a history of cultural practices.[3]

2. See, in particular, Mona Ozouf, *La Fête révolutionnaire* (Paris: Gallimard, 1976);
François Furet, *Pensée la Révolution française* (Paris: Gallimard, 1978); Lynn Hunt, *Politics,
Culture, and Class in the French Revolution* (Berkeley and Los Angeles: University of Cali-
fornia Press, 1984); and Lynn Hunt, ed., *The New Cultural History* (Berkeley and Los
Angeles: University of California Press, 1989).

3. The socio-cultural historians who descend from the French *Annales* school offer a
valuable orientation for such a project; since the publication of *L'Apparition du livre* by
Lucien Febvre and Henri-Jean Martin in 1958, there has been what can only be described
as an explosion of research in the history of printing, publishing, reading, and "the book"
in early modern Europe, and particularly in early modern France. Main landmarks of this
historiography include Febvre and Martin, *L'Apparition du livre* (Paris: Albin Michel, 1958);
Marshall McLuhan, *The Gutenberg Galaxy* (Toronto: University of Toronto Press, 1962);
Geneviève Bollème et al., *Livre et société dans la France du XVIIIe siècle* (Paris: Mouton, 1965);
Henri-Jean Martin, *Livre, pouvoirs et société à Paris au XVIIe siècle*, 2 vols. (Geneva: Droz,
1969); Natalie Z. Davis, "Printing and the People," in *Society and Culture in Early Modern
France* (Stanford: Stanford University Press, 1975), 189–226; Natalie Z. Davis, "Beyond
the Market: Books as Gifts in Sixteenth-Century France," *Transactions of the Royal Historical
Society*, 5th ser., 33 (1983): 69–88; Daniel Roche, *Le Siècle des lumières en province. Académies
et académiciens provinciaux (1680–1789)* (Paris: Mouton, 1978); Elizabeth Eisenstein, *The*

This book thus sets out to explore not the political culture of the Revolution, but rather its cultural politics. It asks what kind of cultural system the Enlightenment philosophers envisioned, and what kind of cultural world their revolutionary heirs ultimately created. Was cultural power redistributed along with political power after 1789? If so, according to what principles and along what lines? What was the relationship of political authority to revolutionary cultural life, and how did this relationship evolve over the course of the Revolution? Was there simply one "revolutionary culture," or did revolutionary politics open up the cultural world to competing cultural visions and practices? Who produced the culture, or cultures, of the Revolution and toward what ends?

The book begins by examining the revolutionary movement to liberate Enlightenment thought from the repressive cultural institutions of the Old Regime through the battle cry for "freedom of the press." Both the meaning and the consequences of the declaration of press freedom encompassed far more than simply an end to prepublication censorship. This declaration brought down the entire literary system of the Old Regime, from the royal administration of the book trade, with its system of literary privileges and its army of censors and inspectors, to the monopoly of the Paris Book Guild on the professions of printing, publishing, and bookselling. Between 1789 and 1793, the mandate to liberate the Enlightenment from censorship and to refound cultural life on enlightened principles translated itself into a massive deregulation of the publishing world. By 1793 anyone could own a printing press or engage in publishing and bookselling. What is more, with the abolition of privileges and prepublication censorship, it appeared that anyone could print or publish anything. Thus the first few years of the Revolution saw the corporatist literary system of the Old Regime entirely dismantled and replaced with a free market in the world of ideas.

These changes did not, however, inaugurate the kind of cultural life their authors had envisioned. Cultural anarchy ensued in the wake of the declaration of "freedom of the press." The collapse of royal regulation

---

Printing Press as an Agent of Change, 2 vols. (Cambridge: Cambridge University Press, 1979); Robert Darnton, *The Business of Enlightenment: A Publishing History of the Encyclopédie, 1775–1800* (Cambridge, Mass.: Harvard University Press, 1979); Robert Darnton, *The Literary Underground of the Old Regime* (Cambridge, Mass.: Harvard University Press, 1982); Roger Chartier and Henri-Jean Martin, eds., *Histoire de l'édition française*, 4 vols. (Paris: Promodis, 1983–); Roger Chartier, *Lectures et lecteurs dans la France d'ancien régime* (Paris: Seuils, 1987); and Roger Chartier, ed., *Les Usages de l'imprimé (XVe–XIXe siècle)* (Paris: Fayard, 1987).

put the notion of authorship itself into question. Pamphleteers reveled in anonymity, while literary pirates exploited the demise of authors' "privileges." Far from propagating enlightened ideas, the freed presses of Paris poured forth incendiary, and often seditious, political pamphlets, as well as works that appeared libelous or obscene to the new men in power. Once legalized and freed for all to copy and sell, the great texts of the Enlightenment fell out of print. The revolutionary reading market demanded novels and amusements, not science and useful knowledge. In the face of these first consequences of the freeing of the press, the cultural policy-makers in successive national assemblies came to recognize that they would have to intervene directly in the world of publishing if their ideal of an enlightened republic was to be realized. As a result, between 1793 and 1799 the republican government deployed a series of new initiatives intended to refound cultural life on liberal principles.

These republican experiments in democratizing the publishing world, however, were unable to avert a continuing commercial crisis in Paris publishing after 1799. Why did the laissez-faire policies of the republican government fail to produce a viable commercial book trade? How did the Napoleonic regime succeed in wedding the commercial interests of big printers and publishers to its own political needs? Finally, what were the consequences of the Napoleonic re-regulation of the printing and publishing world in 1810 for the character and future of French literary culture in the nineteenth century?

The cultural history of the French Revolution is above all a story of political conflict over cultural power—the power to create and circulate meanings, and the power to interpret them. How was this power to be embodied, distributed, organized, and regulated? The modern publishing world in France emerged as a result of repeated political struggles and negotiations between Paris publishers and the cultural policy-makers of the revolutionary governments between 1789 and 1810, as they tried to reconcile their capitalist economic impulses with their enlightened cultural ideals. It is only by reconstructing this story of the political revolution in publishing that we can begin fully to understand the process by which French literary culture issued from the salons of Voltaire into the commercial publishing world of Balzac.

CHAPTER ONE

The Freeing of the Presses, 1788–1791

What did "freedom of the press" mean in practice? Traditional histories of press freedom in France have limited their inquiries to the story of the abolition of royal censorship.[1] As important as this subject is, it does not begin to capture the meaning or the magnitude of the cultural revolution that occurred as a consequence of the freeing of the press in 1789. The struggle against royal censorship was simply one aspect of a much broader assault on the entire literary system of the Old Regime. The destruction of that system would completely transform the legal, institutional, and economic realities of printing and publishing and, ultimately, the character of France's literary culture.

Consider a few examples of what the freedom of the press meant to revolutionaries in 1789. The novelist Restif de la Bretonne wrote: "If you want freedom of the press, establish freedom of the professions.

Unless otherwise noted, all citations from French sources have been translated into English by the author.

1. See, for example, Gustave Le Poittevin, *La Liberté de la presse depuis la Révolution, 1789–1815* (Geneva: Slatkine Reprints, 1975 [orig. ed. Paris, 1901]); Gabriel Peignot, *Essai historique sur la liberté d'écrire chez les anciens et au moyen âge, et sur la liberté de la presse depuis le quinzième siècle* (Geneva: Slatkine Reprints, 1970 [orig. ed. Paris, 1832]); Louis-Eugène Hatin, *Histoire politique et littéraire de la presse en France*, 8 vols. (Paris: Poulet-Malassis, 1859–1861); Maurice Tourneux, "Le Régime de la presse de 1789 à l'an VIII," *Révolution française* 25 (1893): 193–213; Alma Söderhjelm, *Le Régime de la presse pendant la Révolution française*, 2 vols. (Geneva: Slatkine Reprints, 1971 [orig. ed. Paris, 1900–1901]); Claude Bellanger, ed., *Histoire générale de la presse française*, 5 vols. (Paris: PUF, 1969); Natalie Lambrichs, *La Liberté de la presse en l'an IV. Les Journaux républicains* (Paris: PUF, 1976).

Without this, thirty-six privileged printers will become more cruel ty-rants of thought than all of the censors!"[2] For Restif it was the corporate monopoly of the Paris Book Guild, rather than royal censorship and surveillance, that most constrained freedom of expression and the press. This view was expanded upon by the playwright Marie-Joseph Chénier:

> Let us now recall all the kinds of tyranny . . . the inquisition of the Royal Censors, the inquisition of the Lieutenant-General of Police, . . . of the Administration of the Book Trade, . . . of the Keeper of the Seals . . . , of the Minister of Paris . . . , of the Stewards of Court Entertainments . . . , of the Gentlemen of the Bed Chamber . . . , of the lawyers . . . , of the Sor-bonne . . . , of the issuers of mandates and pastoral letters . . . , of the prosecuting attorneys . . . , of the minister of foreign affairs . . . , of the local governments and the royal officials of the provinces . . . , of the postal system, of the book guilds . . . , of all the valets at Versailles. In all, seventeen inquisitions exercised in France upon the minds of citizens.[3]

According to Chénier, royal censorship was only the first in a long list of "inquisitions exercised . . . upon the minds of citizens." To Chénier's seventeen inquisitions an eighteenth was added by Louis-Félix Guyne-ment de Kéralio, a former royal censor, who wrote two pamphlets in 1790: *De la Liberté de la presse* and *De la Liberté d'énoncer, d'écrire et d'imprimer la pensée*. In these pamphlets de Kéralio asserted that "printed matter sold to the public belongs to the public."[4] He thus concluded that there should be no private claims to ownership of ideas or texts by authors or pub-lishers. All texts should be freed from particular claims or "privileges" because "public interest is preferable to the mercantile interests of a few booksellers."[5] In the eyes of these men the freeing of the press was to entail the demise of the entire legal and institutional infrastructure of publishing under the Old Regime: the royal patronage of letters; the royal Administration of the Book Trade and its army of censors, inspec-tors, and spies; the system of literary privileges that gave publishers and authors exclusive publication rights to texts; and finally, the monopoly of

2. Restif de la Bretonne, *Les Nuits révolutionnaires* (Paris: Livre de Poche, 1978 [orig. ed. 1789]), 79.

3. Marie-Joseph Chénier, *Dénonciation des inquisiteurs de la pensée* (Paris: Lagrange, 1789), 41.

4. Louis-Félix Guynement de Kéralio, *De la liberté d'énoncer, d'écrire et d'imprimer la pensée* (Paris: Potier de Lille, 1790), 51; in Archives Nationales (hereafter cited as AN), ser. ADVIII, carton 38.

5. Ibid., 52.

the Book Guild over printing, publishing, importing, and selling printed matter in France.

The struggle for the freedom of the press was a struggle to found a new cultural regime based on principles derived from Enlightenment philosophy rather than divine right absolutism. This would require a reworking of the very terms and conditions by which ideas emerge and circulate in the world. And it could only be achieved by dismantling and reconstructing the laws and institutions that organized the most basic elements of literary culture: authorship, printing, publishing, and book-selling. The *philosophes* of the mid-eighteenth century had reworked the epistemological basis of the origins and transmission of ideas. The revolutionaries sought to embody and give life to this "revolution of the mind" in practice.

The theoreticians of press freedom between 1788 and 1791 were not arguing simply about the policing of thought. They were arguing about where ideas come from, how they are to be transmitted, how and by whom the truth should be determined and, then, made known. Who had sovereignty in the world of ideas? A series of philosophical questions suddenly became political ones.

The Politics of Publishing Under the Old Regime

In November 1788, Augustin-Martin Lottin *l'aîné*, printer-bookseller and devoted member of the Paris Book Guild, set out to publish his *Catalogue chronologique des libraires et des libraires-imprimeurs de Paris*.[6] This trade directory cum genealogy of one of the most privileged and exclusive sectors of cultural commerce in early modern France, the Paris Book Guild, burst into print in the same few months that the Estates General proclaimed itself the National Assembly; abolished all "privileges," at least in principle; and in the Declaration of the Rights of Man and the Citizen announced that "the free communication of thought is one of the most precious rights of man. All citizens can, therefore, speak, write, and print freely."[7] With the declaration of the freedom of the press, a mania to produce and consume the printed word swept across the nation. Over the

6. Augustin-Martin Lottin, *Catalogue chronologique des libraires et des libraires-imprimeurs de Paris, 1470–1789* (Paris: Lottin, 1789).

7. Article 11 of the Declaration of the Rights of Man and the Citizen, promulgated August 26, 1789; an edited version appears in Jacques Godechot, ed., *Les Constitutions de la France depuis 1789* (Paris: Flammarion, 1979), 34.

next several years new printing presses popped up left and right, igniting France, and especially its capital, with the flames of incendiary pamphlets of every political bent. Along with so many other trade manuals, legal handbooks, and government directories, Lottin's *Catalogue* became obsolete—not to say antiquarian—almost overnight. Or did it?

It is worth pausing briefly over Lottin's *Catalogue* because, broadly conceived, it presents us with a view of the world from one of the key nodes of state regulation of the printed word in Paris on the eve of the Revolution. In both its form and intent it reveals the place that one of the more conservative members of the Paris Book Guild sought to preserve for this institution in the larger order of things.

The title page of Lottin's work (plate 1) is in itself a kind of catalogue of the essential features of licit publication of the printed word under the Old Regime. The symmetry and classical beauty of this work is a modest, but nonetheless monumental, testimony to Colbert's programmatic vision of the organization of commerce under the absolutist state. Reading from the bottom up, we find the king and his approbation of the publication of the work; the royally licensed printer-bookseller in Paris; and the dedication to the university, which was, at least in title, the governing body under whose purview the Paris Book Guild fell within the infrastructure of the royal administration.[8] Finally, the printers and booksellers themselves are announced, chronologically and alphabetically, by edict, in royal procession. The author of this tableau of the official process of publication figures nowhere on the title page. The king, as God's first representative on earth, is depicted as the sponsor of all knowledge made public through the medium of the printed word. Thus the work discloses its divine origin through the approbation of the king.[9]

On one side of his chronological tableau, Lottin presents the practitioners of the typographic arts, including not only printers and booksellers, but engravers and type and paper manufacturers as well. Listed alongside in parallel columns are the individuals whom Lottin describes as the "judges and protectors" of the typographic arts, those royal officials who inspected all printed matter and assessed its quality in both

8. In 1789 the Paris Book Guild still appeared under the rubric for the university in the *Almanach royal* (Paris: Debure-d'Houry, 1789).

9. The legal privilege to publish a book began with the formula "Louis, par la grâce de Dieu, Roi de France. . . ." The text of the privilege, by law, had to appear at the beginning or end of any work published with official approbation in France in the eighteenth century.

CATALOGUE
CHRONOLOGIQUE
DES LIBRAIRES
ET
DES LIBRAIRES-IMPRIMEURS
DE PARIS,

Depuis l'an 1470, époque de l'établissement de l'Imprimerie
dans cette Capitale, jusqu'à présent :

ON Y A JOINT

I°. Le Catalogue des mêmes Libraires , &c. difposé par ordre
alphabétique des noms propres.

II°. Le Catalogue des mêmes Libraires , &c. difposé par ordre
alphabétique des noms de baptême.

III°. Le Tableau des XXXVI Imprimeurs de Paris , avec la chronologie
de leurs prédéceffeurs , en remontant à l'Edit de 1686 , qui les fixe
à ce nombre.

IV°. La Notice Chronologique des Libraires, Libraires - Imprimeurs,
& des Artiftes qui fe font occupés , à Paris, de la Gravure & de
la Fonte des Caractères Typographiques , depuis l'établissement de
l'Imprimerie dans la Capitale , jusqu'à préfent.

In tenuitate copia.

DÉDIÉ A L'UNIVERSITÉ.

A PARIS,

Chez *Jean-Roch* Lottin de S. Germain , Imprimeur - Libraire
Ordinaire de la Ville , rue S. André-des-Arcs , N° 27.

M. DCC. LXXXIX.

Avec Approbation , et Privilége du Roi.

Plate 1. Title page of Augustin-Martin Lottin's *Catalogue chronologique des libraires et des libraires-imprimeurs de Paris, 1470–1789* (Paris, 1789). General Research Collection, The New York Public Library, Astor, Lenox and Tilden Foundations.

formal and substantive terms before it reached the public. Beneath the king and his ministers, the prescribed audience of printed works is divided into four columns: (1) the university, (2) the Parlement, (3) the royal police at Châtelet, and (4) the king's Council of State.

Time divides neatly into centuries, reigns of kings, directorships of the Paris Book Guild, and, most importantly, family cycles, ordered chronologically and also alphabetically by both first and last names so as to emphasize every possible genealogical link. As centuries roll by, we see families rise and fall and rise again. The figures change, yet the essential structure persists. The *Catalogue* is organized to place Paris at the center of French publishing, to disclose and stress the continuity and coherence of a closed corporate system of production, and to facilitate and encourage its persistence.

The Chambre Syndicale de la Librairie et Imprimerie de Paris (the Paris Book Guild) was a self-regulating corporation of printers and booksellers in Paris, who by royal privilege enjoyed an exclusive monopoly on the production and distribution of printed matter in the capital city.[10] Since 1686, when Louis XIV had fixed the number of printers in the city at thirty-six, channels of entry into the Parisian printing trade had narrowed steadily in proportion to the increase in population and demand for printed works.[11] Successful entry into the guild required an apprenticeship and examination by both guild masters and the university. To become a printer also required the timely death of one of the select thirty-six and considerable savings to buy a shop and pay the stiff entrance fees exacted by the guild.[12] Except for widows of guild members who chose not to remarry, the law prohibited women from printing, publishing, or selling printed works. According to Lottin, in 1788 the guild comprised 241 printers and booksellers.[13] Initially under the jurisdiction of the University of Paris and the Parlement of Paris, over the

10. See the *Almanach de la librairie* (Paris: Moutard, 1781); Chartier and Martin (eds.), *Histoire de l'édition* 2:64–93; and Philippe Minard, *Typographes des lumières* (Seyssel: Champ Vallon, 1989).

11. Henri-Jean Martin, "La Prééminence de la librairie parisienne," in Chartier and Martin (eds.), *Histoire de l'édition* 2:262–282.

12. On apprenticeship in the eighteenth-century printing and book trades, see Paul Chauvet, *Les Ouvriers du livre en France*, 2 vols. (Paris: Marcel Rivière, 1964); and Minard, *Typographes des lumières*, esp. 74–100.

13. Lottin, *Catalogue chronologique des libraires*. An edited version of Lottin's list appears in Paul Delalain, *L'Imprimerie et la librairie à Paris de 1789 à 1813* (Paris: Delalain, [1900]), li–lx. The 1788 *capitation* tax roll for the Paris Book Guild shows 213 members, of which 37 are printers and 32 are women; see Bibliothèque Nationale (hereafter cited as BN),

course of the seventeenth and eighteenth centuries the guild became tied ever more closely to the royal administration.[14]

Three separate branches of the Crown's administration were intimately related to guild affairs. The single most important was the Administration of the Book Trade, a division of the Great Chancellery. The director of the book trade reported directly to the keeper of the seals, who in turn consulted, in particularly sensitive matters pertaining to the book trade, with the king's Council of State. This administration occupied itself at the national level with the organization of the book guilds in the major cities of France and supervised a national network of royal inspectors of the book trade. The royal inspectors oversaw the activities and duties of the guilds in the cities to which they were assigned and, in conjunction with the postal service, were charged with surveillance of the foreign book trade at designated ports of entry into France.

The Administration of the Book Trade also dispensed and registered literary "privileges," which were at once an official approbation of a work, a permission to print, and a kind of copyright, in that they gave the bearer an exclusive monopoly on the publication of a particular work or on publications in a given area of knowledge. Finally, this office was charged with the delegation of manuscripts to the appropriate member of the corps of royal censors. In light of the censor's report, the Administration of the Book Trade then determined the legal status of a work submitted for publication.[15] By the end of the eighteenth century a work might receive one of six categories of legal sanction: (1) a *privilège en librairie*, which gave an exclusive monopoly on the publication of a work for a fixed period of time (usually ten to twenty years) to a particular licensed guild publisher; (2) a *privilège d'auteur*, which gave the author of a work and his or her heirs an exclusive monopoly on the publication of the work in perpetuity; (3) a *permission simple*, which gave legal authorization to a publisher to produce a single edition of a particular work; (4) a *permission tacite*, which gave no legal sanction to a work but insured that the authorities would permit and protect its publication and circulation unless

---

Fond Français (hereafter cited as mss. fr.) 21861, "Registre de la communauté des libraires et imprimeurs de Paris, 1787–1791" (see table 2).

14. Henri-Jean Martin, "Conditions politiques. La Librairie et les pouvoirs," in Chartier and Martin (eds.), *Histoire de l'édition* 2:64–93.

15. See Daniel Roche, "Censorship and the Publishing Industry," in *Revolution in Print: The Press in France, 1775–1800*, ed. Robert Darnton and Daniel Roche (Berkeley and Los Angeles: University of California Press, 1989), 3–26.

it was denounced, whereupon they might withdraw the permission; (5) a *tolérance,* which simply meant that the authorities would tolerate at their contingent discretion the circulation of an illegal work; and finally (6), a *suppression,* which meant that a work and its publisher would be actively pursued by the authorities, the work confiscated and destroyed, and the publisher and author fined and perhaps arrested or banished.[16]

By law, no one but a registered member of one of the officially sanctioned royal book guilds was allowed to engage in the activities of printing, publishing, or selling printed works in France. In 1777 this regulation was modified to permit authors to publish and sell their own works.[17] Sample copies of every printed work over three printer's sheets in length produced or marketed in the city of Paris had to be deposited and registered at the offices of the Paris Book Guild.[18] Shorter publications were registered directly with the lieutenant-general of police. The guild then sent the manuscript to the Administration of the Book Trade, where it was again registered and then sent on to a royal censor for evaluation. Upon the censor's report, the administration determined whether the publisher would be permitted to circulate the book and, if so, what level of approbation and protection the edition would receive. Any pirate editions or illicit works not bearing the name and address of a licensed guild publisher, a royal "privilege," and the approbation of a royal censor printed at the back of the book were confiscated to the advantage of the actual privilege holder, the Paris Book Guild, and the Administration of the Book Trade. The printers and publishers of the city thus enjoyed protection against competition for their labor force and the licit literary market that they monopolized.

Two other branches of the royal administration concerned themselves with the production and dissemination of printed works in the capital under the Old Regime. Of second most importance, in Lottin's view, was the Châtelet, the law courts and offices of the royal police force

---

16. Raymond Birn, "The Profits in Ideas: 'Privilèges en Librairie' in Eighteenth-Century France," *Eighteenth-Century Studies* 4, no. 2 (Winter, 1971): 131–168.

17. Codes of the book trade for 1723 and 1777; see *Almanach de la librairie.* An *arrêt* of the king's Council of State of 1700 prohibited authors from selling their own works. The *arrêts* of 1777 reversed this decision, making it possible for authors to sell their own works. See H.-J. Martin, "Conditions politiques"; and Birn, "Profits in Ideas"; also Carla Hesse, "Enlightenment Epistemology and the Laws of Authorship in Revolutionary France, 1777–1793," *Representations* 30 (Spring 1990): 109–137.

18. On this procedure, see Robert Estivals, *Le Dépôt légal sous l'ancien régime de 1537–1791* (Paris: Marcel Rivière, 1961).

of Paris, under the jurisdiction of the minister of Paris and, in particular, the lieutenant-general of police and his corps of inspectors of the book trade and undercover spies. These men were charged with the censorship of works printed and published in the capital shorter than three printer's sheets. They made regular visits, in conjunction with the book guild officers, to the establishments of the printers and booksellers of the city. They were further charged, along with the postal service and the Paris customs officers, with the inspection of shipments of printed matter moving into or out of the city.[19] Finally, the minister of foreign affairs controlled the dispensation of "privileges" for the publication of periodical literature and surveillance of the foreign book trade.

The research findings of historians of eighteenth-century literature and the book trade allow us to flesh out the scheme left to us by Lottin and to situate his Paris-centered depiction in the context of the national administration of the book trade.[20] The system of legal publishing on the eve of the French Revolution is shown graphically in figure 1, table 1, and map 1.

This corporatist system, the godchild of divine-right absolutism, was not, however, without its imbalances. The most striking disproportion, concealed by diagrams and maps, involved the increasing preeminence of the Paris Book Guild within the national system over the course of the seventeenth and eighteenth centuries.[21] Parisian commerce as a whole tended to be privileged by the monarchy as the crowning jewel of royal civilization, the more cultivated and protected because it lay close beneath the royal eye. It was also the most susceptible to surveillance. By royal decree, the number of Parisian printing establishments was fixed at three

19. For vivid depictions of the careers and activities of these officials, see Darnton, *Literary Underground;* and Robert Darnton, "A Police Inspector Sorts His Files: The Anatomy of the Republic of Letters," in *The Great Cat Massacre and Other Episodes in French Cultural History* (New York: Basic Books, 1984), 145–189.

20. See, in particular, Estivals, *Dépôt légal;* Robert Estivals, *La Statistique bibliographique de la France sous la monarchie au XVIIIe siècle* (Paris: Mouton, 1965); H.-J. Martin, *Livre, pouvoirs et société;* Chartier and Martin (eds.), *Histoire de l'édition;* Birn, "Profits in Ideas"; François Furet, "La Librairie du royaume de France au 18e siècle," in Bollème et al., *Livre et société;* E. P. Shaw, *Problems and Policies of Malesherbes as Directeur de la Librairie in France* (Albany: State University of New York Press, 1966); J.-P. Belin, *Le Commerce des livres prohibés à Paris de 1750 à 1789* (Paris: Belin frères, 1913); John Lough, *Writer and Public in France* (Oxford: Clarendon Press, 1978); and Nicole Hermann-Mascard, *La Censure des livres à Paris à la fin de l'ancien régime (1750–1789)* (Paris: PUF, 1968).

21. See Martin, "Prééminence de la librairie." See also Jean Queniart, "L'Anémie provinciale," in Chartier and Martin (eds.), *Histoire de l'édition* 2:283–284.

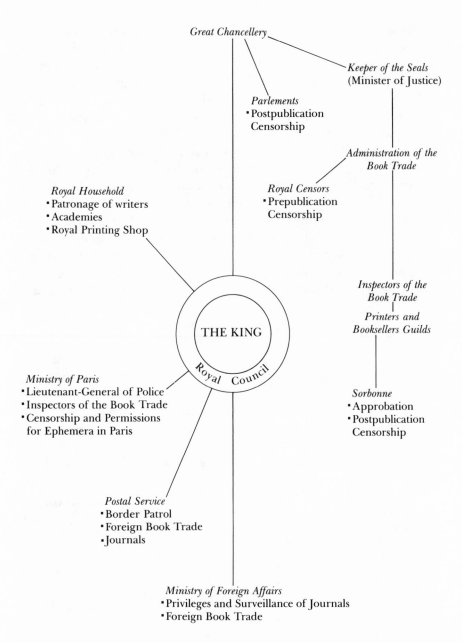

Figure 1. The Royal Administration of the Book Trade: Administrative Organization, 1789

Source: AN, ser. V1, cartons 549–553.

Table 1   The Royal Administration of the Book Trade:
Personnel, 1789

The Administration of the Book Trade, 1788–1790; suppressed on Jan. 1, 1791,
by decree of the National Assembly of July 21, 1790, sanctioned August 15,
1790.

Great Chancellery becomes Ministry of Justice, 1790

The Keepers of the Seals
1784–1787, Villedieu
1787, Miromesnil
1788, Barentin; resigns 1789 and emigrates
1789–1790, Champion de Cicé, archbishop of Bordeaux

The Director-Generals of the Book Trade
1787, Neville; becomes intendant of Bordeaux by 1790
1788; Vidaud de La Tour
1789, Poitevin de Maissemy; resigns July 1789, becomes Commander
General of the National Guard in the
Oise, 1790

Paris Office of the Book Trade
Manager: Dieudonné Thiebault, Responsible for reports and
correspondence
Assistant Managers: Dumirail, Responsible for the Book Guilds of France
LeMercier, Registers works, privileges and permissions,
etc.
Secretaries: Delegue
Clapier
Cuvelier
Office boy: Malasson

SOURCE: AN, ser. V1, cartons 549–553.

times the number of any provincial city.[22] In terms of location they also
benefited from the most intensive, if not extensive, reading market in
France. As Lottin's attention to genealogy suggests, during the seventeenth and eighteenth centuries Paris-centered family empires steadily
consolidated a hegemonic grip on licit publishing under the Old Regime.
Lottin was right to put Paris at the center of official publishing. It was.

22. See Roger Chartier, "L'Imprimerie en France à la fin de l'ancien régime. L'Etat
général des imprimeurs de 1777," *Revue française d'histoire du livre,* n.s., no. 6 (1973):
253–279; and Roger Chartier, "La Géographie de l'imprimerie française au XVIIIe
siècle," in Chartier and Martin (eds.), *Histoire de l'édition* 2:290–291. The figures for 1701
are fifty-one printing shops in Paris to thirty in Lyon (nearest competitor); and for 1777,
thirty-six in Paris to twelve in Lyon (nearest competitor).

Nancy:	Chassel	Lille:	Wiartz
Toulouse:	Cory de Villeneuve	Dijon:	Cortois
Lyon:	La Tourrette	Versailles:	LeClos
Strasbourg:	Saltzmann/Brack/Gérard	Amiens:	Boullet de Varennes
Orléans:	Miron	Montpellier:	Ballainvilliers
Caen:	Fouquet	Reims:	Dessain de Chevieux
Rouen:	Havas	Bordeaux:	Martignac
Nîmes:	Roustan	Besançon:	de Hemmey/Fenouillet
Nantes:	Grélier (Pierre)	St-Malo:	Hovins
Sedan:	de Beyne	Marseille:	Pastoret
Metz:	Chenu	Rennes:	Chaillou

Paris Inspectors

Decrosne, Lieutenant-General of Police
D'Hemery, Honorary Inspector
Sirebeau, Commissioner
Chénon, Commissioner
Gérard, Inspector of the Book Trade
Le Prince, Inspector of the Book Trade
Henry, Inspector of the Book Trade
Willemin, Inspector of the Book Trade
Villemain, Police Inspector

• Inspectors of the Book Trade
○ Book Guilds of France

Map 1. Royal Inspectors of the Book Trade and the Book Guilds of France, 1789. Source: AN, ser. V1, cartons 549–553.

Advantageously positioned at the heart of national administrative life, police power, and royal patronage, Parisian publishers steadily accumulated monopolies on the most lucrative privileges for the major texts of classical literary, religious, and legal civilization. In general, Parisian establishments were large and specialized in what the French call *grande édition:* the publication of multivolume editions, standard reference works, and educational and religious texts with huge press runs.[23]

Massive bibliographic studies of the registers of the literary privileges and permissions granted by the royal Administration of the Book Trade and of officially sanctioned periodical literature in the eighteenth century have provided us with a fairly clear sense of what this system of licit publication produced. The picture of official literary culture that emerges from the studies of François Furet, Robert Estivals, and Jean Ehrard and Jacques Roger is essentially one of cultural stagnation and a steadily consolidated reproduction of the traditional religious and literary inheritance of the seventeenth century.[24] Heavily patronized, protected, and policed, Paris publishers dominated official publishing. And, with a few notable exceptions, they also proved relatively inflexible in the face of new literary and intellectual movements or shifts in the demands of the reading market.[25] Seeking the literary civilization of the eighteenth century, literary historians who have studied licit publishing have found instead the cultural inheritance of the seventeenth century. The official world of corporate publishing in Paris was preeminent, but fossilized.

But Lottin himself, despite his desire to present a world of coherence and symmetry, was unavoidably aware that licit publishing was not the only publishing in Paris or in France. And in the mere act of documenting the official system over time, history inevitably intruded in Lottin's account. "Interesting facts," "clandestine presses," and "supposed presses that do not exist" could not be ignored and had to be tacked on, disrupting the symmetry of his picture.[26] Moreover, in his neat four-column classification system, some columns bulge at the expense of others. Thus, as the centuries of the tableau roll by, the thirty-six printers of Paris become slowly engulfed by increasing numbers of royal officers.

23. H.-J. Martin, "Prééminence parisienne"; and Queniart, "Anémie provinciale."

24. Estivals, *Statistique bibliographique;* Furet, "La 'librairie' du royaume de France au 18e siècle," in Bollème et al., *Livre et société,* 3–32; Jean Ehrard and Jacques Roger, "Deux périodiques français du 18e siècle," in Bollème et al., *Livre et société,* 33–60.

25. Martin, "Prééminence parisienne."

26. Lottin, *Catalogue chronologique des libraires,* xx, xxiii.

While the columns of names under the university and the Parlement remain essentially static, those under the police of Châtelet and the king's Council of State run wild: sometimes they must be doubled; finally whole pages must be given over to them. The business of "judging and protecting" the printed word clearly thrived in the eighteenth century.[27]

Clues like Lottin's unintentional revelations have led historians to uncover and map out a labyrinth of illegal publishing, which seethed underground and across the borders of France during the eighteenth century. Following the theses of Alexis de Tocqueville and Daniel Mornet, these scholars have sought to retrace the dissemination of revolutionary ideas in the century before the Revolution became a reality.[28] They have revealed widespread production and diffusion of subversive ideas through the medium of the printed word, beyond the laws and institutions of the Old Regime.[29] Thus, despite the picture that emerged from studies of official registers of literary privileges, we now know that Enlightenment literature was widely diffused in eighteenth-century French society, and that the spread of this new cultural movement was intimately linked with the elaboration of an underground subculture of printers, publishers, literary smugglers, and book dealers in border cities like Neuchâtel, Bouillon, Geneva, Avignon, in the Low Countries (especially Amsterdam), and in Kehl, Germany.[30] This illicit world also spread within the borders of France, in cities like Troyes and Lyon, in Paris and its suburbs (such as St-Denis, Bourg-la-Reine, or Petit Montreuil), and especially in the Palais Royal.[31] The realities of eighteenth-century pub-

27. Ibid., 244.

28. Alexis de Tocqueville, *The Old Regime and the Revolution* (New York: Doubleday, 1955); and Daniel Mornet, *Les Origines intellectuelles de la Révolution française, 1715–1787* (Paris: Armand Colin, 1967 [orig. ed. 1933]).

29. Robert Darnton, "Philosophy Under the Cloak," in Darnton and Roche (eds.), *Revolution in Print: The Press in France, 1775–1800*, 27–49.

30. On Neuchâtel, see Darnton, *Business of Enlightenment;* Darnton, *Literary Underground;* and Robert Darnton, "Le Livre prohibé aux frontières. Neuchâtel," in Chartier and Martin (eds.), *Histoire de l'édition* 2:342–361. On Bouillon, see Raymond Birn, "Le Livre prohibé aux frontières. Bouillon," in ibid., 334–341. On Geneva, see B. Lescaze, "Commerce d'assortissement et livres interdits. Genève," in ibid., 326–333. On Avignon, see René Moulinas, "La Contrefaçon avignonnaise," in ibid., 294–303. On the Low Countries, see Ch. Berkvens-Stevelinck, "L'Edition française en Hollande," in ibid., 316–325. And on Kehl, see Henri-Jean Martin, "Le Voltaire de Kehl," in ibid., 310.

31. On Troyes, as well as Paris, see Darnton, *Literary Underground*, 122–147. On Lyon, see Darnton, *Business of Enlightenment*. On Paris, see Belin, *Commerce des livres prohibés;* and Henri Carré, "Quelques mots sur la presse clandestine à la fin de l'ancien régime," *Révolution Française* 25–26 (1893–1894): 102–126. And on Parisian suburbs and the Palais

lishing and literary culture thus lay hidden beneath the Colbertian ideal depicted by Lottin and inscribed in the laws, institutions, and programmatic vision of the absolutist state.

Under the Old Regime there were thus two intersecting yet distinct systems of cultural production. In political terms, the one was legal and privileged: it received its justification and legitimation in the idea of the divine origins of all knowledge and in the right of the king as God's first representative to interpret God's knowledge and grant or revoke the privilege to make it public within his kingdom.[32] The other, in contrast, was illegal and unprivileged: its legitimation inhered solely in the notion of the author as the originator and first owner of a work, freely alienated by contract to a publisher, as with any other form of property. Economically, the one relied on corporate monopolies and closed markets; the other depended on market demand in the "booty capitalist" world beyond the law.[33] Geographically, the one was centered in Paris and the traditional provincial cities; the other operated underground, beyond the borders of France, or in free zones like the Palais Royal in Paris, which enjoyed immunity from surveillance by the king's police. Culturally, the one was dominated by the classical, legalistic, and religious worldview of the seventeenth-century court; the other propagated *les lumières* and the romantic spirit of Rousseauism.[34]

Of course, characterizations of this sort are never as neat as they seem. By the end of the eighteenth century many, if not most, publishers, printers, and book dealers, as well as the royal officials who policed them, in reality conducted their businesses on both sides of the law. Nonetheless, it should now be apparent that when, in 1789, Chénier denounced the "seventeen inquisitions exercised in France upon the minds of citizens," he was calling for the destruction of the entire institutional infrastructure of legal publishing under the Old Regime and for the legalization of the commercial literary culture that lay beyond the law. Alternately, when Lottin, the former chief officer of the Paris Book Guild and official printer for the city of Paris and the king, set out to

Royal, see BN, mss. fr. 22070, fols. 198–199, "Mémoire sur l'introduction des libelles dans le royaume et chez l'étranger" (n.d.).

32. This is the actual language of the royal literary privilege, which appeared at the end of all works published with official approbation.

33. See, for example, Darnton, *Business of Enlightenment*, 520–530.

34. On the eve of the Revolution, for example, the *Oeuvres* of Voltaire were being published in Kehl, Rousseau's *Oeuvres* in Geneva, the *Encyclopédie* in Neuchâtel, and Mirabeau's pamphlets in Avignon.

publish his *Catalogue* in 1789, he had no intention of singing a commemorative swan song to a world he had lost. Rather, he intended to be the Paris Book Guild's most erudite polemicist.

The Declaration of Press Freedom

Freedom of the press was declared through the convergence of mounting public demand for free exchange of political ideas in the 1780s and the Crown's decision to permit discretionary tolerance in the months preceding the meeting of the Estates General in 1789. Historians usually date the beginning of the period of "unlimited freedom of the press" from the royal *arrêt* of July 5, 1788, which called on "educated persons" to express their views on the procedures for convening the Estates General, or from the *arrêt* of the Parlement of Paris of December 5, 1788, which gave the first legal sanction to the abstract principle.[35] Whatever the exact moment of official sanction, there can be no doubt that 1788 marked the beginning of a period of de facto freedom on the streets. The prevailing mood of tolerance, reform, anticipation, and uncertainty surrounding the convocation of the Estates General gave rise to a storm of public debate, which expressed itself in a flurry of pamphlet literature and ephemeral journals.[36]

It was not, however, until the Declaration of the Rights of Man and the Citizen on August 26, 1789, that the government sanctioned the freedom of the press as a natural and inalienable right.[37] But in what particular form was this principle to be embodied? From the official recognition of the abstract principle of press freedom a seemingly endless debate ensued in the National Assembly. The crux of the debate centered on the problem of drawing a just line between liberty and libel, and between opinion and sedition. To what extent could authors be held responsible for the consequences of their ideas? What would be the appropriate channels of recourse against slander?

35. See, for example, Bellanger (ed.), *Histoire générale de la presse française*, 1:423–431; Claude Labrosse and Pierre Rétat, *Naissance du journal révolutionnaire* (Lyon: Presses Universitaires de Lyon, 1989), 9–17; Louis-Eugène Hatin, *Manuel théorique et pratique de la liberté de la presse* (Paris: Pagnerre, 1868), 22; Peignot, *Essai historique sur la liberté d'écrire*, 148; Ralph Greenlaw, "Pamphlet Literature in France," *Journal of Modern History* 29 (1957): 349; Tourneux, "Régime de la presse," 193.

36. See Labrosse and Rétat, *Naissance du journal révolutionnaire*, 9–25; Greenlaw, "Pamphlet Literature"; Tourneux, "Régime de la presse"; Bellanger (ed.), *Histoire générale de la presse française*, vol. 1, chap. 5.

37. Article 11 of the Declaration of the Rights of Man and the Citizen, promulgated August 26, 1789; an edited version appears in Godechot (ed.), *Les Constitutions de la France*, 34.

In reading through the record of the National Assembly for 1789 and 1790, one cannot help but be struck by what appears to be a major shift, almost overnight, in the orientation of state policy concerning the regulation of the printed word. It appears that the whole system of preventative censorship and corporate privilege, which the Bourbons had so ambitiously developed and Lottin had so painstakingly documented, became an instant nonissue. The endless records of the discussion of press rights contain virtually no references to how printers and the book trade itself should be regulated. True, the debates in the Assembly were focused principally on the future constitution rather than on the present administration. But did that mean anyone could print anything? Could anyone open a printing shop or go into the publishing business, or launch a newspaper or periodical? And what happened to the literary "privileges" of authors, printers, publishers, and booksellers?[38] What were the consequences of the freedom of the press for the publishing and printing world?

Although the royal *arrêt* of July 5, 1788, precipitated an era of tolerance for free expression, on April 3, 1789, by another *arrêt*, the Crown explicitly reaffirmed the entire code that had regulated the French book trade since 1744, and ordered the royal Administration of the Book Trade to enforce it.[39] Five cartons of reports and correspondence from the Paris office of the Administration of the Book Trade from the years 1788 to 1790 make it possible to recapture the meaning and consequences of the declaration of the freedom of the press from the perspective of those whose job it was to interpret and enforce it.[40]

When the Crown announced the convocation of the Estates General and invited "educated persons" to comment, the Administration of the Book Trade, located in Paris, was already floundering in unsolicited

38. See the list of particular privileges in Lottin, *Catalogue chronologique des libraires*, xx.

39. A royal *arrêt* of April 3, 1789, reaffirmed the *règlements* of the book trade; AN, ser. V1, carton 551. Royal *arrêts* of May 6–7, 1789, reaffirmed the prohibition on publishing any journal without official permission; see Tourneux, "Régime de la presse," 195–196. For the actions taken against Jacques-Pierre Brissot de Warville; Honoré-Gabriel Riqueti, comte de Mirabeau; and Louis Prudhomme in May 1789 by the royal Administration of the Book Trade, see the letters from the bureau's director, Poitevin de Maissemy, reprinted in Pierre Manuel, *La Police de Paris dévoilée* (Paris: Desenne, 1791), 61–70. For the attempt of the Estates General to restrict the publication of their proceedings to official journals, see Tourneux, "Régime de la presse," 196.

40. AN, ser. V1, cartons 549–553.

opinions regarding this great event. Poitevin de Maissemy, a former *parlementaire* and *maître des requêtes*, had been appointed to the post of director-general of this administration in late October 1788:[41] he was thus new on the job. The real driving force and determining character of the office on the eve of the Revolution was its manager, Dieudonné Thiebault, a minor man of letters.[42] Thiebault had managed the administration since 1785, with the aid of two assistants and three secretaries. It was he who drafted all reports; who framed all policy questions for the keeper of the seals, Charles-Louis-François de Paule de Barentin; and who corresponded with the provincial inspectors and guild officials.

In the first few months of 1789 the Administration of the Book Trade faced an unprecedented problem: who would be permitted to document, report on, or discuss the Estates General in print? The king's appeal to the people for advice may have been interpreted as establishing liberty on the streets of Paris, but the Administration of the Book Trade was simultaneously marshaling all of its resources to retain its official monopoly on publications discussing the event. By late January, a flood of pirate editions of the royal *Lettre de convocation* was inundating France.[43] The administration issued a series of bulletins affirming the exclusive monopoly of the director of the Imprimerie Royale, Etienne-Alexandre-Jacques Anisson-Duperron, over publication of the document.[44] A royal privilege for the German translation was granted to Frédéric-Rodolphe Saltzmann, the royal inspector in Strasbourg.[45] But disobedience and contest were endemic within the ranks of the official publishers themselves. The *imprimeurs du roi* of the various cities of

41. Siméon-Prosper Hardy, "Mes loisirs," BN, mss. fr. 6687, 8:136 (entry for November 2, 1788). According to Hardy, Maissemy was received as a *conseiller de la Cour des Aides* on May 18, 1770, and became a *maître des requêtes* in 1783.

42. Dieudonné Thiebault (1733–1807). By his own description, the high moment of Thiebault's literary career was his nomination through the influence of D'Alembert and D'Olivet to the Academy of Berlin in 1764. A student of Fénélon, Thiebault edited a *Dictionnaire de locution française* and authored an *Essai sur le style*, an *Adieu de M. le duc de Bourgogne*, and an *Adieu de M. de Fénélon*. On the eve of the Revolution he also composed a *Plan d'enseignement public;* AN, ser. V1, carton 553 [1790].

43. AN, ser. V1, carton 549, Letter from Barentin to Maissemy, January 23, 1789.

44. A reaffirmation of Anisson's privilege was issued by the king's Council of State on April 18, 1788, and registered at the Administration of the Book Trade in January 1789; AN, ser. V1, carton 549. See also AN, ser. ADVIII, carton 7, "Arrêt . . . qui défend . . . à tous libraires et imprimeurs de la ville de Paris ou des provinces . . . d'imprimer . . . ni débiter . . . des ouvrages, édits [etc.] imprimés de l'ordre de sa majesté à la dite Imprimerie Royale," March 26, 1789.

45. AN, ser. V1, carton 549.

France challenged the monopoly of the Imprimerie Royale in Paris. The inspector of the book trade in Orléans upheld the local printer for the king, Louis Jacob, and seized Anisson-Duperron's shipment of the *Lettre* to that city.[46] The inspector in Caen wrote to the Paris Office requesting clarification of Anisson-Duperron's jurisdiction.[47] Lyon, according to its inspector, Latourette, was awash with pirate editions.[48] Cory de Villeneuve, the inspector in Toulouse, reported similar circumstances.[49] By February, even the German translation was being pirated in Strasbourg.[50] Anisson-Duperron protested to the Administration of the Book Trade, and Maissemy consequently sent a circular to all the book guilds of France ordering them to respect and protect Anisson-Duperron's privilege. Nonetheless, during the next few months the problem spread to Douai, Nîmes, Bordeaux, and Nancy.[51] The royal administration held fairly firm in face of the onslaught, but it was clear that the Crown was losing its grip on its own publications.

The pirating of official proclamations was the least of their problems. The Crown clearly had every intention of maintaining control over public discussion of the Estates General. Indeed, by February 1789 the keeper of the seals had appointed a royal censor to devote himself exclusively to works concerning the Estates General.[52] But by early March the authorities were less sure of their political footing in both Paris and the provinces. Roysans, a royal censor, appealed to the Administration of the Book Trade for clarification of official policy: "M. Fouquet [the inspector at Caen] assured me during his last voyage that it was the government's intention to permit much greater liberty than before to discussions of political matters. . . . I would be extremely obliged, sir, to know what works are to be permitted."[53] And Roysans was not alone with these questions. By the end of March even Thiebault was beginning to have doubts about

46. AN, ser. V1, carton 549, contains several letters from January and February pertaining to this incident, in particular, one dated February 15, 1789.

47. AN, ser. V1, carton 549, Letter from Caen inspector, February 1789.

48. Ibid., Letter from Latourette, inspector at Lyon, February 1789.

49. Ibid., Letter from Villeneuve, inspector at Toulouse, February 1789.

50. Ibid., Letter from Saltzmann, inspector at Strasbourg, February 1789.

51. Ibid., Reports from Douai, March 1789; Nîmes, March 20, 1789; Bordeaux, April 3, 1789; and Nancy, June 8, 1789.

52. Ibid., Letter to the Administration from G. Pouvin, "Commis par Msgr. le Garde des Sceaux pour l'examen des ouvrages concernant les états-généraux," February 5, 1789.

53. AN, ser. V1, carton 550, Letter from Roysans to Maissemy, March 10, 1789.

the authority of the Crown to censor works pertaining to the Estates General. Thus he inquired delicately of the keeper of the seals:

> Without wanting to tire you unduly, sire, I should draw to your attention that by all accounts it is clear that an infinite number of "Instructions" for the deputies to the Estates General are going to be published; that these "Instructions" are public acts, signed by those who edited them, and intended to serve as official mandates. . . . Under these circumstances how are they to be censored? It is impossible to submit them to the formality of a "permission" without compromising their status. These documents must be permitted to circulate freely. . . . This is an irregularity, but it is involuntary and temporary.[54]

Thiebault's policy of temporary and discretionary suspension of censorship became the order of the day. Thus he responded, for Maissemy, to the censor Roysans:

> Any publication that is not going to get people riled up or pitch the orders against one another can be advertised and analyzed in the periodical press. . . . I had thought that I had devised a plan . . . that would have instituted a lawful and very extended freedom in place of this unchecked license, but the King has determined that the assembled Estates General should decide on this matter. So we must resign ourselves to live in this disorder and to wait, with resignation, for happier times.[55]

The Administration of the Book Trade thus found itself in limbo.

This was true not only in matters of censorship, but also in relation to the pressing question among journalists as to who would receive the royal privilege to cover the Estates General in the periodical press. From January through May, the office was swamped with requests for privileges from various editors wishing to launch newspapers or journals under the title "The Estates General."[56] Royal policy was expressed in one of Thiebault's many responses to solicitors, that "it would be useless at present to authorize a privilege that the freedom of the press could render null, or that the Estates General itself could decide to award to someone else."[57]

By the end of March, however, royal policy on press coverage took

54. Ibid., Letter from Thiebault to the keeper of the seals, March 30, 1789.

55. Ibid., Response to Roysans, March 1789.

56. AN, ser. V1, cartons 549–552. Between January and June 1789 the Administration of the Book Trade received over twenty requests for exclusive privileges on a journal entitled "The Estates General."

57. AN, ser. V1, carton 549, Undated response by Thiebault from January–February; similar responses are given in March as well.

another turn. Thiebault now felt "that the best plan is to permit the *Journal de Paris*, the *Journal général de France*, and the *Mercure de France* to publish whatever prudence might authorize" concerning the Estates General.[58] Charles-Joseph Panckoucke, the press magnate and encyclopedist-publisher, took advantage of this shift in the wind and attempted to shortcut the red tape of the Administration of the Book Trade. In a letter of April 17, 1789, he appealed directly to the minister of finance, Jacques Necker, arguing that he had the most rightful claim to exclusive coverage of the Estates General because, first, he owned the most extensive privileges for periodical publishing and, second, one of his journals, the *Mercure*, had given "detailed coverage of the Estates General of 1614." Panckoucke also added a political warning to his request: "If the government does not have one authorized newspaper . . . the capital and the provinces will be infected with huge amounts of false information . . . that could do a great deal of damage and stir up trouble."[59]

But Panckoucke ran up against a dead end: the royal government, Thiebault announced to a solicitor, had decided to leave to the Estates General itself the power and responsibility of "authorizing and monitoring" any publication pertaining to the assembly.[60] On May 19, 1789, the Estates General adopted the policy Thiebault had earlier suggested to the keeper of the seals: they gave permission to the three journals whose privileges covered political affairs—that is, the *Gazette de France* (also known as the *Journal général de France*), the *Journal de Paris*, and the *Mercure de France*—to report on their proceedings.[61] Panckoucke, among others, however, would continue to negotiate with the representatives of the nation throughout the fall, in the hope of acquiring an exclusive monopoly on coverage for one official journal.[62]

58. AN, ser. V1, carton 551, Report by Thiebault, March 17, 1789.

59. AN, ser. AA, carton 56, doc. 1524, Letter from Panckoucke to Jacques Necker, April 27, 1789.

60. AN, ser. V1, carton 551, Undated report of Thiebault from April–May 1789. On Panckoucke's continuing efforts to create an official journal, see Paul Rapheal, "Panckoucke et son programme de journal officiel en 1789," *Révolution française* 64 (1913): 216–219. See also Suzanne Tucoo-Chala, *Charles-Joseph Panckoucke et la librairie française, 1736–1798* (Pau: Marrimpouey, 1977).

61. Tourneux, "Régime de la presse," 196.

62. AN, ser. AA, carton 56, doc. 1524, Letter from Panckoucke to Armand-Gaston Camus, president of the National Assembly, November 2, 1789, in which he reasserts the same arguments he made to Necker in the spring. See Panckoucke's article in the *Moniteur*, November 26, 1789, 3, where he solicits a contract for a "journal de l'Assemblée Nation-

In the months leading up to the meeting of the Estates General, the Crown was slowly ceding its sovereignty over the publication, and hence public interpretation, of political events. Thiebault wrote to the inspector at St-Malo in the early summer of 1789 that in matters of publishing and the press "we must await the future for laws, rules, or principles established by the Estates General. But for now I can only uphold the old regulations."[63] The Administration of the Book Trade, though affirmed in its powers by the royal *arrêt* of April 3, had thus begun to await the orders of a new master. But by the summer of 1789 the administration was collapsing from within.

There were signs from early 1789 that the world of official publishing was beginning to fall apart. Fouquet, the inspector at Caen, requested a "leave of absence" in January.[64] Then the book guild of Toulouse went into revolt against the central administration.[65] By March, the Paris Book Guild was also mobilizing against the royal *règlement* of 1777, which had revoked its hereditary claims to privileges on texts.[66] In April the insubordination of the Toulouse Guild became even more strident.[67] By May 30, the inspector in Lyon had ceased to send in his reports, and in June, the inspector in Marseille, Marin, resigned his post.[68] Chenu, the inspector at Metz, held fast but was forced to concede by early July that he had lost control over the situation.[69] The inspector at St-Malo, Hovins, admitted defeat at the same point.[70] The situation in Nîmes was

ale." See also the documents edited in Rapheal, "Panckoucke et son programme de journal officiel."

63. AN, ser. V1, carton 552, Undated report by Thiebault, June–October 1789.

64. Ibid., carton 549, Undated letter from Fouquet, inspector at Caen, January–February 1789.

65. Ibid., Undated report from Villeneuve, inspector at Toulouse, January–February 1789.

66. Ibid., carton 550, Memorandum from the Paris Book Guild, March 1789.

67. Ibid., carton 551, Undated report from Villeneuve, inspector at Toulouse, April–May, 1789.

68. Ibid., Letter from Maissemy to Latourette, inspector at Lyon, May 30, 1789; and carton 553, Letter from Marin, inspector at Marseille, June 26, 1789.

69. Ibid., carton 553, Letter from Chenu, inspector at Metz, July 11, 1789, and Maissemy's response.

70. Ibid., carton 552, Letter from Hovins, inspector at St-Malo, and response, undated [July 11–28, 1789?].

likewise in total disarray.[71] In La Rochelle, the book guild began to meet illegally to discuss a pamphlet circulated by the printer Chauvet calling for the abolition of all guilds.[72] The officers of the postal service reported the refusal of the printers and publishers of Nantes to abide by the royal regulations "on the pretext that the National Assembly has decreed the freedom of the press."[73] Order also broke down in Nancy.[74] By July 22, the director of the book trade, Poitevin de Maissemy, wrote a long letter to Villeneuve, the diligent inspector at Toulouse, in his own hand, acknowledging the chaos in Paris and Versailles and his own despair.[75] Within a week, Maissemy himself abandoned ship; by late July, the keeper of the seals likewise had disappeared.[76]

By August 1789 the whole system of censorship began to break down. Nicolas-Joseph Sélis, professor of eloquence and censor of the *Mercure de France,* wrote on August 11 asking for "clarifications" of his duties.[77] Three weeks after the declaration of the freedom of the press, the *Mercure's* owner, Panckoucke, was refusing to pay him.[78] The Ministry of Foreign Affairs, however, stepped in and ordered Panckoucke to pay the censor's pension—though he would not have to submit to censorship—"until laws concerning the book trade have been definitively enacted."[79]

The baron de Dietrich, censor in Strasbourg, was out of work as well.[80] In September the editors of the *Journal encyclopédique* began refusing to submit to, or pay, their censor. The report on this affair reveals that censorship of both foreign and domestic periodicals had broken down completely.[81] The chevalier de Gaigne, censor in Paris, also wrote lamenting the freedom of the press and begging for further employ-

---

71. Ibid., Report from Royez, inspector at Nîmes, August 14, 1789.

72. Ibid., carton 553, Letter from the office of the "sénéchaussé du siège présidal et de la police de La Rochelle" to the Administration of the Book Trade, June 9, 1789.

73. Ibid., Letter from the postal inspectors, October 9, 1789.

74. Ibid., Letter from Chassel, inspector at Nancy, November 12, 1789.

75. Ibid., carton 552, Letter from Maissemy to Villeneuve, inspector at Toulouse, July 22, 1789.

76. Ibid., Maissemy's last letter as director, dated July 28, 1789, to Villeneuve, inspector at Toulouse, announcing his resignation; see also Siméon-Prosper Hardy, "Mes loisirs," BN, mss. fr. 6687, 8:396 (entry for July 18, 1789, noting Barentin's resignation).

77. Ibid., carton 553, Letter from Sélis, August 11, 1789.

78. Ibid., Letter from Sélis, September 9, 1789.

79. Ibid., Letter from the Ministry of Foreign Affairs to Panckoucke, November 12, 1789.

80. Ibid., carton 552, Letter from Dietrich, August 13, 1789, and response.

81. Ibid., Correspondence between Thiebault and viscomte de Toustain, September 18 and October 10 and 25, 1789.

ment.[82] The abbé Gentry, censor of the *Journal d'Orléans*, was told that "under the present circumstances, he could be tolerant of the conduct of the journalists."[83] Thiebault began receiving letters from censors renouncing their titles and pensions as well. The abbé LeRoy, Demeunier, and Béranger, for example, asked to be struck from the list of censors in the *Almanach royal*, which was being prepared for the following year.[84] The comte de Kéralio made his views clear in his pamphlets on the freedom of the press.[85] Even the bishop of Boulogne formally renounced his censor's pension before it was suppressed.[86] The censor Bondy, too, rallied to the Revolution, leading the publisher Siméon-Prosper Hardy to note cynically in his journal: "He knows how to profit from all the latest events."[87] Conversely, the censor Moreau, "known as a zealous apologist of arbitrary authority and ministerial power," packed his bags and fled Paris.[88]

Thiebault and his assistants held out alone over the course of 1789 and 1790. A new keeper of the seals, Jérôme-Marie Champion de Cicé, was appointed on August 5, 1789.[89] He oversaw the work of Thiebault, who managed to carry on with the aid of a few faithful die-hards like Villeneuve in Toulouse, Havas in Rouen, Hovins in St-Malo, Grélier in Nantes, the baron de Dietrich in Strasbourg, and the officers of the postal service.[90] These men continued on through the fall, supervising censors, granting privileges, and policing shipments of printed matter.[91] Convinced that the freedom of the press could not mean the end to government regulation of the book trade, they awaited the new order,

82. Ibid., Letter from de Gaigne, October 22, 1789.
83. Ibid., carton 553, Letter to the abbé Gentry, November 17, 1789.
84. Ibid., Report from Thiebault, November 12, 1789.
85. Kéralio, *De la liberté;* AN, ser. ADVIII, carton 38.
86. AN, ser. V1, carton 553, Letter from the bishop of Boulogne, February 3, 1790.
87. Siméon-Prosper Hardy, "Mes loisirs," BN, mss. fr. 6687, 8:424 (entry for August 6, 1789).
88. Ibid.
89. Ibid., 8:422 (entry for August 5, 1789).
90. AN, ser. V1, carton 552, Letter from Villeneuve to Thiebault, October 24, 1789; carton 553, Letter from Havas, October 22, 1789; carton 552, Letters from Hovins, October 6, 1789, and Grélier, September 1789; and carton 553, Letter from Dietrich, September 9, 1789, and correspondence with the postal service, September 17 and October 9, 1789.
91. See the register of privileges for September 30–October 28, 1789; AN, ser. V1, carton 552.

which they expected from the National Assembly as soon as it could attend to the problem of commerce in the world of ideas.

But when the National Assembly did finally legislate on the Administration of the Book Trade in August 1790, it was to suppress what was by then a mere skeleton.[92] Thiebault's closing report to the keeper of the seals at the end of 1790 states:

> The municipality of Paris reserves for itself all that concerns the book trade in this city, and the other municipalities of the kingdom will doubtless follow this example. It seems likely, moreover, that by a natural extension of the freedom of the press, the nomination of censors will no longer take place. . . . If the municipalities take control of policing the book trade, they will want to decide for themselves on the number and selection of printers and booksellers. . . . The general administration of the book trade will not continue in all these areas.[93]

The royal Administration of the Book Trade had fallen to pieces before his eyes.

———————

The declaration of the freedom of the press and the demise of the royal Administration of the Book Trade, as Thiebault's final report suggests, did not mark an end to public regulation of the printed word. Nor, by 1790, had the National Assembly turned its attention to the implications of press freedom for the world of publishing and printing. Nonetheless, between 1788 and 1790 the character of state sovereignty in the world of ideas had been radically transformed.

The system of publishing instituted by the divine-right absolutist monarchy had been brought to the ground. The seat of sovereignty in the publishing world had shifted from the king and his administration to the National Assembly and the Commune of Paris. It was now in these public assemblies rather than in the antechambers of Versailles that the meaning of freedom in the world of ideas would be interpreted and implemented. Prepublication censorship of the printed word had been suppressed. The notion of privilege, in principle if not in substance, had

92. AN, ser. F17, carton 1258, doss. 2, "Loi relative à la dépense publique," August 10, 1790. Article 13 reads, "La dépense de douze mille livres affectée au bureau de la librairie sera supprimée à compter du premier janvier 1791."

93. AN, ser. V1, carton 553, Report "on the book trade," undated [1790], in Thiebault's hand.

been abolished. But most significantly, the whole centralized administration of the publishing world had collapsed.

As the Administration of the Book Trade crumbled the nation was rapidly inundated with an unprecedented volume of printed matter. And behind this craze lay a rapidly expanding printing trade. As early as December 1789, royal officials reported that "the desire for printing shops has become so intense and so widespread that even hamlets will end up demanding them."[94] If Paris had been the nova of French publishing under the Old Regime, it became a supernova in the first few years of the Revolution.[95]

On November 12, 1789, Mlle Louise-Félicité Guynement de Kéralio wrote to the Administration of the Book Trade to announce her intention to open a new printing shop.[96] The daughter of a royal censor and herself the author of a noted biography of Queen Elizabeth, she was not foreign to the publishing or printing trades. In fact, bankruptcy papers in the Archives de Paris, filed under the name of the Paris publisher Jean Lagrange, reveal that Mlle de Kéralio was, on the eve of the Revolution, the silent partner in a very substantial publishing business run under Lagrange's name.[97] With correspondents across continental Europe, Kéralio and Lagrange dealt in a wide variety of genres, including novels, medical tracts, histories, philosophical works, and political writings.[98]

According to the book trade regulations of the Old Regime, Louise de Kéralio, as a woman, was legally prohibited from opening either a publishing house or a printing shop in her own name. Yet when in August 1789 the National Assembly declared the freedom of the press, she jumped at the chance of having her own business. The Administration of the Book Trade reported to the keeper of the seals: "In consequence of article 11 of the Declaration of the Rights of Man and the Citizen, Mlle de Kéralio has announced her intention to . . . establish a printing shop under the title *National Printing Shop of the District of the Daughters of St-Thomas.* She begs you, sire, to honor her establishment with your

94. Ibid., Report by Thiebault, December 24, 1789.

95. Ibid., Report from the Paris Book Guild to this effect, November 12, 1789.

96. Ibid., Report on Mlle de Kéralio, from Thiebault to the keeper of the seals, November 12, 1789.

97. Archives de Paris (hereafter cited as AP), Fond Faillite, ser. D4B6, carton 105, doss. 7454, March 30, 1789.

98. Ibid.

protection."[99] Mlle de Kéralio was playing the politics of publishing both ways. On the one hand she asserted her natural right, while on the other she appealed for the privilege of royal protection. Yet the royal approbation she sought was denied on two grounds: "The article that Mlle de Kéralio cites does not state that everyone will be free to print. . . . Never, in particular, has a woman been permitted to acquire a printing shop. She can only keep one if she is the widow of a master printer."[100] According to the royal agents, the Declaration of the Rights of Man was restricted to men. Further, they insisted, "freedom of the press" did not necessarily mean the freedom to print.

But the royal administration was crumbling. And de Kéralio's was not the only instance of printing and publishing operations surfacing from the cultural underground of the Old Regime. They came rolling across the borders as well. Pierre-Augustin Caron de Beaumarchais wrote to the Administration of the Book Trade on January 16, 1790, announcing that he intended to "have his printing shop"—where he was printing his famous edition of Voltaire's *Oeuvres*— "shipped from Kehl to Paris."[101] Thus Voltaire was to reenter Paris, yet again victorious (this time in spirit), on printing presses shuttled across the border in carts. The printers of Avignon, too, began to crawl over the borders into the newly liberated kingdom of France.[102] Jean-Georges Tretteul and Jean-Godefroy Wurtz, known in Strasbourg as dealers in illicit works, announced their intention, because of the freedom of the press, to set up two printing shops in that city.[103] Rousseau's *Oeuvres,* produced across the border by the Société Typographique de Genève, by 1789 openly bore on the title page the name of the royally licensed publisher Claude Poinçot and Paris as the place of publication.[104] And Poinçot further appealed to the Commune of Paris for restitution of his editions of the abbé Raynal's *Histoire philosophique* and Rousseau's *Confessions,* which had been released from the Bastille as it fell.[105] In 1789 Charles-Joseph Panckoucke, too,

99. AN, ser. V1, carton 553, Report on Mlle de Kéralio, from Thiebault to the keeper of the seals, November 12, 1789.

100. Ibid.

101. Ibid., Report of Thiebault, January 16, 1790.

102. Ibid., Reports of Thiebault, December 12, 1789, and January 16 and February 11, 1790.

103. AN, ser. ADVIII, carton 20, doc. 2.

104. AN, ser. V1, carton 549, Dossier from January–February 1789.

105. For his negotiations with the Paris Commune, see Sigismond Lacroix, ed., *Actes de la Commune de Paris (1789–1791),* 1st ser. (Paris: LeCerf, 1895), 2:656–657, 671–672; 4:13,

brought the whole publishing operation of the *Encyclopédie* back to the city where it had first appeared underground.[106]

As the legal and institutional infrastructure of official publishing folded between 1789 and 1790, it was not just ephemeral literature that boomed in Paris. The underground subculture of Enlightenment publishing, which had evolved over the course of the century, at last emerged into the light of day from prisons, back alleys, and obscure suburbs, and crossed the borders to open shop in its spiritual home. Paris, once the crowning jewel of absolutist publishing, was rapidly becoming the center from which to "spread light in all directions."[107]

385; and 5:60 (May–June 1790). For a list of some of his *livres embastillés*, see his declaration of bankruptcy: AP, Fond Faillite, ser. D4B6, carton 109, doss. 7739, Claude Poinçot, March 16, 1789.

106. Darnton, *Business of Enlightenment*, 481–487.

107. Jacques-Pierre Brissot de Warville, cited in Hatin, *Histoire politique et littéraire de la presse* 5:22–23.

CHAPTER TWO

The Fall of the Paris Book Guild, 1777–1791

Royal Reform and Revolutionary Mobilization

The royal Administration of the Book Trade in France had collapsed by January 1791, and it was not to be resuscitated for almost twenty years. But the most powerful cultural institution of the Old Regime, the Paris Book Guild, did not fall with the Bastille. In fact, its members were quietly holding a meeting to admit a new printer into their ranks on the very day that the Parisian masses toppled what had become the preeminent symbol of royal tyranny.[1] To historians of the French Revolution, the last register of the meetings of the Paris Book Guild, which recorded the group's formal activities from 1787 to 1791, has appeared to be a profoundly disappointing source.[2] In it we read endlessly of the reception of apprentices, booksellers, and printers; their examinations; the attestations to their religious faith and moral standing; their participation in the processions of the rector at the university and in the parish; and the annual roll call for the royal "capitation" tax. Indeed, the entries for the eighty-eight meetings of the guild over this period depict a world more reflective of urban corporate life during the late reign of Louis XIV than of Paris in the throes of revolution (plate 2).

Upon closer reading, of course, the great events of these years are visible, refracted dimly and elliptically through the lens of corporate

1. BN, mss. fr. 21861, "Registre de la communauté des libraires et imprimeurs de Paris," entry for July 14, 1789.
2. Ibid., December 7, 1787–March 18, 1791. For mentions of the source, see, for example, Chauvet, *Ouvriers du livre* 2:28; and Estivals, *Dépôt légal,* 100.

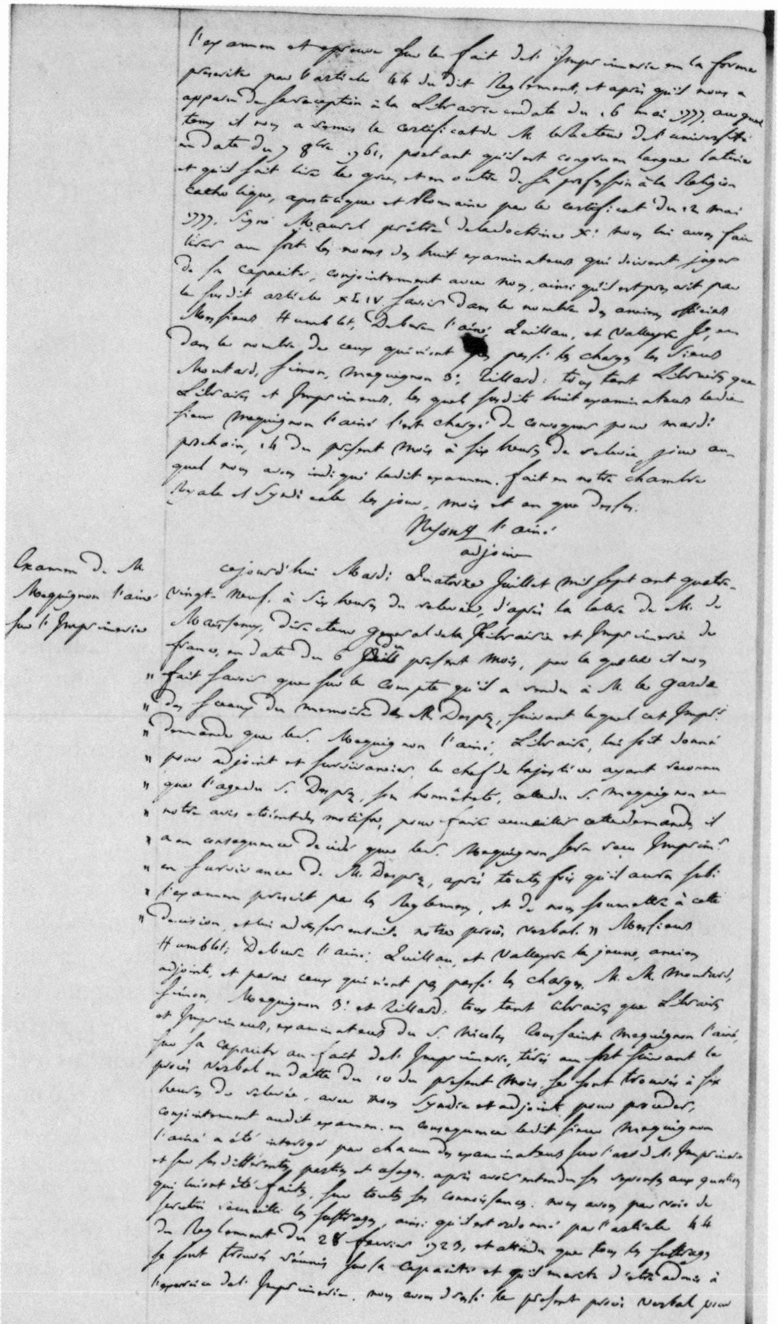

Plate 2. Register of the Paris Book Guild: Entry for the meeting of July 14, 1789. The Paris Book Guild was quietly admitting a new printer into its ranks as the masses toppled the Bastille. Bibliothèque Nationale, Cabinet des Manuscrits.

ritual. The exile of the Parlement of Paris, for example, is quietly acknowledged by a notation of the absence of parliamentary representatives at the rector's procession on August 7, 1788.[3] And later, on April 24, 1789, the register records that the guild's officers had "assembled the entire community through written notice . . . to nominate commissioners and examiners to draft the 'cahiers de doléances' of the publishers and printers of Paris."[4] Still, with the exception of a few similarly unrevealing disclosures, the register of the Paris Book Guild rolls over 1788, 1789, 1790, and 1791 without ever noting even the formal suppression of the guild's existence.

Yet it is the very historical dissonance of the register of the Paris Book Guild as a document *of the Revolution* and its anachronistic character that present the historical problem: What was the position of the Paris Book Guild on the eve of the Revolution? What role did it play in the Revolution itself? Did the Guild form part of a corporatist-aristocratic reaction, as some historians have suggested?[5] Did its members passively or stoically submit to their fate, as others have supposed?[6] The answers lie beneath and beyond the circumspect inscriptions of the guild's cautious official guardians.

———

The Paris Book Guild was quick to mobilize its presses and its members to insure that it would be represented at the Estates General as a corporation. On December 6, 1788, Siméon-Prosper Hardy, a bookseller on the rue St-Jacques and member of the guild, recorded in his journal the receipt from guild officers of a copy of a memorandum submitted to the king: the judges and counsellors of the city of Paris requested a special separate delegation of representatives from the Corporations of the Arts and Trades of Paris to the Estates General to assist the Crown in reestablishing the "credit and confidence" of the realm.[7] The printer

3. BN, mss. fr. 21861, entry for August 7, 1788.

4. Ibid., entry for April 24, 1788.

5. Louis Radiguer, *Maîtres imprimeurs et ouvriers typographes* (Paris: Société Nouvelle de Librairie et d'Edition, 1903), 141–146.

6. William Sewell, Jr., *Work and Revolution in France* (London: Cambridge University Press, 1980), 87.

7. Siméon-Prosper Hardy, "Mes loisirs," BN, mss. fr. 6687, 8:164 (entry for December 6, 1788). See also Etienne Martin St. Léon, *Histoire des corporations de métiers* (Paris: Alcan, 1909), 601.

of this memorandum was the highest officer of the Paris Book Guild, the syndic André-François Knapen (see table 2). The pamphlet went straight from his presses to its constituency, the guilds that elected the judges and counsellors of the city of Paris.

By December 16, 1788, Hardy records having acquired a copy of a petition of the Six Corporations of Paris calling for a more proportional representation of the Third Estate—that is, one cleric to two nobles to three members of the Third Estate, giving the Third Estate an assured representation of 50 percent.[8] Hardy judged this to be a "configuration that today appears to conform most closely to equity . . . and to the spirit of the institution." And he was not the only member of the Paris Book Guild who held this opinion. On December 22, 1788, the guild register recorded that "several members of the guild requested a general assembly of the guild in order to propose that the guild adhere to the petition of the Six Corporations."[9] The following day Hardy received a sealed copy of the petition from the guild officers and a notice for a general assembly of the guild.[10]

The guild officers dared to mention the purpose of this meeting only in a marginal note in the official register.[11] And they recorded no account of the deliberations or their outcome. Fortunately, Hardy was more forthcoming in his private journal:

> Sieur Cellot, publisher and former printer . . . held forth very directly and with great vehemence in favor of the petition; he urged that everyone support it, and that we do so hastily by giving it our unanimous signature. But he was wisely and forcefully countered by sieur Charles-Guillaume LeClerc, publisher, former syndic, and former judge-counsellor of the city . . . , who argued vigorously that we should not give formal written support to the petition so quickly. . . . His proposal passed by a vote of nineteen to fourteen. . . . But as all of those who wanted to support the petition announced their discontent and left having refused to sign anything, this tumultuous assembly decided to defer the final deliberation.[12]

We have no trace of the final outcome of the debate over the adherence of the Paris Book Guild to the petition for proportional representation. However, the Parlement did allow the Six Corporations to submit their

8. Hardy, "Mes loisirs," BN, mss. fr. 6687, 8:172 (entry for December 16, 1788).
9. BN, mss. fr. 21861, "Registre de la communauté," entry for December 22, 1788.
10. Hardy, "Mes loisirs," BN, mss. fr. 6687, 8:185 (entry for December 23, 1788).
11. BN, mss. fr. 21861, "Registre de la communauté," entry for December 24, 1788.
12. Hardy, "Mes loisirs," BN, mss. fr. 6687, 8:186 (entry for December 24, 1788).

petition to the king.[13] And only a week later, on December 27, 1788, Minister of Finance Necker persuaded the king to decree the doubling of the number of representatives of the Third Estate.

The debate in the Paris Book Guild over the petition made clear that their disagreement was over strategy rather than substance. The division—and it was close—was between the strident and the cautious. At bottom guild members had firmly allied their interests with the Third Estate and were agitating, even if not officially, for enlarging that group's representation. At a purely legalistic level, this is not at all surprising. Nor was it particularly revolutionary by the end of December 1788. After all, the publishers, printers, and booksellers of Paris were formally members of the Third Estate. Furthermore, others were beginning to point out that real political change lay not merely in increasing the number of representatives of the Third Estate, but rather in putting an end to a political order based on the division of society into separate privileged estates.

The cultural politics behind the guild's support for the movement to double Third Estate representation were soon elucidated in a pair of anonymous pamphlets, *Remerciment des libraires de la rue S. Jacques à M. Necker* and *Réponse des libraires du Palais Royal, au remerciment de leurs confrères de la rue Saint Jacques, à M. Necker,* which appeared in early January "chez Desenne, Gattey, and Petit, libraires, au Palais Royal."[14] The *Remerciment* was a grub-street satire of the corporate cultural vision of the Paris Book Guild, in which the booksellers of St-Jacques offer profuse thanks to the minister of finance for the decree doubling the number of representatives of the Third Estate. Why? Because, the pamphlet explained, the decree would restore political order and in so doing put an end to public interest in the political ephemera sold in "that magical palace [the Palais Royal], which, like a sun sucking up water and leaving the plains desiccated, has consumed all the business in the capital."[15] Necker had thankfully put an end to the political crisis and hence to the craze for political pamphlets sold beyond the jurisdiction of the king and his book guild by booksellers in the Palais Royal. Readers

13. Martin St. Léon, *Histoire des corporations,* 601–602.

14. *Remerciment des libraires de la rue S. Jacques à M. Necker, suivi de quelques autres pièces relatives aux circonstances* (Paris: Desenne, Gattey, Petit, 1789); and *Réponse des libraires du Palais Royal au remerciment de leurs confrères de la rue Saint Jacques, à M. Necker* (Paris: Desenne, Gattey, Petit, 1789).

15. *Remerciment,* 6.

would now mercifully return to the literary fare offered by the privileged publishers on the rue St-Jacques.

The pamphlet thus transformed the cultural geography of Paris into an allegory of the political debate between reformers, who wanted to modify the system of representation by orders, and revolutionaries, who wanted to abolish distinctions by order altogether. From the perspective of the Palais Royal, the doubling of the Third Estate was far from revolutionary. On the contrary, it only served the interests of those bent on maintaining corporate privileges and distinctions—like those of the Paris Book Guild, whose members worked and lived on the rue St-Jacques. The privileged publishers, the booksellers of the Palais Royal taunted, could not survive in a competitive cultural world based on consumer demand rather than state monopolies.

The *Réponse des libraires du Palais Royal, au remerciment de leurs confrères de la rue Saint Jacques,* in contrast, sounded a conciliatory note—one stressing the potential symbiosis rather than the conflict—between the publishers of St-Jacques and the Palais Royal:

> You feign jealousy of our place in the magic palace, but in reality it is you who control big publishing and bring so many volumes to the light of day. And you have an interest in our being there, to expose your books to the gaze of the curious . . . We are there, from the first sound of the trumpet in the journals, to distribute [your works]. You know, dear colleagues, everything depends on timing, and no one knows better than us how to make the most of it.[16]

The real division within the publishing world, the *Réponse* suggested, lay not between the privileged and the unprivileged, nor between book and pamphlet publishing, but between publishing books and retailing them. The publishers of the rue St-Jacques, they urged, should abandon their defense of privileged orders and cultural monopolies and instead work together with the booksellers of the Palais Royal to take advantage of the opportunities that a publishing world based on free-market principles could offer in compensation.

Some members of the Paris Book Guild were soon won over by arguments calling for an end to the division of public life into privileged orders. Hardy himself, one of the hesitators in the guild debate over the petition, soon enthusiastically noted the publication of Emmanuel Sieyès's

16. *Réponse,* 11–12.

Qu'est-ce que le tiers-état? in his journal and its author's call for an end to the division of the nation into privileged estates.[17] But others within the guild remained firm in defense of their privileges and the old corporate publishing world. Nor was it merely the reestablishment of "credit and confidence" that the guild hoped to achieve from the opportunity for reform presented by the convocation of the Estates General.

On January 5, 1789, a week after the debate on the doubling of the Third Estate in the Paris Book Guild, Poitevin de Maissemy, director of the royal Administration of the Book Trade, received a memorandum from "the Printers and Publishers of Paris."[18] Dieudonné Thiebault, chief officer of the administration's Paris bureau, informed his newly appointed superior that the memorandum was "well known"; indeed, it had already been presented to the former director in the same terms.[19] Another copy of the same memorandum dated 1787 confirms Thiebault's report.[20] This *mémoire* had served as a position piece for the Paris Book Guild and was presented to each new head of the royal Administration of the Book Trade with the hope of gaining a ministerial ear for guild interests. It allows us to locate the posture of the guild in relation to the royal administration on the eve of the Revolution. The *mémoire* opened in the following terms:

> Your elevation to Minister of Laws has given hope to the Book Trade. Ruined, devastated by the six *arrêts* of the Royal Council of August 30, 1777, we dare to beg you to restore the regulations of 1723. . . . Ten years have sufficed to reveal the vices of the new regime. . . . Of these *arrêts*, those concerning pirate editions and the duration of privileges are the ones that have dealt the worst blows to the Book Trade.[21]

On the eve of the Revolution, the Paris Book Guild was already at war with the Crown and its administration, and had been for over ten years. As far as the guild was concerned, the "old regime" had come under

---

17. Hardy, "Mes loisirs," BN, mss. fr. 6687, 8:223 (entry for February 3, 1789). Emmanuel-Joseph Sieyès, *Qu'est-ce que le tiers-état?* [Paris, 1789].

18. AN, ser. VI, carton 550, Report by Thiebault, February 5, 1789.

19. Ibid.

20. BN, mss. fr. 21822, "Archives de la chambre syndicale des libraires et imprimeurs de Paris," fols. 2–10.

21. AN, ser. VI, carton 550, "Mémoire," February 5, 1789, fol. 1r.

assault in 1777. For the officers of the Paris Book Guild, the convocation of the Estates General represented an opportunity to restore rather than to dismantle the corporate publishing monopolies of the Old Regime.

The dispute between the Paris Book Guild and the Crown was no small squabble. The decrees of 1777 had represented the culmination of a fifty-year debate between the Crown and the Paris Corporation of Printers and Publishers concerning the nature and duration of royal literary privileges. The royal *Code de la librairie*, established to regulate the Parisian publishing world in 1723, and extended to the entire nation in 1744, had defined a literary "privilege" as at once an official approbation of the work, a permission to publish, and a kind of copyright, in that a privilege assured its holder a legal exclusivity on the commercial publication of the work.[22] While in principle the Crown could revoke or extend privileges at will, by the end of the seventeenth century the centralizing and corporatistic royal administration had in practice encouraged the consolidation of a monopoly by the Paris Book Guild on the lion's share of the literary inheritance of France.[23] It did this by conferring extensive privileges for publication of both individual texts and whole areas of knowledge to particular Paris publishers and then renewing these privileges automatically over generations.[24]

To protect their monopoly against the protests of excluded provincial publishers, the Paris publishers began in the late seventeenth century to evolve their own interpretation of the meaning of the literary privilege. In 1726, the Paris Book Guild commissioned the jurist Louis d'Héricourt to write a legal brief arguing that a privilege was not a royal "grace" to be conferred or revoked at the king's pleasure, but rather a royal confirmation of an anterior property right. Invoking John Locke's notion of the origins of property in appropriation, d'Héricourt argued that the property in ideas is derived from labor: "It is the fruit of one's own labor, which one should have the freedom to dispose of at one's will."[25] According to the Paris Book Guild, privileges were nothing more than the legal confirmation of a preexisting property right founded in the

---

22. For the text of the *Code* of 1723, see Jourdan, Decrusy, and Isambert, eds., *Recueil général des anciennes lois françaises,* (Paris: Belin-Leprieur, 1826), 21:216–252.
23. H.-J. Martin, *Livre, pouvoirs et société;* H.-J. Martin, "Prééminence de la librairie parisienne"; and Birn, "Profits in Ideas."
24. See Birn, "Profits in Ideas," esp. 139.
25. Cited in ibid., 144.

author's labor and transmitted to the publisher through a contract. Ironically, the argument that ideas were the property of the individual author was first advanced in defense of the monopoly of the Paris Book
Guild on texts whose authors were long since dead.[26]

By the middle of the eighteenth century the issue of literary privileges became caught up in a more general movement by enlightened royal
officials to deregulate commercial life, including commerce in ideas, by
dismantling the corporate monopolies created by Colbert. Although the
royal reformer A.R.J. Turgot had exempted the book guild from his
famous decrees of 1776 suppressing commercial monopolies, the Crown
heeded the advice and counsel of successive officers of the royal Administration of the Book Trade and through six *arrêts* on August 30, 1777,
announced an important shift in its policies concerning the book trade.[27]
The king's Council of State issued a series of decrees intended definitively
to refute the guild's interpretation of literary privileges as confirmations
of property claims and to decentralize the publishing world by breaking
up the Parisian monopoly on the nation's cultural inheritance.

In the 1777 decrees the king's council made its interpretation of "privilege" explicitly clear: "A privilege for a text is a grace founded in Justice. . . . The perfection of the work requires that the publisher be
allowed to enjoy this exclusive claim during the lifetime of the author . . .
but to grant a longer term than this would be to convert the enjoyment

26. Mark Rose makes a similar observation about the source of property arguments in
the English context; see "The Author as Proprietor: Donaldson v. Beckett and the Genealogy of Modern Authorship," *Representations* 23 (1988): 56.

27. Chrétien-Guillaume de Lamoignon de Malesherbes, the director of the royal Administration of the Book Trade between 1750 and 1763, argued for revising the code on the
book trade to allow authors to publish and sell their own works, rather than requiring them
to use licensed publishers and booksellers, in his "Memorandum on the Necessary Regulations to Prevent the Printing, Selling, and Importing of Bad Books," written sometime
during his tenure and first published in his *Mémoires sur la librairie et sur la liberté de la presse*
(Edited by E. Rodmell [Chapel Hill: University of North Carolina Press, 1979; orig. ed.
Paris: Agasse, 1809], 175–178). Notes for a second memorandum, advancing similar arguments, were written by François Marin, general secretary of the Administration of the
Book Trade, at the request of Joseph d'Hemery, inspector of the book trade in Paris, and
submitted to the new director of the royal administration, Antoine-Raymond-Jean-
Gaulbert de Sartine, in 1764. See BN, mss. fr. 22183, "Représentations et observations en
forme de mémoire sur l'état ancien et actuel de la librairie et particulièrement sur la
propriété des privilèges, etc., présentées à M. Sartine par les syndic et adjoints, et en marge
les observations que M. Marin a faites sur chaque article, d'après les notes instructives que
je [d'Hemery] lui ai remises par ordre du magistrat" (March 1764); cited by Birn, "Profits
in Ideas," 153–154.

of a grace into a property right."[28] The Crown thus reaffirmed the absolutist interpretation of royal privileges as an emanation of the king's grace alone and not the recognition of a property right.

The decrees created two categories of literary privilege. *Privilèges d'auteur*, which legally recognized the author for the first time, were to be granted to authors in recompense for their labor and held by them and their heirs *in perpetuity*, unless sold to a third party. Authors were thus for the first time in fifty years permitted, indeed encouraged, to hold on to their manuscripts and to engage in publication rather than sell their manuscripts to publishers. Publishers' privileges, or *privilèges en librairie*, by contrast, were to be limited to the lifetime of the author and nonrenewable. After the author's death, these texts returned to the "royal domain" to be enjoyed by any royally licensed publisher, with the king's permission. The Crown hoped that by making these lucrative legal books available to provincial publishers they could be wooed away from the booming traffic in pirated and illicit works. In an effort to institute these reforms on a new footing, the Crown, by another *arrêt* of the same date, legitimized all pirate editions anterior to the *arrêt*.[29] Thus in 1777, with a stroke of the royal pen, the cultural capital of the Paris Book Guild, as embodied in inheritable literary privileges, had been threatened with extinction.

Not surprisingly, the Paris Book Guild did not receive any of these *arrêts* passively, and it outlined its position succinctly in its *mémoire* to Maissemy of January 1789:

> The *arrêt* concerning the duration of privileges . . . renders the property rights of authors illusory. . . . The dispositions of this *arrêt* are founded upon the principle that a publisher's "privilege" is no more than a "grace founded in justice." . . . But . . . a "privilege" is nothing more than the guarantee of the author's property in his work. . . . If property is incontestable there can be no distinction between an author's "privilege" and that of a publisher. . . . Why this violence against the sacred principle of property?[30]

In its most strident moment, the guild denounced the arbitrary manner in which the royal council determined the matter: "No authority can take our property from us and give it to someone else."[31]

The positions of the Crown and the Paris Book Guild in this debate

28. Jourdan, Decrusy, and Isambert (eds.), *Recueil général des anciennes lois françaises* 25:108–123.

29. Ibid., 121, 123.

30. AN, ser. V1, carton 550, "Mémoire," February 5, 1789, fols. 1v, 2.

31. Ibid., fol. 2v.

ring with dissonance and irony to the modern ear. On the one hand, the Crown, in defining the legal claims on a text as a royal "grace," revocable and mutable at the king's will, had sought to liberate the literary inheritance of France from the monopoly of a privileged corporate elite, to acknowledge the author as the creator of his or her works, and to create a competitive commercial market in ideas. On the other hand, the Paris Book Guild sought to defend its corporate monopoly on the entire literary inheritance of France by defining literary privileges as royal confirmations of sacred and inalienable property rights, inhering originally in a contract between author and publisher. Inviolable by any human authority, property in texts was, according to the guild, a natural right merely ratified by royal privilege.

The dispute between the Crown and the Paris Book Guild in 1789 over the meaning of privilege and who had power to determine this question was not, however, purely theoretical. A good deal of evidence suggests that the guild had, in effect, gone on strike against the efforts of the royal Administration of the Book Trade to implement the six *arrêts* of 1777 and was still in full resistance to the Crown on the eve of the Revolution.

Following the proclamation of the *arrêts* of 1777, the Administration of the Book Trade began to implement the reforms pertaining to the new limits on the literary privileges held by members of the Paris Book Guild. The exclusive claims of guild members over thousands of titles were systematically limited or revoked.[32] The Crown then began to give permission to provincial publishers to produce and market works that had previously been the exclusive privilege of members of the Paris Book Guild.[33] The Paris guild, however, refused to register the six *arrêts*,

32. BN, mss. fr. 22004, "Archives de la chambre syndicale de la librairie et imprimerie de Paris, bureau de la librairie: état des privilèges; état des titres de propriété fournis par les libraires de Paris" [1777]; 22005, "Archives de la chambre syndicale . . . , feuilles des jugements des privilèges derniers et définitifs conformant à l'article XIe de l'arrêt de conseil du 30 août 1777 sur la durée des privilèges"; and 21832, "Archives de la chambre syndicale," feuilles 26–40, "No. 2, Tableau des ouvrages jugés communs ou qui le deviendront à l'expiration des privilèges dont ils sont revêtus, par l'arrêt de conseil du 30 août 1777, portant règlement sur la durée des privilèges en librairie." Another *arrêt* of July 30, 1778, further increased the discretionary power of the administration by allowing the keeper of the seals to extend the duration of privileges beyond ten years at his own will; see Augustin-Charles Renouard, *Traité des droits d'auteur dans la littérature, les sciences et les beaux arts* (Paris: Renouard, 1838), 180.

33. See BN, mss. fr. 1682, Collection Joly de Fleury, "Librairie, imprimerie et censure des livres: règlements sur la matière, 1607–1789," feuilles 168–235 (1779–1780) and 250–268 (1780).

to enforce them, or to recognize the legality of the claims of those who did. Instead, its members mounted a public campaign against the *arrêts* in a series of pamphlets.[34] And they took their case to the Parlement of Paris, which remonstrated in favor of the guild position.[35] The guild succeeded in keeping its cause alive in the courts well into the 1780s, thus lending legal credence to their obstruction of the royal administration.[36]

Sometime after January 1782, at the behest of the Parlement of Paris, the guild prepared a *Compte rendu par les syndics et adjoints de la librairie des faits relatifs à l'exécution des arrêts du Conseil du 30 août 1777 concernant la librairie.*[37] According to this report, the *arrêt* pertaining to pirate editions had been settled amicably with the royal administration: the keeper of the seals had agreed to let the Paris guild prohibit the sale of the newly legitimated provincial pirate editions in Paris.[38] With the most controversial *arrêts*, however, those pertaining to privileges, the situation was different, in part because the guild was not fully able to prevent the implementation of the *arrêts*, nor at every point was it in its interest to do so. Thus, the guild recognized and registered authors' privileges because these conformed to its view that exclusive commercial claims should be perpetual.[39] But when it came to publishers' privileges the situation was more complex. The guild refused to implement any policy that either explicitly or tacitly recognized the new royal "permissions" to publish formerly privileged works.[40] In fact, the guild was seizing any shipment of books from the provinces for which a privilege had once been held by a member.[41] The Paris Book Guild was thus engaged in a full-scale war

34. For examples of Paris Book Guild propaganda against the *arrêts,* see [Charles-Guillaume LeClerc], *Lettre à M*** [sur la propriété littéraire]* [Paris, December 19, 1778], BN, imprimés; and the *Lettre d'un libraire de Lyon à un libraire de Paris* [Paris, 1779], Musée de l'Imprimerie & de la Banque, Lyon.

35. AN, ser. V1, carton 550, "Mémoire," February 5, 1789, fol. 7v.

36. The legal history of the Paris Book Guild's case in the Parlement is documented in BN, mss. fr. 1682, Collection Joly de Fleury, "Librairie, imprimerie et censure," feuilles 168–235, 250–268. See also Renouard, *Traité des droits d'auteur,* 166–193. The guild ultimately lost.

37. BN, mss. fr. 1682, Collection Joly de Fleury, "Librairie, imprimerie et censure," feuilles 168–173.

38. Ibid., feuille 170.

39. Ibid., feuille 169.

40. Ibid.

41. The *Compte rendu* presented to the Parlement by the Paris Book Guild in 1782 gives examples of this practice: "Un S. Baume, libraire à Nîmes, conçut, il y a quelques années, le dessin de faire une édition de *l'Histoire ecclésiastique* de M. de Fleury. Il en existait une

with the royal council and the Administration of the Book Trade when the Estates General was convoked in May 1789. The guild placed its hopes first on the Parlement and then on the Third Estate to defend its corporation and its perpetual monopoly on literary privileges, as they had been interpreted under the Code of 1723.

Corporate Politics in Paris and Versailles

Throughout the summer and fall of 1789 the city of Paris was swept into a revolutionary fervor, propagated and sustained by an unprecedented and seemingly relentless outpouring of printed matter. The task of restoring a modicum of public order fell on the municipal authorities.[42] Among the first acts of the Police Committee of the Commune of Paris were measures to define the limits of legal publication. On July 24, the committee issued an ordinance prohibiting the distribution of any printed matter without the name of the printer.[43] The printer, in the event that he or she could or would not identify the author, was to be held legally accountable. During the fall of 1789, the municipal police, in concert with Lafayette at the head of the National Guard and the royal police force connected to the Châtelet, set out to quell this tidal wave of placards, journals, and pamphlets through a series of regulatory and repressive measures.

Every effort was made to control the practice of colportage, first by requiring colporteurs to identify the source of their merchandise, then by prohibiting the sale of any "calumnious printed matter" or "inflammatory writings."[44] They were then prohibited from crying their wares.[45] And finally, in December, the municipal government attempted to limit the number of colporteurs to three hundred, who were to be registered with the police.[46] On August 25, the National Guard made

---

somme considérable de in-12 et de in-4 dans les magasins des Libraires de Paris qui en avaient le privilège. . . . Depuis les arrêts de 1777 . . . , il [le S. Baume] a voulu faire venir [l'édition] à l'adresse du S. Baume: Nous l'avons suspendue"; ibid., feuilles 171–172.

42. Lacroix (ed.), *Actes de la Commune de Paris*, 1st ser., 1:v.

43. Ibid., 82. See also Gary Kates, *The Cercle Social, the Girondins, and the French Revolution* (Princeton: Princeton University Press, 1985), 31, 181–183.

44. Lacroix (ed.), *Actes de la Commune de Paris*, 1st ser., 1:82, 117, and 211 (July 24 and 31 and August 2, 1789); 2:550 (November 4, 1789); and 1:421, 432–444 (August 31 and September 1, 1789).

45. Ibid., 2:215–216 (October 8, 1789).

46. Ibid., 3:174, 179 (December 21, 1789).

the first of its raids of the Palais Royal, thus violating the police immunity of that cultural free zone of the Old Regime.[47] A wave of raids of printing shops, booksellers, and newsstands and arrests of colporteurs ensued in the Palais Royal and throughout the city, conducted both by the Old Regime police force of the Châtelet and by the revolutionary Commissioners of Police of the Paris Districts.[48]

These regulatory and repressive measures did not go unnoticed. Pamphlets like the *Enterrement des feuilles volantes. De profundis des petits auteurs. Agonie des colporteurs* decried this assault on political ephemera and its producers.[49] In a series of articles published in the *Révolutions de Paris* beginning on October 17, 1789, entitled "Conspiracies Against the Freedom of the Press," the ultrarevolutionary journalist Elysée Loustallot depicted the formation of a fatal coalition of the king's ministers; corrupt deputies in the National Assembly; representatives of the Commune of Paris; the mayor of Paris, Jean-Sylvain Bailly; and the head of the National Guard, the marquis de Lafayette, against unlimited freedom of the press. The military authorities, he wrote, "have made fair game of the freedom of the press throughout the city."[50] The decree registering colporteurs, he cautioned, was a means of recruiting "three hundred spies."[51] Further, the officers of the Paris bureau of the royal Administration of the Book Trade "are still occupying their offices at the town hall."[52] In view of the persecutions of writers, printers, and colporteurs by the Commissioners of Police of the Paris Districts, he wrote, one would be tempted to believe that the French had only changed masters.[53]

47. Hardy, "Mes loisirs," BN, mss. fr. 6687, 8:448 (entry for August 25, 1789).

48. See, for examples of Châtelet-conducted arrests, AN, ser. Y, "Procès-verbal du Châtelet, saisies des libelles par les commissaires de police sous les ordres de M. le lieutenant-général de police," nos. 10012, 11441, 11518, 12083, 12085, 13016, 13582, 14353, 14583, 14584, 15022, 15100, 16008 (January 13, 1789–December 9, 1790). For examples of arrests by the *commissaires de police des districts*, see BN, Nouvelles Acquisitions Françaises (hereafter cited as nouv. acq. fr.) 2696, fol. 109, "Procès-verbal du district de St. André des Arts, saisies des libelles," October 9, 1789; and 2666, "Procès-verbal du Comité du district de St. Roch," fols. 29, raid chez Vaufleury, Palais Royal, July 9, 1790; 62, raid chez S. Pain, Imp.-Lib., Palais Royal, July 1790; 84, arrest of colporteurs, Palais Royal, August 11, 1790; 105, arrest of colporteurs, Palais Royal, September 9, 1790.

49. *Enterrement des feuilles volantes. De profundis des petits auteurs. Agonie des colporteurs* ([Paris]: P. de Lormel, [1790]).

50. *Révolutions de Paris*, no. 15, October 17, 1789, 2–6.

51. Ibid., no. 24, December 19, 1789, 30.

52. Ibid., no. 21, November 28, 1789, 28.

53. Ibid., no. 62, September 11, 1790, 550.

Indeed, it appeared that the revolutionary government was carrying through with enhanced vigor the policy of the Crown's cultural police against grub-street literary culture. After all, it was the keeper of the seals who had initially enlisted the Paris Book Guild in 1788 to regulate and register colporteurs.[54] And it was the royal council in 1787 that had taken the first legal measures to permit raids of bookshops within the Palais Royal.[55] The Palais Royal, the source of sedition under the Old Regime, became an equally insidious fomenter of dissent under the new, and the government, now concerned to check further radicalization of the Revolution, ironically was authorized to apply the total license of martial law to bring about its demise as a center of sedition.

As municipal authorities took over, and even extended, the policing powers of the crumbling royal administration, the Paris Book Guild, too, sought to remake itself as a municipal, rather than a royal, institution. On August 4, 1789, the National Assembly abolished the principle of privilege, but it deferred resolution of the question of corporate monopolies and privileges.[56] The problem was handed over to the Committee on Public Contributions and was not to resurface in the assembly until February 1791. The administrative fate of the Paris Book Guild for the next two years, however, had been largely determined before the famous proclamation of August 4.

According to a report in the *Révolutions de Paris*, the director of the royal Administration of the Book Trade, Poitevin de Maissemy, began meeting with the municipal Committee of Police in late July 1789 to instruct them "on the best means of preventing the circulation of inflammatory pamphlets." The report added that the meeting "suggested that the municipal government will support the conservation of the book guild."[57] These suppositions of the *Révolutions de Paris* were soon vividly confirmed.

On August 2, the Commune of Paris decreed that all publications circulating in Paris had to bear the name of either the author, the printer,

---

54. BN, mss. fr. 21861, "Registre de la communauté des libraires et imprimeurs," entry for January 19, 1788.

55. BN, mss. fr. 22102, Collection Anisson-Duperron, feuilles 258–259: "Arrêt du conseil d'état du roi, concernant le commerce de librairie dans les lieux privilégiés, du 4 septembre 1787."

56. See Sewell, *Work and Revolution*, 86. For the National Assembly's discussion, see Jérôme Madival and Emile Laurent, eds., *Archives parlementaires de 1787 à 1860*, 1st ser. (Paris: Dupont, 1898), 8:349.

57. *Révolutions de Paris*, no. 4, August 6, 1789, 30–31.

or the bookseller and had to be registered with the Paris Book Guild with the deposit of a sample copy.[58] This decree, at least formally, allowed the guild to retain its policing functions intact.[59] Thus, under the authority of the municipality, the guild recovered its power to determine, if not what was printed or who printed it, at least what could legally make its way to the Parisian marketplace, and thus the ability to protect the literary privileges of its members. The royal Administration of the Book Trade was left merely to reaffirm this municipal initiative retroactively.[60] Two days before the National Assembly formally decreed an end to privilege, then, the Paris Book Guild appeared to recover its authority under the wing of municipal authorities.

This victory did not go unnoticed in the Parisian press. The day after the publication of the municipal decree, the following statement, written by Elysée Loustallot, appeared in the *Révolutions de Paris:* "At a moment when freedom of the press has insured a victory for public and personal freedom . . . , the Provisional Committee [of Police] has passed an ordinance concerning the Book Trade that is more repressive than were all the absurd regulations of the inquisitorial police that existed before the Revolution." From Loustallot's perspective, the demise of the royal Administration of the Book Trade had served only to enhance the power of the Paris Book Guild to control what made its way into print: "It is as though a prisoner were told that he was free because he was permitted to stroll in the prison yard." And the economic, as well as the political implications of the decree were clear:

> [A] league exists between the printers and publishers against men of letters, and this incredible situation forces them either to pay very high rates for printing or to share the profits from their works with the publishers. These are profit-making professions, and because authors need a publisher's name in order to get a work printed, it is simple to make them pay for using it.[61]

In essence, for a work to be approved by the Paris Book Guild, it had to bear the name of a printer or bookseller that the guild would recognize.

58. P.-J.-B. Buchez and P.-C. Roux, eds., *Histoire parlementaire de la Révolution française* (Paris: Paulin, 1834), 2:191, 246; and LaCroix (ed.), *Actes de la Commune de Paris,* 1st ser., 1:82.

59. This interpretation of the decree is confirmed by a report on the policing and registering of privileges by the Paris Book Guild found in the papers of the Administration of the Book Trade, AN, ser. VI, carton 553, November 3, 1789.

60. Ibid., Report from Dieudonné Thiebault to the keeper of the seals concerning the registration of permissions at the office of the Paris Book Guild, November 3, 1789.

61. *Révolutions de Paris,* no. 4, August 3, 1789, 43–44.

The guild appeared to have devised a means of preserving its monopoly on the book trade in the city. Within a month after the National Assembly had declared the freedom of the press, the *Révolutions de Paris* was calling for the retraction of that "strange article in the Declaration of the Rights of Man, whose glaring equivocations leave citizens vulnerable to all sorts of despotic and intolerant abuses."[62]

But the guild's victory soon appeared illusory. In October the reorganized commune appointed Pierre Manuel as its chief administrator of the "division of the book trade." Manuel was no friend of the guild or its monopolies. The *Révolutions de Paris* reported that under Manuel's administration "the police issued permits to all citizens allowing them to receive book shipments directly at the customs office" rather than at the office of the book guild, thus checking the power of the guild to control what could be imported into the city.[63] Until Manuel left this post at the end of 1790, the power of the guild to defend their privileges was thus effectively circumvented.

Nonetheless, the book guild continued to meet straight through 1789 and 1790. But in face of the popular enthusiasm for freedom of the press, its members opted to lay low and to conduct their business and their politics behind the scenes. They ceased appearing in public processions, and many members refused to sign the register of their meetings.[64] In October 1789 the guild's officers ceased to perform their regular inspections of the shops of printers and booksellers of the city (figure 2).[65]

Still, the officers of the guild continued to make every effort to protect their privileges and interests in both theory and practice. And after Manuel's departure, Syndic Knapen and the guild managed once again to succeed in gaining the sympathies of the municipal authorities. As late as January 1791, for example, an article in the *Révolutions de Paris* entitled "Vexations of the Book Guild" reported that

> M. Villette, publisher, ordered some books from Maëstricht. The parcel was seized at the office of the book guild reputedly because it contained "incendiary pamphlets." These pamphlets were several copies of *The Adventures of Télémaque*. M. Villette . . . went to City Hall, where one of [Mayor]

62. Ibid., no. 10, September 13, 1789, 11.
63. Ibid., no. 73, November 27–December 4, 1790, 409.
64. BN, mss. fr. 21861, "Registre de la communauté des libraires et imprimeurs," entry for October 7, 1789.
65. BN, mss. fr. 21946, "Registre des ordres de MM. les directeurs-généraux de la librairie et imprimerie de la France," July 1, 1770–October 1, 1789.

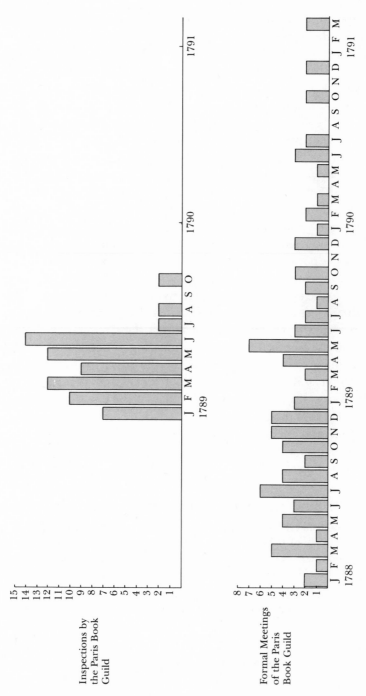

Figure 2. Inspections and Meetings of the Paris Book Guild, 1789–1791

Source: BN, mss. fr. 21936 and 21861.

Bailly's men . . . responded, on the mayor's behalf, that "he was aware of the situation; that the publishers of the book guild were right to want to protect their privileges, and that the books had been fairly confiscated."

The *Révolutions de Paris* was so outraged by this renewal of the guild's prerogatives that it could not resist further comment: "Because [the Paris inspector of the book trade] d'Hémery and his comrade Knapen took *Télémaque* for *an incendiary pamphlet*, an honest citizen has had his property confiscated, his commercial relations disrupted, and it should be no surprise why these men cling to their vile functions with such tenacity."[66] Moreover, the tenacious chief officer of the guild, Knapen, appeared to have succeeded with the municipal authorities where he had failed with the royal administration: any privilege on *Télémaque* could be upheld only on the basis of the Code of 1723, not that of 1777.[67] The author of *The Adventures of Télémaque*, François de Salignac de la Mothe-Fénélon, had been dead for well over ten years.

And while the Paris Book Guild made every effort to retain its grip on the Parisian market in the printed word, it was also marshaling its resources to gain attention and interest for its cause from the deputies of the National Assembly at Versailles. Thus on September 9, 1789, the officers of the guild convened its membership, "in the manner prescribed by the . . . regulations of . . . 1723," in order to vote to make a gift of 20,000 *livres* to the National Assembly.[68] This symbolic overture to the new sovereign was soon followed, on November 12, by a direct appeal to the new keeper of the seals, Champion de Cicé, soliciting "the suppression of the private unlicensed printing shops that have been established in Paris."[69] Champion de Cicé, in consultation with the minister of foreign affairs, counseled the guild to be patient for new regulations, which they assured would be forthcoming from the National Assembly.[70]

The Paris Book Guild awaited the promised legislation. But when,

66. *Révolutions de Paris*, no. 80, January 15–22, 1791, 89. Fénélon's *Aventures de Télémaque* was originally published in 1699.

67. For the history of the dispute between the guild and the royal administration over LaVillette's status as a book dealer and his business practices, see AN, ser. V1, carton 552, Correspondence between Poitevin de Maissemy and the Paris Book Guild, June 9, July 10, and August 12, 1789.

68. BN, mss. fr. 21861, "Registre de la communauté," entries for September 29–30 and October 1, 1789.

69. AN, ser. V1, carton 553, Report from Thiebault to the keeper of the seals, November 12, 1789.

70. Ibid.

three months later, a proposal concerning freedom of the press did emerge from the Committee on the Constitution, it was silent on both the issue of who had the right to own a printing press and the status of the Paris Book Guild. And where it addressed the question of literary property, it proposed only a slight modification of the dispositions of the royal *arrêts* of 1777 regarding the duration of publishers' commercial claims.[71] This first effort by the National Assembly to offer a positive legal definition of freedom of the press did not bode well for the Paris Book Guild or its interests. But fortunately for the guild, the law, presented by Emmanuel Sieyès on behalf of the committee, was defeated by the assembly.[72]

The guild was quick to respond to the threat represented by the Sieyès proposal. During 1790 the guild's officers redoubled their efforts to sway the National Assembly to support the maintenance of the book guild, limitation of the number of presses in Paris, and recognition of publishers' literary privileges as property rights. In February, the officers paid a visit to the president of the merged Committees on Agriculture and Commerce. Not finding him in, they left a letter and a memorandum pleading against revocation of their monopolies on the publishing and printing trades:

> An infinite number of people who can barely read have established boutiques in all the quarters of the capital, putting their names and the sign Bookseller on their doors, a title which they have unscrupulously usurped. . . . We dare to hope that . . . the National Assembly will soon want to turn its attention to the Book Trade: this guild has always been exempted when corporate monopolies have been suppressed, as much because of abuses and piracy . . . as because the sale of bad books will soon infect France if everyone is free to enter the book trade.[73]

And they continued: "Those who have opened new printing shops have taken the words 'Freedom of the Press' to the letter, interpreting them

---

71. France, National Constituent Assembly, Committee on the Constitution, "Projet de loi contre les délits qui peuvent se commettre par la voie de l'impression et par la publication des écrits et des gravures, etc., présenté à l'Assemblée Nationale, le 20 janvier 1790, par le Comité de Constitution," in *Procès-verbal de l'Assemblée Nationale* (Paris: Baudouin, 1790), 11:1–24. For an extensive discussion of this proposal, see chapter 3.

72. Ibid.

73. AN, ser. DXIII, carton 1, doc. 12, Letter from the Paris Book Guild to the Committee on Agriculture and Commerce, February 24, 1790, signed by Knapen, syndic; and Cailleau, Mérigot *le jeune,* Nyon *l'aîné,* and Delalain, adjoints.

to mean the 'freedom of the presses.' All of France . . . has an interest in limiting this freedom of the presses. You are witnesses to the dangers to which this liberty, today degenerated into license, can expose the nation."[74] The Committees on Agriculture and Commerce recorded the memorandum and letter on March 5, 1790, and then forwarded copies to the Committee on the Constitution.[75]

Along with these private negotiations, the guild publicly circulated a printed *Mémoire* addressed to the National Assembly that, in a newly acquired revolutionary idiom, vividly evoked and denounced the consequences of the declaration of press freedom:

Since last January the professions of the printers and publishers of the university have been shamelessly swallowed up: insurrection gave birth to license, and disorder reigned through anarchy. The aristocrats had their incendiary writings printed, lighting the fire of revolt in the hearts of the French: clandestine presses were . . . insufficient to quench their rage; they needed an even greater number. They evolved this false interpretation of *freedom of the press.*[76]

The guild officers violently denounced the municipal police's "division of the book trade," as well, for "pretending to be competent in the affairs of the book trade," for insisting that the municipal government was capable of taking over the functions of the royal Administration of the Book Trade, for permitting the establishment of "supernumerary printing shops" and for justifying the existence of these printing shops with the assertion that "freedom of the press is a right that . . . no one can be denied."[77] As a consequence of this municipal policy, they testified to the National Assembly, in the year following the declaration of the freedom of the press the number of printing presses in the capital had grown from thirty-six to two hundred! And it was these new printers, financed by counterrevolutionary aristocrats, they asserted, who were fueling the flames of popular insurrection and preventing the restoration of public order.

74. Ibid., fol. 3r.
75. AN, ser. AFI, Procès-verbal des Comités d'Agriculture et de Commerce, 51st session, March 5, 1790. For the copy sent to the Committee on the Constitution, see AN, ser. DIV, carton 50, doc. 1452.
76. [Jean-Augustin Grangé] *Mémoire présenté à l'Assemblée Nationale pour le corps des libraires et imprimeurs de l'Université* (Paris: Grangé, 1790), 4.
77. Ibid., 8.

The guild did not miss this opportunity to lash out at its great adversary, the *Révolutions de Paris:*

> Antipatriots have given the printer of the *Révolutions de Paris,* which is devoted to the aristocracy, the necessary sum to establish a beautiful printing shop, and in less than two years this new printer has acquired houses in both the city and countryside, and he is keeping a carriage. Marat, who is in the pay of the enemies of the state, also has a printing shop of which he makes such bad use.[78]

These "suspect men," they asserted, were responsible for the Sieyès proposal and had, moreover, "succeeded in winning over the Committee on the Constitution, by arguing that the freedom of the press belongs equally to the intruders, who have arbitrarily appropriated [these professions] without authorization."[79] The guild officers again pleaded that the only way to prevent continuous assaults on the government and on respectable people was for the government to revive the regulations of 1723 limiting the number of printers and controlling the book trade. Even that great advocate of free trade Turgot, they observed, had exempted the book guild from his famous decrees of 1776 because of the political dangers of an unregulated circulation of printed matter.

These appeals did not fall on entirely deaf ears. The National Assembly was becoming increasingly aware of the range of issues uncovered by the principle of press freedom. The problem could not be reduced to municipal policing of libelous or seditious ephemera produced locally for local consumption. The keeper of the seals himself was at a loss as to how to proceed. He appealed for guidance in a letter to the president of the National Assembly's political watchdog, the Committee on Investigations, on June 22, 1790:

> While awaiting . . . the promulgation of regulations that could affect the printing trades I have not upheld the old regulations and have only enforced those that concern essentially the property rights of authors and printers. In accordance with this policy a bundle of books was brought to the office of the book guild and inspected by the printer-publishers. The pamphlet [one found in the bundle] is not pirated, and it threatens no one's property, but nonetheless the officers of the guild thought that they should request my advice, as [the pamphlet] is directed against the work of the National Assembly. . . . The shipment will not be released until I give

78. Ibid., 5.
79. Ibid., 15.

the order, and I did not think I should make this decision without knowing your wishes.[80]

The keeper of the seals's inquiry raised large questions: How was literary property to be protected? How were the national and international markets in printed matter to be regulated or policed? Who, if anyone, had the right to inspect shipments of printed matter?

It also evidenced the undeniable fact that the Paris Book Guild was performing essential functions, not only in policing literary property but also in protecting the National Assembly against the criticisms of its opponents. Despite the formal declaration of "freedom of the press," that summer the Committee on Investigations pragmatically solicited the services of the guild to inspect shipments of books and pamphlets into the capital in order to identify and suppress counterrevolutionary printed matter.[81] Elysée Loustallot's charges of a conspiracy among deputies of the National Assembly, municipal authorities, and the guild was not without truth.

This unofficial solicitation of guild services by the Committee on Investigations did not resolve the larger question of the future role of the government in the regulation of the publishing world. But it did inspire new hopes for the guild officers that their services might be rewarded in the anticipated legislation on the book trade. They sent another memorandum to the National Assembly, which was forwarded to the Committees on Agriculture and Commerce on September 6, 1790.[82]

Then in early 1791 the keeper of the seals wrote again, with yet greater eloquence and urgency, to the president of the Committee on Investigations: "I want my decisions to be constitutional, and to conform to the principle of liberty as it has been conceived by the National Assembly. . . . Whose right is it to judge . . . a book and to give the order for it to be seized?"[83] He recommended that the Committees on Investigations, on

80. AN, ser. DXXIX *bis*, carton 32, doss. 334, doc. 17, Letter from the keeper of the seals to the Committee on Investigations, June 22, 1790.

81. For the committee's dealings with the Paris Book Guild, see ibid., doc. 16, Letter from the keeper of the seals to the Committee on Investigations, June 28, 1790; doc. 13, Letter from the keeper of the seals to the Committee on Investigations concerning a meeting between the Paris Book Guild and the committee, August 10, 1790; and doc. 12, Report from the guild to the Committee on Investigations, August 13, 1790.

82. AN, ser. AFI, Procès-verbal des Comités d'Agriculture et de Commerce, 124th session, September 6, 1790.

83. AN, ser. DXXIX *bis*, carton 16, doss. 182, doc. 7, Letter from the keeper of the seals to the president of the Committee on Investigations, January 9, 1791.

the Constitution, and on Agriculture and Commerce convene together to settle the question.[84] The Committees on Agriculture and Commerce received the same letter and took the initiative to convene the committees "in order to propose a law concerning these matters of great importance to the book trade and to literature."[85] The Committees on the Constitution and on Agriculture and Commerce finally met in May 1791 and recommended a formal legislative proposal "concerning the property in scientific and literary productions."[86] But there was no mention of the Paris Book Guild in the proposal. This was because the Paris Book Guild, along with all other Corporations of the Arts and Trades, had been suppressed definitively on March 17, 1791, two months earlier.[87]

Ironically, the law that served as the death warrant of the Paris Book Guild concerned guilds or corporations only indirectly. It was a tax law, sponsored by the Committee on Public Contributions. This law suppressed all corporations and then created a new license tax, the *patente*, which was to be levied on all businesses. The ideology of freedom of commerce was here deployed as much in the service of state revenues as in that of social, economic, or cultural freedom: more businesses meant more business taxes.

On March 18, 1791, the day after the formal suppression of all guilds and corporations, the officers of the Paris Book Guild assembled for a rector's procession at the church of St. Jacques des Hauts-Pas to send their last collective prayers to God.[88] They soon began to register at the City Hall for individual business licenses in conformity with the new

84. Ibid.

85. AN, ser. AFI, Procès-verbal des Comités d'Agriculture et de Commerce, January 12, 1791; and AN, ser. DXXIX *bis*, carton 16, doss. 182, doc. 10, Letter from the Committees on Agriculture and Commerce to the Committee on Investigations, January 13, 1791.

86. AN, ser. AFI, Procès-verbal des Comités d'Agriculture et de Commerce, 224th session, May 23, 1791; and François Hell, *Rapport fait à l'Assemblée Nationale par M. Hell, député du Bas-Rhin, sur la propriété des productions scientifiques ou littéraires* (Paris: Imprimerie Nationale, 1791), AN, ser. ADVIII, carton 16.

87. France, National Constituent Assembly, Committee on Public Contributions, Decree of March 17, 1791, in *Collection générale des décrets rendus par l'Assemblée Nationale* (Paris: Baudouin, 1791), 52–62.

88. BN, mss. fr. 21861, "Registre de la communauté des libraires et imprimeurs," entry for March 18, 1791.

patent law.[89] The liquidation of the corporation was conducted by the "department of domains" of the Paris Commune.[90] Disputes over the fate of the guild's funds and over ownership of suspended books held in the guild's warehouses dragged on into 1796.[91] The archives of the Paris Book Guild at our disposal today were finally transmitted to the Bibliothèque Nationale by the keeper of the National Archives in 1801.[92] The legacy of the official records of the guild, however, leaves many crucial questions unanswered. Why did the guild so stubbornly and persistently maintain the reactionary posture it did in face of the national mandate for the freedom of the press and the abolition of privileges? Were the official politics of the guild's officers representative of the views of its 220 members? After holding out so long against the current of opinion, why is there not more evidence of protest against the law suppressing the guild when it was finally passed?

The Paris Book Guild comprised diverse constituencies. The roll call for the royal *capitation,* the head tax for 1788, along with Augustin-Martin Lottin's *Catalogue . . . des libraires et libraires-imprimeurs* of 1789, enables us to determine the relative wealth of guild members and to distinguish the select 36 printer-publishers from the remaining 194 publishers and booksellers.[93] Table 2 presents a roll call of the guild on the eve of the Revolution, divided by relative wealth into the twenty classes of payment of the head tax.[94] It also allows us to locate the officers of the Paris Book Guild within the larger corporate structure.

89. For traces of the implementation of this patent law, see AN, ser. H2, carton 2103, "Bureau de la Ville de Paris, Lettres Patentes, 1791–1797."

90. Lacroix (ed.), *Actes de la Commune de Paris,* 2d ser., 3:196 (March 18, 1791) and 4:183 (May 19, 1791).

91. For disputes over the adjudication of the guild's holdings, see *Pétition des membres du ci-devant corps de la librairie et imprimerie de Paris, présentée à l'Assemblée Nationale* (Paris: Knapen, June 10, 1791); and AN, ser. F17, carton 1233, doc. 3, Report by the Temporary Commission on the Arts, 15 vendémiaire, an IV (October 7, 1795).

92. Henri Omont, ed., *Catalogue général des manuscrits de la Bibliothèque Nationale, ancien petit fond français* (Paris: Leroux, 1898), 1:403.

93. BN, mss. fr. 21861, "Registre de la communauté," *Capitation* roll prepared by the Lieutenant-General of Police, along with the officers of the Paris Book Guild, entry for August 12, 1788; Lottin, *Catalogue chronologique des libraires.* In fact, there were thirty-seven legally registered printers in Paris in 1789.

94. By an *arrêt* of the Council of State of March 14, 1779, the *capitation* tax for each corporation in Paris was established at a fixed sum. The members of a given corporation were divided, according to relative wealth, into twenty classes, each of which was assigned a proportional amount of the total *capitation* to be paid by the corporation. For the *arrêt,* see Jourdan, Decrusy, and Isambert (eds.), *Recueil général des anciennes lois françaises* 26:48–51.

André-François Knapen, the guild's highest officer, the syndic, was the key intermediary between the guild and the government. He was one of the thirty-six printers and also held the titles of printer for the Court of Aides and printer for the Parlement of Paris.[95] In the seventh class on the head-tax roll, he was relatively well off but by no means one of the wealthiest members of the guild. Knapen had been hit hard by the royal council *arrêts* of 1777 concerning the duration of literary "privileges." The royal administration, according to its own figures, had revoked his exclusive privileges on at least sixty-two titles.[96] Jean Luc III Nyon *l'aîné*, a second officer (*adjoint*), was a bookseller and member of one of the largest family empires within the guild. Four other immediate family members and at least one cousin, Paul-Denis Brocas, appear on the 1788 head-tax roll.[97] An uncle, Nicolas-Henri Nyon, was one of the thirty-six privileged printers, and among his other titles was that of printer of the Parlement of Paris.[98] Nyon *l'aîné* figured in the ninth class for the head tax and, with the rest of his family, fell into the wealthiest half of the guild, though not near the top. André-Charles Cailleau, the second *adjoint,* was also one of the thirty-six city printers and fairly wealthy, falling into the fourteenth head-tax class.[99] The third *adjoint,* Nicolas-Augustin Delalain *l'aîné,* bookseller, fell into the eleventh head-tax class, as did his son. Being solely in the book publishing and selling business, the Delalain family had been hit extremely hard by the *arrêts* of 1777, which revoked their privileges for 227 titles.[100] Nonetheless, Delalain *l'aîné* was still well off in relation to the guild at large. Jean-Gabriel Mérigot *le jeune,* the fourth and last *adjoint,* remains the most obscure. A book publisher and retail dealer, he fell into the eighth *capitation* class; he was thus relatively well off compared to both the other officers and the guild as a whole.

95. See Delalain, *Imprimerie et la librairie,* lvi.

96. BN, mss. fr. 21832, fols. 26–40, "No. 2 Tableau des ouvrages jugés communs ou qui le deviendront à l'expiration des privilèges dont ils sont revêtus, en exécution de l'article XI de l'arrêt du conseil du 30 août 1777 portant règlement sur la durée des privilèges en librairie." This document catalogues at least some of the privileges suppressed by the *arrêt,* and the names of the publishers who held them.

97. For the connection between the Brocas and Nyon families, see BN, mss. fr. 21896, "Registre de déclarations pour la contribution patriotique, 1789–1791," entry no. 3, December 27, 1789. Nyon *l'aîné* identifies Mme Brocas as his aunt.

98. For the names, titles, and addresses of the Nyon family, see Delalain, *Imprimerie et la librairie,* lviii.

99. Ibid., lii.

100. BN, mss. fr. 21832, fols. 26–40, "No. 2 Tableau des ouvrages jugés communs."

The guild's officers were not its wealthiest members, but they were some of its most privileged, and thus had more to lose with the demise of their monopolies. Three of the five were either printers or had family ties to the printing trade. Two were tied closely to the Parlement, and at least two had suffered serious losses as a consequence of the *arrêts* of 1777. Not surprisingly, they became virulent defenders of their hereditary literary privileges, their monopoly on the printing presses of the capital, and the power of the guild to inspect shipments of books into the city. They were joined in their struggle to preserve traditional guild privileges by other privileged printers, like Augustin-Martin Lottin, the guild's scholarly polemicist, and Philippe-Denis Pierres, one of the king's printers, who inscribed his vituperative rage against press freedom alongside his forced "patriotic contribution."[101] It was precisely these "old printers . . . who sell to the rich, and only to the rich," that Restif de la Bretonne, among others, had hoped the freedom of the press would drive under.[102]

However, the guild's officers and the privileged thirty-six printers of Paris were not the only members of the guild to defend this institution's continuance after the declaration of the freedom of the press. Charles-Joseph Panckoucke, the encyclopedist publisher and press magnate, and by far the wealthiest member of the guild, also mobilized both his pen and his journal, the *Mercure de France,* to argue for retaining some form of a guild after 1789. In two articles published in the *Mercure* on January 23 and March 6, 1790, Panckoucke argued for the formation of an "unrestricted book guild."[103] But Panckoucke's guild differed significantly from the Bourbon corporation that the officers of the Paris Book Guild sought to preserve. His guild was conceived more like a modern businessman's association. The trade should be open to all, and the guild should admit any honest businessman capable of paying its fee. The guild would provide paternalistic charitable services for workers within the trade and thus woo them away from fly-by-night operations. Its essential function, however, would be to serve as a surveillance network, in coordination with public authorities, to police the property rights of authors and publishers.

---

101. For Lottin, see chapter 1. On Pierres, see BN, mss. fr. 21896, "Registre des déclarations pour la contribution patriotique," entry no. 111, May 11, 1790.

102. Restif de la Bretonne, *Nuits révolutionnaires,* 230.

103. Charles-Joseph Panckoucke, "Sur les chambres syndicales," *Mercure de France,* January 23, 1790; and "Sur l'état actuel de l'imprimerie," ibid., March 6, 1790, esp. 35. See also Darnton, *Business of Enlightenment,* 501–502.

Table 2 The Paris Book Guild in 1788 by *Capitation* Class

Capitation Roll, 1788:

1e
1. Panckoucke

2e
*2. Moutard
*3. Barbou

3e
*4. Debure, le jeune
5. Desaint, Vve
*6. Laporte
*7. Desprez

4e
*8. Herissant, Vve

5e
9. Duchesne
*10. Pierres
11. Samson

6e
12. Barrois, l'aîné
13. Brocas
14. Debure, fils
*15. Didot, l'aîné
16. Fournier
*17. Quillau
*18. Stoupe

7e
19. Barrois, le jeune
*20. Knapen, père et fils
*21. Lamesle
22. Martin
*23. Prault, l'aîné

8e
*24. Chardon
*25. Clousier
26. D'Houry, Vve
27. Didot, le jeune
28. Durand et fils
*29. Gueffier
30. Mérigot, le jeune
*31. Nyon
*32. Simon
*33. Valade, Vve et fils
34. Vincent

9e
35. Bailly
36. Cuchet
37. D'Houry
38. Desenne, Victor
39. Esprit, Vve
40. Froullé
41. Nyon, l'aîné et fils
42. Tillard, Vve et fils

10e
43. Belin
44. Buisson
45. Colombier
46. Demonville
47. Gando, père et fils

11e
48. Berton
*49. Cellot, père
50. Debure, Vve
51. D'Houry, Vve
52. Gattey
53. Lamy

12e
54. Barrois, Vve
55. Bastien
56. Delalain, l'aîné et fils
*57. Desaint
*58. Hérissant, Vve (St. Jaq.)
*59. Lottin de St-Germain
60. Onfroy
61. Santus
62. Savoye
63. Visse

13e
*64. Ballard
65. Cellot, fils
*66. Couturier
67. Crapart
68. Debure St. Faubin
69. Didot, fils
70. Guillot
71. Jombert
72. Langlois, père
73. LeClerc, L.F.
74. Méquignon, l'aîné
75. Méquignon, le jeune
76. Nyon, quai des 4 Nations
77. Royez

14e
78. Alix, Vve
*79. Cailleau
80. Colas
*81. Delormel
82. D'Houry, Vve
83. Durand de Sugères
84. Etienne, le jeune
85. Fournier, J.-B.
86. Humblot
87. Gibert
88. Laurent
89. Legras
90. Née de la Rochelle
91. Séguy-Thiboust
92. Servières
*93. Valleyre, le jeune
94. Voland

15e
*95. Baudouin
96. Briand
97. Brunet
98. Crapart, Vve
99. Cussac
*100. Delaguette, Vve et fils
101. Delalain, le jeune
102. Desnos
103. Devéria
104. Duplain
105. Durand-Dufresnoy
106. Fabre
107. Gueffier, Vve Rich. Sim.
*108. Jorry
109. Lamesle
110. LeBouges
111. LeClerc, quai des Aug.
112. LeClerc, rue St-Martin
113. Lejay, fils
114. LeRoy
115. Maradan
116. Molini
117. Nyon, Vve
118. Périsse
119. Prault, Marcel
120. Prault, St. Martin
121. Prévoste, l'aîné
122. Saugrain, le jeune
123. Séguin
*124. Valleyre, l'aîné
125. Barin
126. Plassan

16e
127. Belin, le jeune
128. Bleuet, rue de Seine
129. Lagrange
130. LeComte
131. Lejay, père
132. Petit
133. Planche
134. Poincot
135. Piré
136. Regnault
*137. Thibout, Vve
138. Vastaud

17e
139. Babuty
140. Boudet
141. Crescend
142. Croullebois
143. Debray
144. Desrois
145. Gastelier
146. Godefroy
147. Grégoire
148. Guillaume, fils
149. Hardy
150. Lallemant de Sancières
*151. Lambert, Vve
152. Lotin, le jeune
153. Louette
154. Masson
155. Prisard
156. Pissot, père et fils
157. Prévoste, le jeune

18e
158. Bacos
159. Bleuet, père
160. Bleuet, fils, de la Barillière
161. Boulard
162. Deschamps
163. Despilly
164. Dufresne
165. Gogué, Vve
166. Guillyn, Vve
167. Langlois, fils
168. Lesclapart
*169. Morin
170. Vente

19e
171. Bichois, Vve
172. Blanchon
173. Brocas, Vve
174. Butard
175. Caille
176. Couturier, Vve
177. Desauges
178. Gobreau
*179. Grangé, père
180. Guillaume, Pl. Pont St. Mich.
181. LaCloye
182. Lefevre-Sordet
183. Lemoine
*184. Lesclapart, Vve
*185. Lottin, l'aîné
186. Marisaud, Vve
187. Mérigot, l'aîné
188. Monory
189. Morin
190. Moureau
191. Musier
192. Pierres, Vve
193. Robin, Vve
194. Rouquier
195. Vallet-la-Chapelle

20e
196. Capon, Vve
197. Delevaque, Vve
198. Dorez
199. Dubois, père
200. Goguery
201. Grangé, fils
202. Guillaume, Vve
203. Hilaire
204. Jolly
205. Momoro
206. Poilly
207. Poiree, Vve
208. Prault, Vve
209. Robuffet
210. Saugrain, père
211. Serveron
212. Sorin
213. Vatar, père

*printer

The Paris Book Guild Officers: *Syndic:* Knapen, Printer; *Adjoints:* Nyon l'aîné, Publisher; Cailleau, Printer; Delalain, l'aîné, Publisher; Mérigot, je., Publisher; Mérigot, jeune, Publisher. Total no. of members = 213 (32 women); Total no. of bookseller/publishers = 176; Total no. of printer/publishers = 37 (5 women); Total no. of family names = 163. SOURCE: BN, mss. fr. 21861, "Registre de la communauté des libraires et imprimeurs."

Panckoucke's publishing background and interests differed significantly from those of the officers of the book guild.[104] As early as 1777 he had proclaimed himself against perpetual privileges on literary texts for publishers; his own greatest ventures had been conducted beyond the world of privileged texts.[105] Nor did he believe in a corporate monopoly on the means of producing the printed word: the presses. In fact, he badly needed more presses in Paris to meet the production schedule of his *Encyclopédie.*[106] Panckoucke's crucial motive for defending the concept of the guild, in short, was to regain control over the work force and to aid in the policing of property.

Panckoucke was not alone in believing that maintenance of the Paris Book Guild and freedom of the press were not incompatible goals. A whole second stratum of the Paris Book Guild shared his vision of a guild open to all: the younger and less well-off booksellers of the guild and the myriad of ambitious printing-shop workers who held little prospect of advancing within the old structure of the guild. With the declaration of freedom of the press, they jumped at the chance to become the thirty-seventh, thirty-eighth, or thirty-ninth printer of Paris. Such was the case with the bookseller Pierre Leroy, who made his request to the keeper of the seals on October 20, 1789.[107] He was followed by the son of the widow Valade on November 15; Jean-Baptiste-Nicolas Crapart, bookseller, on December 12; and Jacques-Denis Langlois, also a licensed bookseller, on January 19, 1790.[108] Quickly, and more spontaneously, other minor book dealers from the bottom of the Paris Book Guild ranks joined in, such as Martin-Sylvestre Boulard, the future author and printer of the *Manuel de l'imprimeur* (1791), and Antoine-François Momoro, a man soon to leave his mark in Parisian revolutionary politics.[109]

104. The definitive study of Panckoucke's career is Tucoo-Chala, *Charles-Joseph Panckoucke.* See also Darnton, *Business of Enlightenment.*

105. [LeClerc], *Lettre à M***.*

106. Ibid.; and AN, ser. V1, carton 553, Report on a letter from Panckoucke to the keeper of the seals, June 6, 1789. The edition in question is Charles-Joseph Panckoucke, ed., *Encyclopédie méthodique,* 166 vols. (Paris, 1789–1832).

107. AN, ser. V1, carton 553, Letter from Pierre LeRoy, Paris book dealer, October 20, 1789.

108. Ibid., Letters from Valade, Paris bookseller, November 15, 1789; Jean-Baptiste-Nicolas Crapart, Paris bookseller, December 12, 1789; and Letter in favor of Langlois *fils,* Paris bookseller, January 19, 1790.

109. On Boulard, see BN, nouv. acq. fr. 2666, fol. 6 [1790]. And on Momoro, see Lacroix (ed.), *Actes de la Commune de Paris,* 2d ser., 3:16, 340, 574, 719, 768, 771; 4:460;

To these can be added, Pierre Plassan, Gillé *fils,* Jacques Mérigot *l'aîné,* Laurent-Mathieu Guillaume *le jeune,* Jean Cussac, François Belin, Jean-François Colas, and Honoré-Clément DeHansy.[110] In sum, many of the new printers of Paris came from within the ranks of the old guild (see table 2). While these men evidenced desire for reforms within the guild, they were not necessarily against the guild, because as book publishers and sellers they were aware of the commercial necessity of policing the publication of printed matter.

In the first few years of the Revolution, the members of the Paris Book Guild held together as a coalition in defense of their guild. But it was a negative coalition formed out of two competing but seemingly inseparable conceptions. For the old guard, whose fortunes were based on printing monopolies and a closed market in privileged texts, the guild was defended as a productive entity. Yet there were significant new elements at both the top and bottom of the guild's spectrum of fortunes, men and women whose careers had been or were to be made in a competitive market, beyond the borders and on the margins of the corporatist system. For these individuals the imperative to maintain the guild resided in the commercial need to police property and to assure the financial stability of their ventures. Over the course of 1789, 1790, and 1791, these two visions were inextricably interwoven in defense of the same institution. As with many issues, however, the Revolution sorted out old contradictions in new ways. By 1791 it became clear that the legislative process of the National Assembly would resolve the issues of freedom of commerce and protection of property in the world of ideas independently of each other. The Gordian knot had been cut, and the coalition within the guild collapsed. And with it went many of the oldest Parisian publishing fortunes.

5:391, 432, 485; 6:99–100, 105, 648, 658; 7:29, 48, 50, 643; and 8:621. For more on Momoro's career, see below, chapter 5.

110. See AN, ser. F18, carton 11A, plaque 1, Letter from Plassan to the Ministry of the Interior detailing his career since 1789, January 28, 1810; ibid., Letter from Gillé to the Ministry of the Interior detailing his career since 1789, January 11, 1810; Lacroix (ed.), *Actes de la Commune de Paris,* 1st ser., 1:386 (November 25, 1790), wherein Mérigot *l'aîné* proposes the establishment of a new printing shop; AN, ser. Y, no. 15021, doss. Bossange, February 14, 1790, in which Guillaume is charged with printing pirate editions; and, on Cusac, Belin, Colas, and DeHansy, AN, ser. F18, carton 25, "Notes sur les imprimeurs ci-après désignés," [1811].

A Cultural Elite in Economic Crisis

The king's printer Philippe-Denis Pierres was not alone when he proclaimed in 1790 that his profession was "lost and prostituted."[111] Similar laments echoed both publicly and privately throughout the Paris publishing world from 1789 through 1793. In August 1789, the printer Jean-Baptiste-Paul Valleyre protested to the Administration of the Book Trade that he was being menaced and ruined by a new printer.[112] Louis-François-André Godefroy, a bookseller, wrote to the office in September testifying that "our sales are nearly dead."[113] In November, Pierre-François Gueffier, one of the wealthiest printers of the Paris Book Guild, decried "the decimation of the industry."[114] Guillaume Debure *l'aîné*, a publisher from one of the oldest and wealthiest families in the guild, testified in December: "I am losing considerable sums on books."[115] The bookseller Méquignon *l'aîné* acknowledged "the extreme penury of the business" in the spring of the following year.[116] So, too, the bookseller Jean-Baptiste Gobreau remarked a few months later on "the considerable losses I have taken" and "the current radical loss of business."[117] Even Charles-Joseph Panckoucke commented on "the extreme distress in which the book trade finds itself."[118] At the end of 1790, the bookseller Jean-Augustin Grangé presented a collective *Mémoire* to the National Assembly on behalf of the printers, publishers, and booksellers of the capital. Here he queried before the representatives of the nation, "Are we now to be without means and out of business?"[119]

Laments and testimonies continued over the next several years.

---

111. BN, mss. fr. 21896, "Registre des déclarations pour la contribution patriotique," entry no. 111, May 11, 1790.

112. AN, ser. V1, carton 552, Letter from Valleyre to Poitevin de Maissemy, August 19, 1789.

113. Ibid., Letter from Godefroy to the Administration of the Book Trade, September 11, 1789.

114. For Gueffier's position in the guild, see table 2. For his protest, see BN, mss. fr. 21896, "Registre des déclarations pour la contribution patriotique," entry no. 10, November 24, 1789.

115. For the position of the Debure family in the guild, see table 2. For his testimony, see ibid., entry no. 34, December 24, 1789.

116. Ibid., entry no. 79, March 12, 1790.

117. Ibid., entry no. 108, May 7, 1790.

118. Charles-Joseph Panckoucke, "Avis sur l'encyclopédie par ordre de matières," *Mercure de France,* February 27, 1790, 155.

119. Cited in Radiguer, *Maîtres imprimeurs et ouvriers typographes,* 143.

Jacques-Denis Langlois, a bookseller, wrote to the Committee on the Constitution that he had "greatly suffered in his bookselling business because of losses."[120] The publishers of religious books Vincent Petit and the widow Despilly protested to the Ecclesiastical Committee that six hundred families in the religious book trade were on the verge of ruin.[121] In the National Assembly, the deputy Charles de Lameth testified on behalf of a Paris bookseller that, "earning nothing by printing good books," he was being driven to produce incendiary pamphlets.[122] In 1793, Nicolas-Léger Moutard, a printer and the second wealthiest member of the guild, wrote to fellow printer and bookseller Antoine-Louis-Guillaume-Catherine Laporte lamenting "the enormous losses that I have suffered."[123] So, too, Jean-Luc III Nyon *l'aîné*, former officer of the Paris Book Guild, testified to the minister of the interior that "our business is totally wiped out."[124] Several months later, his brother Pierre-Michel Nyon *le jeune* was to use almost identical terms to describe his plight: "From 1789 to this day, my business has been completely demolished."[125]

Were these men and women telling the truth? Or were they merely evoking a picture of financial plight for political and economic purposes, to defend and enhance their monopoly on the printed word? After all, testimony of material duress was almost a required credential of good citizenship during the first years of the Revolution. Furthermore, the statements cited above appeared in somewhat suspect contexts, such as justifications of the modesty of their "patriotic contributions," deferrals of payments to creditors, and requests for government subsidies or contracts.[126] Elysée Loustallot, the vigilant watchdog of press freedoms

120. AN, ser. DIV, carton 50, doc. 1452, Letter from Langlois *fils* to the Committee on the Constitution, [1790–1791].

121. AN, ser. DIX, carton 81, doc. 623, Letter from Petit and Despilly, publishers, to the Ecclesiastical Committee, January 10, 1791. See also AN, ser. ADVIII, carton 20, *Mémoire présenté à l'Assemblée Nationale au nom des imprimeurs-libraires, propriétaires des privilèges des divers liturgies de France* (Paris: N.-H. Nyon, 1790).

122. Buchez and Roux (eds.), *Histoire parlementaire de la Révolution française* 4:270, proceedings of the National Assembly for January 12, 1791.

123. AN, ser. BB16, carton 703, doss. 17, Ministry of Justice, Letter from Moutard to Laporte, May 11, 1793.

124. AN, ser. F17, carton 1004c, doss. 650. Committee on Public Instruction, Letter from Nyon *l'aîné* to the minister of the interior, June 30, 1793.

125. Ibid., carton 1008a, doss. 1374, Committee on Public Instruction, Letter from Nyon *le jeune*, 8 frimaire, an II (November 28, 1793).

126. See BN, mss. fr. 21896, "Registre des déclarations pour la contribution patriotique," entry nos. 10 (November 24, 1789), 34 (December 24, 1789), 79 (March 12, 1790),

for the *Révolutions de Paris,* adopted this latter interpretation, persistently decrying the Paris Book Guild, its members, and "their scandalous profits."[127] But the bankruptcy records in the Archives de Paris suggest that for once Loustallot was wrong.

The Paris head-tax roll for 1788, declarations for the national "patriotic contribution" (1789–1791), and declarations of bankruptcy (1789–1793) together offer a fairly accurate picture of the wealth of the members of the Paris Book Guild and the fate of their affairs during the first few years of the Revolution. Figure 3 gives a breakdown of guild members according to head-tax class and profession.[128] Declarations of total assets at bankruptcy by seventeen members between 1789 and 1793 provide a rough estimate of the thresholds of actual wealth within the guild; these figures are presented beneath the *capitation* classes.[129]

Figure 3 can be cross-checked by an alternative measure of relative wealth provided by individual declarations for the "patriotic contribution" (figure 4).[130] Taken together, figures 3 and 4 show the extreme

---

and 108 (May 7, 1790). On deferrals of payments, see AN, ser. BB16, carton 703, doss. 17, Ministry of Justice, Letter from Moutard to Laporte, May 11, 1793. And on requests for government subsidies or contracts, see AN, ser. DIV, carton 50, doss. 1452, Committee on the Constitution, Letter from Langlois *fils* [1790–1791]; and AN, ser. F17, carton 1004c, doss. 650, Committee on Public Instruction, Letter from Nyon *le jeune,* 8 frimaire, an II (November 28, 1793).

127. See *Révolutions de Paris,* no. 23, December 12–19, 1789, 17.

128. It should be noted that whereas *libraires* (publishers and/or booksellers) were prohibited by law from owning printing shops, *imprimeurs* were legally allowed to print as well as to publish and retail books. Thus, while all members of the guild were technically *libraires,* only some were *imprimeurs.* The character of these enterprises varied widely. The assessment for each of the twenty *capitation* tax classes was established along a sliding incremental scale (4–200 *livres*), the ratio narrowing toward the bottom. Figure 3 plots the twenty classes on an absolute scale, correlating each class according to its assessment in *livres* to reveal the relative metric "distance" between them.

129. For the exact figures on which these estimates are based, see appendix 2, "Declarations of Bankruptcy."

130. The *contribution patriotique* was a forced loan levied by the National Assembly in 1789. It required all citizens to sacrifice, one time only, one-quarter of their net revenue to the service of the state. In contrast to the *capitation* tax, the "contribution" to be paid was determined by each individual rather than by the lieutenant of police and the guild officers. It also differed from the *capitation* in that the "contribution" was based on a percentage of the individual's actual revenue, rather than on a fixed sum paid by the guild as a whole and divided proportionally among its members. Figure 4 correlates the range of

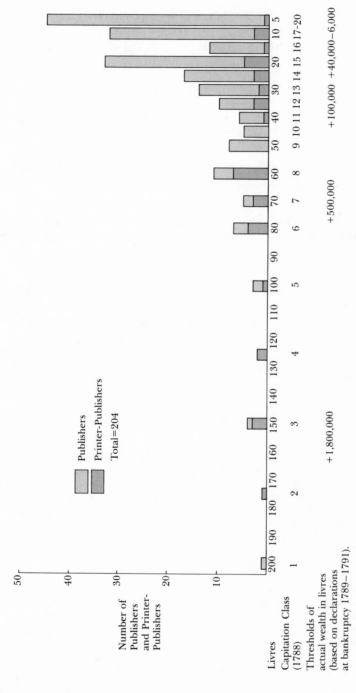

Figure 3. Estimates of the Relative and Actual Wealth of the Paris Book Guild By Correlation of Capitation Tax and Declarations of Bankruptcy, 1789–1791

Note: On the distinction between publishers and printer-publishers, see further chapter 2, note 128.

Sources: BN, mss. fr. 21861, "Registre de la communauté des libraires et imprimeurs"; and AP, Fond Faillite, ser. D4B6.

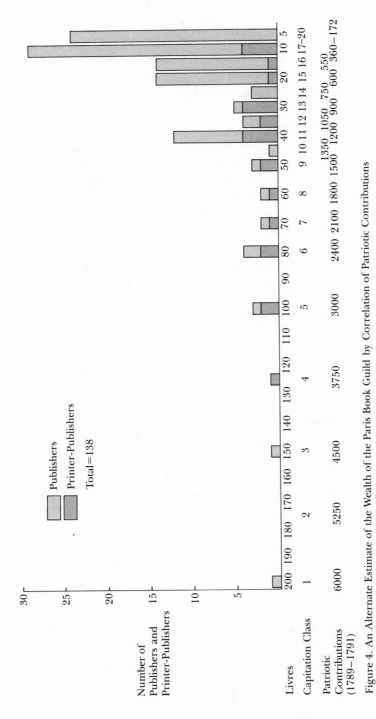

Figure 4. An Alternate Estimate of the Wealth of the Paris Book Guild by Correlation of Patriotic Contributions and Declarations of Bankruptcy, 1789–1791.

Note: On patriotic contributions, see further chapter 2, note 130.

Sources: BN, mss. fr. 21861, "Registre de la communauté des libraires et imprimeurs"; and 21896, "Registre des déclarations pour la contribution patriotique."

polarization of wealth among the privileged purveyors of literate culture in Paris, whose assets spanned practically the entire wealth spectrum of the Parisian population above indigence.[131] Charles-Joseph Panckoucke, Nicolas-Léger Moutard, Joseph-Gérard Barbou, François-Jean-Noël Debure *le jeune*, the widow Desaint, and Antoine-Louis-Guillaume-Catherine Laporte formed a kind of superelite, living in a different world from the hundreds of small book dealers and modest printers who swelled the lower ranks of the guild. The contrast between these two groups could not have been sharper, as there were relatively few medium-scale establishments to bridge the enormous gap in material wealth and social milieu that divided them. Of the 123 guild members who provided the information requested for the "patriotic contribution"—that is, concerning living situation and property holdings—only 18 declared themselves owners of their residence, and only 4 identified themselves as the principal tenants of the houses in which they lived.[132]

In 1788, Panckoucke boasted eight hundred workers and employees in his pay. He owned elegant homes in Paris and Boulogne and maintained personal relations with both the most famous literary figures of the period and the most powerful ministers at the court of Versailles.[133] A man as at home in fashionable salons as in noisy printing shops, Panckoucke formed part of the politico-cultural elite that ruled France on the eve of the Revolution.[134]

The Debure-d'Houry establishment, formed by a marriage between two of the oldest families in the Paris Book Guild, cut a similar profile in the social landscape of the late eighteenth century. François-Jean-Noël Debure *le jeune* declared his total wealth (minus his wife's dowry) at 1,870,247 *livres* in 1790. The couple owned a country house in the village of Massy, with "outbuildings, a garden, and landholdings comprising

---

declarations for the "contribution" (72–6,000 *livres*) with the incremental scale used to determine the payment of the *capitation*, for purposes of comparison.

131. For estimates of the socio-economic breakdown of the Parisian population in the second half of the eighteenth century, see Adeline Daumard and François Furet, *Structures et relations sociales à Paris au XVIIIe siècle* (Paris: Armand Colin, 1981), 76–100.

132. BN, mss. fr. 21896, "Registre des déclarations pour la contribution patriotique," 1789–1791.

133. For a description of Panckoucke's social milieu, see David I. Kulstein, "The Ideas of Charles-Joseph Panckoucke, Publisher of the *Moniteur universel*, on the French Revolution," *French Historical Studies* 4, no. 3 (Spring 1966): 307–309.

134. Pierre Goubert, *L'Ancien Régime*, vol. 2: *Les Pouvoirs* (Paris: Armand Colin, 1973), 210, 218.

around seventy acres," assessed at 95,650 *livres;* a *maison bourgeoise* in Paris, with "a coach entry and garden, . . . on the rue Copeau" and "half of an entire establishment . . . on the rue Neuve Saint-François, also with a coach entry, a garden, and ice cellar." They were creditors of the Estates of Brittany and Languedoc and of the duc d'Orléans, among numerous others.[135]

These *grands bourgeois,* despite having the same official profession and "privileges" as their fellow guild members, lived in worlds apart. More representative, at least quantitatively, of the Parisian merchants of the printed word on the eve of the Revolution were types like Antoine-François Momoro, on the rue de la Harpe with a stock of eleven titles in his boutique, his entire fortune;[136] or Jean Fabre, a bookseller on Pont St-Michel whose 30,245 *livres'* worth of books constituted nearly all he had in the world.[137] These two were joined by hundreds of other small printers and booksellers, like Charles Guillaume on the place du Pont St-Michel, who assessed his entire "belongings and merchandise" at 1,500 *livres;*[138] or Lefevre on the rue des Mathurins, who estimated his merchandise at 1,500 *livres* and his "furniture, suits, linens, and the everyday clothing worn by husband, wife, and children" at the same sum.[139] In second-floor printing shops and wooden storefronts, the majority of the "privileged" members of the Paris Book Guild produced and disseminated the printed word in Paris, with neither hope nor aspirations of entry into the literary salons of Panckoucke or the genteel country-manor circles of the Debure-d'Houry family.

The members of the Paris Book Guild, then, were dramatically polarized, related, it would seem, only by inverse correlation. But statistics do not tell the entire story, of either fortunes or personal destiny. Money flows. And individuals live or work together, marry and do business with one another. However extreme the contrasts of wealth and social standing within the guild, the Paris publishing world was in reality a very tightly woven community. And it was the weave of this fabric as much as its constituent threads that would shape and determine its fate.

135. AP, Fond Faillite, ser. D4B6, carton 110, doss. 7844, July 26, 1790.
136. See table 2 for his position in the guild (20th *capitation* class); and AP, Fond Faillite, ser. D4B6, carton 110, doss. 7811, June 8, 1790.
137. See table 2 for his position in the guild (15th *capitation* class); and AP, Fond Faillite, ser. D4B6, carton 109, doss. 7763, April 3, 1790.
138. AP, Fond Faillite, ser. D11U3, carton 2, January 22, 1793.
139. Ibid., ser. D4B6, carton 108, doss. 7711, February 20, 1790.

While the count provided by the head-tax roll for 1788 lists 213 guild members, only 163 family names appear on the list (see table 2). Moreover, at least eleven of the largest of these families were related by marriage: Nyon-Brocas, Knapen-Delaguette, Didot-Barrois, Didot-Regnault, Lottin-Pierres, and Debure-d'Houry.[140] The Paris publishing community was, above all, a community of blood relatives and in-laws who sought to consolidate and enhance their family empires. And guild members also lived together and rented from one another. For example, Cellot *fils* lived with Cellot *le jeune*.[141] Tillard, Duchesne, and Crapart all lived with their mothers.[142] And Mme Didot, the widow of Barrois, shared a roof with Didot *l'aîné*.[143] Cohabitation and space sharing, moreover, did not require formal family and apprenticeship bonds. Plassan worked as Panckoucke's agent, and Ruault as the director of his printing shop.[144] The two widows Tillard and Leroy shared a household.[145] The printer Stoupe rented from Debure.[146] The publisher Hardy lived with the widow Desaint; Babuty with the Debures; Ballard with Mlle Simon; Lamy with Leroy; Froullé with Didot *fils aîné;* Gueffier *le jeune* with Onfroy; and Saugrain *le jeune* with Leroy.[147] Thus in daily life, family, household, and social ties frequently spanned the great divisions in wealth and living standards, rendering them less sharp.

Even more important, perhaps, than kinship bonds or social connections was the high degree of financial interdependence among Parisian printers, publishers, and booksellers, a result of their labyrinthine business transactions. The detailed business accounts of seventeen members

140. For Nyon and Brocas, see BN, mss. fr. 21896, "Registre des déclarations pour la contribution patriotique," entry no. 3, December 22, 1789; Knapen and Delaguette, no. 73, March 9, 1790; Didot and Regnault, no. 97, March 29, 1790; Didot and Barrois, no. 27, December 22, 1789; Lottin and Pierres, no. 16, December 9, 1789; and for Debure and d'Houry, see AP, Fond Faillite, ser. D4B6, carton 110, doss. 7844, July 26, 1790.

141. BN, mss. fr. 21896, "Registre des déclarations," entry no. 11.

142. Ibid., entry nos. 58 (February 26, 1790), 110 (May 7, 1790), and 120 (May 14, 1790).

143. Ibid., entry no. 27, December 22, 1789.

144. See AN, ser. F18, carton 25, "Notes sur les imprimeurs ci-après désignés," [1811], entries for Plassan and Agasse.

145. BN, mss. fr. 21896, "Registre des déclarations pour la contribution patriotique," entry no. 58, February 26, 1791.

146. Ibid., entry no. 7, November 17, 1789.

147. For each of these shared households, see, respectively, ibid., entry nos. 23, December 18, 1789; 40, December 27, 1789; 53, February 23, 1790; 54, February 23, 1790; 86, March 23, 1790; 80, March 16, 1790; and 114, May 11, 1790.

of the Paris Book Guild for the years 1789 to 1793 held at the Archives de Paris enable one to reconstruct a partial, but nonetheless significant, picture of the maze of business relations among guild members (see appendix 1).[148] Strikingly, ninety members—almost half the guild's total membership—appear in fifteen of these accounts.

Nor were patterns of indebtedness unidirectional. Individuals sometimes appeared as both creditors and debtors in a single account, and some of the wealthiest members of the guild, such as Debure-d'Houry and Moutard, were debtors to more minor figures like Valleyre and Briand. Debits and credits flowed in both directions. In the publishing world, debts were an index not of simple dependency, but of ongoing reciprocity. Indebtedness was not simply an unavoidable, or even a regrettable, *fact* of economic life; it was rather a *way* of life, the essence of good business relations in a world where financial institutions were few, metal coins scarce and cumbersome, communication slow, and transportation time-consuming, expensive, and often dangerous. All these factors combined to encourage the conduct of business as the elaboration of a continuous and, if successful, expanding web of debts and credits, negotiated through bills of exchange and letters of credit.

The evidence suggests that the guild functioned as a kind of credit union in a time of highly unpredictable production and distribution and uneven and episodic markets. It was better business to keep creditors at bay and uncollected debts in the coffer. Debts and credits were passed on through multiple countersignatures rather than squared up, because unsettled accounts functioned as a kind of private currency that at once maximized options and insured the continuance of business relations. Credit, as much and perhaps more than capital, was the stuff of economic life. Hence the members of the Paris Book Guild, both rich and poor, were inextricably tied to one another's economic fate.

Although the practice of pursuing indebtedness could lead to a positive mutual interdependence, it often led to illiquidity as well. The figures provided by guild members in declaring their "patriotic contributions"—a requirement that citizens offer the government one-quarter of net revenues and 2.5 percent of their precious metals—warrant fur-

---

148. The list in appendix 1 cites members of the Paris Book Guild *only*. Of course, many of these businesses had extensive financial relations beyond the guild, in Paris, the provinces, and abroad.

ther examination (figure 4).[149] Because these declarations were made
under written oath at the office of the Paris Book Guild,[150] they should
in principle offer us an index of the net revenues of declarants.

The declarations of Paris Book Guild members ranged from 72 to
6,000 *livres,* surprisingly modest figures in light of the declared assets
presented in figure 3 and appendix 2. Louis-François Prault, for example, declared on March 16, 1790, that his net revenue for that year
amounted to 1,200 *livres.*[151] But seven months later when, on November
20, Prault filed for bankruptcy, he estimated his total assets at 329,935
livres.[152] When Charles-Joseph Panckoucke, the guild's wealthiest member, declared his contribution on April 30, 1790, he estimated one-
quarter of his net revenue at 6,000 *livres.*[153] One current expert on
Panckoucke's publishing business estimates that his total assets at this
time were somewhere near 2,500,000 *livres,* that is, close to one hundred
times his declared annual net revenue.[154] Were Prault and Panckoucke
simply guilty of unpatriotic tax evasion? Evidence suggests otherwise.

While Panckoucke, Prault, and others no doubt took advantage of any
loopholes the law afforded, it is unlikely that they, or the other
declarants, resisted conformity to the letter of the law. A week before he
made his contribution, Panckoucke had published an article under his
own signature in the *Moniteur universel* in which he declared that "only a
complete execution of the patriotic contribution can save the state" and
the French business classes as well. He then held up the corporations of
Paris as models of conformity to the law and urged all citizens to follow
their example.[155]

If we take Panckoucke and other guild members at their word, they
had substantial assets and credit but little revenue. This fact suggests an
alternative interpretation of the contrast between their large assets and

149. France, National Constituent Assembly, *Procès-verbal de l'Assemblée Nationale,* October 6, 1789, 5:1–12.

150. Ibid., arts. 3 and 5.

151. BN, mss. fr. 21896, "Registre des déclarations pour la contribution patriotique,"
entry no. 82, March 16, 1790.

152. See appendix 2.

153. BN, mss. fr. 21896, "Registre des déclarations," entry no. 31 (undated).

154. The estimate was given by Robert Darnton, author of *The Business of Enlightenment,*
a study of Panckoucke's business, in conversation with the author at Princeton University
in February 1985.

155. Charles-Joseph Panckoucke, "Sur la contribution patriotique," *Moniteur universel,*
no. 97, April 7, 1790 (Reprint Paris: Panckoucke, an III [1795–1796]), 396.

their modest declarations: the corporate publishing and printing establishments of Paris were incredibly insolvent on the eve of the Revolution.
This situation left them unable to respond effectively to the rapidly
changing circumstances, legal, political, and institutional, that ensued
from the declaration of the freedom of the press and the suppression of
the guild.

---

*Everyone is talking bankruptcy: someone has even dared to utter this word in the
National Assembly: it has reverberated in public squares, in cafés, and in the clubs.*
CHARLES-JOSEPH PANCKOUCKE, *MONITEUR UNIVERSEL*, ARPIL 7, 1790

In the spring of 1790, Panckoucke was worried about bankruptcy.
Indeed, the frightening possibility of a declaration of default by the
French state was on many people's minds during this first uncertain year
of National Assembly rule. The royal government's suspension of payments to the Caisse d'Escompte in 1788 precipitated a financial crisis that
reverberated through the French commercial world from Marseille to
Le Havre.[156] Far from exempt from this crisis, Parisian merchants found
themselves at its epicenter.[157] And the realities of bankruptcy were even
closer to home for Parisian publishers like Panckoucke. Between 1789
and 1793 at least twenty-one Paris publishers, booksellers, and printers—seventeen of whom were members of the Paris Book Guild—declared themselves in default, with more than half the total bankruptcies
occurring in 1790 alone. For the Paris Book Guild, clearly, 1790 was a
year of financial reckoning. Significantly, as these figures reveal, pub-

---

156. For a general overview of credit, risk, and business failure in the eighteenth
century, see Julian Hoppit, *Risk and Failure in English Business, 1700–1800* (Cambridge:
Cambridge University Press, 1987). For the difficulties of the Caisse d'Escompte and the
ensuing credit shortage in the early years of the Revolution, see Robert Bigo, *La Caisse
d'escompte (1776–1793) et les origines de la Banque de France* (Paris: PUF, 1927), 117–148. For
the consequences of this crisis in the commercial world, see Pierre Dardel, *Commerce,
industrie et navigation à Rouen et au Havre au XVIIIe siècle* (Rouen: Société Libre d'Emulation
de Seine-Maritime, 1966), esp. 394–395; Charles Carrière, *Négociants marseillais au XVIIIe
siècle* (Marseille: Institut Historique de Provence, 1973), esp. 427–464; and, for Paris, Tom
Luckett, "Credit and Society in Eighteenth-Century France" (Ph.D. diss., Princeton University, forthcoming). Dardel, Carrière, and Luckett find an upsurge in bankruptcies in
Rouen, Le Havre, Marseille, and Paris in 1788–1789. I am grateful to Tom Luckett for
drawing my attention to these studies, and for sharing his yet unpublished findings on
bankruptcies with me.
157. Luckett, "Credit and Society."

lishers declared nearly as many bankruptcies between 1789 and 1793 as in the preceding twenty-year period, 1770–1789 (see figure 5 and appendix 2). The total liabilities on the twenty-one bankruptcies from 1789 to 1793 ran over 4,000,000 *livres*.[158] Bankruptcy was not simply a looming possibility within the Paris publishing world: it was a frightening reality (figure 5).

As Jean-Clément Martin has observed, the causes and the economic significance of declarations of bankruptcy are not at all self-evident.[159] Broadly speaking, in a given industry they are as often an index of economic growth—albeit unstable—as of decline. Nonetheless, in revolutionary France, businessmen, unless they were engaged in fraud, generally sought to avoid declaring default; and when they were forced to do so, it was because they found themselves overextended and hence unable to make their payments. Furthermore, as Martin points out, however general a crisis appears, its causes are most frequently best understood through analysis of the particular situation of each industry rather than of broader price or credit trends. The accounts of the bankruptcies of Parisian publishers between 1789 and 1793 confirm the value of this localist approach: financial interdependence and illiquidity set off a domino reaction in the publishing world, transforming a series of discrete crises into collective catastrophe.

On January 21, 1789, the publisher Siméon-Prosper Hardy entered the following information in his journal:

Jean Lagrange, book dealer . . . on the rue St-Honoré near the place Palais Royal, where he seemed to conduct a thriving business and to have extensive dealings . . . in modern speculations, has just closed up shop, abandoned his establishment, . . . supposedly to go to London, leaving in commercial circulation a considerable number of notes all covered with fictional and false endorsements, having had the temerity to allow himself to forge the signatures of *four* businessmen . . . , of whom three are his

158. This estimate is based on a computation of the individual declarations of bankruptcy extant in the Archives de Paris. Louis Radiguer estimates the total *passif* of Paris printers and publishers in 1790 at 30,000,000 *livres* but does not indicate how he arrived at that figure (I assume that he is quoting the figure given by the publisher Jean-Augustin Grangé in his *Mémoire présenté à l'Assemblée Nationale*, 11). Grangé's estimate suggests that my own is probably extremely conservative. See Radiguer, *Maîtres imprimeurs et ouvriers typographes*, 143.

159. For the most penetrating assessment of the problems involved in the historical interpretation of bankruptcies, see Jean-Clément Martin, "Le Commerçant, la faillite et l'historien," *Annales E.S.C.* 35, no. 6 (November–December 1980): 1251–1268.

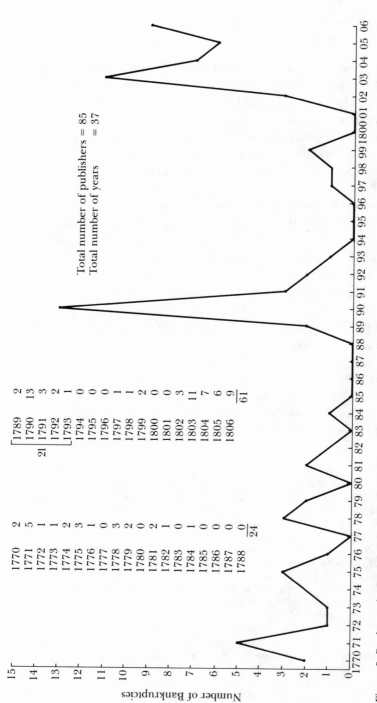

Figure 5. Bankruptcies Declared by Paris Publishers, 1770–1806

Source: AP, Fond Faillite, ser. D4B6 and D11U3.

partners: namely MM. *Debure-d'Houry,* printer-publisher, *Durand neveu,* and *Cuchet,* publishers.[160]

Ironically, this "speculator" in Enlightenment works helped to trigger a crisis in the publishing world of the Old Regime, not by conquering markets or reading publics, but by abusing his credit and credibility within the old corporate structure. The irony went further: Mlle Louise de Kéralio, a member of the aristocratic literati and Lagrange's invisible partner, was forced to file bankruptcy papers for the business after he fled.[161]

Within a year, two of the victims of Lagrange's forgery, Durand *neveu* and Debure-d'Houry, filed for bankruptcy as well.[162] As figure 5 illustrates, bankruptcies led to more bankruptcies. Debure-d'Houry, for example, appeared in the accounts of nine of the seventeen declarants of bankruptcy in the guild between 1789 and 1793, while Durand figured in six (see appendixes 1 and 2). And the consequences reverberated far beyond the fates of those forced to formal declarations. Debure *l'aîné* lost 8,000 *livres* in the Durand bankruptcy;[163] Panckoucke stood to lose 30,000 *livres* in three other bankruptcies (those of Debure, Poinçot, and Savoye).[164] Over half of the guild families (90 of 163) figured in accounts of the seventeen declarants, who alone owed at least 800,000 *livres* to members of the book guild.[165] There are indications, moreover, that the crisis of 1790 threatened to spread from Paris to the provinces.[166] The publishing world of the Old Regime was on the verge of collapse.

Matters would have been even worse had it not been for the intervention of the Crown. In its proceedings for June 8, 1790, the royal

160. Hardy, "Mes loisirs," BN, mss. fr. 6687, 8:207 (entry for January 21, 1789).

161. AP, Fond Faillite, ser. D4B6, carton 105, doss. 7454, March 30, 1789.

162. For the Debure-d'Houry bankruptcy, see ibid., carton 110, doss. 7844, July 26, 1790. The papers of the Durand bankruptcy are no longer extant, but evidence of its occurrence can be found in BN, mss. fr. 21896, "Registre des déclarations pour la contribution patriotique," entry no. 34, December 24, 1789.

163. BN, mss. fr. 21896, "Registre des déclarations," entry no. 34, December 24, 1789.

164. AP, Fond Faillite, ser. D4B6, carton 110, doss. 7844; carton 109, doss. 7399; and carton 111, doss. 7944.

165. This estimate is based on the declared debts of members of the Paris Book Guild in the accounts of the bankruptcies found in the Archives de Paris, Fond Faillite. See appendix 2 for detailed references.

166. AN, ser. DIV, carton 30, doss. 728, Committee on the Constitution, "Liberté de la presse, commerce de la librairie, réhabilitation des faillites. Février 1790–janvier 1791 (7 pièces)," especially the letters from Toulouse decrying the collapse of the book trade and an increase in bankruptcies. See also BN, mss. fr. 11708, "Procès-verbal des délibérations du bureau de Paris," June 8, 1790.

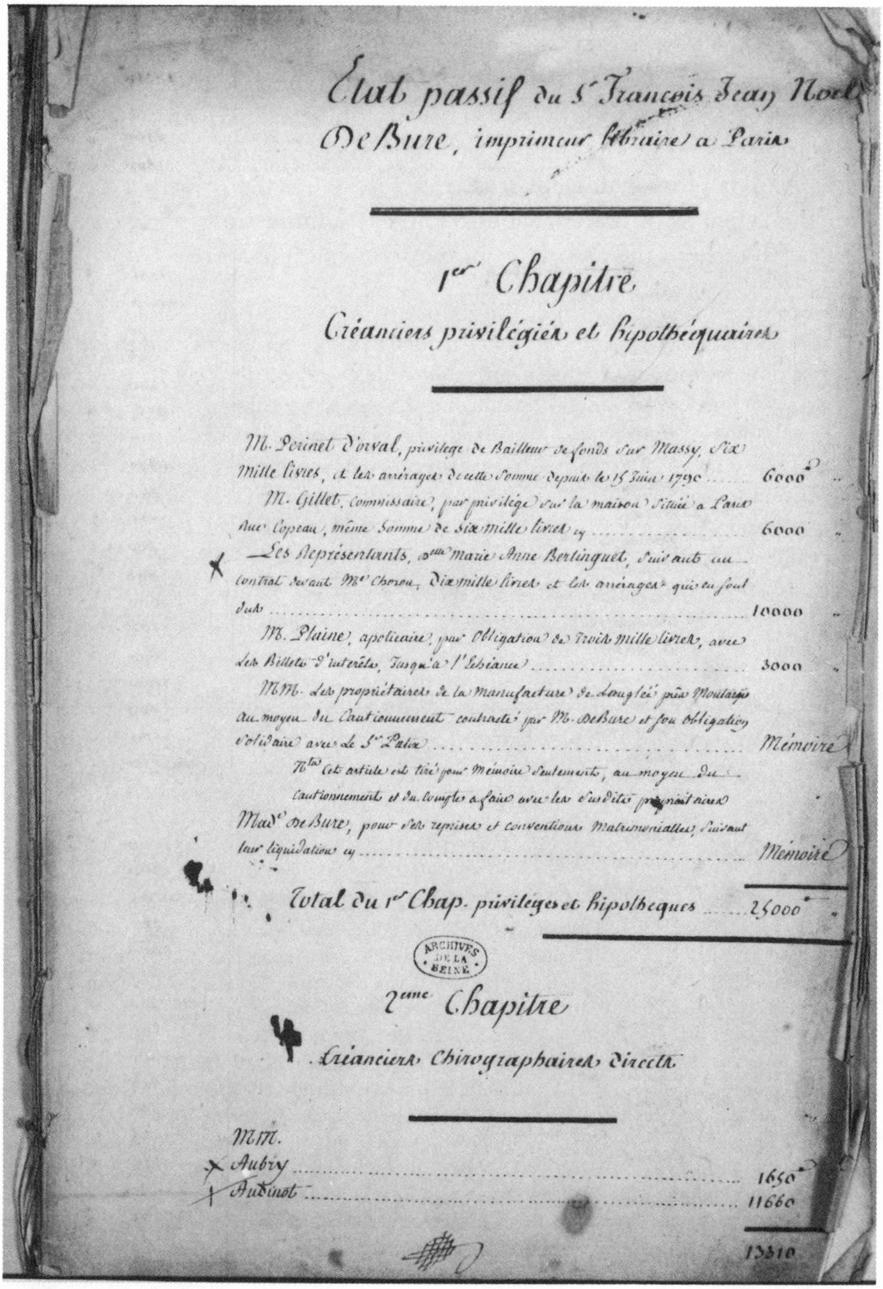
État passif du Sr François Jean Noël
De Bure, imprimeur libraire à Paris

1er Chapitre
Créanciers privilégiés et hipothécaires

M. Perinet d'orval, privilege de Bailleur de fonds sur Massy, six mille livres, et les arrérages de cette somme depuis le 15 Juin 1790 ... 6000
M. Gillet, commissaire, par privilège sur la maison située à l'aux rue Copeau, même somme de six mille livres cy ... 6000
Les Représentants, Dlle Marie Anne Berlinguet, suivant un contrat devant Me Choron, dix mille livres et les arrérages qui en sont dus ... 10000
M. Plaine, apoticaire, par obligation de trois mille livres, avec les billets d'interêts, jusqu'à l'échéance ... 3000
MM. les propriétaires de la manufacture de Langlée près Montargis au moyen du cautionnement contracté par M. DeBure et son obligation solidaire avec le Sr Patix ... Mémoire
Nota. Cet article est tiré pour mémoire seulement, au moyen du cautionnement et du compte à faire avec les susdits propriétaires
Madme DeBure, pour ses reprises et conventions matrimoniales, suivant leur liquidation cy ... Mémoire
Total du 1er Chap. privileges et hipotheques ... 25000

ARCHIVES DE LA SEINE

2eme Chapitre
Créanciers chirographaires directs

MM.
Aubry ... 1650
Audinot ... 11660
13310

Plate 3. Declaration of bankruptcy by Sieur Debure-d'Houry, one of the wealthiest members of the Paris Book Guild, July 26, 1790. Archives de Paris.

Administration of the City of Paris registered receipt of a memorandum presented by MM. Nyon *l'aîné*, Didot *le jeune*, Moutard, Cuchet, Guillot, and Huguet, publishers, printers, engravers, type and paper manufacturers in Paris, containing an exposé on the dangers with which they were threatened by the default of funds in circulation and by the personal bankruptcy of M. Debure-d'Houry, who was the principal creditor for the activities of their business. The city administrators summarized their response to the associates in the following manner:

> Considering that the ruin of the six partners would entail that of several thousands of persons, in the capital as well as in the provinces, and that the reaction to this disastrous event could have unheard-of consequences, even for the public weal . . . ; that the shareholders enjoy the most unimpeachable reputations and constitute one of the most important sectors of the book trade, . . . [the administration] has resolved to send its good officers to procure the access they desire to the National Assembly and the government, in order to obtain an open line of credit for 1,200,000 *livres* in bills of exchange . . . endorsed by the six partners. . . . MM. de Joly and de Juissieu have, moreover, been authorized to present themselves to the minister of finance and to do in this manner all that they deem necessary to insure its success.[167]

A series of negotiations ensued over the summer of 1790 between the city administration, the associated members of the Paris guild, Minister of Finance Necker, and the king himself.[168] A cache of letters and doc-

---

167. BN, mss. fr. 11708, "Procès-verbal des délibérations du bureau de Paris," June 8, 1790.

168. The documents of these negotiations were removed from the king's *armoire de fer* in 1793 by the Committee on Domains and have since been lost. However, at the time of their removal the following inventory of their contents was prepared by the committee and is still extant in AN, ser. C, carton 183, portfolio 107, nos. 384–393, "Inventaire des papiers saisis aux Tuilleries: armoire de fer." It reads as follows: "no. 384, chemise d'une liasse de papiers titrés de la main du roi; affaires des libraires de Paris [n.d.]; no. 385, lettre des libraires sociétaires de Paris, dans laquelle ils demandent au roi un provisoire de cent-cinquante mille livres [n.d.]; no. 386, écrit de la main du roi par lequel il annonce qu'il a cautionné sur les fonds de la liste civile, les libraires associés pour une somme de 1,050,000 livres [n.d.]; no. 387, lettre de M. Necker au roi, relative au cautionnement accordé aux libraires associés. La date est de la main du roi, 29 juillet 1790; no. 388, lettre du roi à Necker dans laquelle il announce son intention de faire une avance de 150,000 livres aux libraires associés, et de les cautionner sur la liste civile du surplus de la somme dont ils ont besoin pour remplir leurs engagements, St Cloud, le 27 juillet; no. 389, lettre des libraires dans laquelle ils se plaignent au roi des lenteurs du ministre des finances à remplir les voeux du roi à leur égard [n.d.]; no. 390, écrit de la main du roi, par lequel il prend les mêmes engagements que dans la lettre no. 388 [n.d.]; no. 391, arrêt du Bureau

uments discovered by the revolutionary government after August 10, 1792, in the king's secret *armoire de fer* revealed that by July 1790 the king had decided to subsidize the guild and had made them a personal advance of 150,000 *livres*.[169] By August the full subsidy of 1,200,000 *livres* received notarial authorization.[170] The king thus succeeded in averting an immediate and total collapse of the old elites of the Paris Book Guild. The monarchy, after all, needed their presses and markets. Retaining cultural power was crucial to the fate of the regime. Over the rocky course of 1789, for example, it was the head of this partnership, Nyon *l'aîné*, who faithfully propagated works affirming monarchical authority, such as the *Tableau des droits réels et respectifs du monarque et de ses sujets*.[171]

The *Révolutions de Paris* was quick to elucidate the broader implications of this royal act of cultural patronage:

> On August 4, the king stood security for the funds on the civil list for the associated booksellers in the amount of 1,200,000 *livres*. This act of benevolence is founded on the concern inspired in the king for the fate of these booksellers and the numerous artisans whom they employ, and who would find themselves without work. . . . The benevolence of his majesty makes a striking contrast with the unjust pursuits of the civil and military leaders of Paris against the press. It is well known that the associated booksellers do not employ a tenth part of the workers who are supported by the enterprises that the freedom of the press has allowed to blossom.[172]

The journal was right. The forces of cultural production were shifting elsewhere, and the Crown, in a desperate effort to maintain control over public opinion and cultural life, was bailing out a dying literary civilization.

Four months after the Crown's subsidy was enacted, the Paris publishing world was still in crisis. In a meeting of December 24, 1790, the

---

de la Ville de Paris portant témoignage honorable en faveur des libraires associés [n.d.]; no. 392, mémoire de la société des libraires qui demande au roi de venir à son secours; cette société sollicite une avance à divers époques d'une somme de 1,200,000 livres [n.d.]; no. 393, actes notaires relatifs au cautionnement accordé par le roi à la société des libraires de Paris, 16 août, 11 et 28 septembre, 1790."

169. Ibid., nos. 386, 387.

170. Ibid., no. 393.

171. For the royal approbation of Nyon's timely publication of the *Tableau des droits réels et respectifs du monarque et de ses sujets, depuis la fondation de la monarchie jusqu'à nos jours, ou théorie des lois politiques de la monarchie française*, see AN, ser. VI, carton 552, Letter from Nyon to the Administration of the Book Trade, and response, September 25, 1789. This edition ultimately received a royal subsidy.

172. *Révolutions de Paris*, no. 56, August 4, 1790, 172.

Committees on Agriculture and Commerce of the National Assembly heard a report concerning "a petition from the publishers of Paris, presented by the municipality, in which they make public how their businesses continue to suffer."[173] The committees responded in much the same fashion as the Crown. On the same day they decreed:

> There shall be entrusted to the municipality of Paris *assignats* in an amount up to 1,500,000 *livres* against the sale of national lands, to be distributed under the direction of the municipal government in various loans to different publishing houses in Paris that demonstrate that, as a consequence of public circumstances, they find themselves unable to meet the terms of their former obligations.[174]

Thus during the fall of 1790 at least 2,700,000 *livres* poured from royal and municipal coffers to the aid of the foundering cultural elites of the Old Regime. But the National Assembly had thrown good money after bad.

The *Révolutions de Paris* had correctly linked the crisis in the Paris Book Guild to the declaration of the freedom of the press and the revolutionary mandate to "spread enlightenment." The guild crisis was not, in origin, a fiscal crisis. The source of the problem lay in the allegiance of many prominent guild members to a system of cultural production and a literary civilization that were both rapidly becoming obsolete. The economic crisis in the guild was, in that sense, a symptom of cultural revolution.

The publishers of Paris lamented in their petition to the Committees on Agriculture and Commerce that "the Revolution completely obliterated the value of the major books that they stocked in their shops, of the costliest articles, and of those whose sale formerly was most assured."[175] Within a few years, the Revolution had swept their way of life and the culture it produced into the past. The stock of the most prominent publishers of Paris—spiritual, legal, pedagogical, and historical—lost its commercial value as *nouveautés* and *lumières* flooded the capital. Thus Debure *l'aîné* declared in December 1789: "I am losing considerable

173. AN, ser. AFI, "Procès-verbal des Comités d'Agriculture et de Commerce," 179th session, December 24, 1790.
174. Ibid.
175. Ibid.

sums on works of jurisprudence."[176] So, too, Antoine Maugard listed in his declaration of bankruptcy on June 26, 1790, "works whose sale has been suspended by circumstances: *Code de la noblesse, Remarques sur la noblesse, Lettres sur les dangers des abrégés des lois.*"[177] Petit and Despilly, publishers of liturgies, wrote to the National Assembly in January 1791 to protest the ruin of six hundred families which would result from the division of France into departments, the consequent suppression of sixty-two bishoprics, and the proposal to standardize the liturgy of those remaining. They stood to see their privileges on the extant liturgies evaporate into thin air: "Twelve to fifteen million in commercial value . . . will be lost."[178] Nyon *le jeune* protested as well:

> Citizen legislators, from 1789 until this day my business has been completely wiped out by the suppression of the religious houses charged with education, by the inactivity of the colleges; elementary books for classes and for religious use that composed almost the whole of my stock are a total loss. . . . I can estimate the nonvalue of my classical books at 60,000 livres . . . as they are no longer in use.[179]

The classical, legal, and religious culture of the Old Regime ceased to reproduce itself.

The elites of Old Regime cultural commerce were driven under along with the culture they produced. Between 1789 and 1793 eighteen members of the guild were forced to bankruptcy. Another twenty-two gave evidence of being on the verge of default. These were not establishments on the margins of Old Regime publishing but those at its very heart: the Debures, Nyons, Moutards, and Méquignons. The king's printer Philippe-Denis Pierres sold his printing shop in 1792 and was to die an employee of the postal service in Dijon in 1808.[180] His former rival, the director of the Imprimerie Royale, Jacques Anisson-Duperron, saw his

176. BN, mss. fr. 21896, "Registre des déclarations pour la contribution patriotique," entry no. 34, December 24, 1789.

177. AP, Fond Faillite, ser. D4B6, carton 110, doss. 7829.

178. AN, ser. DIX, carton 81, no. 623, "Adresse à l'Assemblée Nationale au nom et par les chargés du pouvoir des libraires et imprimeurs propriétaires des privilèges des différents liturgies de France," January 10, 1791. See also *Mémoire présenté à l'Assemblée Nationale au nom des imprimeurs-libraires, propriétaires des privilèges des divers liturgies de France* (Paris: N.-H. Nyon, 1790), AN, ser. ADVIII, carton 20.

179. AN, ser. F17, carton 1008a, doss. 1347, Letter from Nyon *le jeune*, 8 frimaire, an II (November 29, 1793).

180. BN, nouv. acq. fr. 12684, feuilles 2–12, 23–24, Letters from Pierres to the minister of justice and bibliographic note [1803].

monopoly on royal publications eclipsed by the new printer of the National Assembly, François-Jean Baudouin.[181] Anisson-Duperron was to
fall under the blade of the guillotine in 1793.[182] By the year III (1794–
1795) Debure *l'aîné* was working as an employee of the Temporary Commission on the Arts, cataloguing the libraries confiscated from émigrés.[183]
Knapen *fils*, the son of the last syndic of the Paris Book Guild, left the
publishing business and went to work as a functionary of the Ministry of
the Interior.[184] Those who held out would be faced with the task of
remaking themselves and their enterprises as the Revolution remade the
literary world.

181. AN, ser. V1, carton 552, Letter from Anisson-Duperron to the Administration of
the Book Trade, and response, concerning the purview of Baudouin's printing shop.
182. AN, ser. BB16, carton 703, doss. 17, May–August 1793; and *Pétition des créanciers-
fournisseurs d'Anisson-Duperron* (N.p., [1793]), AN, ser. ADVIII, carton 20.
183. AN, ser. F17, carton 1199, doss. 1, Temporary Commission on the Arts, 20 germinal, an III (April 9, 1795).
184. Ibid., carton 1204, doss. 7, Memorandum from Knapen *fils*, employee in the
fourth division of the Ministry of the Interior, to the Committee on Public Instruction
[1800?].

CHAPTER THREE

The "Declaration of the Rights of Genius" in 1793

By the end of September 1792 the French monarchy had been formally abolished by the nation's new sovereign, the National Convention. With the Crown and its administration went the entire system of licit publishing under the Old Regime: the royal Administration of the Book Trade, the king's printers and the royal printing shop, the Court's patronage of writers, the academies, the royal censors, the system of literary privileges, the inspectors of the book trade, and the printers' and booksellers' guilds.[1] Once preeminent, the Parisian publishing community found itself in default. The revolutionary movement to "spread enlightenment" had succeeded through the declaration of freedom of the press in liberating productions of the mind from the tyrannical institutions of the Old Regime. Within four years of Marie-Joseph Chénier's denunciation, the "seventeen inquisitions exercised . . . upon the minds of citizens" were gone.[2]

Could anyone now print or sell anything—including works already published by someone else? The royal laws on the book trade defined the exclusive commercial monopoly on the publication of a work as a royal privilege, granted to the author or publisher by the king's "grace" alone. Had the abolition of privilege on August 4, 1789, abolished literary privileges? Retrospectively and prospectively? What about authors'

---

1. An earlier version of this chapter appeared as "Enlightenment Epistemology and the Laws of Authorship in Revolutionary France, 1777–1793," in *Representations* 30 (Spring 1990): 109–137.

2. See above, chapter 1. Chénier, *Dénonciation des inquisiteurs de la pensée*, 41.

rights? What distinguished a privilege from a property right? Were ideas in fact a form of property? The cultural capital of the Old Regime, as embodied in literary privileges for books, hinged on these questions. So did the future of the publishing industry. How did the French Revolution redefine the laws on authorship and literary property?

Although the history of modern authorship has long been of interest to historians and literary critics, no single essay has been more influential in current investigations and discussions than Michel Foucault's meditation "What Is an Author?"[3] Michel Foucault wrote, "The coming into being of the notion of the 'author' constitutes a privileged moment of *individualization* in the history of ideas. . . . It would be worth examining how the author became individualized in a culture like ours." He continued, "Since the eighteenth century, the author has played the role of the regulator of the fictive, a role quite characteristic of our era . . . of individualism and private property."[4] Thus Foucault established a parallelism. The relation between the "author" and the "text," he suggested, emerged historically as the cultural incarnation of a new axis in sociopolitical discourse: the inviolable relation between the rights-bearing individual and private property. According to Foucault, this "privileged moment of individualization" was also a moment of *privatization* of knowledge claims as property, in which the individual author came to be the exclusive principle by which meanings are composed, manipulated, and determined, or, to use his word, "regulated."

Two recent historical investigations have responded to Foucault's invitation to "examin[e] how the author became individualized." Both

3. Michel Foucault, "What Is an Author?" in *Textual Strategies: Perspectives in Post-structuralist Criticism,* ed. Josué V. Harari (Ithaca: Cornell University Press, 1979), 141–160. For the influence this essay has had on critical debates, see Harari (ed.), *Textual Strategies;* Peggy Kamuf, "Criticism," *Diacritics* 12, no. 2 (1982): 42–47; the response by Nancy K. Miller, "A Feminist Critic and Her Fictions," *Diacritics* 12, no. 2 (1982): 48–53; and Biddy Martin, "Feminism, Criticism, and Foucault," *New German Critique* 27 (1982): 3–30. For the impact of the essay in orienting historical research, see Martha Woodmansee, "The Genius and the Copyright: Economic and Legal Conditions of the Emergence of the 'Author,'" *Eighteenth-Century Studies* 17, no. 4 (1984): 425–448; Molly Nesbitt, "What Was an Author?" *Yale French Studies* 73 (1987): 229–257; Rose, "Author as Proprietor"; and Carla Hesse, "Reading Signatures: Female Authorship and Revolutionary Law in France, 1750–1850," *Eighteenth-Century Studies* 22, no. 3 (1989): 469–487.

4. Foucault, "What Is an Author?" 141, 159.

Martha Woodmansee's study of the development of the concept of the author in eighteenth-century Germany and Mark Rose's exploration of the legal debates on authorship and literary property in eighteenth-century England tend to confirm Foucault's thesis; the concept of the individual author as proprietor of his work, they conclude, emerged as a result of the rapid commercialization of the book trade.[5] For both these scholars, the advent of the modern cultural system can be marked by the translation of these new bourgeois socio-economic relations and cultural values into laws of copyright (in England in 1709 and in Prussia in 1794), that is, by their institutionalization as a system of legal regulation. Does the legal history of French authorship and copyright confirm this picture presented by Foucault and his successors? Did the French Revolution invent the "bourgeois author"? The answer to these questions lies in the cultural struggles in the opening years of the Revolution.

The Legal Contingencies of Liberty

The abolition of the principle of privilege by the National Assembly on August 4, 1789, threw the parameters of commercial publishing into doubt—and not just book publishing. Under the Old Regime all periodical publications had to bear a privilege as well. These privileges were granted on the basis of the particular area of knowledge that the journal intended to cover. Thus, for example, the journal of the Académie des Sciences was granted exclusive coverage of scientific developments; the *Mercure de France* enjoyed a monopoly on literary subjects; and so forth. But over the course of the eighteenth century two publishing concerns succeeded in accumulating and consolidating particular privileges to produce journals covering a wide variety of interests and subjects: namely, the *Gazette de France,* the *Mercure de France,* and the first Parisian daily, the *Journal de Paris.*[6] These general journals were created through the calculated purchase and combination of narrower privileges, or by payment of usage rights to the bearers of those privileges.

After August 4, 1789, the system of privileges in periodical publishing fell apart. The owners of the *Journal de Paris,* for example, refused to continue to pay a *rente* to M. Palissot and the Dame Devaux for the right to report on events covered under their privilege for the *Journal des*

5. Woodmansee, "Genius and the Copyright," 426; Rose, "Author as Proprietor," 56.
6. Bellanger (ed.), *Histoire générale de la presse française* 1:188, 240.

deuils de la cour et du nécrologie des hommes célèbres.[7] MM. Romilly, Cadet, Corancez, and Xhrouet, who owned the *Journal de Paris,* argued that the suppression of privileges applied equally to journals, and therefore they were no longer obliged to pay the *rente.* Palissot and Devaux took their complaint to the royal law courts at Châtelet and on May 18, 1790, won a judgment upholding their privilege.[8] The owners of the *Journal de Paris,* however, in turn appealed the case before the newly constituted civil courts in July 1791. On July 22, the new court reversed the decision of Châtelet, determining that "as a result of the abolition of privileges, privileges on journals are suppressed as well."[9] Palissot and Devaux thus lost their monopoly on covering court mourning rituals and the obituaries of famous men in the periodical press.

As trivial as this dispute may appear on its surface, the underlying legal issue had broad implications. The court's decision in effect abolished the internal barriers and tolls regulating the Old Regime periodical press. Journals and newspapers would no longer be required to limit their coverage to a particular area of knowledge. The abolition of these commercial publishing privileges, as much as the abstract declaration of the principle of freedom of the press, opened up the possibility for any individual to engage in the production of "news" of any sort.

Moreover, the abolition of the privileges of specialized journals simultaneously allowed the press empires of the eighteenth century to effect a de facto consolidation of their monopolies and an extension of their purview, for it freed them from the legal and economic constraints of the royal censors and the particular privilege holders to whom they had been accountable. While hundreds of new small pamphlet-newspapers poured onto the streets of Paris, the specialized journals of the Old Regime either disappeared or were swallowed up by the larger multi-genre dailies.[10]

But did the abolition of privileges mean that all newspapers could

7. Aristide P. Douarche, ed., *Les Tribunaux civils de Paris pendant la Révolution (1791–1800). Documents inédits recueillis avant l'incendie du Palais de Justice de 1871 par Casenave* (Paris: Le Cerf, 1905–1907), 1:94 and note. See also AN, ser. ADVIII, carton 38, "Réclamation d'un homme de lettres contre MM. Romilly, Cadet, Corancez et Xhrouet, entrepreneurs-associés du Journal de Paris," n.d.

8. Ibid.

9. Ibid.

10. For two extremely interesting discussions of the consequences of these developments for newspaper publishing, see Labrosse and Rétat, *Naissance du journal révolutionnaire;* and Jeremy D. Popkin, *Revolutionary News: The Press in France, 1789–1799* (Durham, N.C.: Duke University Press, 1990). See also Jeremy D. Popkin, "Journals: The New Face of the News," in Darnton and Roche (eds.), *Revolution in Print,* 141–164.

print exactly the same thing? Or did the owners and editors have exclusive commercial rights? Jacques-Pierre Brissot de Warville's journal the *Patriote français* is perhaps the most frequently celebrated example of the revolutionary challenge by journalists to the authority of the Crown to determine what was put into print and by whom.[11] Yet within eight months of the first issue of the *Patriote français*, Brissot's journal fell prey to the consequences of the very ideology of unlimited freedom of the press that it had espoused. Brissot had joined in a partnership with the Paris publisher François Buisson to produce the *Patriote français*. The famous prospectus for this journal appeared in early April 1789, bearing Buisson's bookshop as the address for subscriptions.[12] But when the royal Administration of the Book Trade suppressed the prospectus and prohibited publication of the journal, Buisson wrote to the administration denying any relation to Brissot and claiming that his name had been abused by the author.[13]

After the declaration of press freedom in August 1789, however, Buisson acknowledged his contract with Brissot. Further, he now charged Brissot with a breach of contract for producing the journal with clandestine presses.[14] Buisson asserted that Brissot's actions were sufficient cause for dissolution of the partnership and, further, that Buisson was thus free to publish his own journal under the title *Journal patriote* or any title he might choose—including Brissot's.[15] Brissot's journal was an extraordinary success, and Buisson wanted to hold on to a share of it. Ironically, but not surprisingly, the fledgling royal Administration of the Book Trade now came to the defense of Buisson.[16] If the press was totally free, the administration reasoned, then Buisson had as much right to publish a *journal patriote* as did Brissot.

The *Révolutions de Paris,* another ardent voice for unlimited freedom of the press, ran into similar problems. On November 3, 1789, the editor

11. See, for example, Bellanger (ed.), *Histoire générale de la presse française* 1:424–425; and Söderhjelm, *Régime de la presse* 1:76.

12. AN, ser. V1, carton 553, Correspondence between the director of the Royal Administration of the Book Trade, Poitevin de Maissemy, and the Paris Book Guild, April 14 and September 7, 1789.

13. Ibid.

14. Ibid., Correspondence between François Buisson and the Administration of the Book Trade, November 12, 1789.

15. Ibid., Memorandum concerning Jacques-Pierre Brissot de Warville and François Buisson, September 17, 1789.

16. Ibid.

and proprietor of this journal, Louis Prudhomme, wrote the National Assembly denouncing a "libel entitled no. XVI of the Révolutions de Paris, chez Froullé," which he claimed was a pirate edition.[17] His only recourse was publicly to disown the issue in question because, after all, it was his own journal that argued there should be no civil laws limiting the press.[18]

The Chaignieau brothers, owners of the popular *Journal du soir*, felt otherwise. The victims of repeated efforts to pirate both the title and contents of their journal, they finally filed a suit before the civil tribunal charging "usurpation of title and piracy" in March 1793.[19] The court resolved that the Chaignieau brothers did in fact own the title of their journal, as well as their family name.[20] They could not, however, claim ownership to the contents of their newspaper because the information belonged to everyone. Nonetheless, the auspices under which that information became public, in the form of title, format, and signature, belonged to those who first claimed them. In newspaper publishing, the legal claim to an exclusive commercial publishing right was rapidly shifting from the contents of the publication to its form—from the text to what Gérard Genette has called the "paratext."[21]

But what about books? Had the abolition of privilege meant the abolition of particular claims on texts as well? Even those of living authors? The manager of the Administration of the Book Trade, Dieudonné Thiebault, worried about this in his closing report to the keeper of the seals in late 1790: "People may soon feel the need to establish or reestablish some general public mechanism . . . to protect authors' property against the abuses of piracy."[22] But a "general public mechanism" was not forthcoming. Instead, with the suppression of the Administration of the Book Trade and then the Paris Book Guild, the job of policing what printers and booksellers produced and distributed devolved on local authorities. In Paris this meant the Commissioners of Police of the newly constituted Sections.

17. AN, ser. AA, carton 56, doc. 1524, Letter from Louis Prudhomme, November 3, 1789.
18. "De la liberté de la presse," *Révolutions de Paris*, no. 29, January 23–30, 1790, 17–18.
19. Douarche (ed.), *Tribunaux civils* 1:401–402 and notes, 497–498.
20. Ibid.
21. Gérard Genette, *Seuils* (Paris: Seuils, 1987).
22. AN, ser. V1, carton 553, Report from Thiebault to the keeper of the seals, [1790–1791].

When the Commune was reorganized in October 1789, it established a Police Committee composed of several administrators who were assigned to particular departments and accountable to the mayor. On October 10, 1789, Pierre Manuel was appointed administrator of the committee's division of the book trade and thus took charge of policing the book trade in Paris.[23] In this capacity Manuel gained access to the archives of the lieutenant-general of police pertaining to the book trade, including copies of the registers of royal literary privileges. Over the course of 1789 and 1790 he mined these papers, exposing the tyrannical exploits of the cultural police of the Old Regime in his book *La Police de Paris dévoilée*.[24] Ironically, only by virtue of having taken over their tasks did he gain access to the evidence to expose them.

Manuel had openly opposed the Paris Book Guild and its monopoly on the professions of printing and publishing. But what about the notion of literary privileges sanctioned by the regulations of 1777? And what about authors' rights? Would Manuel now take over the task of policing and protecting the literary privileges of authors and publishers? The few remaining records of the police of the Parisian districts from the years 1790–1793 enable us to reconstruct some of the realities of Parisian book publishing after the collapse of royal regulation.

By the end of 1789 pirate publishing was flourishing in Paris. Laurent Mathieu-Guillaume *le jeune*, a former member of the Paris Book Guild, was one of the many young booksellers who took advantage of the declaration of freedom of the press to open a printing shop.[25] And the administrative chaos that ensued from that declaration no doubt put some risky ideas into his head. In late January 1790, the presses at the shop of Pierre-François Didot *le jeune* on the rue Hurepoix were occupied with the production of *Charles IX ou l'école des rois,* a tragedy by Marie-Joseph Chénier, for the publisher Martin Bossange. Guillaume struck a deal with an apprentice printer named Morin who worked in Didot's shop. He got Morin to pass on the sheets of the *Charles IX* as they came off the presses; Guillaume then had the sheets reset by his own compositors, and he printed off pirate copies as fast as they emerged from Didot's

23. Paul Robiquet, *Le Personnel municipal de Paris pendant la Révolution* (Paris: Jouaust, 1890), 257.

24. Manuel testifies to this effect; see Lacroix (ed.), *Actes de la Commune de Paris,* 2d ser., 8:551–608. See also Manuel, *Police de Paris dévoilée.*

25. The following account is reconstructed from the *procès-verbal* of the "plainte de S. Bossange et Cie.," found in AN, ser. Y, no. 15021, February 14, 1790.

presses. Apparently Morin came through with the entire work because Guillaume succeeded in completing the pirate edition and getting it onto the streets as fast as Bossange. He stored the bound copies in the Hôtel d'Orléans, where his foreman distributed them to two young men just arrived from Bordeaux in search of work, with instructions to sell the works in the Palais Royal.

Guillaume had distributed approximately six thousand copies of the tragedy in Paris before the scheme was discovered. When it became clear that a pirate edition was circulating in Paris, Morin apparently got cold feet and confessed that he had been bullied into delivering the sheets to Guillaume's workers under threat of violence. On February 5, 1790, Bossange appealed to the Police Committee to stop the pirate edition. Pierre Manuel signed orders for the deputies of the committee of the district of St-André des Arts to raid Guillaume's printing ship and the depot at the Hôtel d'Orléans, to confiscate any copies of the tragedy, and to break all the press forms for the edition. These tasks were successfully accomplished with the assistance of Bossange and his foreman, with André-François Knapen, former head of the Paris Book Guild, as a witness.

Bossange testified at the royal court at Châtelet that he owned the manuscript of *Charles IX,* having purchased it from Chénier for 15,000 *livres,* and that Guillaume was guilty of theft and that he had used criminal means to acquire the sheets of the edition. Guillaume had, to be sure, deprived Bossange of six thousand prospective customers. No trace of the outcome of this case remains, unfortunately. Nonetheless, it is evident that under Pierre Manuel's administration the Police Committee had taken over the surveillance and seizure functions of the Paris Book Guild and that the municipal authorities intended to do everything in their power to protect the property rights of living authors and the publishers to whom those authors had ceded their property.

Nor was the Bossange-Guillaume case an isolated incident. In October 1791, the noted moralist and satirist Jean-Pierre Claris de Florian complained to the police that a pirate edition of his historical work *Numa Pompilius* was being printed by Rochelle, a new printer on the rue St-Jean Beauvais.[26] A visit to Rochelle's shop by the police commissioners of the district bore out his accusation. They found composed forms for the

---

26. Archives de la Préfecture de Police de Paris (hereafter cited as APP), ser. AA, carton 200, feuilles 177–179, "Procès-verbal de police, section de St. Geneviève, 22–25 octobre 1791."

edition, which they smashed, and proof sheets, which they confiscated. Rochelle testified that he did not know the author and that he had been contracted to print the edition by a man named Prieur, a bookseller on the Quai Voltaire. The police searched Prieur's warehouse but failed to uncover any positive evidence of Prieur's role.

Rochelle and Prieur turned out to be quite a team. The day after Florian's complaint, the author Henri Bernardin de St. Pierre and Didot *le jeune* denounced Rochelle again as the source of a pirate edition of *Paul et Virginie,* which St. Pierre had contracted Didot to print.[27] The following day the district police commissioners made another visit to Rochelle's shop, where they found the printing of *Paul et Virginie* in progress. Rochelle was out and his son claimed to know nothing of his father's business. But the commissioners confiscated the evidence and requested that the son inform his father that,

> according to the Declaration of the Rights of Man, liberty means only the freedom to do what does not harm others; and that it harms others to appropriate the work of an author, because it is an infringement of the sacred right of property; and that such an enterprise, if it were to remain unpunished, would deprive citizens of the instruction they await from celebrated authors like M. Bernardin de St. Pierre, because no author would want to consecrate his labors to the instruction of his age if piracy were ever authorized.[28]

St. Pierre and Didot then sought to find the entire edition in the hands of the publisher, Prieur, and prevent its distribution. In June 1792, they finally received a court order to search his bookshop on the Quai Voltaire and his warehouse on the rue Bourbon, at their own risk and expense.[29] This time they charged Prieur with pirating *Etudes de la nature, Paul et Virginie, Des Voeux d'un solitaire,* and *La Chaumière indienne.* The search turned up two copies of *Paul et Virginie* and three of *La Chaumière indienne.* St. Pierre filed a suit against Prieur in the civil tribunal of Paris on February 27, 1793, charging him with piracy.[30] The court declared that St. Pierre could not prove that the copies were unauthorized and required him to pay the court costs. St. Pierre, however, appealed the case on May

27. Ibid., feuilles 182–183, "Procès-verbal de police, section de St. Geneviève, 23–24 octobre 1791."

28. Ibid.

29. Ibid., ser. AA, carton 148, feuilles 75–76, "Procès-verbal de police de la section de la Fontaine de Grenelle, 26 juin 1792."

30. Douarche (ed.), *Tribunaux civils* 1:390–391.

25, and finally won a reversal.[31] The court ordered Prieur to pay a fine "prescribed by the law," but it did not say what law. In fact, no law protecting literary property existed until July 19, 1793.

These cases suggest, however, that the principle of the property rights of living authors was upheld by both the police and the local courts in the absence of national legislation or regulation. They also reveal that in the absence of guild surveillance, pirating was easy and prosecution both difficult and costly. Proof was hard to produce, and by the time the courts ruled in favor of the author or publisher the financial losses were already great.

But what about works by authors no longer living? Could anyone lay claim to their works? What about heirs, or publishers? After all, the cultural capital of the publishing elites of the Paris Book Guild resided largely in royal privileges on texts whose authors could no longer claim them. It was Pierre Manuel, former administrator of the police book trade division, whose actions brought the issue to the courts in December 1791.[32]

With the keys to the offices of the former lieutenant-general of police in his hands, between October 1789 and October 1790 Pierre Manuel found himself sitting on a literary gold mine that contained not only the reports of the former cultural police but also much of the literature and correspondence they had suppressed.[33] Among these papers was a cache of love letters from Honoré-Gabriel Riqueti, comte de Mirabeau, to his mistress Sophie Monnier, written during his imprisonment at the Château de Vincennes from 1777 to 1780 and intercepted by the police. As Mirabeau rapidly distinguished himself as the most famous orator of the Revolution after 1789, the potential commercial value of the letters soared.

In October 1790, Manuel retired to the countryside to edit several works, including these letters. After Mirabeau's death on April 2, 1791, Manuel returned to Paris intending to publish the collection of letters in association with the Paris publisher Jean-Baptiste Garnery.[34] Didot *le*

31. Ibid., 471.
32. The following discussion is based primarily on the dossier entitled "Affaire des lettres de Mirabeau," compiled in Lacroix (ed.), *Actes de la Commune de Paris*, 2d ser., 8:551–608 (app. II).
33. Ibid., 569.
34. Notices to this effect appeared in the *Patriote français* (July 23, 1791) and in the *Journal de la cour et de la ville* (November 20, 1791). See Lacroix (ed.), *Actes de la Commune de Paris*, 2d ser., 8:556–557.

jeune was contracted to print them.[35] Notices announcing the imminent publication of the letters appeared in the *Patriote français* on July 23 and in the *Journal de la cour et de la ville* on November 20, 1791.[36] The collaborators planned to capitalize on the timely interest of a nation now in mourning over the death of one of its greatest revolutionary heroes.

By December 19, 1791, Garnery had five thousand copies of the edition ready to be folded and bound in his warehouse.[37] But that night, the commissioner of police of the section Henri IV paid a visit to both Garnery and Didot on behalf of the family and creditors of the late Mirabeau. Didot did not hesitate to declare that he was in the process of printing the edition, but, he said, the manuscript was with Garnery. They proceeded to Garnery's, where they confiscated the manuscript and nine printed sheets, leaving the five thousand copies under Garnery's oath that they would not be removed or sold.[38]

Was Pierre Manuel guilty of theft? If so, from whom—the police, Mirabeau's family, his creditors, or Sophie Monnier's family?[39] Or rather, was he guilty of violating state security, or the privacy of the family? Alternatively, were the police guilty of violating the freedom and immunities of domicile and the presses? Why had they conducted the raid late at night? Was the raid merely a plot instigated by Manuel's political opponents within the Commune of Paris? If the Mirabeau family was really concerned with their privacy, why had they waited until the edition was completed before attempting to have the work, now quite valuable, confiscated? Manuel's intention to publish the letters had been publicly announced six months prior to the raid. Why had they not protested then? Were *they* in fact guilty of theft from the editor, publisher, and printer? What claim did they have on letters addressed to Sophie Monnier (now dead), then confiscated by the police, and which Mirabeau had willed to no one?

The case became a cause célèbre of the Parisian press the following morning. Didot *le jeune* filed a complaint, probably written by Manuel, with the City of Paris, charging the police with violation of domicile, freedom of the press, and property rights of the business associates.[40]

---

35. Ibid., 552–553.
36. Ibid., 556–557.
37. Ibid., 553.
38. Ibid.
39. Sophie Monnier died in September 1789.
40. Lacroix (ed.), *Actes de la Commune de Paris*, 2d ser., 8:554–555.

Certain to suffer a loss of 36,000 to 40,000 *livres* because of the raid, they were suing for damages. On December 28, 1791, the Sixth Criminal Tribunal of Paris found the police proceedings to have been legally conducted.[41]

At bottom, however, the issue was not one of police proceedings but of the disputed property claims on Mirabeau's letters. The family and the commissioner of police charged:

> The proposed publication of secret papers, that should have remained at the police office until they were restored to the representatives of the deceased M. Mirabeau, is a crime, not only against his representatives but against the police administration itself. . . . M. P. Manuel claims that his domicile and his "sacred presses" have been violated. . . . But the freedom of the press only means that you can print freely your own opinions, and not the work of another.[42]

The conservative *Journal de la cour et de la ville* rallied to the defense of family rights and state security in a sarcastic tone: "This faithful administrator in 1790 had confiscated works sold for his own profit. This abuse of confidence, which would have sent him to the Grève in a well-policed country, instead has brought him the trust of a people inspired by Jacobinism."[43] They proposed to "enrich the language with the word *manueliser* . . . to be applied to simple operations of the hand [*la main*]."[44] He was, they suggested, a mere thief.

But Manuel depicted himself as a champion of the freedom of the press. In a speech at the Jacobin Club he intoned: "The laboratory of the printer ought to be inviolable, because it is the sanctuary of thought."[45] And the *Révolutions de Paris* disputed the police interpretation of press freedom: "If the freedom of the press consists only of the right to print one's 'own opinions,' then no man in the world would have the right to print Mirabeau's letters, and freedom of the press would be reduced to

---

41. Ibid., 555.

42. *Rapport fait au Corps Municipal par le Département de la police relatif à M. Manuel* [Paris, 1791]; cited in ibid., 567–570.

43. *Journal de la cour et de la ville,* November 20, 1791; cited in Lacroix (ed.), *Actes,* 2d ser., 8:557–558.

44. *Journal de la cour et de la ville,* December 26, 1791; cited in Lacroix (ed.), *Actes,* 2d ser., 8:565.

45. The speech was printed in the *Chronique de Paris,* December 21, 1791; cited in Lacroix (ed.), *Actes,* 2d ser., 8:563.

very little."[46] Thus, as the conservative press and the police defended the property claims of Mirabeau's heirs and the security of the state, Manuel and his allies in the revolutionary press succeeded in depicting Manuel as the champion of Mirabeau's memory and of the rights of citizens to immortalize a national hero in print.

Manuel based his claim to the manuscript on two grounds. First he asserted that the author of the letters had given him verbal permission to publish the letters before he had died.[47] Had Manuel been able to offer any proof of that conversation, the case might have ended there. But he could not. He was therefore pushed to adopt a second line of reasoning that advanced an entirely new distinction in notions of literary property. Manuel argued that he did not own the *text* of Mirabeau's letters but, rather, the *edition* of those letters that he had prepared. Thus he wrote in his own defense:

> I spent a year collecting them, deciphering them, and arranging them, for the honor of the man who is to open the French Pantheon. . . . O you who have wanted to steal from me a work that was inspired by love, glory, and the nation, I will put you at the foot of Mirabeau's statue like the slaves who were at the feet of Louis XIV.[48]

The *Révolutions de Paris* rallied to Manuel's interpretation of literary property: "After the suppression of the book guild, what right do the police have to make nocturnal searches in printing shops. . . . These are letters . . . collected and edited by a third party after the death of the author . . . which, because they are the works of a man of genius, are public property."[49] The *Courrier des 83 départements* also accused the police of daring to "withhold from posterity letters that attest to the immortality of Mirabeau."[50] But Manuel summarized his position most eloquently when the case finally went to trial in May 1792: His "conduct in these circumstances was that of a citizen who researched in a public library in order to extract a manuscript, which, through additions, be-

---

46. *Révolutions de Paris,* December 31, 1791–January 7, 1792; cited in Lacroix (ed.), *Actes,* 2d ser., 8:573.
47. *Chronique de Paris,* December 28, 1791; cited in Lacroix (ed.), *Actes,* 2d ser., 8:572.
48. Ibid.
49. *Révolutions de Paris,* December 17–24, 1791; cited in Lacroix (ed.), *Actes,* 2d ser., 8:564.
50. *Courrier des 83 départements,* January 19, 1792; cited in Lacroix (ed.), *Actes,* 2d ser., 8:574.

came his property."[51] These arguments challenged not only the notion of exclusive privileges on literary works whose authors were dead, but also the idea of perpetual literary property, that is, of an author's *absolute* property rights.

Both the proponents of royal privileges and advocates of absolute property rights asserted that their claims lay in the possession of the text itself and that authors, and by extension their heirs, had the legal right to determine the fate of the text in perpetuity. Manuel and his allies in the revolutionary press departed radically from this position. They argued that after the death of an author the text belonged not to the family, or to any particular publisher, but to everyone—to the public. Further, they asserted that after the author's death, property claims could inhere only in the *edition* of the text, which became the editor's property through his labor, and not in the text itself, which could belong only to the public at large. In forwarding this position, they challenged the entire legal and economic basis of the largest sector of the publishing industry: that which engaged in the publication of texts whose authors were no longer living. The commercial fate of the entire literary inheritance of the Old Regime hung on this point of interpretation.

By 1792, new lines of legal reasoning were emerging from such street-level cultural politics. There was a connection, moreover, between the case of the Chaignieau brothers' *Journal du soir* and that of Manuel's edition of the *Lettres*. Despite their differences, both cases involved arguments for exclusive commercial claims to the published form, rather than the eternal content, of the works in question. The Chaignieau brothers owned their name and the title and format of their journal, the judge at the civil tribunal reasoned, but information that was available to all belonged freely to all to make use of as they would. Similarly, Manuel argued that upon an author's death his works fell from his hands into the public domain, whereupon they could be freely published by all. Only a particular edition of these works, distinguished by its notes, organization, format, and so forth, could be claimed as the exclusive commercial property of the editor and publisher. That is, the publisher owned the paratext, rather than the text itself.

The affair of Mirabeau's letters ended on a doubly ironic note. First, the publisher, Garnery, succeeded in getting a lower court to grant him

---

51. *Intérrogation de Pierre Manuel devant le premier tribunal criminel, 22 mai 1792* [Paris, 1792], cited in Lacroix (ed.), *Actes*, 2d ser., 8:593.

permission to sell the *Lettres* before the property dispute between Manuel and Mirabeau's heirs went to court.[52] Then, when the case finally came before the First Provisional Criminal Tribunal of Paris in June 1792, the court dropped all criminal charges against Manuel for removing the manuscripts from the police archives and referred Mirabeau's mother to the civil courts. Mirabeau's mother, however, the last remaining plaintiff, withdrew her case.[53]

In the Jacobin Club that evening Manuel's supporters claimed a victory, boasting that Mme de Mirabeau had withdrawn only because she was certain of defeat.[54] But it was merely a victory de facto. There was still no law determining the legal status of the works of authors, living or dead. After 1789, the legal basis of publishing could be found only in the legal contingencies of discontinuous and often contradictory decisions, meted out by the municipal police and lower courts. Over ten years later, cases were still in the courts disputing whether editions published between 1789 and 1793 were to be settled on the basis of the *règlements* of 1777 or the legislation of 1793.[55] From where would the new legal basis of publishing emerge and in what terms?

The First Legislative Initiative (1789–1791)

The first legislative attempt definitively to resolve the legal standing of claims on ideas appeared as a subsection of a comprehensive law on sedition and libel presented to the National Assembly by Emmanuel Sieyès on behalf of the Committee on the Constitution on January 20, 1790.[56] The law was born out of a convergence of the commercial interests of book publishers and the political imperatives of the National Assembly.

Within a year of the collapse of the royal Administration of the Book Trade, Paris publishers who had in no way lamented the fall of the old

52. Lacroix (ed.), *Actes*, 2d ser., 8:597.
53. Ibid., 604.
54. Ibid.
55. See, for example, AN, ser. ADVIII, carton 7, "Consultation pour la citoyen Dugour, propriétaire de *Cours d'agriculture*," [1803], 88.
56. France, National Constituent Assembly, Committee on the Constitution, "Projet de loi contre les délits qui peuvent se commettre par la voie de l'impression et par la publication des écrits et des gravures, etc., présenté à l'assemblée nationale, le 20 janvier 1790, par le Comité de constitution," in *Procès-verbal de l'Assemblée Nationale* 11:1–24; also in Buchez and Roux (eds.), *Histoire parlementaire de la Révolution française* 4:273–288.

publishing world or the literary culture it had produced began to issue public calls for national legislation to protect their publications from literary pirates. Thus the Paris publisher Jean-François Royer, a cultural revolutionary of unimpeachable credentials, observed that while ephemeral and periodical literature poured from the presses of the capital, *book* publishing had ground to a virtual halt: Paris, he wrote, "will soon cease to be the capital or the center of literature."[57] He lamented that "pirate editions are one of the principal reasons for the losses in the publishing business."[58]

Moreover, as Royer pointed out, the problem of literary piracy was not exclusively municipal, or even national, in character. The specter of local piracy was driving Parisian publishers and printers into the less capital-intensive, and hence less risky, business of ephemeral and periodical literature. Thus authors of serious, or "long-winded," works, as he put it, could no longer find Parisian or even French publishers willing to take the risk of a book-length publishing venture: "Our neighbors are making the first profits from our immense book trade." Something, he insisted, had to be done to "destroy or gradually diminish piracy."[59] It was neither the old publishing elites and their monopolies nor the literary civilization of the Old Regime that Royer sought to preserve, but rather the civilization of "the book" itself.

Such observations soon percolated upward into the discussions of the National Assembly. Publishers sent testimony that they were being driven to produce seditious and libelous material in order to stay afloat. In the session of January 12, 1790, for example, the deputy Charles de Lameth testified: "A Paris publisher has just reported to me that, unable to make any profit printing good books, he is being forced to go into the business of printing and selling libelous matter. . . . There are few

57. Jean-François Royer, *Avis intéressant aux gens de lettres et aux amateurs de bons livres et des bonnes éditions* (n.p., [1789–1790]), AN, ser. F17, carton 1010d, doss. 4102. In a cover letter to the Commission on Public Instruction, dated thermidor, year II (July–August 1794), Royer states that he composed this letter "four years earlier." A report to the Committee on Public Instruction describes Royer in the following terms: "He gave proof of his patriotism well before the beginning of the Revolution by sacrificing part of his fortune to spread works attacking the abuses of the former government. This is proven by the fact that he was banned from his trade by order of Breteuil [the former keeper of the seals]"; see AN, ser. F17, carton 1010d, doss. 4102, Royer, Paris publisher, 30 thermidor, an II (August 17, 1794).

58. Royer, *Avis intéressant aux gens de lettres,* AN, ser. F17, carton 1010d, doss. 4102.

59. Ibid.

printers in Paris who can afford not to."[60] Hoping to gain the ear of the National Assembly, publishers thus linked the economic issue of literary property and its protection to the political questions of sedition, libel, and authorial accountability.

The National Assembly itself was in the throes of a conservative backlash against the collapse of all regulation of the printed word. In the face of a flood of anonymous, libelous, and seditious pamphlet literature, the assembly heard repeated outcries like that found in an anonymous conservative pamphlet, *Contre la multiplicité et le danger des brochures,* that demanded laws requiring authors to sign published works and holding authors accountable for their publications.[61] The economic complaints from publishers thus converged with political demands in the National Assembly, such as that of Jacques-André d'Emeri for "a law on the freedom of the press" to outlaw seditious publications, or of the deputy Louis-Marie, marquis d'Estourmel, for a law requiring authors, publishers, and printers to sign, and thus lay claim to, the works they produced as a means of holding them accountable.[62] As a consequence of this agitation, the assembly moved that "the Committee on the Constitution will be charged to present forthwith a proposal for a law regulating the freedom of the press."[63]

The Committee on the Constitution faced no small task. In order to determine the legal accountability of authors and publishers as well as their legal claims on the texts they wrote, edited, and published, the committee had to rework the legal definitions of the most basic elements of the literary civilization of the Old Regime: the author and the text. Although theories of authorial and literary property were widely circulated and debated throughout the eighteenth century, under the Old Regime there was, legally speaking, no "property" in ideas or in the texts that embodied them. Ideas were a gift from God, revealed through the author and made public by a printer-publisher. The king alone, as God's first representative on earth, had the power to determine, through his censors, what God's knowledge was, and also who would have the privilege to publish it. Having abolished privileges,

---

60. Buchez and Roux (eds.), *Histoire parlementaire de la Révolution française* 4:270.
61. *Contre la multiplicité et le danger des brochures, par l'auteur de l'écrit intitulé: Je ne suis point de l'avis de tout le monde* (n.p., 1789).
62. Buchez and Roux (eds.), *Histoire parlementaire de la Révolution française* 4:271–272.
63. Ibid., 272.

the revolutionary legislators now had to find a way to reground the legal definitions of accountability and exclusive commercial claims within the framework of a constitution based on natural rights rather than divine sanction. In order to do this they would have to replace the doctrine of revelation, that had provided the epistemological basis for the Old Regime system of privileges. They would, in other words, have to legislate Enlightenment epistemology into law. Fortunately, they were not working without precedents.

The dispute between the Paris Book Guild and the royal Administration of the Book Trade that led to the formulation of the royal decrees of 1777 had drawn key Enlightenment figures directly into the debate on literary property. Consequently, the mid-eighteenth century witnessed several systematic efforts to reground the discussion of the origins and nature of claims on knowledge in terms of Enlightenment epistemology. Two distinct positions emerged within enlightened circles.

In 1763, Denis Diderot was hired by André-François LeBreton, the chief officer of the Paris Book Guild and publisher of the *Encyclopédie,* to write a treatise to be presented to the new director of the royal Administration of the Book Trade, Antoine-Raymond-Jean-Gaulbert-Gabriel de Sartine, defending the guild's view of their privileges as a form of property. In his "Lettre historique et politique adressée à un magistrat sur le commerce de la librairie," Diderot argued that ideas are the most inviolable form of property because they spring directly from the individual mind; they are a creation of the mind, indeed the very substance of the mind, the means by which it constitutes itself. Thus he writes:

> What form of wealth *could* belong to a man, if not a work of the mind, . . . if not his own thoughts, . . . the most precious part of himself, that will never perish, that will immortalize him? What comparison could there be between a man, the very substance of man, his soul, and a field, a tree, a vine, that nature has offered in the beginning equally to all, and that an individual has only appropriated through cultivating it?[64]

Diderot's argument was radically individualistic. Although his epistemological stance, and his ideas on aesthetics, are rife with complexities, in

---

64. Denis Diderot, "Lettre historique et politique . . . sur le commerce de la librairie" (1763), in *Oeuvres complètes,* ed. Roger Lewinter (Paris: Club Français du Livre, 1970), 5:331.

this 1763 *Lettre* Diderot depicted ideas as emerging sui generis from the mind, rather than taking the more Lockean line of argument that they were appropriated through the labor of combining sensations that emanate from nature. Diderot admitted that property in land is merely a social claim, based on appropriation through labor and thus susceptible to social mediation. But ideas, originating in the individual mind, original to it and not acquired through appropriation or labor, are, rather, the most natural and most inviolable form of property.[65]

Diderot therefore argued that privileges for the texts of living authors should be recognized as legal confirmations of a perpetual property right. Similarly, works whose private lineage could no longer be traced should also be considered the perpetual property of the privilege holder, justified by the theory of "right of first use." In contrast, then, to his general condemnation of commercial privileges, Diderot made an exception for those conferred on texts, arguing that the protection of exclusive and inheritable property claims, rather than free market competition, was the best guarantee of the progress of knowledge and the spread of enlightenment.[66]

The legal implications of Diderot's line of reasoning were cogently formulated by the lawyer-journalist Simon-Nicolas-Henri Linguet in his *Mémoire sur les propriétés et privilèges exclusifs de la librairie* of 1774:

> What is a literary privilege? It is a recognition made by public authority of the property of the author or of those to whom he has ceded it. It is the literary equivalent of a notarial act which . . . assures the rights of

---

65. For a more extensive treatment of the complex subject of Diderot's epistemology, its relation to the development of French aesthetic theory, and the idea of authorial originality in particular, see Jacques Chouillet, *La Formation des idées esthétiques de Diderot* (Paris: Armand Colin, 1973), esp. 403–417; Jacques Chouillet, *L'Esthétique des lumières* (Paris: PUF, 1974), 73–82, 120–125; and Roland Mortier, *L'Originalité. Une Nouvelle Catégorie esthétique au siècle des lumières* (Geneva: Droz, 1982), 153–163. The Renaissance beginnings of the idea of authorial originality are treated extensively in David Quint, *Origin and Originality in Renaissance Literature* (New Haven: Yale University Press, 1983). The classic work on the epistemology of the French Enlightenment is Ernst Cassirer, *The Philosophy of the Enlightenment* (Princeton: Princeton University Press, 1951). For a discussion of the complexities of Diderot's epistemological stance in relation to both Locke and Descartes, see Robert Darnton, "Philosophers Trim the Tree of Knowledge: The Epistemological Strategy of the *Encyclopédie*," in *Great Cat Massacre* 191–214. Both Martha Woodmansee and Mark Rose note the contribution of the idea of authorial originality to arguments for authors' property rights in Germany and England; see Woodmansee, "Genius and the Copyright," 427; and Rose, "Author as Proprietor," 56.

66. Diderot, "Lettre historique et politique," 349.

citizens. . . . The privilege is a seal that guarantees peaceful enjoyment; but it is not the source of that enjoyment. . . . A privilege grants nothing to the author, it only insures protection.[67]

These arguments, both philosophical and legal, advanced by two key figures of the French Enlightenment, are consistent with—indeed, they would seem further to confirm—the recent assertions of Michel Foucault and others that the modern author was first conceived as individual property owner.

There was, however, a second Enlightenment position on the issue of literary privileges and property, articulated in France by the marquis de Condorcet in 1776, on the eve of the new royal regulations of the book trade, in a pamphlet entitled *Fragments sur la liberté de la presse*. Although the original context of the composition of this pamphlet remains obscure, it undoubtedly formed part of Condorcet's effort to assist the French Minister of Finance, Anne-Robert-Jacques Turgot, in his attempt to liberalize French commerce by suppressing the monopolies of the royal guilds.[68] The pamphlet was clearly intended to present a complete revision of the current royal code organizing and regulating the book trade.[69] Like all Old Regime codes on the book trade, Condorcet's pamphlet treats the issues of censorship, liability, commercial regulation, protection, and policing together, as interconnected elements of a single regulatory vision. The lion's share of the document was devoted to a refutation of prepublication censorship and the commercial monopolies

67. Simon-Nicolas-Henri Linguet, *Mémoire sur les propriétés et privilèges exclusifs de la librairie: Présenté en 1774* (n.p., n.d.); cited in Renouard, *Traité des droits d'auteur*, 175. For further discussion of Linguet's views on the organization of the book trade, see his *Mémoire signifié pour le sieur Luneau de Boisgermain, défendeur, contre les syndic et adjoints des libraires et imprimeurs de Paris, demandeurs* (Paris, 1769).

68. Elisabeth Badinter and Robert Badinter, *Condorcet. Un Intellectuel en politique* (Paris: Fayard, 1988), 99–142.

69. I have been unable to find any earlier reference to the pamphlet *Fragments sur la liberté de la presse* than the edition of Marie-Jean-Antoine-Nicolas Caritat, marquis de Condorcet, in *Oeuvres complètes*, ed. M. F. Arago (Paris: Didot, 1847), 11:253–314. Arago provides the date 1776, but without explanation. The text is mentioned in neither Keith Michael Baker's *Condorcet: From Natural Philosophy to Social Mathematics* (Chicago: University of Chicago Press, 1975) nor the most recent biography by Elisabeth and Robert Badinter, *Condorcet*. Although Nina Ratner Gelbart notes that Condorcet contributed a series of articles, including one on the freedom of the press, to the *Journal des dames* in the latter half of 1775, the *Fragments* are clearly too extensive to have been intended only for publication as a journal article; see Gelbart, *Feminine and Opposition Journalism in Old Regime France: "Le Journal des Dames"* (Berkeley and Los Angeles: University of California Press, 1987), 229.

of the book guild. He proposed replacing these regulations with liberal laws on sedition, libel, and freedom of commerce in the printing, publishing, and book-selling trades. Under such laws, the "author of the publication," as distinct from the author of the work, would be held legally accountable and liable for its public consequences.[70]

The issue of accountability led Condorcet logically to a sustained discussion of the problem of authorial claims and literary privileges as well. Drawing on arguments formulated in sensationalist epistemology, Condorcet attacked both the royal theory of literary privilege and the theories of authorial property rights advanced by Diderot and the lawyers for the Paris Book Guild.[71] "There can," he wrote, "be no relationship between property in ideas and that in a field, which can serve only one man. [Literary property] is not a property derived from the natural order and defended by social force, it is a property founded in society itself. It is not a true right, it is a privilege."[72] Unlike a piece of land, an idea can be discovered, inhabited, and used by an infinite number of people at the same time. Ideas are not the creation of individual minds, be it through revelation, appropriation, or cognition. Rather, they inhere in nature and hence are equally and simultaneously accessible through the senses to all. They can belong to no single individual.

Furthermore, Condorcet rejected any social value to individual claims on ideas. Since true knowledge was objective, particular, individual claims on ideas could consecrate and protect nothing more than the style, the individual form, rather than the substance, of an idea. Far from viewing originality as the hallmark of the modern bourgeois author, Condorcet condemned particularities of style as attributes of aristocratic culture. Any privileges that might be derived from these attributes, he argued, should be abolished; style distorts nature's truths, and thus to privilege it encouraged the production of pleasant fictions and personal gain rather than the pursuit of useful knowledge and the public good: "It is thus uniquely for expressions, for phrases, that privileges exist. It is not for the substance of things [*les choses*], for ideas; it is for words [*les mots*], for the name of the author." Further, legal privileges

70. Condorcet, *Fragments*, in *Oeuvres complètes* 11:294.

71. For the definitive treatment of the intellectual origins, character, and development of Condorcet's epistemology, see Baker, *Condorcet*.

72. Condorcet, *Fragments*, in *Oeuvres complètes* 11:308–311.

derived from individual style inhibit the spread of ideas by restricting access to them. "Privileges of this sort, like all others, are inconveniences that diminish activity by concentrating it in a small number of hands. . . . They are neither necessary, nor useful, and as we have seen, they are unjust."[73]

Condorcet argued against individual claims on knowledge as either property or privilege. He imagined an authorless world of free manipulation and circulation of information and ideas. These observations led Condorcet to conclude that a commercial publishing industry that sold ideas rather than authors, substance rather than style, could be organized according to the principles of periodical publishing as opposed to book publishing, as with the proceedings of the Académie des Sciences or the *Encyclopédie:* through reader subscriptions to a genre of knowledge rather than through the marketing of unique works distinguished by the author's signature.[74]

The debate between Condorcet and Diderot played out a tension inherent in Enlightenment epistemology (found in John Locke's *Essay on Human Understanding* itself) concerning the origins of ideas and hence the kinds of claims that could be made on them. Did knowledge inhere in the world or in the mind? To what extent was it discovered and to what extent invented? Condorcet argued that knowledge was objective, found in nature, and thus fundamentally social in character, belonging to all. Diderot viewed ideas as inherently subjective and individual, originating in the individual mind and thus constituting the most inviolable form of private property.

The revolutionary legislators then, did not have at their disposal simply one modern position on the nature of the author and his relation to the text (that is, the property-bearing individual); rather, they confronted a modern *tension* between Diderot's conception of the author as the original creator, and hence inviolable proprietor, of his works, on the one hand, and Condorcet's depiction of the ideal author as a passive midwife to the disclosure of objective knowledge, on the other.[75] How

73. Ibid.

74. Ibid. Interestingly, Woodmansee finds a similar line of argumentation advanced in the German context, although she does not explore its implications; see "Genius and the Copyright," 440.

75. While it is beyond the scope of this inquiry, it could be argued that despite the conclusions of Woodmansee and Rose, their evidence suggests that a similar tension was present in the English and German contexts as well. Although each of these authors clearly

was the Committee on the Constitution to resolve this tension? Would it legally consecrate Diderot's notion of the author as the inviolable proprietor of his text, as Michel Foucault, among others, has recently suggested it did? Or would it prefer Condorcet's view of ideas and the texts that embody them as a cultural commons, best cultivated freely and collectively by all?

On January 20, 1790, Sieyès presented a proposal for a law on sedition, libel, and literary property to the National Assembly on behalf of the Committee on the Constitution.[76] Initiation of this proposal was part of an effort by moderates in Paris and the assembly to restore order and check the radicalization of the Revolution in the wake of the popular revolt that swept the cities and countryside after the fall of the Bastille.[77] By the end of 1789, Sieyès was meeting with the group of moderates who had split from the Jacobin Club, including Condorcet, Lafayette, the duc de La Rochefoucauld-Liancourt, and Dupont de Nemours. In early January 1790 these men officially founded the Society of 1789.[78] There can be little doubt that this group, and in particular Condorcet, played a crucial role in drafting the National Assembly's first legislative effort to regulate the printed word.

Significantly, the proposal was publicly attributed to Condorcet as well as Sieyès.[79] There is good evidence to support this attribution. In both

---

establishes the presence of arguments for unlimited property in ideas in eighteenth-century England and Germany, in fact these arguments did not go uncontested, and ultimately, the laws that ensued from the debates in these countries did not reflect a victory for unlimited property rights. See Woodmansee, "Genius and the Copyright"; and Rose, "Author as Proprietor."

76. France, National Constituent Assembly, Committee on the Constitution, "Projet de loi," in *Procès-verbal de l'Assemblée Nationale* 11:1–24; also in Buchez and Roux (eds.), *Histoire parlementaire de la Révolution française* 4:273–288.

77. On the political reaction of the propertied classes to the popular revolution, see Georges Michon, *Essai sur l'histoire du parti feuillant. Adrien Duport* (Paris: Payot, 1924). For the connection of cultural elites to this conservative backlash of 1790–1791, and especially of writers and publishers, see Darnton, *Business of Enlightenment*, 505.

78. See Baker, *Condorcet*, 272.

79. See François Lanthenas, *De la liberté indéfinie de la presse* (Paris: Visse, 1791), 6: "A proposal from the Committe on the Constitution of the National Assembly to regulate the press, attributed to MM. Condorcet and Sieyès, appeared a few months after this glorious Revolution."

form and content the proposal presented by Sieyès in 1790 bears a striking resemblance to Condorcet's *Fragments sur la liberté de la presse* of 1776.[80] Indeed, close comparison of the two texts suggests that the Sieyès document was drafted directly from Condorcet's pamphlet. The two share virtually the same organizational structure, and the substantive parallels between the two texts are equally striking. Ironically, then, Condorcet in 1790 revived a pamphlet he had originally circulated as a radical indictment of the inquisitorial institutions of the Old Regime, now to serve as a conservative check on the flood of ideas unleashed by the collapse of those very institutions by proposing a law that would hold authors, publishers, and printers legally accountable for their publications.

This conservative turn is further disclosed in the one substantive change made to Condorcet's earlier pamphlet in the new proposal: the section on privileges and literary property. In 1776 Condorcet had argued that ideas were social rather than individual in origin and as a consequence they could not be considered a form of private property to be protected as a natural right. He had also argued that privileges, as private claims on texts, inhibited rather than aided the spread of enlightenment. By 1790, Condorcet had evidently reconsidered his position in light of recent events. Now, instead of denouncing literary property as a privilege, Condorcet and Sieyès claimed that "the progress of enlightenment, and consequently the public good, united with notions of distributive justice to necessitate that the property of a work should be guaranteed to the author by law."[81] They went on to specify, however, that this property right was to be limited to the author's life plus ten years, the length of time deemed necessary to complete and sell an edition. The Sieyès proposal thus consecrated the notion of property in ideas, but in a restricted form. The notion of limiting authors' property rights reflected the continuing influence of Condorcet's original concern that the "progress of enlightenment" depended on public access rather than private claims to ideas.

Article 21 of the proposed law concluded the section on literary property with an effort to smooth the transition from the old regime of privileges to the new regime of property: "Publishers or others who at present have acquired for any work a privilege for a fixed term will

---

80. Condorcet, *Fragments*, in *Oeuvres complètes* 11:253–314; and France, National Constituent Assembly, Committee on the Constitution, "Projet de loi."
81. Buchez and Roux (eds.), *Histoire parlementaire de la Révolution française* 4:283.

continue to enjoy this privilege for its entire duration."[82] In direct contrast to Condorcet's original position, then, the Sieyès proposal argued that the spread of enlightenment was best achieved not by liberating ideas from particular claims entirely, but by ensuring the viability of the authored book as a legally defined and protected commodity.

The main concern of the debates on freedom of the press in the assembly, and of the Sieyès proposal itself, was to stem the flood of libelous and seditious pamphlets that poured forth after the collapse of the Old Regime systems of censorship and surveillance. The proposal was primarily an effort to determine the limits of what could be said in print and to establish the legal accountability of authors, printers, and booksellers for what they made public. Consequently, the repressive aspects of the proposal have received the most attention from historians.[83] But the assembly, the Committee on the Constitution, and Sieyès and Condorcet had all taken Lameth's comments about the state of the book trade seriously. The connection between the crisis in book publishing and the boom in periodical and ephemeral literature was not lost on them. If the commercial insecurity of book publishing was driving printers and publishers into ephemeral printed matter, then the flood of ephemeral matter—that is, seditious and libelous pamphlets—might abate if book publishing could be restored to a commercially secure and profitable footing. Only in the light of these political concerns can we understand why the National Assembly's first legislative effort to define and protect literary property emerged within a law on sedition and libel, and why Condorcet's original position had been reversed.

The first revolutionary attempt to give legal recognition to the author's claim on the text, then, was *not* a granting of freedom to the author, but the imposition of accountability and responsibility. Politically, it formed part of a conservative pro-order move, a police measure. The law made the author legally responsible for the text by defining it as his property.

Nor were the commercial motivations behind the law concerned with enhancing the power of the author over the text. In comparison with the royal decrees of 1777, authors were being given a rather poor deal by the revolutionary legislators. The proposal rejected the Crown's grant of authorial claims in perpetuity. Instead it argued for limiting such claims

82. Ibid., 4:284.
83. See, for example, Söderhjelm, *Régime de la presse* 1:118–127; and Bellanger (ed.), *Histoire générale de la presse française* 1:432.

to ten years after the author's death in the interest of the "progress of enlightenment" and "the public good." Thus, while declaring that texts are authors' property, the law in fact severely *diminished* the author's power to determine the fate of his texts, and put an end to the perpetual private claims—privileges—granted by the Crown on the literary inheritance of the nation. True to the spirit of Condorcet's original pamphlet, he and Sieyès wanted to free those texts for the use of all citizens. This was no mere theoretical matter. By advancing the notion of "limited property," the two men were proposing that the entire literary inheritance of the nation pour forth from the hands of private publishers and the heirs of authors into the public domain: Rousseau and Voltaire, as well as Racine and Molière, had all been dead for well over ten years. They would now be freely publishable, in any form, by all citizens.

While the proposal rendered publishers, authors, and heirs equal before the law, it failed to address or resolve the philosophical issue at the heart of the late-eighteenth-century debate. If property rights were inviolable natural rights, as the Declaration of the Rights of Man and the Citizen had recently proclaimed, what power did the state have to limit them or regulate their distribution? If claims on property were instead socially constituted, were they not then just privileges by another name? The proposed law appeared incoherent and arbitrary: on the one hand it recognized a property right; on the other, by defining that right as noninheritable, it advanced an instrumentalist notion of the public good that flew in the face of natural rights theory and explicitly undermined the actual power of individuals to exercise their constitutionally guaranteed right. It was an attempt at a compromise between two epistemological stances, between individual and collective claims on ideas.

The Condorcet-Sieyès proposal of 1790 broke on the shoals of its own contradictions. While applauded upon presentation in the assembly, the proposal suffered such virulent criticism from so many quarters that it was never even brought to a vote. Much of this criticism focused on the issues of libel and sedition, in particular on the articles that proposed authors and printers be held accountable for the seditious and criminal actions that their works could be construed as intending to incite.[84] Radicals were quick to detect the repressive and conservative character of the entire proposal (plate 4). The militant journalist Elysée Loustallot

---

84. For an extensive discussion of the critical response of journalists and pamphleteers to the clauses on sedition and libel, see Söderhjelm, *Régime de la presse* 1:123–128.

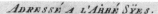

De ce Pretre, craigues l'Air fin et Seducteur,
L'imposteur est caché sous son masque Hypocritte,
La vérité jamais ne pénétra son Cœur,
Francais il vous trompa, voila tout son merite.

Ne me trahis pas, ou je ....?

l'Abbé Sÿes cathéchisant des Citoyens sur l'heureuse révolution
et le Succes de la liberté française. Dans les même circonstances,
il faisait à Paris des motions et presentait à l'Assemblée
Nationale des projets contre la liberté de la presse, voulant
restraindre jusqu'aux pensées des gens de lettres, voulant étouffer
la vérité: mais cette Deésse, le flambeau à la main, brise les vitres
du temple qu'il profane et lui fait appercevoir qu'il renverse la
Religion par des Sophismes...t. un de ces gens passant pour des
Aristocrates S'écrie: Eh bien! Ne vous disaje pas qu'il vous trompait?

Plate 4. Anonymous engraving attacking the Sieyès proposal on the press and
literary property of January 20, 1790. Sieyès is lewdly depicted as "violating the
liberty of the press." Bibliothèque Nationale, Cabinet des Estampes.

decried any law that limited the exercise of a natural right: "The patriotic public does not ask for a law *granting* freedom of the press. . . . The only true limits of freedom are those in the nature of things themselves."[85] There should be no civil laws, according to Loustallot, limiting or regulating what could be said in print—even if what was said seemed libelous or seditious to the men in power.

Apart from sedition and libel, the measure was also criticized for its treatment of the issues of literary privileges and property. This section was attacked from three different positions during 1790–1791. The first line of attack came from pamphleteers who took up Condorcet's position of 1776 specifically to denounce any measure that would reimpose private claims on ideas. Thus the comte de Kéralio attacked the very notion of property in ideas as a threat to freedom of thought and, consequently, to the progress of enlightenment:

> [The National Assembly] has negated all privileges as destroyers of liberty. . . . And as liberty cannot be maintained without enlightenment and knowledge, a wise legislator will guard himself from conserving even the smallest of privileges, which, by limiting the freedom of the press, restrain freedom of thought and inhibit the expansion of human knowledge.[86]

He viewed the Condorcet-Sieyès proposal as an unprincipled and misguided effort to translate a regime of privilege into a rhetoric of property. According to Kéralio, the cause of "authors' property rights" was no more than a political smokescreen, serving to conceal the commercial interests of publishers.[87] The publishing world offered ample evidence to support these charges. Like Condorcet in 1776, Kéralio believed knowledge should be freely accessible to all—even to print, publish, and sell.

A second line of attack on the Condorcet-Sieyès proposal was advanced by the old corporate monopolists of the Paris Book Guild and the royally privileged theater directors. These men, reviving and deploying Diderot's arguments in a campaign to have their privileges recognized as unlimited property rights, mounted a lobbying effort to kill the proposal in committee. The playwright Jean-François de LaHarpe protested to the National Assembly on August 24, 1790: "Your decrees have pronounced the abolition of all privileges. Having enjoyed such privileges for over one hundred years, the directors of the Comédie Française . . . claim that all

---

85. Elysée Loustallot, "De la liberté de la presse," *Révolutions de Paris*, no. 29, January 23–30, 1790, 17–18; emphasis in the original.
86. Kéralio, *De la liberté*, 51–53.
87. Ibid.

the plays that they have been given the exclusive privilege to perform since the establishment of their theater are now their eternal and inviolable property."[88] A few weeks later, on September 6, the officers of the Paris Book Guild joined in this corporatist reaction and presented a *mémoire* to the assembly in which they proposed to "put before the eyes of the Committee on the Constitution the Code [of 1723] for the Publishing and Printing Trades edited by the great d'Aguesseau."[89] It was this code that had provided the basis for arguments that publishers' privileges were automatically and perpetually renewable and hence actually confirmed an anterior property right.[90] How could a revolution that had declared property a natural and inalienable right now take steps to limit that right?

These arguments were forcefully reiterated in 1791 as the forces of cultural reaction mobilized with greater intensity to advance their corporatistic cause under the guise of defending "authors' rights." The Committees on Agriculture and Commerce reported on a letter from the keeper of the seals in which he testified that the lack of a law guaranteeing literary property was ruining French letters:

> It is impossible to doubt that the vigilant and active protection that the government has always accorded the property of authors and those to whom they cede their works was one of the principal reasons that literature has flourished in France more than with any other modern people. There can be no doubt that pirates of our best books will incessantly inundate the kingdom, ruin proprietors, intimidate those who are in a position to purchase manuscripts, and exhaust, in a word, the most precious branch of our national industry.[91]

The keeper of the seals recommended that the Committees on the Constitution, on Agriculture and Commerce, and on Investigations meet together to resolve this question. The Committees on Agriculture and Commerce took the initiative to convene all three "to propose a law on these issues, which are crucial to the book trade and to literature."[92]

---

88. Jean-François de LaHarpe, *Adresse des auteurs dramatiques à l'Assemblée Nationale, prononcé par M. de LaHarpe dans la séance du mardi soir 24 août* ([Paris, 1790]), 8.

89. Fernand Gerbaux and Charles Schmidt, eds., *Procès-verbal des Comités d'Agriculture et de Commerce* (Paris: Imprimerie Nationale, 1906), 1:518–519 (124th session, September 6, 1790).

90. Birn, "Profits in Ideas," 139.

91. Gerbaux and Schmidt (eds.), *Procès-verbal* 1:756.

92. AN, ser. DXXIX *bis,* carton 16, doss. 182, doc. 10, Letter from the Committees on Agriculture and Commerce to the Committee on Investigations, January 13, 1791.

The formal abolition of the Paris Book Guild in March 1791 dealt a severe blow to the corporate lobby.[93] But individual publishers of the old guild, as well as public officials, continued to agitate for the protection of literary property. On May 22, the minister of justice (formerly the keeper of the seals) wrote to the Committees on Agriculture and Commerce urging action.[94] The following day committee member François Hell received a letter from

> MM. Jean-Marie Bruysset and Pierre-Marie Bruysset and son, printers of Lyon, requesting a law that will assure authors the property in their works and prohibit pirating. . . . They state that this law is urgently needed, as at this moment someone has pirated a fifteen-volume edition of Valmont's *Dictionnaire* that appeared only fifteen days ago, which cost 500,000 *livres* to produce, and the loss of which would reduce the author and printers to the state of beggars.[95]

The Committees on Agriculture and Commerce and on the Constitution resolved as a consequence of this report to charge Hell with the drafting of a new law.

The Hell *projet du loi,* published by order of the National Assembly sometime in the summer of 1791, gave legislative embodiment to the principles long advocated by the Paris Book Guild and Diderot. Thus Hell announced to the National Assembly:

> The first of all properties is that of thought; it is independent, it is anterior to all laws. . . . All other forms of property are nothing but conventions, social concessions; those of the mind and of genius are gifts from nature, they ought to be beyond any restriction. . . . The Old Regime named the act by which one guaranteed literary property a "literary privilege." A privilege! What a gross abuse of words. You have destroyed the word . . . now you can consecrate the thing.[96]

Nothing could have been further from the views presented a year earlier by Sieyès and Condorcet. The specific clauses of the Hell proposal upheld all former privileges on the entire literary inheritance of France, which had been accrued by publishers in consequence of the Code of

93. France, National Legislative Assembly, Decree of March 17, 1791, in *Collection générale des décrets rendus par l'Assemblée Nationale* (Paris: Baudouin, 1791), 52–62.

94. Gerbaux and Schmidt (eds.), *Procès-verbal* 2:256.

95. Ibid.

96. Hell, *Rapport fait à l'Assemblée Nationale,* 5–8, in AN, ser. ADVIII, carton 16. I have been unable to determine if this proposal was actually presented on the floor of the National Assembly.

1723, as titles of property. Literary property was to be inheritable and transmissible in perpetuity like any other form of property. The law, moreover, was to be printed at the end of every publication, "replacing the text of the former privilege."[97] This was precisely the interpretation that the Comédie Française and the Paris Book Guild had long hoped to advance.

A third line of attack on the Condorcet-Sieyès proposal came from within the camp of those who sympathized with the principle of a limited property right. Three days after the proposal was presented to the assembly, Charles-Joseph Panckoucke published the first of two articles in the *Mercure de France* exposing his own views on how the crisis in book publishing could be resolved.[98] Like Sieyès and Condorcet, he expressed ideological concerns about unlimited exclusive claims on ideas: "An author or a publisher who would be the eternal proprietors of their books, would necessarily be monopolists."[99] Panckoucke did not believe in monopolies in ideas; he shared Condorcet's concern that perpetual monopolies on texts left the fate of public enlightenment and the spread of enlightened ideas totally in the hands of private individuals. Limits on private claims, he insisted, were justified by public interest.

He felt, however, that the limits on private claims proposed by Sieyès and Condorcet were too severe. Instead, he suggested that France adopt the model put into place by the English in 1774:

> Every author enjoys at first a fourteen-year claim on his work. If he survives that term, he obtains another fourteen years of enjoyment of his claim. At the expiration of that term, the book belongs to the public. The [English] nation has thought, with reason, that this is the proper means of reconciling private interest with the public good, and that as good books contribute to its enlightenment . . . it is just to favor its writers with these dispositions.[100]

As a publisher of multiauthored, multivolume works, Panckoucke sought to extend the legal definition of the time deemed necessary to complete an edition from ten to fourteen years. Nonetheless, the arguments of even this large commercial publisher rested not on the invio-

---

97. Ibid., 15.

98. Charles-Joseph Panckoucke, "Sur les chambres syndicales," *Mercure de France,* January 23, 1790; and "Sur l'état actuel de l'imprimerie," ibid., March 6, 1790.

99. Panckoucke, "Sur l'état actuel de l'imprimerie," 37–38.

100. Ibid. There is much more to be said about the role of English copyright law in the French revolutionary debates. While Panckoucke here invokes it, the Hell proposal, for example, explicitly refuted arguments in favor of adopting the English model; see *Rapport fait à l'Assemblée Nationale.*

lability of property rights but on the ideal of an enlightened nation. Writers merited special favor, not as property holders, but because they were the source of the "good books" through which the public received enlightenment. Once they had received their compensation, the public good dictated that these texts belong to all.

By 1791, then, the mid-century debate between Diderot and Condorcet had resurfaced within the Revolution itself. Caught between their interest in liberating public circulation of ideas from the inquisitorial and monopolistic institutions of the Old Regime and their fear of the political consequences of the cultural anarchy that followed the "freeing of the press," Condorcet and Sieyès had advanced the notion of a "limited property right" in an attempt to effect a legislative compromise between private interests and public enlightenment. But cultural libertarians like Kéralio took up Condorcet's arguments of 1776 and protested violently against any private claims on ideas, whereas the Paris Book Guild and directors of the Comédie Française mobilized a corporate lobby to argue for the inviolability of authors' property rights. Even men like Panckoucke, who agreed with the basic premise of a limited right, found the particular stipulations of the proposal unacceptable. The Condorcet-Sieyès proposal of 1790 foundered in a sea of criticism. There was to be no law regulating claims on ideas until 1793.

The Second Initiative (1791–1793)

The revolutionary law of July 19, 1793, which defined the legal limits and powers of the author and laid the foundation for republican publishing, has served as the basis for French publishing to this date. It is still the first standard citation in French law school textbooks on literary property.[101] In order to understand how a law was finally passed and why it took the form it did, critical changes in the revolutionary context between 1791 and 1793 must be considered.

In 1791 there was a crucial shift in the balance of forces for and against the notion of a limited property right. The suppression of the Paris Book Guild in March 1791 had dealt a severe blow to the pro-property corporate lobby. A distinct law on libel and sedition was incorporated into the constitution in September, leaving the property question to be resolved independently of the issue of censorship. This

---

101. See, for example, Henri Desbois, *Le Droit d'auteur en France*, 3d ed. (Paris: Dalloz, 1978), 416; or Claude Colombet, *Propriété littéraire et artistique* (Paris: Dalloz, 1980), 6.

separation significantly depoliticized the property issue. The Hell proposal, which circulated for public discussion in those uncertain months of the summer of 1791, appears never to have reached the floor of the assembly for a vote. By autumn it had become clear that the advocates of perpetual private property in ideas had wasted their energies by courting the wrong legislative committee.

The transfer of power from the Constituent to the Legislative Assembly on October 1, 1791, was accompanied by a structural reorganization of the assembly's committees. Jurisdiction over the question of literary property now passed from the Committees on Agriculture and Commerce to the newly formed Committee on Public Instruction, headed by Condorcet.[102] He was joined by, among others, Sieyès.[103] Thus the question of literary claims, raised first in 1790 as part of a repressive police measure and then as a commercial interest, was, by virtue of changing circumstances, recontextualized as a question of education and the encouragement of knowledge.

By 1791, moreover, the results of a second wave of agitation for authors' rights reached legislative formulation. This agitation came not from corporate interests, but rather from playwrights protesting the monopoly of the Comédie Française on dramatic works. Since the founding of the Comédie Française in 1680, only theater directors could legally receive privileges to present and publish theatrical works.[104] This monopoly had not been affected by the royal recognition in 1777 of authors' literary privileges. The agitation of "unprivileged" playwrights was therefore crucial in disassociating the cause of authors' rights from a rearguard defense of Old Regime privileges and realigning it politically within the prorevolutionary attack on privileged interests.

Playwrights began their agitation in 1790 with the creation of a committee led by Pierre-Augustin Caron de Beaumarchais to assert the rights of dramatic authors to their own works and to call for abolition of the privileges of the Comédie Française. A protest petition bearing the signatures of twenty-one writers was presented to the National Assembly

102. M.-J. Guillaume, ed., *Procès-verbaux du Comité d'Instruction Publique de la Convention Nationale* (Paris: Imprimerie Nationale, 1891), 1:iv.

103. Ibid., iv–xiii. Although the exact composition of the committee was constantly changing, Condorcet and Sieyès were continuous and influential presences.

104. See Renouard, *Traité des droits d'auteur*, 211–225. See also Michele Marie Root-Bernstein, *Boulevard Theater and Revolution in Eighteenth-Century Paris* (Ann Arbor: UMI Research Press, 1984).

by LaHarpe on August 24, 1790. This petition was essentially an effort to reintroduce into the assembly the clauses of the Sieyès proposal that had pertained to the theater and to property in dramatic works. Anyone, the signers argued, should be free to open a theater. The works of authors dead more than five years should be considered public property, but no one should be allowed to represent or publish the works of living playwrights without their written consent.[105] The petition was sent to the Committee on the Constitution.[106]

LaHarpe's plea did not fall on deaf ears. In fact, supporters of the Comédie Française charged that the petition drive had been instigated by a key member of the very committee to which it was submitted: "It's chez M. de Mirabeau . . . that this petition was cooked up."[107] Whether true or not, there can be little doubt that Honoré-Gabriel de Mirabeau helped to advance the cause of the petitioners.[108] Less than a month later, on January 13, 1791, Issac-René-Guy LeChapelier, for the Committee on the Constitution, presented to the National Assembly a *projet de loi* drafted by Mirabeau on behalf of the petitioners.[109]

The Mirabeau proposal was essentially a redrafting of the articles of the Condorcet-Sieyès proposal pertaining to literary property, but this time focused on theater authors alone. In contrast to the earlier proposal, however, the preamble of the new *projet* stressed not authors' rights, but the rights of the public. Thus LeChapelier argued:

> In soliciting for authors . . . exclusive property rights during their lifetime and five years after their death, authors acknowledge, even invoke, the rights of the public, and they do not hesitate to swear that after a period of five years the author's works are public property. . . . The public ought to have the property of great works. . . . But despotism invaded that communal property and carved it up into exclusive privileges.[110]

The authors represented themselves as servants of the public good, of its enlightenment, in opposition to the private interests of publishers and

---

105. LaHarpe, *Adresse des auteurs dramatiques*, 37–39.
106. Ibid., 44.
107. Article by M. de Charnois in *Le Modérateur*, cited by LaHarpe, ibid., 45.
108. Renouard, *Traité des droits d'auteur*, 305–306.
109. For the attribution of the *projet* to Mirabeau, see the letter written to the National Assembly on behalf of the authors of dramatic works on September 18, 1792, in Guillaume (ed.), *Procès-verbaux du Comité d'Instruction Publique* 1:52.
110. Issac-René-Guy LeChapelier, *Rapport fait par M. Le Chapelier au nom du Comité de Constitution sur la pétition des auteurs dramatiques, 13 janvier 1791* (Paris: Imprimerie Nationale, 1791), 4–6, in AN, ser. ADVIII, carton 16.

theater directors. Hence the authors themselves rejected the Diderotist argument for unlimited and absolute claims on their texts and, reviving the compromise position of Sieyès and Condorcet, presented themselves as contributors to "public property" and guardians of the public claim to the nation's cultural commons. The author was now depicted as a hero of public enlightenment, rather than as a selfish property owner. Unlike the Sieyès proposal, that of LeChapelier passed into law on January 13, 1791, abolishing all past privileges and recognizing the playwright's claims as exclusive property rights until five years after the author's death, at which point they would become part of the public domain.

This law, however, covered only the work of authors in the theater. The initiative to define the legal status of *all* authors therefore passed to the newly formed Committee on Public Instruction. Ironically, it was the recently empowered authors of dramatic works who again brought the issue to the committee's attention. On December 6, 1791, the Committee on Public Instruction received a request from a deputation of authors headed by Beaumarchais to hear new charges against theater directors for noncompliance with the law of January 13. It seems the theater directors had chosen to interpret this law as applying only to future works, leaving them free to present any work, even by a living author, that had already been printed or published. Further, they claimed publication rights on any work contracted by their companies prior to the law.[111]

Following a series of meetings, the committee drafted a *projet de loi* that was presented by Gilbert Romme and passed in the National Assembly on August 30, 1792.[112] This law, however, represented a victory for the theater directors: it upheld all contracts between authors and the theaters and sustained the exclusive right of the theaters to stage any work performed prior to the passage of the law of January 13, 1791. Needless to say, the law met with a vociferous outcry from authors. This time the playwright Marie-Joseph Chénier headed up the protest with a

111. A succession of meetings and debates on the retroactive implications of the law ensued between the authors and the theater directors in the Committee on Public Instruction on December 9 and 23, 1791, and January 2, 6, 9, 13, and 23, 1792. See M.-J. Guillaume, ed., *Procès-verbal du Comité d'Instruction Publique de l'Assemblée Législative* (Paris: Imprimerie Nationale, 1889), 47–8, 76, 78–9, 83, and 94. See also Pierre-Augustin Caron de Beaumarchais, *Pétition à l'Assemblée Nationale . . . contre l'usurpation des auteurs* ([Paris]: Dupont, [1791–1792]).

112. Presentation of the proposal was first attempted on February 5, 1792, but was deferred, first to February 8 and finally to August 30, 1792. See Guillaume (ed.), *Procès-verbal du Comité d'Instruction Publique*, 96.

letter and petition to the Committee on Public Instruction dated September 18, 1792. The law, Chénier argued, had been slipped through by Romme without the support of the majority of committee members.[113] Consequently, the committee reopened the question.[114]

Those expressing discontent in 1792 were not just writers of dramatic works. On January 2, 1792, the committee received a petition from thirty authors and editors of music who begged the National Assembly, "in all its wisdom, to find a means to protect their property and prevent pirating."[115] The novelist Jean-Baptiste Louvet de Couvray wrote to the National Assembly as well, requesting permission to present a petition "calling for a law against piraters, who are destroying the book trade and bringing me to ruin."[116] These appeals did not go unnoticed. On February 20, 1793, the Committee on Public Instruction finally assigned Chénier the task of drafting a general law against pirate editions in all genres.[117] News of the forthcoming proposal was announced in the *Moniteur* in April, but Chénier did not succeed in getting the convention floor during the troubled spring of 1793.[118]

---

113. Guillaume (ed.), *Procès-verbaux du Comité d'Instruction Publique* 1:52–53. For the original letter, the reference is now AN, ser. F17, carton 1001, doss. 39, doc. 1.

114. The struggle between the theater owners and authors was as byzantine as it was, ultimately, fruitless; see ibid., 1:51. In February, P.-C.-L. Baudin was charged by the committee to draft yet another law concerning the rights of authors of dramatic works, with the intention of abrogating the law of August 30, 1792; see Baudin, *Rapport et projet de décret sur la propriété des auteurs dramatiques présentés au nom du Comité d'Instruction Publique par P.C.L. Baudin* (Paris: Imprimerie Nationale, [1793]), in AN, ser. ADVIII, carton 16. The report was announced in the *Journal des débats et des décrets*, no. 168 (March 4, 1793); cited in Guillaume (ed.), *Procès-verbaux du Comité d'Instruction Publique* 1:347, 349n.1. On February 28, the playwright Michel-Jean Sedaine sent a letter and a petition to the committee demanding that the heirs of Jean Racine receive perpetual royalties on the presentation or publication of his works—but to no avail; see AN, ser. F17, carton 1004b, doss. 447, doc. 1, Letter and petition from Sedaine to the Committee of Public Instruction. On March 4, Baudin's proposal, which abrogated the law of August 30, 1792, and reaffirmed the original law of January 13, 1791, was published by the committee and distributed to the members of the National Convention. Protest against the proposal was registered by the committee on March 19. The proposal was pursued no further. See Guillaume (ed.), *Procès-verbal du Comité d'Instruction Publique*, 367, 369–371, 392n.3.

115. AN, ser. F17, carton 1004a, doss. 397, Letter from authors and editors of music to the National Assembly, January 2, 1792. This letter and a petition were forwarded to the Committee on Public Instruction on June 2, 1792.

116. AN, ser. C, carton 147, no. 167, Letter from Jean-Baptiste Louvet de Couvray to the National Assembly, February 23, 1792.

117. Guillaume (ed.), *Procès-verbaux du Comité d'Instruction Publique* 1:347 (session of February 20, 1793).

118. Cited in ibid., 348.

After the "revolution" of May 31–June 2, 1793, which purged the Girondist faction from the National Convention, Condorcet ceased appearing at committee meetings. A month later he was in hiding.[119] Sieyès took over the committee presidency on May 23, but he and Chénier both soon withdrew as well.[120] Denounced as Girondists, all three were formally excluded from the committee on October 6, 1793.[121] It is ironic that the Girondist law on which modern French publishing is based should emerge precisely at the moment of the Jacobin victory that suppressed its authors. Indeed, it was the Jacobin consolidation of power that made it possible for the law to pass. On July 19, 1793, the convention at last heard Chénier's proposal, presented on behalf of the Committee on Public Instruction by Joseph Lakanal.[122] It was passed with no recorded discussion.[123]

The decree amounted to yet another version of the Condorcet-Sieyès proposal of 1790. No longer perceived as a "Girondist" police measure intended to insure the accountability of authors, or as a commercial regulation to protect the private property interests of publishers, it was now presented as a mechanism for promoting public enlightenment by encouraging and compensating intellectual activity—that is, by granting limited property rights to authors:

> Citizens, of all the forms of property the least susceptible to contest, whose growth cannot harm republican equality, or cast doubt upon liberty, is property in the productions of genius. . . . By what fatality is it necessary that the man of genius, who consecrates his efforts to the instruction of his

119. Ibid., xiii.
120. Alfred Jepson Bingham, *Marie-Joseph Chénier: Early Political Life and Ideas (1789–1794)* (New York, 1939 [privately printed]), 123–126.
121. Ibid., 125.
122. For a textual analysis of the provenance of the *projet,* see Guillaume (ed.), *Procès-verbaux du Comité d'Instruction Publique* 2:80. My hypothesis is that Chénier drafted the version of the law but for political reasons did not present it himself. It was ultimately presented by Lakanal. In both the contemporary press and the Committee on Public Instruction's proceedings, Chénier is assumed to be the author, and the proposal conforms closely to the views expressed in his petition of September 18, 1792. This theory is also supported by Bingham, *Marie-Joseph Chénier,* 123. It should be noted, however, that Joseph Lakanal later claimed credit for the proposal; see his *Exposé sommaire des travaux de Joseph Lakanal* (Paris: Didot, 1838), 9–12.
123. Madival and Laurent (eds.), *Archives parlementaires* 69:186–187. A little over a month later, on September 1, 1793, the convention added a new clause to the law to clarify explicitly that this law was intended to supersede the LeChapelier law on theater authors of 1791 and to cover equally authors of dramatic works; see ibid., 73:293–294.

fellow citizens, should have nothing to promise himself but a sterile glory
and should be deprived of his claim to legitimate recompense for his noble
labors?[124]

Like the Sieyès proposal three years earlier, this law guaranteed authors, their heirs, or those to whom they ceded the text by contract an
exclusive claim on the publication of the text for the lifetime of the
author plus ten years. The royal Administration of the Book Trade,
which had registered the literary privileges of the Old Regime, was to be
replaced by a national depository at the Bibliothèque Nationale, where
all property claims were to be legally registered. The decree differed
from the Sieyès proposal in one crucial respect: it gave no retroactive
protection to the former holders of *privilèges en librairie* or *privilèges d'auteur*. With the law of July 19, 1793, then, the cultural capital of the Old
Regime was definitively remanded from the private hands of heirs and
publishers into the public domain. As Condorcet had dreamed, the authors of the Enlightenment as well as those of the classical age became
the inheritance of all.

The severing of the clauses on literary property from their original
context in the Sieyès proposal on sedition and libel, the deletion of
the clause reaffirming current privileges, the mobilization of authors,
and the new stress on public enlightenment significantly transformed
the law's political meaning and impact. Initially part of a concerted
moderate effort to re-regulate and police the printed word and insure
publishers profits, the recontextualized clauses were presented by
Lakanal as a "declaration of the rights of genius"—a Jacobin effort to
abolish the vested interests of inherited privileges, to consecrate the
bearers of enlightenment, and to enhance public access to the ideas of
the Enlightenment.

But the law did not resolve the epistemological tension between Condorcet and Diderot. Instead it produced an unstable synthesis of the two
positions. Although it drew on a Diderotist rhetoric of the sanctity of
individual creativity as an inviolable right, it did not rigorously respect
the conclusions Diderot drew from this position. In contrast to the *privilège d'auteur* of 1777, the law did not recognize the author's claim beyond his lifetime but consecrated the notion, advanced first by Pierre
Manuel to defend his edition of Mirabeau, that the only true heir to an

---

124. Lakanal's speech to the National Convention, July 19, 1793, is in Guillaume (ed.),
Procès-verbaux du Comité d'Instruction Publique 2:82.

author's work was the nation as a whole. This notion of a public domain, of democratic access to a common cultural inheritance on which no particular claim could be made, bore the traces not of Diderot, but of Condorcet's faith that truths were given in nature and, although mediated through individual minds, belonged ultimately to all. Progress in human understanding depended not on private knowledge claims, but on free and equal access to enlightenment. An author's property rights were conceived as recompense for his service as an agent of enlightenment through publication of his ideas. The law of 1793 accomplished this task of synthesis through political negotiation rather than philosophical reasoning—that is, by refashioning the political identity of the author in the first few years of the Revolution from a privileged creature of the absolutist police state into a servant of public enlightenment.

This understanding of the history of the formation of the legal identity of the author returns us to Foucault's original question: What is an author? The author as a legal instrument for the regulation of knowledge was created by the absolutist monarchy in 1777, not by the liberal bourgeois democracy inaugurated in 1789. The author was created by a royal regime that exercised power through privilege, rather than by a constitutional regime committed to insuring the protection of the individual as a private property owner. The revolutionary legislation did redefine the author's privilege as property, but not as an absolute right. The intention and the result of this redefinition of the author's claim to his text as property did not, however, enhance the author's power to control or determine the uses and meanings of the text. Quite the opposite, in fact.

What the revolutionaries acknowledged and sought to insure was not the individual dictation of meanings and truths, but their maximum exchange, conflict, and social negotiation. Progress in understanding, they believed, occurred through enhanced access and exchange. In reshaping the cultural regime, the revolutionaries sought to make a world appropriate not to an absolutist police state, but to a liberal state founded on conflict and negotiation. The democratic bourgeois revolution did not mark a further step in the progressive consolidation of the notion of the author. Rather, the revolutionaries explicitly intended to dethrone the absolute author, a creature of privilege, and recast him,

Plate 5. Detail of "La Révolution française." Engraving by A. Duplessis [1790s].
The Revolution celebrated the author as a hero of public enlightenment rather
than as a private individual creator. Musée de la Révolution française, Vizille,
France.

not as a *private* individual (the absolute bourgeois), but rather as a *public*
servant, as the model citizen (plate 5). This civic ideal of authorship was
shared by both liberal statesmen such as Condorcet and Sieyès and the
most capitalistically inclined publishers like Panckoucke. Concern for
the public good explains why the author's regulative powers, rather than
being further consolidated, were eroded and destabilized by the revolutionary legislation.

Contrary to Foucault's Diderotist interpretation, the revolutionary
legislation actually reflected not one but both sides of the Enlightenment
debate, effecting an epistemologically impure and unstable legal synthesis that combined an instrumentalist notion of the public good with a
theory of authorship based on natural rights. Precisely because of this
legal instability, the regime by which the public exchange of ideas was
regulated would be challenged and renegotiated repeatedly throughout
the revolutionary period.

If the Old Regime first accorded Voltaire, Rousseau, or Mirabeau the possibility of legal status as privileged authors with perpetual private lineages for their texts, the Revolution relocated these figures in the public domain, the legal parallel to the civic rituals that unearthed them from private gravesites and reposed their bodily remains in the public temple of the Pantheon. By legally consecrating and protecting the public domain, rather than the private authorial lineage, the French revolutionary laws on authorship shifted the legal basis of exclusive commercial claims on the majority of books from the manuscript to the edition, from the text to the paratext. As a result, the problem of determining the fate and meaning of a text shifted away from its source, the author, and toward its destination, its representation and reception by the editor and reader.[125] In this way the revolutionaries inaugurated a new cultural regime preoccupied as much with paratexuality—that is, with distinctions between different editions and readings of texts—as with epistemological debates about the origins of ideas.[126] The questions "Who is Voltaire?" and "What is Rousseau?" were thus joined by a new set of legal, commercial, and also literary preoccupations: *Whose* Voltaire? *Which* Rousseau? Not until the end of the nineteenth century would the legal recognition of the "moral rights" of authors put limits on how an author's works, once devolved into the public domain, could be edited or represented.[127]

Although there can be little doubt that the eighteenth-century expansion of commerce in the printed word placed unprecedented pressures on public authorities to recognize authorial property, the legal responses of both prerevolutionary and revolutionary authorities did not reflect these socio-economic changes alone. Politics, and a concern for public life, mediated the successive negotiations between the private interests of authors and publishers and the concerns of legal authorities. As a consequence, the revolutionary legislators produced a legal conception of authorial identity that did not merely consecrate, but also limited, the author's power of self-determination, for the sake of the public good.

---

125. For recent developments in the history of reading, see Chartier, *Lectures et lecteurs;* Chartier (ed.), *Usages de l'imprimé;* Roger Chartier, "Texts, Printings, Readings," in *The New Cultural History,* ed. Lynn Hunt (Berkeley and Los Angeles: University of California Press, 1989), 154–175; and Robert Darnton, "Readers Respond to Rousseau: The Fabrication of Romantic Sensitivity," in *Great Cat Massacre,* 215–256.

126. For important theoretical reflections along these lines, see Genette, *Seuils.*

127. See Desbois, *Droit d'auteur.*

With the "declaration of the rights of genius," the power to determine the meaning and fate of ideas devolved from the state, the family, and the corporate publishers to individual authors and to the public at large. The ideal of an enlightened republic was embodied in more than just the "rights of genius"; it lay also in the notion of democratic access to a common cultural inheritance, preserved in the public domain.

CHAPTER FOUR

Cultural Crisis and Literary Politics, 1793–1799

In order to liberate thought and facilitate the progress of enlighten-ment, the National Convention inaugurated an era of freedom of com-merce in the world of ideas. Between 1789 and 1793, the government dismantled the legal and institutional infrastructure that had organized French publishing. With the law of 1793, the National Convention rec-ognized the property rights of living authors but abolished all former literary privileges. As a consequence, the entire literary inheritance of France was released from private hands into the public domain. In place of the vast cultural bureaucracy of the Old Regime, the revolutionary government merely established a voluntary legal depository at the Bib-liothèque Nationale. There would be no national administration to reg-ulate or inspect the book trade during the republican period.

The disastrous consequences of this deregulationist cultural policy for book publishing were immediately apparent. Continuing crisis in the publishing world throughout the republican period prompted the gov-ernment to rethink its laissez-faire policies toward the printed word and to evolve two distinct paths of reintervention into publishing: the cen-tralization and expansion of government printing on the one hand, and subsidies to commercial publishing on the other.

The Cultural Crisis of the Year II

The reign of "the rights of genius" began as the Revolution entered into its darkest moment. On September 2, 1793, the National Convention applied the finishing touches to the law on literary property.[1] Yet the very same day, the deputies also passed an emergency decree requisitioning all Parisian presses for the service of the nation.[2] This was only one of the many ironies of the political riptide in which the purveyors of the printed word, new and old, were to find themselves. Authors had been granted their political rights and publishers given a clear legal footing for their commerce. It was to be near impossible, however, for them to make use of, let alone benefit from, this new legal situation.

The wars at home and abroad wreaked havoc on national and international commerce in the book trade. By July 1793 the *assignat* had lost approximately 75 percent of its face value.[3] The government then responded to soaring inflation with the *maximum,* extended to all goods and services on September 29, 1793.[4] Monetary fluctuations threw the book market into chaos, and then brought it to a standstill. According to the editor of the *Courrier de la librairie,* Chemin *fils,* by the time a book dealer's price list reached customers, it could no longer be guaranteed. He therefore announced that he was discontinuing his catalogue sales until "the market restabilizes."[5] J.-F. Morin and A. Lenoir, the editors of the *Nouvelliste littéraire,* repeatedly echoed similar difficulties with price fluctuations because of the war and the *assignat.*[6] Inflation and monetary restrictions brought Charles-Joseph Panckoucke's production of the *Encyclopédie méthodique* to a halt in 1795. And according to Panckoucke, he was not alone: "The most everyday books are lacking, the stockrooms are empty, and no one dares to go to press."[7]

To make matters worse, because of the war the government prohibited exports of any kind to hostile nations. The book trade with Austria,

1. Madival and Laurent (eds.), *Archives parlementaires* 73:293–294.

2. AN, ser. ADVIII, carton 20, doc. 17, "Décret de la Convention Nationale du 2 septembre 1793 . . . portant que tous les imprimeurs de Paris sont en état de réquisition pour le service public," [Paris: 1793].

3. Alfred Cobban, *A History of Modern France,* vol. 1: *1715–1799* (Middlesex, Eng.: Penguin Books, 1963), 226.

4. François Furet and Denis Richet, *La Révolution française* (Paris: Marabout, 1973), 518.

5. Chemin *fils,* ed., "Avis important," *Courrier de la librairie,* no. 27, prairial, an III [May–June 1795], 1.

6. The *Nouvelliste littéraire* was published in Paris from germinal, an IV, to germinal, an IX (April 1796–April 1806); see especially nos. 7–8, 8; and nos. 9–10, 8.

7. Charles-Joseph Panckoucke, *Mémoire sur les assignats et sur la manière de les considérer dans l'état de la baisse actuelle* (Paris, 1795); cited by Tucoo-Chala, *Charles-Joseph Panckoucke,* 495.

Belgium, England, and Spain therefore ground to a halt. Trade with neutral countries, notably Switzerland, was disrupted as well.[8] Domestic commerce, too, was in a state of chaos as a result of the revolts in the south and the civil war in the west. The Paris publisher Louis Ravier later recalled the wartime loss of sales as the most important cause of the "prolonged stagnation in the book trade."[9] Disruptions of the book trade by the war were so extensive that even the most sought-after works, such as Pierre-Augustin Caron Beaumarchais's famous Kehl editions of Voltaire's works, could not find a market. And if Voltaire could not sell, Ravier reflected, nothing could, because "it would take nothing less than Voltaire to survive such violent blows."[10]

Statistical evidence also suggests that by 1794 book publishing was at a near standstill. The newly established legal depository at the Bibliothèque Nationale registered only 69 works in its first four months of operation (July 21–December 31, 1793).[11] Many of these works were not even new titles from the year 1793, but editions dating back to 1791. In 1794, the *dépôt* recorded receipt of only 396 titles, as compared to the 728 registered by royal authorities in 1787, or the global figure of 1,687 works, both legal and illegal, published in 1788![12] The figures compiled by Angus Martin, Vivienne G. Milne, and Richard Frautschi in their massive *Bibliographie du genre romanesque français* reveal a strikingly similar pattern to those of the *dépôt légal:* the publication of fiction dropped dramatically from over one hundred new novels in 1789 to only *sixteen* in 1794. The number of reeditions of novels reveals a less dramatic, but similar, decline for the same period.[13] Thus, despite the "declaration of the rights of genius," by the year II Paris book publishing was in a state of crisis.

In early March 1794, Jean-Baptiste Lefebvre de Villebrune, the director of the Bibliothèque Nationale, sent separate reports to the Com-

8. AN, ser. AA, carton 56, doc. 1525, Letter from Batilliot, Paris publisher, to the Committee on Public Safety, 12 floréal, an II (May 1, 1794). See also Jean-Baptiste Lefebvre de Villebrune, "Considérations sur le commerce de la librairie," 29 ventôse, [an II] (March 19, 1794), in Guillaume (ed.), *Procès-verbaux du Comité d'Instruction Publique* 3:612, 613, 617.

9. Louis Ravier, *Répertoire de la librairie* (Paris: Crapart, Caille & Ravier, 1807), xv.

10. Ibid., 260.

11. BN, Archives Modernes, CXXIX, "Registres du dépôt légal des livres imprimés," reg. 1, July 1793 to the year VII [September 21, 1799].

12. According to Estivals, *Statistique bibliographique*, 405, 415.

13. Angus Martin, Vivienne G. Milne, and Richard Frautschi, *Bibliographie du genre romanesque français* (Paris: France Expansion; London: Mansell, 1977), xxxvi–xxxix.

mittee on Public Safety and the Committee on Public Instruction declaring a crisis in Paris publishing: "There is total stagnation. Something must be done . . . as much for the general good of the fatherland as to avert the total ruin of the publishers of Paris."[14] Villebrune outlined the central causes of the crisis in book publishing as follows:

> First: Fewer customers; [in former times,] many useless people fastidiously formed libraries that they were incapable of reading. Incapable of being republicans, they have fled the country.
> Second: Those who educate themselves and read in order to educate themselves, absorbed by the defense of the fatherland or by the posts that they occupy, are not reading or are reading much less.
> Third: The interruption of commerce with hostile countries has closed this branch of export.
> Fourth: The obstacles imposed on commerce with neutral countries.[15]

Emigration and war, in short, had closed down literary markets by depriving dealers of aristocratic, bourgeois, and foreign customers.

While the war ravaged the elite book market both within and beyond France, the Terror deprived publishers and printers of the new markets in political literature that had opened up after the collapse of state censorship in 1789. By 1792 repression had begun to send an icy chill across the printing and publishing trades. The laws of December 4, 1792, and especially March 29, 1793, turned political journalism and pamphleteering into potentially lethal professions: any call for the dissolution of the present government became punishable by death.[16] The law against suspects of September 17, 1793, still further smoothed the path from the printing press to the guillotine.[17] In the *Histoire générale de la presse française*, Jacques Godechot writes: "From June 2, 1793, until the fall of Robespierre and the great Committee on Public Safety on 9 thermidor, year II [July 27, 1794] . . . the press no longer enjoyed any freedom."[18]

Not surprisingly, between 1792 and 1793 the number of journals published in Paris dropped by one-half, from 216 to 113. In the year II

14. BN, nouv. acq. fr. 2836, feuille 27, Report from Jean-Baptiste Lefebvre de Villebrune to the Committee on Public Safety, on the state of the book trade, 12 ventôse, an II (March 2, 1794).

15. Villebrune, "Considérations sur le commerce de la librairie française," in Guillaume (ed.), *Procès-verbaux du Comité d'Instruction Publique* 3:613.

16. Jacques Godechot, "La Presse française sous la Révolution et l'Empire," in Bellanger (eds.), *Histoire générale de la presse française* 1:504.

17. For the application of this law against journalists, see ibid., 508.

18. Ibid.

the number of periodicals circulating in Paris hit an all-time low of 106 for the revolutionary period (1788–1799).[19] Further, the repression of unpatriotic printed matter was not limited to political journals. No genre was above suspicion. Surveillance extended from posters and pamphlets to novels and scientific publications.[20] Even the character of a bookseller's clientele could come under scrutiny.[21]

Terror ground the Paris printing presses to a halt. Thus one of the minister of the interior's secret agents in Paris, Le Breton, reported on March 3, 1794:

> Printers are complaining that even at the very modest wage rates for which they are now working, they can no longer find any work because of the large number of printing shops that have been suppressed. They say that if people were allowed to express their ideas freely they would not be in this situation. They would have too much work and there would not even be enough printers in the city.[22]

The stifling of public discussion and dissent left the commercial presses idle.

The war and the Terror thus conspired with scissorlike inevitability to cut down the old book dealers along with the militant young political printers of Paris. Another secret agent of the Interior Ministry, the bookseller Siret, summed up the state of the publishing and printing world in Paris at the end of December 1793:

> The thirty-six formerly privileged printers who used to have an exclusive monopoly on all the typographical work in the capital continuously em-

19. Ibid., 436, 504.

20. For an example of posters, see Chemin *fils,* printer, 26 messidor, an II (July 14, 1794), in AN, ser. F7, carton 4645, doss. 2. For pamphlets, see Jacques-François Froullé, printer, and Thomas Levigneur, bookseller, 8 ventôse, an II (February 26, 1794), in AN, ser. W, carton 332, no. 566, and AN, ser. AF*II, carton 294, docs. 107–108; Philippe-Denis Pierres, printer, and Jean-Nicolas Barba, publisher, 25 nivôse, an II (January 14, 1794), in AN, ser. BB3, carton 81a, docs. 361–364; and Charlier and Senneville (Rioux-Maillon), booksellers, germinal–thermidor, an II (March–August 1794), in AN, ser. F7, carton 4774, doss. 93, doc. 3; AN, ser. F7, carton 4775, doss. 17, doc. 4; AN, ser. F7, carton 4637, doss. 4; and AN, AF*II, carton 294, doc. 145. For an example of novels and scientific publications, see Gaspar-Joseph Cuchet, publisher, 8 thermidor, an II (July 26, 1794), in AN, ser. W, carton 53, doss. 3401, and AN, ser. F7, carton 4658, doss. 4.

21. For suspect clientele, see Victor Desenne, publisher, September 19, 1793, in AN, ser. F7, carton 3688, doss. 3, doc. 2.

22. Pierre Caron, *Paris pendant la Terreur, Rapports des agents secrets du ministre de l'intérieur* (Paris: Picard, 1910–1978), 5:50, "Rapport de Le Breton, 13 ventôse, an II" (March 3, 1794).

ployed twelve to fifteen hundred workers. Four hundred presses running continuously consumed at a minimum, in Paris alone, 250,000 reams of paper a year; today they don't even consume half this much.

The new printing shops to which liberty has given birth, although numerous, have in general very little work, to judge by the number of presses they can keep busy. It is easy to become convinced that, including journals, posters, pamphlets, all varieties of literature, and trade jobs, paper consumption only barely equals what it did in former times.[23]

Bust had followed boom. And although Siret observed that the former members of the Paris Book Guild were suffering the greatest losses, the new presses of Paris, according to his report, now too found themselves underemployed.

To make matters worse, in the fall of 1793 the Committee on Public Safety announced its intention to achieve governmental and national unity by centralizing government patronage and production of printed matter. But this intensification in the production and dissemination of official documents did not lead to an increase in government contracts for Paris printers. It resulted, rather, in the expansion of government printing houses at their expense.

The effort to centralize the publication of laws, begun with the requisitioning of pressmen and presses in September 1793, received new impetus on November 18, 1793, from a report to the National Convention by Jacques-Nicolas Billaud-Varenne on behalf of the Committee on Public Safety.[24] The committee proposed that the government compile one complete and exclusive *Bulletin des lois,* to be printed and distributed exclusively by a national "imprimerie des lois." This measure, he wrote, "is simple because it removes all of the intermediaries so that there will no longer be any separation between the legislator and the people. . . . This luminous idea was conceived under the Constituent Assembly. . . . Be wise enough to draw upon it and make use of it in your turn in order to consolidate the Republic."[25] When the convention promulgated its principles of revolutionary government on 14 frimaire, year II (December 4, 1793), the first section of the decree made provisions to com-

23. Ibid., 1:415–416, "Rapport de Siret, 5 nivôse, an II" (December 25, 1793).

24. Report by Billaud-Varenne to the National Convention, 28 brumaire, an II (November 18, 1793); cited in François-Antoine-Brutus Duprat, *Histoire de l'Imprimerie Impériale de France* (Paris: Imprimerie Impériale, 1861), 144–146.

25. Ibid., 146.

mence implementation of the Billaud-Varenne plan.[26] The "intermediaries"—that is, commercial and departmental printers—were to be removed from the process of government publication.

A decree of 27 frimaire, year II (December 17, 1793), transformed the old printing shop for the royal lottery on the rue Neuve-des-Petits-Champs into a new Imprimerie de l'Administration Nationale.[27] The national Imprimerie des Lois was then constructed in the Maison Beaujon in the faubourg St-Honoré during the winter and spring of the year II. In order to produce a *Bulletin des lois* with press runs estimated at two hundred thousand copies, the printing shop had to contain 120 presses.[28] The new printing house was supplied, in part, by the construction of new presses, but also through confiscation of the presses of suppressed printers.[29] For example, when Jacques Anisson-Duperron, the director of the Imprimerie du Louvre (formerly the Imprimerie Royale), perished in the Terror of the spring of 1794, his presses were moved from the Louvre to the Maison Beaujon.[30] The presses of Momoro, Hébert, Froullé, Nicolas, Parisau, Deschamps, and Tassin de l'Etang—all similarly convicted as counterrevolutionaries—met the same fate.[31] With the printed word as its most powerful medium, the government wielded repression and centralization simultaneously in the effort to produce a unified political culture.

The Committee on Public Safety did not limit its interest in controlling the printed word to the publication of laws. Their propaganda efforts led them into all genres of printed literature. Less than a year after the abolition of the royal academies and literary societies, the committee initiated an effort to establish a corps of official writers.[32] On April 16, 1794, it sent out a call to all poets "to celebrate the principal events of the

---

26. Ibid., 147.

27. Ibid., 154.

28. Ibid., 151.

29. One hundred new presses were ordered from the shop at the Imprimerie du Louvre. According to Duprat, thirty new presses were actually delivered; ibid., 152.

30. Ibid., 165.

31. Ibid., 166. For more on the fate of Froullé's business, see Guillaume (ed.), *Procès-verbaux du Comité d'Instruction Publique* 5:311.

32. The National Convention suppressed all official societies and academies by their decrees of August 8 and 12, 1793. For the plans of the Committee on Public Safety, see AN, ser. F17, carton 1008b, doss. 1487, Letter from the Committee on Public Safety to the Committee on Public Instruction requesting a list of patriotic writers, 17 frimaire, an II (December 7, 1793); AN, ser. F17, carton 1258, doss. 2, for the decree ordering the printing and distribution of the *Recueil des actions héroiques et civiques des républicains français,*

Revolution, to compose hymns and patriotic poems, republican dramatic plays, to publish the heroic actions of the soldiers of freedom . . . to give to history the severity and firmness appropriate to the annals of a great people."[33] These works, the committee promised, would be printed by the government. Further, while systematically repressing independent publishing of journals and pamphlets, the government committed its own presses and millions of *livres,* in the form of secret discretionary funds attributed to various ministries and committees, to both officially sanctioned and unofficially subsidized ephemeral literature.[34]

The consumption patterns of the industry's most critical resource—paper—are telling evidence of the expansion of government publishing. By the winter of 1793–1794 the Commission on Provisions and Subsistence became concerned about potential government shortages of paper.[35] But according to the minister of the interior's agent, Siret, there was no real shortage of paper, only a change in patterns of consumption, which created the appearance of a shortage:

> Paper consumption . . . is not as prodigious as one would think; it is rather its concentration that makes it appear so great to our eyes. Commercial consumption barely equals what it did before the Revolution. There is thus no real increase in consumption but that which is the result of the work of the Convention, the executive power, and of the tasks delegated to other constituted authorities.[36]

Only the government was consuming more paper. Commercial printers were consuming less.

---

13 nivôse, an II (January 2, 1794); and ibid., doss. 8, for the Committee on Public Safety's calls for patriotic poems, hymns, and plays, 27 floréal, an II (May 16, 1794).

33. AN, ser. F17, carton 1258, doss. 8, "Extrait des registres des arrêtés du Comité de Salut Public," 27 floréal, an II (May 16, 1794).

34. For the extent of officially and unofficially subsidized publications, see Alphonse Aulard, "La Presse officieuse pendant la Terreur," *Etudes et leçons sur la Révolution française,* 1st ser. (n.d.): 227–240; Pierre Caron, "Les Publications officieuses du Ministère de l'Intérieur en 1793 et 1794," *Revue d'histoire moderne et contemporaine* 14 (1910): 5–43; Claude Perroud, "Roland et la presse subventionnée," *Révolution française* 62 (1912): 206–213, 315–332, 396–419; Albert Mathiez, "Mélanges. La Presse subventionnée en l'an II," *Annales révolutionnaires* 10 (1918): 112–113; and Bellanger (ed.), *Histoire générale de la presse française* 1:510. The Committee on Public Safety submitted nine technical and educational pamphlets to the *dépôt légal* in its own name in 1794; see BN, Archives Modernes, CXXIX, "Registres du dépôt légal des livres imprimés," reg. 1, July 1793 to the year VII [September 21, 1799].

35. Caron, *Paris pendant la Terreur* 1:414n.5, "Adresse . . . sur la consommation du papier du 9 frimaire [an II]" (November 29, 1793).

36. Ibid., 415–416, "Rapport de Siret, 5 nivôse, an II" (December 25, 1793).

A look at the number of books registered for legal protection at the Bibliothèque Nationale during the revolutionary period, in conjunction with figures for legal and illegal book publishing in the decade before 1789 and for Parisian periodicals produced during the Revolution, provides a vivid depiction of the scissorlike cultural crisis of the year II (figure 6).[37] As Daniel Roche and Roger Chartier have observed, compilation and interpretation of bibliographic statistics from the revolutionary period is a problematic affair.[38] Not only are the sources fragmentary, but basic definitions of what constitutes a "book," a "periodical," or a "publication" vary widely. Two separate studies for the years 1790–1791 and 1799 conclude that current statistics may represent as little as half the actual amount published in this period. Nevertheless, all available evidence, both quantitative and otherwise, suggests that the basic shape of the curve

37. A definitive quantitative study of French publications during the revolutionary period has thus far eluded historians. The discontinuous and fragmentary nature of the extant documentation from the revolutionary period is one of the most telling consequences of the deregulationist cultural policies of the government. Because there was no obligatory national deposit between 1789 and 1810, no definitive national record remains of books in print. Numerous book dealers attempted to fill this gap with commercial trade journals; yet as invaluable as these are, none achieved the comprehensiveness aspired to, and none survived for more than a few years of the period in question. The only known bibliographic source that spans the entire revolutionary period is the manuscript register of the *dépôt légal* at the Bibliothèque Nationale, from its founding on July 19, 1793, to the revival of the national Administration of the Book Trade in 1810, now conserved in the Archives Modernes of the Bibliothèque Nationale, CXXIX. Several decades ago the most noted bibliographer of the Old Regime and the Revolution, Robert Estivals, made a monumental effort to tabulate all official government records of French publications for the eighteenth century, including the revolutionary period; see Estivals, *Statistique bibliographique*, 404–405, 415.

38. For a discussion of the technical problems in arriving at definitive bibliographic statistics for the revolutionary period, and an assessment of the problems with Estivals's work in particular, see Roger Chartier and Daniel Roche, "L'Histoire quantitative du livre," *Revue française d'histoire du livre*, n.s., no. 16 (1977): 480; and Roger Chartier and Daniel Roche, eds., "Les Livres ont-ils fait la Révolution?" in *Livre et Révolution*, Mélanges de la Sorbonne 9 (Paris: Aux Amateurs de Livres, 1989), 12–13. Registration at the *dépôt légal* was completely voluntary, and thus it cannot be considered an accurate account of what was actually in print. As figure 6 reveals, the numbers of works more than doubled when deposit became obligatory with the Napoleonic re-regulation in 1810. Further evidence that the actual number of books in print probably needs to be nearly doubled is cited by Roche and Chartier in "Livres ont-ils fait," 12; see also Jean Dhombres, "Books: Reshaping Science," in Darnton and Roche (eds.), *Revolution in Print*, 178–181. Further, the *dépôt* functioned poorly, as Estivals has shown, and as a consequence is severely biased, largely for the logistical reason of proximity, toward Parisian authors and publishers. The number of works submitted by non-Parisian publishers between 1793 and 1799 totaled only 92 out of 2,593; the first foreign deposit was made only in 1796 (see appendix 5).

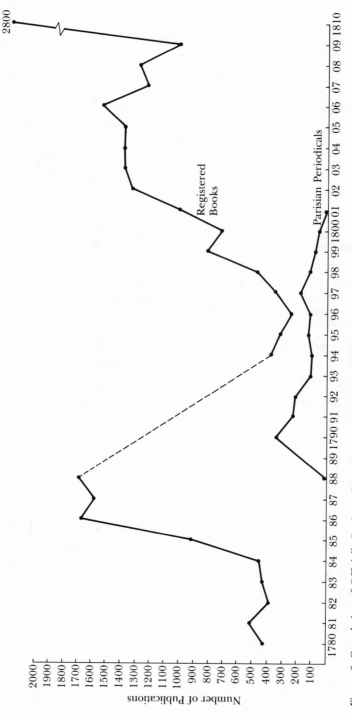

Figure 6. Correlation of Officially Registered Books and Parisian Periodicals Published Between 1789 and 1800

Sources: for books, Robert Estivals, *La Statistique bibliographique de la France sous la monarchie au XVIIIe siècle* (Paris: Mouton, 1965), 404–405, 415; for periodicals, Claude Bellanger, ed., *Histoire générale de la presse française* (Paris: Presses Universitaires de la France, 1969), 1:436.

is essentially accurate.[39] As David Bellos puts it, "The general contours of the evolution are . . . clear enough: expansion toward the end of the eighteenth century, a brutal crash during the revolutionary period, a slow recovery at the end of the eighteenth century, a modest and stable level under the Consulate, [and] growth under the Empire."[40]

After expanding rapidly in the 1780s, book publishing plummeted following deregulation in the early years of the Revolution. Yet whereas book publishing collapsed, between 1789 and 1792 the periodical press boomed, only to be dramatically cut back in 1793 by political repression. By 1793, a crisis in *both* book and periodical publishing is indisputably clear. Finally, a distinct revival in book publishing during the Directory (1795–1799), Consulate, and early Empire (1800–1808) was accompanied by a notable decline (due again to government repression) of the periodical press.

The crisis of the year II crushed the Paris publishing and printing world with multiple blows. Inflation and war completely disrupted the elite book market, both within and beyond France, while political repression shut down the new mass markets in popular political newspapers and ephemera. More harmful still than the contingencies of the Terror and the war was an alarming new development in the government's cultural policies: the centralization of government printing and publishing at the Imprimerie des Lois. Deprived of both elite and popular, foreign and domestic markets, as well as of the work created by the expansion of government publishing, the newly liberated Paris publishing and printing world found itself in desperate straits. Throughout the fall and spring of the year II, Paris printers, individually and collectively, sent desperate appeals for work to the Committee on Public Instruction.[41] Their appeals did not go unanswered.

39. The overall contours of figure 6 are further confirmed by Martin, Milne, and Frautschi in their massive *Bibliographie de genre romanesque français:* the publication of novels dropped dramatically from several hundred new ones in 1789 to only *sixteen* in 1794. Further, some of the limitations of the *dépôt* are in fact virtues: the bias toward Paris, for instance, actually increases its statistical significance for the Parisian publishing community.

40. David Bellos, "La Conjoncture de la production," in Chartier and Martin (eds.), *Histoire de l'édition française* 2:552.

41. See AN, ser. F17, carton 1008c, doss. 1559, Letter from Beauvais, printer, rue de la Sorbonne, to the Committee on Public Instruction, requesting to be requisitioned as a consequence of their decree, [1793–1794]; AN, ser. F17, carton 1009a *bis*, doss. 1992, Letter from Lavoye, printer, to the Committee on Public Instruction, 25 pluviôse, an II (February 13, 1794); and AN, ser. F17, carton 1009b, doss. 2071, Appeal for employment from Deltufo, printer, to the Committee on Public Instruction, 9 prairial, an II (May 28,

Cultural Thermidor

As the Committee on Public Safety pursued its objective of political unity by centralizing and nationalizing the production of printed matter, the Committee on Public Instruction was made painfully aware of the initial results of its fledgling cultural policies pertaining to the printed word. They had liberated man's reason from the inquisitions and superstitions of the Old Regime and given legislative consecration to his genius and its fruits. They had abolished private claims on the great classical and Enlightenment texts and made them the inheritance of all. They had opened the professions of printing, publishing, and bookselling to anyone. But it was clear that "enlightenment" was not spreading in every direction, at least not by means of the printed word.

In early March 1794, the Committees on Public Safety and Public Instruction each received separate reports from Jean-Baptiste Lefebvre de Villebrune, head of the Bibliothèque Nationale, concerning the state of publishing.[42] Something had to be done, he insisted, to reverse the total stagnation of the book trade.[43] With the exception of rare books and military maps, Villebrune argued, there could be no reason to prohibit the export of printed matter, even to hostile nations. The economic benefits of allowing exportation of books were obvious. Villebrune, however, was not a man of narrow commercial concerns. He appealed, in all sincerity, to the cultural vision of the committee as well: "It is important to the French nation that its revolutionary principles be propagated beyond its frontiers, because thus impregnated with liberty, the diverse peoples who surround us will resist all the better the perfidious plots of their tyrants."[44] By relegalizing the export of books, commercial pub-

---

1794). Finally, the committee registered receipt of an appeal from "printers without occupation" on 5 prairial, an II (May 24, 1794); see Guillaume (ed.), *Procès-verbaux du Comité d'Instruction Publique* 4:471.

42. BN, nouv. acq. fr. 2836, feuilles 27–29, Report from Villebrune to the Committee on Public Safety concerning the state of the book trade, 12 ventôse, an II (March 2, 1794), forwarded to the Committee on Public Instruction on 24 ventôse, an II (March 14, 1794); and AN, ser. F17, carton 1009c, doss. 2216, Report from Villebrune to the Committee on Public Instruction entitled "Considérations sur le commerce de la librairie française," received by the committee on 29 ventôse, an II (March 19, 1794). This second report has been reproduced in Guillaume (ed.), *Procès-verbaux du Comité d'Instruction Publique* 3:612–618.

43. BN, nouv. acq. fr. 2836, feuille 27, Report from Villebrune to the Committee on Public Safety concerning the state of the book trade, 12 ventôse, an II (March 2, 1794).

44. Villebrune, "Considérations sur le commerce de la librairie française," in Guillaume (ed.), *Procès-verbaux du Comité d'Instruction Publique* 3:614.

lishing could be revived and at the same time be made to serve as an agent of global revolution.

But it was not just the lack of production and markets that worried Villebrune. It was also the *kind* of works publishers were producing that disturbed him. There was no guarantee that commercial publishing houses, if revived, would rise as a vanguard of republican literary culture. In fact, the streets of Paris offered ample evidence to the contrary. Thus, for example, the agent Mercier reported to the minister of the interior on 17 nivôse, year II (January 6, 1794): "The *marchands des nouveautés* are selling lots of books better suited to corrupting morals than to improving the minds of citizens. Without public morality there will be no true republicans."[45] Villebrune's own observations confirmed these reports of the negative influence of the freed presses on public morals. He offered the following diagnosis of the situation:

> Consider the publisher for a moment as any ordinary manufacturer. His business augments and diminishes in proportion to the orders he receives. The type of product in which he invests his industry is that for which there is the greatest demand. . . . But at the same time as the fashions of the moment determine the nature of his product, he in turn, by the works with which he inundates his fatherland, acts upon the tastes of his fellow citizens, implanting in an ever greater number of heads further fantasies, daydreams, and useless notions which a few opinion makers have made the rage of the moment. Thus there is a relationship between the moral judgment of the publisher and public morality. When the caprices of fashion encourage courses of study that are destructive of reason, or immoral readings, the publisher spreads this venom into all classes of society, and the immorality of the Old Regime Court reaches into even the most remote corners of the country.[46]

In Villebrune's view, a pattern of feedback between the reading public and the commercial publisher made cultural transformation through purely laissez-faire commercial publishing impossible. The vicious circle of cultural reproduction was all the more difficult to break because of the power of the printing press, which multiplied exponentially the culture that it reproduced. The most immediate cultural consequence of the freeing of the press, he concluded, was the uninhibited and contin-

45. Caron, *Paris pendant la Terreur* 3:211, "Rapport de Mercier, 17 nivôse, an II" (January 6, 1794).

46. Villebrune, "Considérations sur le commerce de la librairie française," in Guillaume (ed.), *Procès-verbaux du Comité d'Instruction Publique* 3:614.

uous reinfection, indeed spreading, of the decadent literary tastes of the Old Regime Court.

The problem, as Villebrune saw it, was how to intervene in such a manner as to break the cycle of reproduction without undermining or compromising the newly instituted rights of freedom of commerce, expression, and the press. The answer was not simple:

> Where minds are not already shaped, it is to be feared that the tastes of consumers imbued with prerevolutionary ideas will not be in harmony with the spirit of the nation. In this situation, the mercantile interests of the publisher do not coincide with the national interest, and it becomes necessary for the government to intervene in the publishing world. . . . But in what way? The prohibition of works contrary to republican principles is indispensable. . . . But there are other works, as dull as they are useless to the development of the mind: they cannot be prohibited merely for that. Works of this genre form the large majority of what is printed, they are the most sought after. . . . Among these works are compilations, excerpts, [and] almost all novels. . . . The publisher is not guilty for engaging in this kind of business . . . because these works have no other vice than their uselessness.[47]

If this decadent literary culture of the Old Regime could not be censored, how were the reading habits of the nation to be reformed? Villebrune thought he had an answer:

> The fatherland should offer the publisher a compensation that will balance in his eyes the benefits that he sacrifices for the greater good. . . .
> First: Civic awards to the publishers who in the course of the year have published the greatest number of useful works.
> Second: . . . To honorific awards could be added the acquisition of copies of works judged to be useful [for the national library system]. By this organization of encouragements, the book trade will preserve all the liberty it needs to keep itself alive, and the government, by a constant, but not onerous, policy, could redirect people's minds from their former emptiness toward more useful objectives.[48]

The Old Regime had attempted to shape minds through a system of censorship and privileges. Under the Republic these mechanisms were to be replaced by "awards" and "encouragements." The principles of freedom of commerce, expression, and the press could thus be upheld.

Villebrune's reports reveal an important shift in both the underlying principles and the practical aspects of revolutionary cultural policy. His

47. Ibid., 615.
48. Ibid., 615–616.

proposal betrayed a recognition that a "free market in ideas" was not adequate to insure enlightenment of the nation. The minds of citizens, if freed from prescriptive constraints, might not naturally or easily reason toward enlightenment or the public good. Eighteenth-century France, even after the fall of the Old Regime, was not, after all, a state of nature. Indeed, the very mechanism on which the government had placed so much faith as an agent of enlightenment, the printing press, had proved that it could act equally as a force obstructing the course of reason, by reproducing and multiplying the public's preference for an aristocratic reading diet of books intended for leisure and pleasure, rather than for works that encouraged the republican virtues of productivity and self-improvement. These sober insights of the year II contributed to a significant redefinition and expansion of the revolutionary government's patronage of the printed word.

Villebrune's call for positive government intervention in the nation's cultural life could not have been more timely. Indeed, it is possible that his reports were solicited by the two committees to which they were sent. The Committee on Public Instruction, at any rate, had just been called upon to reassess the question of literary patronage. With the nationalization of state finances in 1790 and the suppression of the royal academies and literary societies in 1793, government patronage of cultural and intellectual life had fallen into total disarray.[49] As early as 1791, the National Assembly had seen the need to encourage the production of patriotic works for educational and political purposes, but persistent suspicion of any official reinstitutionalization of culture prevented anything more than stopgap measures and piecemeal discretionary patronage on the part of the government.[50] In February 1793, therefore, the

---

49. For more on the deinstitutionalization of government patronage, see Roger Hahn, *The Anatomy of a Scientific Institution: The Paris Academy of Sciences, 1666–1803* (Berkeley and Los Angeles: University of California Press, 1971), 228–285; Françoise Waquet, "La Bastille académique," in *La Carmagnole des muses. L'Homme de lettres et l'artiste dans la Révolution,* ed. Jean-Claude Bonnet (Paris: Armand Colin, 1988), 19–36; and Emmet Kennedy, *A Cultural History of the French Revolution* (New Haven: Yale University Press, 1989), 168–192.

50. A decree of the National Assembly of August 3, 1790, assured financial encouragement for "les artistes, savants, gens de lettres, élèves, auteurs de recherches utiles aux progrès des sciences et des arts" (title 2, article 6). Another decree, on August 14, 1790, assured that the assembly would honor all current government subsidies and contracts for the arts, sciences, and letters, and instructed that reports and bills should be submitted to the Committee on Finance. The National Assembly awarded several subsidies and pensions over the course of 1790–1791. See Guillaume (ed.), *Procès-verbal du Comité d'Instruction Publique,* xi, xvi. For early efforts to encourage patriotic, and especially anticlerical,

National Convention ordered the Committee on Public Instruction to prepare a report assessing state financing of cultural patronage. In so doing it offered the occasion for a systematic rethinking of the appropriate relationship of republican government to the cultural and intellectual life of the nation.[51]

The project received new momentum during 1793 from the repeated calls for public assistance from authors as notable as Henri Bernardin de St. Pierre who had lost the pensions and positions they had held under the Old Regime.[52] On July 20, 1793, the committee assigned Henri Grégoire the task of drawing up a major report and proposal for legislation to encourage the arts, letters, and sciences.[53] By early February 1794, the Committee on Public Instruction ordered Grégoire to collaborate on the proposal with the Committee on Public Safety.[54] Villebrune's reports on the state of the book trade were forwarded to Grégoire to assist him in his task.[55]

Grégoire's report, *Sur les encouragements, récompenses et pensions à accorder aux savants, aux gens de lettres et aux artistes*, was finally presented to the National Convention on 17 vendémiaire, year III (October 5, 1794).[56] Grégoire explicitly rejected the noninterventionist, laissez-faire stance that had until then oriented the cultural policies of the revolutionary

---

writing, see the assembly's decree of November 23, 1791, exhorting citizens to produce works against fanaticism and promising public compensation; see ibid., 59.

51. AN, ser. F17, carton 1258, doss. 2, Decree of 13 frimaire, an II (December 3, 1793). Article 4 of the decree is cited by Guillaume (ed.), *Procès-verbaux du Comité d'Instruction Publique* 3:413n.3: "Sur la proposition des Comités de Liquidation et de l'Examen des Comptes, la Convention Nationale chargea le Comité d'Instruction Publique de se faire rendre compte . . . de l'emploi des sommes accordées pour l'encouragement des arts utiles, les genres d'invention, les noms des auteurs, et la récompense à accorder à chacun d'eux."

52. Guillaume (ed.), *Procès-verbaux du Comité d'Instruction Publique* 1:356 (February 22, 1793); 4:14 (March 23, 1794); and 4:1016 (July 6, 1794).

53. Ibid., 2:85 (July 20, 1793), and 2:342 (August 24, 1793).

54. For the collaboration of the two committees on this report, see ibid., 3:432 and 4:93.

55. See the marginal notes on both reports: BN, nouv. acq. fr. 2836, feuilles 27–29, Report from Villebrune to the Committee on Public Safety concerning the state of the book trade, 12 ventôse, an II (March 2, 1794), forwarded to the Committee on Public Instruction on 24 ventôse, an II (March 14, 1794); and AN, ser. F17, carton 1009c, doss. 2216, Report from Villebrune to the Committee on Public Instruction, "Considérations sur le commerce de la librairie française," reproduced in Guillaume (ed.), *Procès-verbaux du Comité d'Instruction Publique* 3:612–618.

56. Henri Grégoire, *Rapport sur les encouragements, récompenses et pensions à accorder aux savants, aux gens de lettres et aux artistes* (Paris: Imprimerie Nationale, an III [1794–1795]). See also Guillaume (ed.), *Procès-verbaux du Comité d'Instruction Publique* 4:758, 766–767.

government. He also sounded a distinctly Thermidorean note. The heart of the problem, Grégoire asserted, lay in the adherence of the convention to the cultural theories advanced by Jean-Jacques Rousseau in his *Discourse on the Sciences and Arts:*

> We are all aware of what Jean-Jacques thought, or at least what he wrote, about the utility of the sciences. But he also contended that a large republic is a chimera, and that a people who delegates representatives to govern for them ceases to be free. We have already, through our acts, rejected his views in resolving these two latter questions: we can proceed in the same manner with the question of the sciences. If the abuse of a thing reflects upon the thing itself, then virtue would be a vice: Instead of arguing about abuses, it is necessary to prove that abuse is inseparable from the sciences. . . . In a country where wealth and vanity carry weight over everything else, where one studies only to draw attention to oneself and to advance in society, and not for self-improvement, virtue diminishes and the price of talent increases. . . . But if talent is only applauded when it embodies the characteristics of the beautiful, the just, and the good, then the arts will soon recover their moral character. Pleasing talents whose sole purpose had seemed only to make life a bit more charming will then reveal their hidden utility. Painting, engraving, poetry, and music will recover their original dignity. With us, as with the ancients, they will become resources in the hands of the government. The hymns of Tyrtheus, that of the men of Marseille, and the happy effects that they have produced are irrefragable proofs.[57]

Grégoire announced a cultural Thermidor: just as representative government was to eclipse direct democracy, so too cultural representation would replace the social ideal of transparent and unmediated exchange between the government and its citizenry, as well as exchange among citizens themselves. Refuting Rousseau, Grégoire argued that there was nothing inherently corrupt or corrupting about culture itself. Rather, cultural life reflected the mores of the society that produced it. Old Regime culture was vain and decadent because Old Regime society had been so. Virtuous societies, like the classical republics, proved that a beneficent and virtuous culture was both possible and desirable. Further, he asserted, citizens would, if given the opportunity, incline naturally toward a more virtuous culture. The government needed to provide that opportunity. Massive government intervention in intellectual and cultural life was necessary, as much to assure the economic and political strength of the nation as to contribute to the happiness of its citizens.

57. Grégoire, *Rapport sur les encouragements,* 10–11.

On a more practical level, Grégoire used the information provided by Villebrune and others to depict for the convention the pitiful situation in which authors, editors, and publishers now found themselves. The great works of men of letters are rarely appreciated by the commercial reading public in their own time, he observed. In revolutionary moments literary tastes become narrowly focused on the immediate concerns of the present, ignoring the more abstract, elevated, and timeless themes of great thinkers. It was not surprising, then, that "Milton's *Paradise Lost,* Winckelmann's history of art, or Stewart's research on political economy had met with public disdain." In times of revolution, such works require even more support than they normally would. Moreover, the laws protecting literary property were so inadequate that "if, on the contrary, a work is well received, every literary pirate will rush to publish it." Thus, he lamented, "the possessors of some of Mably's unpublished manuscripts, amounting to about three volumes, have suspended their publication out of fear of pirate editions."[58] The fate of such important publishing ventures could not be left to the vagaries of the revolutionary market.

The inherent faults of commercial publishing were only further exacerbated by the particular circumstances of the Revolution, Grégoire continued. He denounced the political persecution of men of letters under the Terror. Finally, and most importantly, French publishing had been devastated by the collapse of the international book trade because of the war. Like Villebrune, Grégoire saw the revival of the international market in French books as critical both to the revival of commercial publishing and to the propagation of revolutionary principles: "It is opinion that demolishes thrones: a good book is a political weapon."[59] Thus Grégoire concluded: "The nation should pay for the printing of good books, and compensate their authors by giving them either part or all of the edition: the power to do this is in your hands."[60] Upon hearing Grégoire's report, the National Convention voted 300,000 *livres* to be distributed annually by the Committee on Public Instruction, for "encouragement and awards" to men of letters, scholars, and artists.

Grégoire's report marked the official end of the National Convention's laissez-faire cultural policies. It also marked a crucial turning point in revolutionary patronage of the printed word. Over the next three

58. Ibid., 5.
59. Ibid., 3–5, 12.
60. Ibid., 19.

years the publishing world was to receive millions of *livres* in "encouragements" dispensed through the Executive Commission on Public Instruction (established by the Committee on Public Safety in 1794) and then, after the suppression of the Committee on Public Safety in 1795, by the Ministry of the Interior's Bureau of Encouragement and Awards.

Government cultural patronage that directly or indirectly benefited the publishing world during the republican period took three essential forms: (1) prizes awarded through government-sponsored competitions in the writing and editing of elementary school books, which amounted to 193,000 *livres* and untold profits from sales;[61] (2) subsidies accorded to men of letters by the decree of October 5, 1794, amounting to 605,500 *livres* in 1794–1795;[62] and (3) direct subsidies and public credits, granted first by the Executive Commission on Public Instruction and then the Ministry of the Interior, to the authors, editors, publishers, and printers of individual works or editions that the government wished to encourage.

While the exact amount that reached Paris publishers and printers is impossible to calculate, the budgets for the Commission on Public Instruction for the years II to IV, conserved in the papers of the commission's director, Pierre-Louis Ginguené, suggest the dimensions of republican cultural patronage after Thermidor: 2.5 million *livres* went directly into cultural patronage, and another 16.25 million *livres'* worth of credit was extended![63] The year III (1794–1795), in particular, marked a moment of intensive government intervention in cultural production, even after accounting for unprecedented inflation. To put these sums into

61. For commissions of school textbooks, see Guillaume (ed.), *Procès-verbaux du Comité d'Instruction Publique* 1:36, 57, 84, 85, 92–101, 493, 495; 2:lxii, 127, 216, 306; 3:xi, 364, 371, 372; 4:ix, xxx, xxxi, 41, 42, 45, 370, 751, 768, 917, 934; 5:xxvi, xxxiv, xxxv, xxxvi, 541; and 6:xiii, 82, 173, 502, 544, 569, 634, 642, 852, 897, 898. See also AN, ser. F17, carton 1258, doss. 2, 9 pluviôse, an II (January 28, 1794); and AN, ser. F4, carton 2554, Report to the Ministry of the Interior on the results of the competition for elementary schoolbooks, 13 floréal, an IV (May 2, 1796).

62. For the decrees authorizing these expenditures, see *Rapport fait à la Convention Nationale, au nom du Comité d'Instruction Publique, par Marie-Joseph Chénier . . . 14 nivôse, an III* (January 2, 1795); *Rapport sur les récompenses à distribuer aux savants et aux artistes, présenté au nom des Comités d'Instruction Publique et des Finances dans la séance du 27 germinal, an III* (April 16, 1795); and *Rapport et projet de décret présenté à la Convention Nationale dans la séance du 18 fructidor . . . sur les encouragements destinés aux savants, gens de lettres et artistes, par Villar* (September 4, 1795), all in Guillaume (ed.), *Procès-verbaux du Comité d'Instruction Publique* 5:380–387 and 6:86–90, 624–631.

63. BN, nouv. acq. fr. 9192–9193, "Instruction Publique: Collection Ginguené"; also in Guillaume (ed.), *Procès-verbaux* 4:948 and foldout.

perspective, we can compare them to total expenditures over the same period for the other activities of the commission. "Encouragement and awards" figured second in priority only to educational institutions in the commission's budget.[64] Indeed, with the exception of educational institutions (5,349,174 *livres*), the commission spent twice as much on this category (2,550,830 *livres*) as it did on any other item. But who were to be the beneficiaries? And what were "useful works"?

Protest and Patronage in the Years III and IV

The French victory at Fleurus on 8 messidor, year II (June 26, 1794), marked not only the reconquest of Belgium but also the reversal of the nation's position in the European theater. The country was no longer in imminent danger of invasion. In the next year France would make peace with Prussia (April 5, 1795), Holland (May 16), and Spain (July 22). The civil war in the Vendée ended as well, in February 1795. Victory and peace brought an end to the Terror, the fall of Robespierre (July 27–28, 1794), and the abolition of the *maximum* (December 24, 1794). Release from danger both within and without also elicited a flood of grief and protest across the nation. And the publishing community, in Paris as well as the departments, had plenty to complain about.

In late December 1794, the National Convention, with its Girondist members restored, registered the wrath of printers nationwide against the laws passed under the Terror that had centralized government document printing at the newly formed Imprimerie des Lois and Imprimerie de l'Administration Nationale in Paris.[65] The convention also received a lengthy exposé from the Agence des Lois extolling the efficiency and economy of the Imprimerie des Lois.[66] The government decided to reexamine the question and as a result, on 8 pluviôse, year III (January 27, 1795), issued a new decree concerning government printing. While it met the demands of the departmental printers, this law could not have been less favorably disposed to the interests of the commercial printers of Paris.

64. BN, nouv. acq. fr. 9193, feuille 49, "Collection Ginguené. Compte sommaire des expenditures de la Commission de l'Instruction Publique, an II–IV" (1793–1796), also edited in Guillaume (ed.), *Procès-verbaux* 4:948 and foldout.

65. For the laws of 14 and 27 frimaire, year II (December 4 and 17, 1793), see Duprat, *Histoire de l'Imprimerie Impériale*, 169.

66. Ibid.

The law reestablished the system whereby national laws were reprinted in the departments from samples sent by the Imprimerie des Lois, thus returning a significant amount of government work to departmental printers. But the convention decreed additionally that because the Imprimerie des Lois—now to be called by the much grander title of Imprimerie Nationale—would lose the work of printing huge runs of the *Bulletin des lois* for the provinces, its purview was to be extended far beyond the speeches, laws, committee reports, and administrative documents of the convention and other offices of government: "[The National Printing Shop] will be charged with printing . . . the first editions of all works intended for public instruction that are adopted by the convention, and all scientific and artistic works that are to be printed by order of the convention and at the expense of the Republic."[67]

Through a series of laws passed during the spring of 1795, the convention consolidated and extended the domain of the new Imprimerie de la République (renamed again in April) from government laws to national education and patronage of the "arts and sciences." Then in June they again confirmed the legal monopoly of the Imprimerie de la République on all areas of printing, advising all official agencies that "in no case were they permitted to have printing done at government expense in either commercial or foreign printing shops."[68] Far from quelling the discontent of Paris printers, these laws outraged an even wider segment of the Paris printing community.[69]

The response was vociferous (plate 6). In a series of petitions and memoranda presented to the National Convention during the spring of 1795, seventy-five Paris printers denounced the national printing houses as monopolistic instruments of state tyranny that violated the basic rights

67. Cited in ibid., 173. For more on the development of artistic, scientific, and educational printing at the Imprimerie de la République, see Guillaume (ed.), *Procès-verbaux du Comité d'Instruction Publique* 3:255–256, 486, 494; and 4:94, 631.

68. The law renaming the Imprimerie Nationale as the Imprimerie de la République was passed on 18 germinal, year III (April 7, 1795); its attributions were reconfirmed by a law of 21 prairial, year III (June 9, 1795). See Duprat, *Histoire de l'Imprimerie Impériale*, 178, 185.

69. For an example of a Parisian printer who lost his government contract for educational printing to a government printing shop, see the case of Louis Reynier, printer and bookseller, whose job printing the *Journal sténographique des cours de l'école normale* was taken over by the Imprimerie des Lois on September 20, 1795, in Guillaume (ed.), *Procès-verbaux du Comité d'Instruction Publique* 4:706.

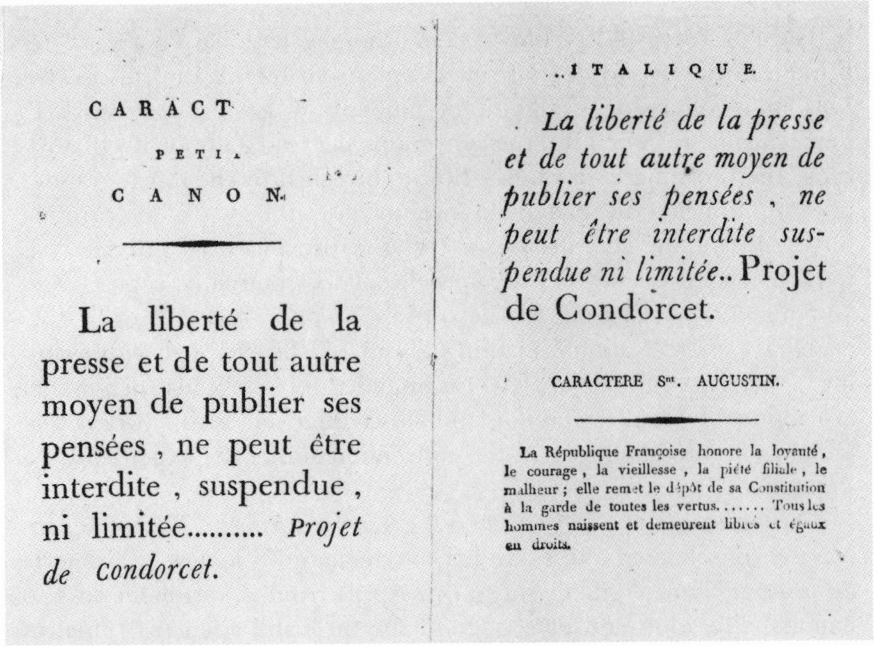
CARACT
PETI
CANON

La liberté de la presse et de tout autre moyen de publier ses pensées , ne peut être interdite , suspendue , ni limitée.......... *Projet de condorcet.*

ITALIQUE.

La liberté de la presse et de tout autre moyen de publier ses pensées , ne peut être interdite suspendue ni limitée.. Projet de Condorcet.

CARACTERE S[nt]. AUGUSTIN.

La République Françoise honore la loyauté, le courage , la vieillesse , la piété filiale , le malheur ; elle remet le dépôt de sa Constitution à la garde de toutes les vertus....... Tous les hommes naissent et demeurent libres et égaux en droits.

Plate 6. A type specimen for the Paris printer Guffroy celebrating "freedom of the press" (1795–1796). Archives Nationales, Paris.

of freedom of commerce, expression, and the press.[70] They queried: "If there is only one printing shop, what meaning can 'Freedom of the Press' possibly have? We protest this system of centralization. It was invented by Robespierre. He created it, as you well know, in order to bring all the reins of tyranny into his own hands: We should need to say no more."[71] These were certainly not trivial accusations in 1795.

The director of the Imprimerie de la République, Duboy-Laverne, responded to these accusations in kind:

> The Revolution gave rise to a huge number of new printing shops directed by men who up until that moment knew absolutely nothing about the typo-

70. AN, ser. AA, carton 56, doc. 1525, Petition to the National Convention from the printers of Paris, [22 pluviôse, an III (February 10, 1795)]; and AN, ser. C, carton 356, doc. 1883, "Mémoire sur les inconvénients et les dangers des deux Imprimeries de l'Agence des Lois et des Administrations Nationales," 22 pluviôse, an III (February 10, 1795); "Pétition des imprimeurs de Paris à la Convention Nationale," [20 messidor, an III (July 8, 1795)]; "Addition au mémoire présenté par les imprimeurs de Paris à la Convention Nationale," [20 messidor, an III (July 8, 1795)].

71. AN, ser. AA, carton 56, doc. 1525, Petition to the National Convention from the printers of Paris, [22 pluviôse, an III (February 10, 1795)].

graphical arts. And their number has grown so great that they are now driven to intrigue in order to find work. . . .

There are now four hundred printing shops where formerly there were thirty-six. . . . Should the public treasury be the guarantor of these shady speculations? . . . And should the Republic renounce an establishment . . . that has proven itself so important as a guarantor of public order?[72]

The director of the government printing shop, in short, blamed unrestricted access to the printing trade and the poor business sense of its new practitioners for the sufferings of Parisian printers. He also reminded the convention that centralized control over the publication of laws and government documents was indeed critical to maintaining both public order and the authority of the convention.

But were the protesters in fact new printers, as the director of the Imprimerie de la République charged? The protest documents of that spring, and their signatories, reveal a different picture. Of the seventy-five printers identified as having signed at least one petition or *mémoire*, thirty were former members of the Paris Book Guild, their in-laws, or their direct successors (see appendix 3).[73] Considering the signatories of just the initial petitions—that is, those who spearheaded the protest—we find that over half were former guild members or their relations. They were also those who had been among the guild's wealthiest or most eminent printers and publishers: André-François Knapen (ex-syndic), Nicolas-Léger Moutard, Joseph-Gérard Barbou, Jean Cussac, Augustin-Martin Lottin, François Belin, the widow Valade, the widow Delaguette, Pierre-Robert-Christophe Ballard, and so on. To these can be added "new printers" like Charles-Joseph Panckoucke's son-in-law, Henri Agasse, and the successors of Philippe-Denis Pierres (former printer for the king), Jean-Michel Eberhart and Baudelot.[74] Thus, far from representing new speculators, the protest was mobilized by a core of the oldest printing establishments in the capital, those who

72. AN, ser. C, carton 356, doc. 1883: *Réponse de l'Agence de l'Envoi des Lois aux mémoires et pétitions adressés à la Convention Nationale par plusieurs imprimeurs de Paris sur les prétendus inconvénients et dangers des Imprimeries executives*" [after 20 messidor, an III (July 8, 1795), 1; and 6].

73. The following signators were associated by familial or business relations: Henri Agasse, son-in-law of Charles-Joseph Panckoucke; Louis Cordier, associate of François Legras; Dupont, successor to Gilles Lamesle; Fuchs, son-in-law of Eugène Onfroy; J.-J. Delance, associate of Auguste-Pierre Belin; Jean-Michel Eberhart and Baudelot, successors to Philippe-Denis Pierres.

74. For the status of these individuals within the Old Regime guild, see figure 5.

had been hit hardest by the abolition of their privileges and the collapse of the book market.[75]

The real irony was the transformation of die-hard corporatists like Knapen and Lottin into vociferous proponents of freedom of commerce and the press:

> These privileged printers . . . intend to grab for themselves the printing of "everything pertaining to legislation, administration, and public instruction," that is, everything worthy of being printed. . . . The printers of Paris . . . are *citizens*. . . . They demand only freedom of competition. They love the fatherland. They are not foreigners.[76]

To give one printing establishment a monopoly on government contracts of all kinds was, they argued, to treat commercial printers as foreigners—indeed, the law of 8 pluviôse (January 27) had attributed the same status to both groups. To be deprived of the possibility to publish and print literary works consecrated by the nation's representative institutions was to be denied a role in the production of a national literary civilization. In fact, if the state itself published and printed all that it deemed worthy of publication, there would be no need for commercial publishers or printers:

> What new work would they dare to undertake? Every author, flattered by the possible suffrage of the convention, will present his manuscript. The convention will decree to have it printed at the expense of the nation if it finds it worthy. And in the contrary case, what printer would want to run the risk of printing a book that, having been rejected by such a solemn judgment, will already have public opinion set against it?[77]

The key issue, of course, concerned the millions of *livres* in government subsidies for publishing made available through the Commission on Public Instruction. With 2.5 million *livres* in subsidies and contracts and 16 million more in public credit at stake, it is not surprising that the printers of Paris responded so violently when the Commission on Public

75. It should be noted that I am advancing a significantly different interpretation of this protest than the one presented by the official historian of the Imprimerie Impériale, François-Antoine-Brutus Duprat, who, not surprisingly, accepts and defends the version put forward by the printers of the Imprimerie des Lois and the Imprimerie de l'Administration; see his *Histoire de l'Imprimerie Impériale*, 354–399.

76. AN, ser. C, carton 356, doc. 1883, "Pétition des imprimeurs de Paris à la Convention Nationale," [20 messidor, an III (July 8, 1795)], 3.

77. AN, ser. C, carton 536, doc. 1883, "Mémoire sur les inconvénients et les dangers des deux Imprimeries de l'Agence des Lois et des Administrations Nationales," 22 pluviôse, an III (February 10, 1795), 5.

Instruction was ordered to deal exclusively with government printing shops.

The government's various agencies and committees, however, were not unanimously pleased with the National Convention's renewed effort to centralize government publishing in one great national printing shop, and there is significant evidence of official resistance to implementation of this policy over the course of 1795.[78] The resistance of the Commission on Public Instruction was particularly notable. On June 14, 1795, the director of the Imprimerie de la République sent that commission a memo demanding that it conform to the laws requiring all printing jobs for public instruction to be executed by the government's printing shop.[79] Indeed, expenditures disclosed by the proceedings and the budget of the Commission on Public Instruction suggest a lack of compliance with both the spirit and the letter of the laws centralizing publications.

After Thermidor, the cultural policies initiated by the Committee on Public Safety and the Commission on Public Instruction, respectively, thus began to come into conflict. The records of the Commission on Public Instruction, government deposit records at the *dépôt légal,* and what remains of the accounts of the Interior Ministry's Division of Public Instruction (1794–1799) leave little doubt that despite their complaints about increased centralization, Parisian publishers and printers in fact began to enjoy significant direct government patronage through the Commission on Public Instruction, under the auspices of encouraging the "arts and sciences" and "public instruction."[80] As fragmentary as the evidence is, these three sources alone allow us to identify at least fifty Paris publishers and printers who enjoyed encouragements or contracts for "public instruction" from 1794 to 1799. Over sixty-two different publications or publishing projects received some kind of government

78. Duprat, *Histoire de l'Imprimerie Impériale,* 180, 187.
79. Ibid.
80. The following discussion is based on a systematic survey of all government contracts with Paris printers and publishers mentioned in the following sources: Guillaume (ed.), *Procès-verbaux du Comité d'Instruction Publique;* the papers of the Ministry of the Interior pertaining to public instruction, found in AN, ser. F4, carton 2554, Ministère de l'Intérieur, "Comptabilité générale, Instruction Publique, Sciences et Arts, an II–IV"; and the register of deposits at the *dépôt légal* from 1793 to 1799, in BN, Archives Modernes, CXXIX, reg. 1, July 19, 1793–an VII (September 21, 1799).

support, whether in the form of actual government purchases or subscriptions, the provision of paper, warehouse space in public buildings, or use of government printing presses. And although the documents often fail to provide the monetary sums of these encouragements and contracts, the sum total of accounts that I have actually been able to locate from this period exceeds 1,000,000 *livres*. Clearly, then, Paris publishers enjoyed considerable patronage from the government as a consequence of the government's new policy to "encourage and reward" the arts and sciences during the republican period.

But what kind of commercial publishing did the Commission on Public Instruction promote? In his report on encouragements and awards of October 1794, Grégoire outlined the basic guidelines of the Commission on Public Instruction's patronage. Grégoire's stress was clearly on the sciences, especially those with practical applications, and on grammar and foreign languages, which were crucial, in his view, to the maintenance and expansion of French economic and political power. First and foremost, the natural and applied sciences, scientific illustration, travel literature, geography, and cartography, were to receive particular attention. And not just research and writing, but intensive scholarly exchange, urgently needed to be facilitated: "There are almost no more periodicals to serve as depositories for new inventions, and to keep a record of the progress in human understanding."[81] The National Convention had been right to abolish the closed corporate academies, but it should not hesitate to support individual authors, scholars, editors, or nonrestrictive literary and scientific societies.

In the course of his report, though, he also celebrated literary pursuits as being vital to the life and health of the Republic: "The art of social life, perfected by Jean-Jacques and Mably, does it not hold an honorable rank among the forms of knowledge? A good poem, does it not have as much merit as a good machine?" He told the National Convention, "You need a new theater, a new history, and a new dictionary of your language"— and so, too, philosophy, poetry, and especially songs. Villebrune was no doubt pleased with the vision of a morally regenerated republican literary culture espoused by Grégoire. Indeed, the only literary form notably missing from Grégoire's list of genres worthy of patronage was that which Villebrune had earlier denounced as the very source of the cultural decadence perpetuated by commercial publishing: prose fiction. Gré-

---

81. Grégoire, *Rapport sur les encouragements*, 15–20.

goire, like Villebrune, reasoned that if the public were presented with a more edifying cultural alternative it would eventually opt for it.

Villebrune and Grégoire were to see their policies implemented by the new head of the Commission on Public Instruction, Pierre-Louis Ginguené.[82] Ginguené cut a distinctly different figure in the cultural landscape than either Villebrune or Grégoire. Despite their radical ideas, both Grégoire and Villebrune had been well established within the official cultural institutions of the Old Regime. Grégoire had been a Jesuit professor, distinguished for his philosophical writings by the Academy of Metz, before his election as a representative of the lower clergy to the Estates General in 1789.[83] It was not surprising that he now advocated the revitalization of an elite scholarly culture.

Villebrune, too, emerged from a traditional scholarly milieu. A classicist, orientalist, and philologist, he was renowned for his knowledge of twelve languages. The younger generation found him tedious. One of Ginguené's assistants described him as a "bitter character." He was one of those "old erudites who bore the Republic of Letters with their tiresome debates."[84] Villebrune became head of the Bibliothèque Nationale in the winter of 1793 as a consequence of an *arrêt* of the Committee on Public Safety that "invited the minister of the interior to nominate citizens of proven patriotism" to replace the Girondists purged from the library administration.[85] In fact, he replaced Ginguené's friend and patron Sébastien-Roch-Nicolas de Chamfort after this Girondist's dismissal.[86] Villebrune, needless to say, was a Jacobin of unquestionable credentials.

82. Regrettably, Ginguené has not yet found a biographer. For more on his revolutionary career, see Joanna Kitchen, *Un Journal "philosophique": "La Décade," 1794–1807* (Paris: Minard, 1965), 3–19.

83. Although he has been the subject of many books, Grégoire, like Ginguené, has not been the subject of a definitive biography. Ruth F. Necheles, *The Abbé Grégoire, 1787–1831* (Westport, Conn.: Greenwood Press, 1971), is the most extensive treatment of the political aspects of Grégoire's struggle for religious and racial equality. The recent, but brief, study by Bernard Plongeron, *Abbé Grégoire ou l'arche de la fraternité* (Paris: Letouzey & Ané, 1989), deals with the religious dimension of Grégoire's life. Most relevant here is the study of Grégoire's linguistic reforms during the Revolution by Michel de Certeau, Dominique Julia, and Jacques Revel, *Une Politique de la langue. La Révolution française et les patois* (Paris: Gallimard, 1975). For biographical information, see also Albert Soboul's foreword to the *Oeuvres de l'abbé Grégoire* (Paris: EDHIS, 1977), 1:ix–xvii.

84. Guillaume (ed.), *Procès-verbaux du Comité d'Instruction Publique* 6:347 (8 messidor, an III [June 26, 1795]).

85. Ibid., 3:142n.3.

86. Ibid. See also Louis-Gabriel Michaud and Joseph-François Michaud, eds., *Biographie universelle ancienne et moderne* (Paris, 1816), 16:476.

Ginguené, by contrast, rose to prominence in the Commission on Public Instruction during the fall of 1794, serving as director from July 1795 through its dissolution three months later. He then continued to serve as head of the Division of Public Instruction in the Ministry of the Interior.[87] He was a man of the Thermidorean moment who, after a brief imprisonment under the Terror, achieved power under the sponsorship of the minister of the interior, Joseph Garat.[88] He could not have been more different, in political as well as cultural terms, from the erudite head of the Bibliothèque Nationale, Jean-Baptiste Lefebvre de Villebrune, or the philosopher turned Jacobin legislator, Henri Grégoire.

Ginguené emerged from the grub-street journalistic circles of the Old Regime, becoming after 1789 a vocal advocate of popular literature in opposition to scholarly culture.[89] An editor of the *Feuille villageoise* from 1791 through 1795, he believed that knowledge had to be taken out of the libraries and into the streets. He articulated his cultural program cogently in 1792 in a proposal for government subsidy of an *encyclopédie populaire et portative:*

> The people hunger for instruction. They don't have time to read volumes, or the means to buy them. In order to put science within their reach, it has to be liberated from the huge tomes where scholars have buried it, and put into little booklets. . . . As a boy I had a love of books which for the longest time was an unhappy passion. My parents were not wealthy enough to be able to satisfy my literary tastes. . . . What a difference it would have made for me, who at that age, and for a good while after, could get my hands on nothing more than the romances of the Twelve Knights of France and the Bibliothèque bleue.[90]

Rather than regenerating scholarly culture, Ginguené wanted to transform it, to democratize it by bringing it out of the libraries and to the people through the medium of chapbooks and periodicals.

Yet despite the contrasts in their cultural visions, Ginguené, Villebrune, and Grégoire all agreed on at least two things: the deleterious

---

87. Guillaume (ed.), *Procès-verbaux du Comité d'Instruction Publique* 4:xviin.1; 5:25n.1, 28 (annexes); 6:452, 835n.2.

88. Ibid. See also Michaud frères (eds.), *Biographie universelle* 16:476 and notes.

89. Michaud frères (eds.), *Biographie universelle* 16:475–476. For his association with the prerevolutionary grub-street milieu, see the entry for Ginguené in Antoine Rivarol's "Petit Almanach de nos grands hommes," in his *Oeuvres complètes*, 2d ed. (Geneva: Slatkine Reprints, 1968 [originally published 1808]), 5:91.

90. BN, nouv. acq. fr. 9192, feuilles 118–121, Pierre-Louis Ginguené, "Copie du projet de *L'Encyclopédie populaire* envoyée à quelques hommes de lettres, citoyens, au mois de mars 1792."

effects of popular novels on the minds of citizens; and the need for the government to commission French publishers to produce enlightened texts, containing useful scientific and moral knowledge, in order to reform the literary tastes of the nation. The subsidies of the Commission on Public Instruction suggest that both the Jacobin scholars and the Girondist populist left their mark on revolutionary literary patronage.

In light of the reports by Villebrune and Grégoire, it is not surprising to discover that the Paris publishing group Smits and Maradan were soon commissioned to produce a new edition of the *Dictionnaire de l'Académie,* in fifteen thousand copies.[91] Or that the Commission on Public Instruction purchased the plates for the comte de Buffon's *Histoire naturelle* from the publisher Charles-Joseph Panckoucke for 50,000 *livres.*[92] Similarly, they ordered one hundred copies of Edmé Mentelle's *Analyse du cours de géographie,* as well as Jean-Gabriel Mérigot *le jeune*'s edition of Simonin's *Traité d'arithmétique.*[93] They also patronized numerous other publishers and printers of scientific works.[94] With Grégoire's call to revive scientific periodical publishing, Gaspar-Joseph Cuchet, having narrowly escaped the guillotine for his counterrevolutionary pamphlets, now found his *Journal de physique, de chimie, et d'histoire naturelle* infused with new life by the patronage of the Commission on Public Instruction.[95] So, too, the *Journal des mines* and the *Bulletin de l'Ecole de Santé* prospered from new-found official support.[96]

As Grégoire had insisted, classical languages, history, and philosophy were not to be neglected either. Thus the printer Haubout was assisted

91. Decree of the National Convention, premier jour complémentaire, an III (September 17, 1795), in Guillaume (ed.), *Procès-verbaux du Comité d'Instruction Publique* 6: 404–405. See also ibid., 443–444, 501, 621, 680, 683, 688.

92. Guillaume (ed.), *Procès-verbaux* 6:561.

93. For the former, see AN, ser. F4, carton 2554, "Ministère de l'Intérieur: Comptabilité générale, Instruction Publique"; for the latter, AN, ser. AA, carton 56, doc. 1524, August 6, 1798.

94. AN, ser. F4, carton 2554, doss. 4, Bernard and Regence, Paris booksellers, 13 thermidor, an III (July 31, 1795), arithmetics, geometries, and algebras by Etienne Bezout; Barrois, *l'aîné,* Paris bookseller, 16 messidor, an III (July 4, 1795), works on meteorology; ibid., doss. 3, Laurent-Eloy Goujon, Paris bookseller, prairial–messidor, an II (May–June 1794), maps and geographical dictionaries.

95. AN, ser. F17, carton 1214, doss. 12, November 23, 1794, in which the Committee on Agriculture orders fifteen hundred copies on the recommendation of the Commission on Public Instruction.

96. For the former, see AN, ser. F4, carton 2554, Dupont, printer of the *Journal des mines,* 23 messidor, an III (July 11, 1795); for the latter, Guillaume (ed.), *Procès-verbaux du Comité d'Instruction Publique* 5:315, 336.

in his effort to bring out an edition of Tacitus's *Histoire romaine,* as were the classicist Johannes Schweighäuser with his *Polybii megalopolitani historiarum* and the publisher Jean-Antoine-Guillaume Bailleul with his *Politique d'Aristote.*[97] The commission also followed through with its mandate to regenerate modern history and philosophy. Thus Jean-Georges-Antoine Stoupe and Jean Servières, a printer and a publisher in Paris, brought out the new edition of Voltaire's *Oeuvres* edited by Charles Palissot de Montenoy, with considerable official aid.[98] Likewise, both Claude-François Poinçot *fils* and Pierre-François Didot *le jeune* received assistance in producing their editions of Rousseau's *Oeuvres.*[99] The commission purchased copies of the Louis-François Barrois *l'aîné* edition of Gabriel Bonnet de Mably's *Oeuvres.*[100] And the commission purchased three thousand copies of the marquis de Condorcet's *Esquisse d'un tableau historique des progrès de l'esprit humain* from the Parisian publisher Henri Agasse, to be distributed "throughout the Republic, in a manner most useful for public instruction."[101] Etienne Bonnet de Condillac's *Logique* was purchased for the students at the Ecole Normale as well.[102] Nor did the commission overlook the need to encourage contemporary historical models, such as those commissioned for the *Recueil des actions héroiques et civiques des républicains français* or depicted in the *Vie de Général Hoche.*[103] Contemporary philosophy and politics, from Jean-Paul Marat to Adam Smith and Moses Mendelssohn, received encouragement too.[104] Moreover, flying directly in the face of the decrees centralizing the printing

97. On Tacitus's *Histoire romaine,* see AN, ser. F18, carton 565, 15 ventôse, an IV (March 5, 1796). On the *Polybii megalopolitani historiarum,* see Guillaume (ed.), *Procès-verbaux* 6:89; and BN, Archives Modernes, CXXIX, "Registres du dépôt légal des livres imprimés," reg. 1. And on the *Politique d'Aristote,* see ibid.

98. AN, ser. F17, carton 1306, doss. 1025, 13 messidor, an III (July 31, 1795). See also Guillaume (ed.), *Procès-verbaux* 4:742, 789–790, 938; 5:360, 384.

99. For Poinçot, see Guillaume (ed.), *Procès-verbaux* 5:106, 410–411, 609–610; and AN, ser. AA, carton 56, doc. 1524, Letter from Poinçot *fils,* publisher, to the Corps Législatif, 17 floréal, an VI (May 6, 1798). The edition was begun in the year III (1794–1795). For Didot *le jeune,* see Guillaume (ed.), *Procès-verbaux* 5:210.

100. Guillaume (ed.), *Procès-verbaux* 4:970.

101. AN, ser. F4, carton 2554, doss. 4, 15 thermidor, an III (August 2, 1795).

102. Guillaume (ed.), *Procès-verbaux* 5:491.

103. For the *Recueil,* see AN, ser. F17, carton 1258, doss. 2, "Secours et encouragements aux sciences et aux arts," and doss. 8, "Extrait des registres des arrêtés du Comité du Salut Public," 27 floréal, an II (May 16, 1794). And for the *Vie de Général Hoche,* see AN, ser. F17, carton 1215, doss. 5, "Secours et encouragements."

104. For support of an edition of Jean-Paul Marat's *Oeuvres,* see Guillaume (ed.), *Procès-verbaux* 3:485, 499, 530, 559; 4:789; 5:609–610. For support of editions of Adam Smith's *Théorie des sentiments moraux* and Moses Mendelssohn's *Oeuvres,* see ibid., 5:169.

and publishing of laws, they purchased an elegant edition of the *Constitution* from Pierre-François Didot *le jeune* and regularly ordered laws from Louis Rondonneau.[105]

But government encouragement extended beyond the scholarly culture of scientific, classical, and Enlightenment books. True to Ginguené's vision of an enlightened popular literary culture, the commission subsidized numerous educational, philosophical, and political journals aimed at a broader reading public, such as the *Journal des censeurs*, the *Journal de l'homme libre*, the *Décade philosophique et littéraire*, the *Feuille du cultivateur*, the *Feuille villageoise*, and the *Républicain français*.[106] They subsidized and distributed educational political pamphlets;[107] so, too, republican almanacs and democratic catechisms, as well as engravings of the republican martyrs Jean-Paul Marat and Louis-Michel Lepeletier de Saint-Fargeau.[108] They commissioned the printing of songs and music to be distributed at revolutionary festivals.[109] Nor did they overlook efforts to win a popular female reading public over to the Thermidorean regime, like Citizeness Boosère's *Triomphe de la saine philosophie, ou la vraie politique des femmes*, which they ordered to be "distributed by her in various departments of the Republic."[110]

105. For Didot *le jeune* ibid., 5:429. For Louis Rondonneau, see AN, ser. F4, carton 2554, doss. 3, Rondonneau, Paris, 25 fructidor, an II (September 11, 1794).

106. The *Journal des censeurs* was printed by Langlois *fils;* see AN, ser. F18, carton 21, Letter to the Commission, December 8, 1795. For the *Journal de l'homme libre*, see AN, ser. AA, carton 56, doc. 1524, 16 thermidor, an II (August 3, 1794). For the *Décade philosophique et littéraire*, see AN, ser. F4, carton 2554, doss. 4, Say, Paris editor and printer, 19 floréal, an III (May 8, 1795); see also Joanna Kitchen, *Journal "philosophique."* For the *Feuille du cultivateur*, see AN, ser. F4, carton 2554, Lefebvre, director of the printing shop of the *Feuille*, 1 fructidor, an III (September 18, 1795). For the *Feuille villageoise*, see ibid., doss. 5, Louis Reynier, printer of the *Feuille*, 30 brumaire and 12 frimaire, an III (November 20 and December 2, 1794); see also Melvin Allen Edelstein, *"La Feuille villageoise." Communication et modernisation dans les régions rurales pendant la Révolution* (Paris: Bibliothèque Nationale, 1977). And for the *Républicain français*, see AN, ser. F4, carton 2554, doss. 4, Goujet-Deslande, 5 messidor, an III (June 23, 1795).

107. AN, ser. F4, carton 2554, Dupont, printer of the *Nouvelle Instruction sur les poids et mesures*, 23 messidor, an III (July 11, 1795); see also the publisher Lemercier's contracts for several political pamphlets, AN, ser. F18, carton 21, May 11, 1797.

108. For almanacs, see Guillaume (ed.), *Procès-verbaux du Comité d'Instruction Publique* 3:296; and for catechisms, see BN, Archives Modernes, cxxix, "Registres du dépôt légal des livres imprimés," reg. 1, *Catéchisme français à l'usage des écoles primaires* (1795), deposited by the Committee on Public Instruction. On the engravings of martyrs, see Guillaume (ed.), *Procès-verbaux* 6:47.

109. Guillaume (ed.), *Procès-verbaux* 4:850.

110. AN, ser. F4, carton 2554, doss. 4, Boosère, 28 vendémiaire, an III (October 19, 1794). See also Guillaume (ed.), *Procès-verbaux* 5:138.

After Thermidor, the government dispensed enormous sums on cultural patronage intended to promote republican values, by wooing the public away from the passions of politics and romance and toward forms of learning and reading that encouraged civic order and contributed to the public good. The political motivations behind the government's new cultural initiatives became even more explicit when the laws of 9 and 13 vendémiaire, year IV (September 30 and October 4, 1797), imposed a stamp tax on all periodicals, with the exception of monthly periodicals relating exclusively to "arts and sciences."[111]

———————

The commercial publishing world of Paris responded rapidly to the cultural initiatives and patronage of the Commission on Public Instruction. In May 1796, the publisher J.-J. Lucet launched a new trade newsletter entitled the *Bulletin de littérature, des sciences et des arts,* to be devoted entirely to announcing "decrees concerning the arts and artists, prizes and honors awarded for technical achievements, discoveries and inventions . . . everything concerning literature, the arts, and the sciences."[112] In his prospectus Lucet hailed Grégoire's report and the legislation on encouragements and awards of October 1794 as the founding of a new cultural regime, when at last men of letters and artists

> can begin to recover their original dignity, and literary commerce to develop its immense resources. Artistic and scientific liberty will give birth to masterpieces, and soon, with the aid of national subsidies, the French Republic of Letters will recover its former splendor. At last we have left the era of horror and barbarism when monsters insisted that men of learning deserved only the guillotine.[113]

His *Bulletin,* he avowed, would insure that the works of men of letters singled out by the commission for encouragements and awards would be made known to the entire publishing community. "Sciences and arts" had become the new catch phrase in the book trade for works supported by the republican government.

Others followed in Lucet's wake. Thus on August 16, 1796, the editors of the *Nouvelliste littéraire,* Morin and Lenoir, announced that they were adding the subtitle "des sciences et arts" to their newsletter. In their

111. Bellanger (ed.), *Histoire générale de la presse française* 1:544–545.
112. *Bulletin de littérature, des sciences et des arts,* 2 vols. (May 1796–1803); see "Prospectus," 1:2.
113. Ibid., 1:1–2.

avis to the reader they, too, sounded the Thermidorean call for a literary culture devoted to reason, utility, and self-improvement:

> O French, so celebrated of old in the sciences, you who were the jewel upon Parnassus, flee, flee forever your political newspapers, those scions of bad taste and passions. Rediscover Voltaire, Racine, and Fénélon: their logic is worth more than that of Babeuf and the Frérons. What good do your political journals serve? To corrupt your taste, to embitter your heart, and to stir up disagreements with your best friends.[114]

Morin and Lenoir offered cultural pursuits as an alternative to politics. They not only reviewed and advertised all new works in the arts and sciences deemed worthy of attention by the government, but they also offered a "varieties" section in their newsletters, which featured poems and articles on various cultural issues and events intended to woo readers away from the passions of partisan politics toward more rational pursuits such as science, philosophy, and poetry. Issue number 31 of May 19, 1797, for example, carried an ode celebrating the powers of the microscope set to a popular vaudeville tune.

A whole new generation of publishers emerged in response to the government's policies. Some, like A.-J. Dugour and Durand, "booksellers for education, the sciences, and the arts" (established 1796), bought out withering old guild establishments like that of Gaspar-Joseph Cuchet. Similarly, Adrien Egron bought out the widow Valade in 1798 and in 1799 Pierre-Henri Genets *l'aîné* took over Jean Servières's business. Others went into association with old elites, like Ballio with Jean-François Colas (1796) or François Legras with Louis Cordier (1797). Then there were those who founded new houses, like P. Bernard, "printer-publisher for mathematics, the sciences, and the arts," in 1797; Adrien-Joseph Marchand, "printer-publisher of agricultural works," in 1798; Marie-Rosalie Vallat-la-Chapelle, the widow of Huzard, "printer-publisher for agriculture and veterinary medicine," in 1798; or J.-B.-M. Duprat, "bookseller for mathematics," in 1797.[115] Villebrune had been right: government initiative and patronage could, at a minimum, redirect the orientation of a sector of the publishing world.

As the reversal after 1796 of the curve of book production in figure

---

114. *Nouvelliste littéraire* (published in Paris from germinal, an IV, to germinal, an IX [April 1796–April 1806]), nos. 15–16, 30 thermidor, an IV (August 17, 1796), 1.

115. See these names in Delalain, *Imprimerie et la librairie*, 7, 15, 69–71, 73, 86, 102, 126, 142.

6 suggests, peace and the consequent reopening of international markets after the Treaty of Basel in 1795, along with the infusion of millions of *livres* in government patronage between 1794 and 1796, stimulated a revival of book publishing during the period of the Directory. For the first time since 1789 book production began to rise, while the production of journals declined.

A Partial Victory for Centralization

But the Thermidorean moment of peace and of encouragement and awards did not last forever. As the contraction of Ginguené's budget for the year IV (1795–1796) suggests, government subsidies for the arts and sciences began to dry up. The Commission on Public Instruction was to see its patronage powers eclipsed in the fall of 1795 by the newly founded Institut National.[116] In fact, on October 26, 1795, the day after the Institut was founded, the commission met for the last time.[117]

In filing his closing report to the minister of the interior, Ginguené expressed his fear that the creation of the Institut would spell the end to the pluralist and democratic patronage system evolved by the commission. The Institut, he argued, by patronizing authors rather than books, would recreate the corporatist and castelike literary culture of the Old Regime Court:

> Despotism, which always had reason to fear scholars and men of letters, thought it best to attach them to the regime, or at least . . . to guarantee their silence, by installing them in academies. . . . Many of these scholars and men of letters believed that although they had accepted these favors, they had not compromised their independence. . . . Yet it is nonetheless true to say that it is among those who were not touched by these perfidious benefits that one finds the energetic and profound writers who have contributed the most to the nation's understanding of its rights, and who did the most to bring about the fall of the monarchy and the founding of a Republic.[118]

116. The Institut was founded by a decree of 3 brumaire, year IV (October 25, 1795); see Martyn Lyons, *France Under the Directory* (Cambridge: Cambridge University Press, 1975), 94; and, for the original decree, AN, ser. F17, carton 1258, doss. 3, 3 brumaire, an IV (October 25, 1795).

117. Guillaume (ed.), *Procès-verbaux du Comité d'Instruction Publique* 6:1.

118. BN, nouv. acq. fr. 9192, feuilles 102–103, [1795], "Projet de rapport à présenter au ministre de l'intérieur (sur l'établissement du Bureau d'Encouragement des Sciences et Lettres)."

The commercial cultural world of grub street and the literary market-place, not the privileged academies and salons of the high Enlightenment, Ginguené reminded the minister, was what had won the nation over to the Republic. "A government founded on enlightened principles," he wrote, should not revive the cultural institutions of absolutism. Indeed, it should not give its official sanction to any single cultural institution. Rather, the government should maintain "varied relations" with the nation and its intellectual luminaries through an "open correspondence." Instead of creating a new caste of officially designated intellectuals, the government should establish an office of cultural patronage open to appeals for cultural assistance from *all* citizens:

> Some will send the government works they have already published, either in simple homage or to propose that they be distributed in the schools and national institutes or to the public at large, or perhaps they will request grants or subsidies; others will send in a completed manuscript, or a draft, or a proposal for a work, or even a simple prospectus, asking that their work be printed by the nation or that they be given the means to complete their work and publish their ideas themselves.[119]

Ginguené believed that the role of a truly democratic and republican government should be to support the spread of good books and ideas—not a closed caste of authors. The government should support the activities of writing and publishing, not writers as individuals. There should be no officially privileged cultural elite. It was this institutional vision that embodied his ideal of a truly democratic and self-enlightening republic, "encouraged" by its government.

As prescient as Ginguené's vision was, it was never to be fully realized under the first Republic. The minister of the interior did create an "Office of Encouragement" to exercise discretionary patronage in cultural matters, under the directorship of Ginguené;[120] but it never achieved the scale of the Commission on Public Instruction, or of the office that Ginguené had proposed.[121]

By the year IV (1795–1796), the nation's economy was plagued by soaring inflation, with the *assignat* falling to less than 1 percent of its face

119. Ibid.
120. See BN, nouv. acq. fr. 9193, feuilles 2, 6, 23, 36, "Papiers Ginguené," pertaining to his directorship of the "Direction Générale de l'Instruction Publique, 5e Division du Ministère de l'Intérieur."
121. Ibid., feuilles 6, 23, 141–147, an V–an VIII (1796–1800).

value.[122] In the following two years, the government was finally driven to partial bankruptcy in order to consolidate its debts.[123] With the fiscal crisis, the government's budget for cultural patronage was drastically reduced and recentralized. The minister's Office of Encouragement was forced to make severe cutbacks, and by November 19, 1796, Ginguené reported that its very existence was imperiled. Literary patronage lost its status as a distinct division of the ministry: henceforth it would figure only as a line item in the minister of the interior's discretionary budget.[124]

The founding of the Institut and the suppression of the Office of Encouragement were not the only events to mark the victory of cultural centralization. On 12 vendémiaire, year IV (October 5, 1795), the printing of laws was recentralized at the national printing shops in Paris.[125] The departmental printers were again dispossessed. To accommodate the reconsolidation and expansion of government publishing in Paris, on 14 brumaire, year IV (November 4, 1795), the Imprimerie de l'Administration Nationale was swallowed up by the Imprimerie de la République.[126] There was now only one government printing house in Paris.

The deregulationist and laissez-faire policies toward commerce in ideas implemented by the National Assembly and the National Convention between 1789 and 1793 spelled economic disaster for commercial book publishing. What is more, they totally confounded the expectations of the cultural legislators who had endorsed them. Far from producing an enlightened Republic, the newly freed printing and publishing world, left to its own devices, could barely produce at all. And what it did produce appeared hardly enlightened to the new men in power.

122. Lyons, *France Under the Directory*, 180.
123. Ibid., 183–184.
124. See BN, nouv. acq. fr. 9193, feuille 23, "Papiers Ginguené," Report to the Minister of the Interior, 29 brumaire, an V (November 19, 1769). For examples of cutbacks, see the letter from the Ministry of the Interior to the Paris printer Jean-Baptiste Brasseur announcing that although they had subsidized the first two editions of his *Vie de Général Hoche*, they could not subsidize the third, though they would like to, "if their financial situation were less difficult." They added that there were many schools that could use this book; AN, ser. F17, carton 1215, doss. 5, 10 brumaire, an VIII (November 1, 1799).
125. Duprat, *Histoire de l'Imprimerie Impériale*, 175.
126. Ibid., 188.

The economic crisis in the printing and publishing world in the year II thus converged with a crucial shift in revolutionary cultural policy. By 1794 the struggle against the monarchy, church, and aristocracy took on an overtly cultural dimension. Cultural legislators were forced to recognize that if left to follow their own desires, citizens, as well as the publishers and printers who satisfied their appetites for reading material, might not naturally incline toward republican ideals. Sobered by this insight, the National Convention abandoned its laissez-faire approach to publishing.

Rejecting the Old Regime model of preventative censorship and corporate regulation, the republican government evolved two distinct new strategies for intervention in the publishing and printing world. The first, spearheaded by the Committee on Public Safety in its decrees on revolutionary government of November–December 1794, involved the expansion and centralization of government printing and publishing, as part of the committee's effort to impose political and cultural unity on the divided nation. This strategy was not checked by Thermidor but continued throughout the Directory and Napoleonic period as well.

A second form of government intervention in publishing came from the Commission on Public Instruction. Rather than attempting to nationalize the production of printed matter, it embarked on an ambitious effort to reshape the commercial literary market by a system of encouragements and rewards for writers and commercial printing and publishing establishments which contributed to the public good. Over the course of 1794–1799 the commission spent huge sums in the form of government encouragements in order to woo publishers away from the tempting profits to be made by exploiting the passions aroused through political journals and romantic literature. Official subsidies and rewards were offered to those publishers proffering the cooler virtues of philosophical inquiry, self-improvement, and public utility.

To implement these policies the government, first through the Commission on Public Instruction and then through the Ministry of the Interior's Office of Encouragement, embarked on an unprecedented experiment in democratic cultural patronage. The committee and the office offered the possibility of cultural patronage to *all* citizens, irrespective, at least formally, of class, occupation, gender, or any other criterion. In so doing they shifted the basis of government patronage from writers to writing, from publishers to books. The democratic cultural policies of the Thermidorean moment, however, were soon eclipsed by the revival of the corporatist model of government patronage embodied in the new Institut National.

These successive developments in revolutionary cultural politics had a significant, and sometimes contradictory, impact on commercial publishing and printing in the capital during the republican period. Already hit hard by the collapse of the book market and then the repression of political literature under the Terror, commercial printers saw themselves further dispossessed by the ever-expanding Imprimerie de la République. Yet at the same time, the peace declared after Thermidor, along with the patronage of the Commission on Public Instruction, opened up a wide range of new opportunities for commercial publishing, both within and beyond France.

CHAPTER FIVE

The New World of the Printed Word, 1789–1799

The Democratization of the Presses

The Paris bookseller Antoine-François Momoro was thirty-three years old when the Revolution began. He had arrived in Paris from his native Besançon in 1780. In 1787 he was admitted as a bookseller by the Paris Book Guild.[1] His bookshop stocked a mere eleven titles, which he estimated in 1790 to have a total value of 19,720 *livres*. Momoro was one of the myriad of small Parisian book dealers with little hope of advancement within the Old Regime book guild. But with the declaration of the freedom of the press in August 1789 Momoro's career prospects suddenly opened up before him. Embracing the revolutionary movement wholeheartedly, he quickly opened a printing shop at 171 rue de la Harpe and boldly declared himself the "First Printer of National Liberty" (plate 7). Within a year he had added four presses, ten cases of type, and a small foundry for making type characters; his business assets now totaled 30,108 *livres*.[2] In the publishing and printing world Momoro was still a very small fry. But he was soon to make a big name for himself in ultrarevolutionary politics.

Momoro understood the power of the press, and he believed in unleashing its revolutionary potential. Further, he knew the business from the bottom up. In 1793, he composed and published a little treatise on

---

1. Lottin, *Catalogue chronologique des libraires,* 126.
2. AP, Fond Faillite, ser. D4B6, carton 110, doss. 7811, Faillite de Antoine-François Momoro, [June 8, 1790].

printing, the *Traité élémentaire de l'imprimerie*, which was intended to put the practical knowledge of printing within the reach of a wide audience.[3] It remains the single best source of eighteenth-century printing shop slang. He also used his press to launch a career in radical revolutionary politics, soon becoming the official "Printer for the Cordeliers Club." His printing business evolved along with the revolutionary politics of the Parisian sections, serving as a propaganda machine, first for the Cordeliers Club and then, by the winter of 1794, for the Hébertists. He produced pamphlets, minutes of meetings of the Cordeliers, and handbills and posters for several of the Parisian sections, and he also did a significant business by sending the publications of the Paris Cordeliers out into the provinces to be read before the tribunals of provincial clubs.[4]

When he was arrested in February 1794, the police inventoried his commercial stock. With the exception of a few sheets of a *Manuel du républicain*—found literally under the presses—Momoro's entire stock consisted of pamphlets, handbills, and, most important, sectional posters.[5] His business was devoted exclusively to, and depended almost entirely on, the printed ephemera that sustained the revolutionary political life of the Paris sections.

Not surprisingly, Momoro worshipped Jean-Paul Marat as a political and cultural idol and modeled his revolutionary career after him. After Marat's death, Momoro aspired to succeed him as the cultural champion of the little people. He convinced the Cordeliers Club to produce a continuation of the *Ami du peuple* under his editorship. His first issue received the number 243, to establish a direct lineage from Marat's last issue, number 242. Its rhetorical style resonated deeply with that of the martyred Marat:

> The Cordeliers Club, justly alarmed by the new dangers that menace the Republic, and convinced of the necessity of enlightening the people to the odious and perfidious plots of new conspirators, has resolved to repair . . . the loss of *Marat*, that ardent defender of the rights of the people, through

---

3. Antoine-François Momoro, *Traité élémentaire de l'imprimerie* (Paris: Momoro, 1793).

4. For examples of provincial dissemination, see AN, ser. W, carton 78, plaque 1, nos. 61, 69, Momoro's correspondence with Richard and Lulier of February 19 and March 7, 1794.

5. For the *Manuel du républicain*, see AN, ser. W, carton 76, plaque 2, no. 106, Minutes of a search chez Momoro, 29 ventôse, an II (March 19, 1794). For the inventory of Momoro's stock, see AN, ser. W, carton 78, plaque 1, no. 68, 10–20 ventôse, an II (February 28–March 10, 1794).

Plate 7. Portrait of Antoine-François Momoro, "First Printer of National Liberty" (n.d.). Momoro was one of the most militant new printers in revolutionary Paris. He was guillotined by the revolutionary government as an agitator in March 1794. Musée de la Révolution française, Vizille, France.

a journal that will be edited in the name of the Club and in the spirit of its principles. Like Marat, the Club will publicize terrible truths; like him, it will stand up to the daggers of assassins; it will denounce all traitors without exception, and tear the masks from the enemies of the fatherland.[6]

Momoro also entered into negotiations with Marat's widow to convince her to collaborate with him in publishing an edition of Marat's *Oeuvres*. Like numerous other Parisian publishers, in 1794 he began soliciting the Commission on Public Instruction in the hope of receiving one of the government's newly authorized publishing subsidies for the project.[7]

Between 1789 and 1794 Momoro had built his entire business around agitational ephemera designed to expose counterrevolutionaries and their perfidious plots. The careers of sectional politicians and municipal bureaucrats were made and broken through his neighborhood terrorist media campaigns. At a moment's notice a flood of handbills and posters could pour forth from his presses, turning public opinion almost instantaneously. These political tactics, however ruthless and demagogic, proved effective—at least in the short run. By 1794 he had become president of the Cordeliers Club and served on the directorate of the department of Paris.

There is also significant evidence to suggest that Momoro did quite well in his business of revolutionary ephemera. The Revolutionary Tribunal heard repeated depictions of Momoro as a greedy opportunist and ambitious parvenu, a man notorious for shady business dealings who had declared bankruptcy twice.[8] They also testified that he had gotten rich—too rich—in recent times: his wife lived in "scandalous luxury," with "sumptuous furniture," a "superb wardrobe," and even a carriage. But it was not just his enemies who remarked on his financial success: his uncle, the local barber, stood up in his defense, describing Momoro as an upstanding and sober businessman who, despite his bankruptcies, was worth, by 1794, 80,000 *livres*.[9] In the first four years of the

6. AN, ser. W, carton 77, plaque 5, no. 334, *L'Ami du peuple*, no. 243 [1793–1794], 1–2.

7. Guillaume (ed.), *Procès-verbaux du Comité d'Instruction Publique* 3:485, 499, 530, 559; 4:789; 5:169.

8. For testimony against Momoro concerning his business dealings and his wealth, see AN, ser. W, carton 78, plaque 1, no. 6; plaque 2, no. 120; plaque 3, no. 191; and AN, ser. W, carton 339, doss. 617, for Fouquier-Tinville's "acte d'accusation," which includes the charge of fiscal opportunism, March 24, 1794.

9. AN, ser. W, carton 78, plaque 3, no. 1919, Testimony of Jean-François Legendre, 29 ventôse, an II (March 19, 1794).

Revolution Momoro's business in printing revolutionary propaganda appears to have expanded, perhaps as much as twofold.

———————

Momoro's career, however dramatic, was not untypical. In 1789 Parisian printing exploded. In the first few years of the Revolution the industry was swept by a new generation of little printers, most of them former printing-shop workers or small book dealers who seized the cultural space opened by the declaration of freedom of the press and commerce, bought a few presses, and entered into the fast-paced world of revolutionary cultural agitation through the production of political ephemera.

Trade journals, commercial almanacs, and government surveys from the revolutionary and Napoleonic periods offer striking testimony to the numbers of these businessmen. In 1789, Lottin's *Catalogue chronologique* listed the 195 *libraires* (publishers and book dealers) and 47 *imprimeurs* (printers who might be publishers and retail book dealers as well) who were legally authorized in Paris. Only a year later, in a memorandum to the National Assembly, the Paris publisher Jean-Augustin Grangé claimed that the number of printing shops in Paris had climbed to 200.[10] Although this was perhaps an exaggeration, ten years later, in 1798–1799, a more neutral source, M. Duverneuil's *Almanach du commerce de Paris*, advertised the names of 337 publishers/book dealers and 223 printers in the capital. And after another decade, an official government survey of 1810–1811 recorded 508 publishers/book dealers and 157 printers.[11] Thus, over the course of the revolutionary decade 1789–1799, the number of active printers had at least quadrupled, while the number of publishers increased by at least one-half as a consequence of the deregulation of these industries. Even after the Napoleonic decrees

10. [Grangé], *Mémoire présenté à l'Assemblée Nationale*, 4.

11. For Lottin's totals for 1789, see Delalain, *Imprimerie et la librairie*, li–lx; and for Delalain's original source, see Lottin, *Catalogue chronologique des libraires*. The three available sources for numbers of publishers and printers in Paris in 1798–1799 are M. Duverneuil, ed., *Almanach du commerce de Paris* (Paris: Vve Valade, an VII [1798–1799]); Henri Tardieu-Denesle, ed., *Almanach typographique* (Paris; an VIII [1799–1800]); and Pierre Roux, ed., *Journal typographique et bibliographique* (Paris, 1797–1810). Finally, for the years 1810–1811, the best sources are the government surveys found in AN, ser. F18, carton 10a, plaque 2, and carton 25. For the figures offered by the government after the re-regulation, see the *Journal général de l'imprimerie et de la librairie* (Paris: Pillet, 1810–1811).

of 1810 limited the number of printers to eighty, the printing world had nearly doubled in size. The Revolution thus marked a moment of unprecedented expansion in both productive power and the sites of distribution of the printed word in the capital.

The available statistical evidence, moreover, suggests that the greatest share of this expansion occurred during the revolutionary decade 1789–1799. In 1900, the publisher and bibliographer Paul Delalain compiled a masterful registry of every printer, publisher, and bookseller he could identify in Paris for the years 1789–1813.[12] Using this register as a base, it is possible to establish the number of active printing and publishing businesses, date their founding, and trace the longevity of their enterprises with some accuracy.[13] It is further possible to distinguish the multitude of ephemeral enterprises that appeared and disappeared in response to the heightened demand for printed debate at critical political conjunctures, on the one hand, from the longer-term printing and publishing businesses that succeeded in installing themselves permanently within the cultural infrastructure of the capital, on the other. The result is a near-complete picture of the new printing and publishing enterprises established during the two decades spanning the Revolution and the Napoleonic period (figure 7).

Over the twenty-six-year period 1788–1813, approximately 1,224

12. Delalain, *Imprimerie et la librairie.*

13. Delalain was a meticulous and conservative bibliophile. As a consequence, he excluded 181 names of individuals or establishments that he determined to be fictive, redundant, or ephemeral, dating principally from the period 1789–1795, and he excluded 75 individuals because he found them in only one source. To avoid redundancies, he lists as a separate index 61 descriptive names, such as the Imprimerie de l'Ami de l'Ordre, de l'Egalité, or des Révolutions de Paris, that printers gave to their establishments. Proper names posed certain problems. Simple questions of spelling variations could be resolved by cross-checking addresses. Less easy to clarify were establishments employing fictive or anagrammatic names, addresses, and dates. Although TEYGAT for Gattey or ROUGYFF for Guffroy were fairly unproblematic, what about "Clairvoyant imprimeur-libraire de leurs Altesses sérénissimes, Nosseigneurs les princes fugitifs, à l'enseigne de la Lanterne," or "Au pays de la liberté, de l'Imprimerie de la Résurrection, l'an de la vraie lumière 5590"? Delalain found at least forty-five titles of this kind in the first five years of the Revolution; he excluded them from his main registry because they did not represent separate establishments; see Delalain, *Imprimerie et la librairie,* xxiv–xxv. Delalain's totals from his index of individuals by profession are 438 printers and 1,177 booksellers/publishers, totaling 1,615 (1790–1813). My calculation of the total number of actual establishments, as opposed to individuals, is 337 printers and 887 booksellers/publishers, totaling 1,224 (1788–1813). In both cases printers are counted only as printers, even if they also performed the services of publishers and booksellers.

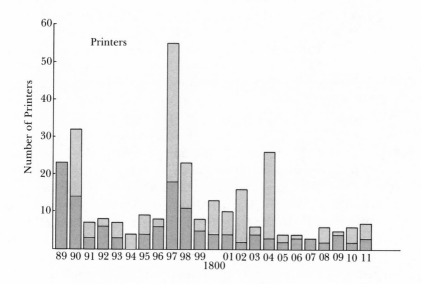

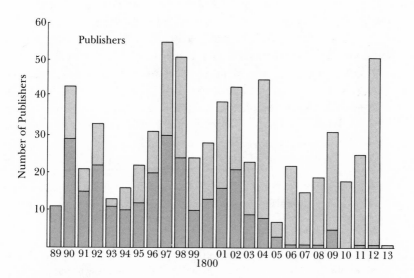

Figure 7. New Printers and Publishers in Paris, 1789–1810

Note: Darker area represents printers and publishers in business for eight or more years; lighter area represents those in business for less than eight years.

Sources: Paul Delalain, *L'Imprimerie et la librairie à Paris de 1789 à 1813* (Paris: Delalain, [1900]) and AN, ser.F18, cartons 10a and 25.

printing, publishing, and bookselling establishments were active in Paris: 337 printing houses and 887 booksellers/publishers. A little fewer than half of these businesses (166 printers and 403 booksellers/publishers) were active for at least one-third of the period. Major changes of regimes (1789–1791, 1795–1796, and 1804) ushered in new generations of printers and publishers.[14] It is not surprising that these political upheavals would be accompanied by spasmodic increases in the production and consumption of printed matter. Interestingly, however, if we consider only the longer-term establishments—those in business for over eight years, or one-third of the period in question—the upsurge of new businesses that otherwise appears to accompany the declaration of the first Empire in 1804 disappears entirely. The new world of printing and publishing, then, was forged during the two great liberal moments of the revolutionary decade: in the wake of the freeing of the press (1789–1791) and in the period of renewed liberalization of press laws during the Directory (1796–1799).

Did this sudden expansion of the power to print and publish transform the cultural topography of the capital? Apparently not. In 1807, the Paris guidebook *Le Pariséum* described a literary landscape much like that found at the end of the Old Regime: "The majority of the publishers have their warehouses and shops on the Quai des Grands-Augustin. *Nouveautés* are sold in the Palais Royal, in the wooden galleries."[15] As Bernard Vouillot has shown, printing and publishing enterprises remained concentrated around the university, where they had formerly been restricted by royal regulation: that is, in the area roughly circumscribed today by the rue St-Jacques, the rue Soufflot, the rue Vaugirard, the rue de Rennes to the place St-Germain des Prés, the rue Bonaparte to Pont Neuf, and the *quais* of the Left Bank back up to St-Jacques. The

14. A quick glance at Delalain's list reveals that because he based his list on published sources alone, his information is weak for the period before 1797. Similarly, his dating of enterprises is strongly biased toward the years of his sources: 1797–1798, 1804, and 1811–1813. Fortunately, the manuscript surveys of Paris booksellers, publishers, and printers, compiled by Napoleonic inspectors between 1810 and 1811 and currently found in the F18 series at the Archives Nationales (cartons 10a and 25), allows the bias in the published sources to be corrected against, because these surveys provide *actual* dates of entry into the profession attested to by some form of written proof, most frequently a privilege or *patente*. Consequently, the dates of the founding for approximately half of the establishments listed in Delalain have been redated.

15. J.-F.-C. Blanvillain, *Le Pariséum, ou tableau actuel de Paris* (Paris: Piranesi, 1807), 205.

largest expansion of printers was eastward up the Left Bank, remaining as close by the old neighborhood as possible. The greatest expansion of book dealers, in contrast, was outward from the Palais Royal into the new wealthy neighborhoods on the Right Bank.[16]

Just as printers remained closely tied to their prerevolutionary neighborhoods, so too, as Philippe Minard has recently shown, did they remain wedded to their old craft mode of production.[17] With the two exceptions of the national printing house and Charles-Joseph Panckoucke's enormous shop with twenty-seven presses, the printing shops of the revolutionary period increased in number but not in scale, containing on average between four and ten presses.[18] Indeed, the most distinctive feature of the revolutionary world of print was the proliferation of many small shops like Momoro's, rather than an expansion of the more established shops.

Furthermore, apart from minor improvements in typesetting and the introduction of night work to produce daily newspapers, the technology of printing (the two-strike wooden handpress) and the basic division of labor between pressmen and compositors remained essentially unchanged from the Old Regime into the nineteenth century. To Philippe Minard, Roger Chartier, and Daniel Roche, in fact, the most striking feature of the world of print during the Revolution is the very persistence of "the old typographical regime":[19] the printing community was enlarged as a consequence of the freedom of the press, but its character was not fundamentally changed.

The crucial transformation in the world of revolutionary print cannot be found in the development of new technologies, or in the reorganization of the relations of production within the printing shop. Rather, it must be sought more broadly in the impact of the transformations of the political and legal institutions within which those technologies and relations of production were embedded, that is, in the collapse of the closed

16. Bernard Vouillot, "La Révolution et l'empire. Une Nouvelle Réglementation," in Chartier and Martin (eds.), *Histoire de l'édition française* 2:533.

17. See Philippe Minard, "Agitation on the Work Force," in Darnton and Roche (eds.), *Revolution in Print,* 107–123.

18. Ibid. See also Robert Darnton, "L'Imprimerie de Panckoucke en l'an II," *Revue française d'histoire du livre,* n.s., no. 23 (1979): 359–369; Duprat, *Histoire de l'Imprimerie Impériale.*

19. The phrase is Roger Chartier's; see his "Ancien Régime typographique," *Annales E.S.C.,* no. 36 (March 1981): 191–209. See also Minard, "Agitation in the Work Force"; Minard, *Typographes des lumières;* Roger Chartier and Daniel Roche, "Les Livres ont-ils fait la Révolution," in Chartier and Roche (eds.), *Livre et Révolution,* 9–20.

corporate printing world of the Old Regime, the introduction of laissez-faire cultural policies, the consequent redistribution of the cultural power to print, and the freeing up of the possible ends toward which that cultural power could be deployed.

Who ran the presses of the Revolution, and to what purposes? A look beyond the raw numbers reveals that three-quarters of the printers and almost two-thirds of the booksellers/publishers of the old Paris Book Guild, though suffering badly, managed to survive at least through the Directory (until 1799). One-third of the guild families still had active members in the professions in 1811, and a full one-quarter of the eighty printers selected by the Napoleonic administration were from families of the eighteenth-century guild.[20] These figures indicate that despite their serious financial difficulties immediately following the freeing of the press and the collapse of the guild, a significant sector of the old eighteenth-century publishing elite maintained a critical presence in the industry.

But they also sustained two large infusions of new blood in the periods of the constitutional monarchy (1789–1792) and the Directory (1795–1799). Old families, such as the Delalains, the LeClercs, and the Barbous, scrupulously restricted their business and marital relations to other families of the old guild.[21] Far more common, however, were those businessmen who followed the instinct not only to band together, but also to draw in new blood and capital. With a few notable exceptions, the new empires of the Revolution thus look more like those of Charles-Joseph Panckoucke, Pierre Didot *l'aîné*, François-Jean Baudouin, and François Belin, who strategically built bridges between the old elites and the new. The Panckoucke family, for example, drew in weaker members of the old guild, like Nicolas Ruault and Pierre Plassan, as managers and directors of their expanding establishments; at the same time, they brought in, through marriage and business, new associates like Henri Agasse and Pierre-Claude-Victor Boiste.[22] The Didot-Maginel-Demonville-Jombert-Léger nexus and the Baudouin-Imbert-Mame-Hacquart-Rondonneau-Prault conglomerate; the associations of Belin-Leprieur-Rozet-Delance

20. For the persistence of the families of the Paris Book Guild, see Delalain, *Imprimerie et la librairie*. For the selection of the eighty printers of Paris in 1811, see AN, ser. F18, carton 25, "Notes sur les imprimeurs ci-après désignés" (1810–1811).

21. See Delalain, *Imprimerie et la librairie*, 52.

22. Ibid.; and AN, ser. F18, carton 25, "Notes sur les imprimeurs."

and Duprat-Letellier; and Crapart, Caille, and Ravier Company all disclose similar patterns.[23] New publishers grafted themselves onto the old elites, forming associations, and fusing new capital to old. However exaggerated, there was an element of truth in what the director of the national printing house had said: the printers and publishers of the Old Regime were not driven under by new speculators who appeared after the freedom of the press; rather, they were engulfed by them.

But what were the characteristics of these new empires? Between 1789 and 1799 the number of printing shops in Paris better than quadrupled, from 47 to 223. When the Napoleonic administration undertook a door-to-door survey of Parisian printers in 1810, the number stood at 157. Of these, the 80 that best met the qualifications established by the administration were allowed to remain in business, provided they swore political allegiance to the new regime and they had the requisite scale—at least four presses and enough type to run them full time—and financial security as printing establishments.[24] These eighty shops constituted a core of the largest and more successful printing establishments to emerge from the revolutionary period.

The majority of the new printing shops of the revolutionary period arose to meet the explosive demand for political news and debate that accompanied the declaration of the freedom of the press in 1789.[25] Of the 196 new newspapers (the publishing of which required many more presses than did book publishing, since extensive press runs and continuous production were necessary)[26] that appeared in Paris in 1789, fewer than half (90) can be attributed to the old printers of the book guild.[27] It is thus not surprising that great numbers of new printing shops emerged in the early years of the Revolution—at least fifty-five in Paris between 1789 and 1790 alone.

But the Terror, and then the dismantling of sectional politics after

23. Ibid.

24. AN, ser. F18, carton 1, "Décret impérial contenant le règlement sur l'imprimerie et la librairie . . . 5 février 1810," title 2.

25. Bellanger (ed.), *Histoire générale de la presse française* 1:436. The number of journals produced in Paris went from 4 in 1788 to 184 in 1789, 335 in 1790, and 236 in 1791. In contrast, from the year II (1793–1794) to the year III (1794–1795) the numbers jumped only from 106 to 137, fell in the year IV to 105, climbed in the year V to 190, and finally settled in the year VI at 115.

26. Ibid., 435.

27. My calculations are based on the information provided in Pierre Rétat, *Les Journaux de 1789. Bibliographie critique* (Paris: CNRS, 1989).

Thermidor, spelled the end to popular political activity and debate, and hence to quick profits in political journals and ephemera. After 1793, political repression cut down the desperate and unprotected along with the militant and outspoken. Thus, formerly wealthy and respected members of the old Paris Book Guild, such as Philippe-Denis Pierres, Jacques-François Froullé, and Gaspar-Joseph Cuchet, having suffered the abolition of their privileges and witnessed the collapse of their businesses, soon found themselves driven into the production of illicit ephemera in order to survive.[28]

Cuchet, who had specialized in publishing scholarly scientific and agricultural works, was one of the wealthiest members of the book guild in 1789.[29] In July 1794, Cuchet presented the following account of his career since the beginning of the Revolution to the Committee on General Security:

> [A] zealous partisan of the Revolution, I embraced it with the enthusiasm of a free man. An elector in 1789, I was one of the first to take up arms. The morning of July 14 I was in town, and in the afternoon I marched among the brave French Guards to take the Bastille. . . . On October 5 I marched with the Parisian army . . . to Versailles. I have proof of all of these facts. . . . After these great events, I was overcome by the darkest misfortunes; I went bankrupt. Heartbroken, pursued by creditors, menaced by captivity . . . I lost my spirit, I lost my reason, and weakened by torment I clung to any branch that could save me from the storm. . . . Citizens, I am not guilty of treason; I succumbed to the excesses of woe. I printed three of four works on the monarchy.[30]

Whatever his actual political beliefs, Cuchet was driven by the collapse of the book trade after 1789 from his business in *grande édition* into the

28. See AN, ser. BB3, carton 81a, fols. 361–364, Pierres, printer, 25 nivôse, an II (January 14, 1794). For Froullé, see AN, ser. F17, carton 1005a, doss. 743*bis*, Letter from Froullé to the Committee on Public Instruction, July 27, 1793; and AN, ser. W, carton 332, no. 566, 8 ventôse, an II (February 26, 1794). Finally, for Cuchet, see AN, ser. F7, carton 4658, doss. 4, 24 messidor, an II (July 12, 1794); and AN, ser. W, carton 53, doss. 3401, 8 thermidor, an II (July 26, 1794). For the corporate status and wealth of Cuchet, Pierres, and Froullé on the eve of the Revolution, see table 2.

29. See AN, ser. F7, carton 4658, doss. 4, 24 messidor, an II (July 12, 1794); this dossier gives a list of some of Cuchet's stock. See also AN, ser. ADVIII, carton 7, "Consultation pour le citoyen A. J. Dugour, propriétaire du *Cours d'agriculture* par Rozier." A.-J. Dugour bought Cuchet's business, including this work, in 1796.

30. AN, ser. F7, carton 4658, doss. 4, Cuchet, publisher, 24 messidor, an II (July 12, 1794). For more of Cuchet's business troubles in the early years of the Revolution, see Gaspar-Joseph Cuchet, *Avis* (N.p., [January 11, 1789]).

shady world of counterrevolutionary ephemera, only to stand trial before the Revolutionary Tribunal.

Yet it was not simply the last relics of the old cultural regime who found themselves in danger. The Terror struck to the left as well as the right, at young as well as old, in its effort to impose political unity on the warring nation. Momoro, too, found himself denounced before the Revolutionary Tribunal in March 1794 as a counterrevolutionary conspirator because of his association with the ultrarevolutionary Hébertist movement.[31] A death sentence on March 24 thus brought to an abrupt end one of the most prominent new printing establishments of the revolutionary period.[32] Momoro instructed his wife in his last letter: "You will not be able to maintain the printing shop. Dismiss the workers. . . . I leave you my memory and my virtues. Marat taught me how to suffer."[33] Momoro's presses were soon confiscated by the government.[34]

Behind ideological hot-heads like Momoro stood numerous new printers of *nouveautés* and peddlers of printed matter who found themselves suddenly at risk of losing their lives for a journal or pamphlet they had simply printed "in consequence of the freedom of the press, and to make a living."[35] By the end of 1794, the honeymoon between youthful revolutionaries and the printing press was definitively over.

Despite the unhappy fate of individuals like Momoro, on the whole it was the new printing shops founded early in the Revolution that survived into the Empire. Twenty-one of the eighty shops selected for retention in 1810 were owned by members of the old guild; thirty-five

31. The entire dossier concerning Momoro's arrest and conviction is conserved in AN, ser. W, cartons 76, 77, 78, and 339.

32. AN, ser. W, carton 339, doss. 617, "Acte de condamnation contre Antoine-François Momoro, et al.," 4 germinal, an II (March 24, 1794).

33. AN, ser. W, carton 77, plaque 1, no. 47, "Billet de Momoro à sa femme," [February–April 1794].

34. Duprat, *Histoire de l'Imprimerie Impériale,* 166.

35. AN, ser. W, carton 339, doss. 8, Jean-Pascal Sétier, printer in Paris, September 4, 1793. For other, similar, cases, see AN, ser. W, carton 21, doss. 1160, Gallier, printer, 9 pluviôse, an II (January 28, 1794); AN, ser. F7, carton 4722, doss. 3, Gérard, printer, 10 prairial, an II (May 29, 1794); AN, ser. F7, carton 4645, doss. 2, Chemin *fils,* 8 messidor, an II (June 26, 1794); and, for a printer named Senneville (Rioux-Maillon), see AN, ser. F7, carton 4775, doss. 17, doc. 4, 21 messidor, an II (July 9, 1794), and AN, ser. F7, carton 4774, doss. 93, doc. 3, 13 thermidor, an II (July 31, 1794).

were founded in the period 1789–1793, nine in the period 1795–1799, and fifteen in the period 1800–1810—that is, almost half of the printers of 1811 came from the time of the constitutional monarchy.[36] The printers of 1811, furthermore, break down by specialization (possible for sixty-four of the eighty) as follows: newspapers and periodicals, 19; administration, 12; literature, belles lettres, and *nouveautés*, 11; classical works, 4; theater, 3; religion, 3; foreign languages, 3; sciences, medicine, and agriculture, 2; arts, 2; almanacs, 2; ephemera, 2; law, 1.[37] Clearly, periodical publications were the single most important source of employment in the new printing world.

It was not just old fortunes like those of Charles-Joseph Panckoucke, Pierre-Robert-Christophe Ballard, Jean-François Colas, or Antoine Demonville that followed the winds of revolutionary literary culture and shifted toward newspaper and ephemeral publishing.[38] New fortunes were made from the periodical press as well. Thus, the Napoleonic inspector who wrote up "notes" on the eighty largest printing establishments in Paris recorded a whole new generation of wealthy printers as well: François Chaignieau *l'aîné*, "rich from his *Courrier universel*"; Henri Agasse, "printer of the *Moniteur*, . . . stockholder and editor at 3,000 *livres* a year"; Jean-Baptiste-Etienne-Elie Lenormand, "former worker, a parvenu who can always be reproached for having printed pamphlets. But the presses of the *Journal de l'Empire* have cured him of that"; or Louis Prudhomme, "rich, *Révolutions de Paris*, a hot-head."[39] The association of the freedom of the press with both "the presses" and *la presse* is not a phonetic coincidence or a mere play on words: it is a historical reality.

The freeing of the press and the consequent deregulation of printing and publishing after 1789 led to an unprecedented democratization of the printed word. The number of printing and publishing establishments in Paris more than tripled during the revolutionary period, allowing much broader social initiative and participation in the production of the printed word than ever before and, consequently, in the public exchange of ideas. Not surprisingly, the literary forms created by the freed presses were more democratic as well. Ephemeral publishing was less capital-intensive than book production, and its success depended on

36. See Delalain, *Imprimerie et la librairie;* and AN, ser. F18, carton 25, "Notes sur les imprimeurs ci-après désignés" (1810–1811).

37. Ibid.

38. Ibid.

39. Ibid.

extensive, as opposed to intensive, markets. These literary forms were made for (and often by) people who inhabited the world of Momoro rather than that of Condorcet and Sieyès, with little money to spend and little leisure time to read. This is not to suggest that there was no popular literary culture prior to the French Revolution. But with the declaration of press freedom and the collapse of the literary institutions of the Old Regime, the center of gravity in commercial printing shifted perceptibly from the elite civilization of the book to the democratic culture of the pamphlet, the broadside, and the periodical press.

The Publishers of the Republic

In contrast to the world of ephemeral printing and newspapers, book publishing and bookselling saw their most dramatic expansion during the period of the Directory (1795–1799) (figure 6).[40] After a precipitous crash in 1789, the number of new titles registered annually at the *dépôt légal* turned steadily upward: from 287 in 1796 to 657 in 1798, and reaching 740 in 1799 (see figure 7).[41] The number of novels published in France (but not necessarily registered), after a dramatic drop from 1789 to 1795, also began to expand dramatically after 1796, peaking in 1799.[42] These trends attest to a new infusion of capital, both government and commercial, into book publishing after the end of the Terror, and in particular after the Treaty of Basel (1795), when European markets were reopened to French businesses. But how many book publishers were there? And what did they publish?

Because it was less closely monitored, the world of revolutionary book publishing and selling is more difficult to reconstruct than that of printers and the periodical press. Furthermore, the French word *libraire* is a murky term, used indiscriminately to describe anyone engaging in a whole series of related activities, from retail bookselling to investing in, or coordinating, the printing, publication, or distribution of an edition.

40. One hundred twenty-one new publisher-booksellers appeared between 1789 and 1793, and 183 appeared between 1795 and 1799.

41. For reasons I cannot explain, my own calculations differ slightly from those presented in Estivals, *Statistique bibliographique*, 415. Estivals's figures are as follows: 1794, 371; 1795, 308; 1796, 240; 1797, 345; 1798, 475; 1799, 815.

42. Martin, Milne, and Frautschi, *Bibliographie du genre romanesque français*, xxxvi–xxxix. The number of new titles appearing in 1794 was 16; 41 appeared in 1795, 54 in 1796, 73 in 1797, 96 in 1798, and 174 in 1799.

In his listing of 887 Paris *libraires,* for example, Delalain included any-one who sold books from a fixed location—even the *bouquinistes* along the *quais*—together with the largest publishers in the capital. But how are the publishers to be distinguished from the booksellers? And who were the biggest Parisian publishers of the revolutionary period? How did the shape of the publishing world evolve after it was freed from the con-straints of corporate monopoly and regulation?

Business records of individual publishers during the revolutionary period are scarce and fragmentary. Fortunately, the records of the *dépôt légal* prove more illuminating. In order to guarantee legal protection for individual editions, the law of July 19, 1793, required publishers or authors to deposit two copies of their work at the *dépôt* at the Bib-liothèque Nationale, for which they received a *récépiscé,* a receipt that served as legal proof of ownership of the edition. Because the names of each depositor, along with the date, title, and format of each publication, were recorded in the register, it is possible to reconstruct a complete record of legally documented publications for the period July 1793– December 1799.[43] The register thus offers an illuminating record of publishers of new editions during the period, as distinct from distribu-tors and booksellers.

No single group, including individual authors, made greater use of the *dépôt légal* than Paris publishers. In the six years between 1793 and 1799, 272 publishers with businesses in Paris deposited at least one work; their submissions account for 1,969 of the total 2,778 works reg-istered—nearly two-thirds of the total (see appendix 5). Thus, more than one-quarter of the 887 establishments listed as Paris *libraires* by Delalain between 1789 and 1813 can be shown to have engaged directly in publishing.[44] The number of publications deposited per publisher over the six-year period ranged from 1 to 90 for books, and as high as 286 for music and song sheets. As with printers, approximately one-third (72 of 272) of the publishers of the revolutionary period can be identified as former guild members or their relations.

While 213 publishers made only one deposit, 37 deposited between five and fifteen books, and an elite core of 15 publishing houses regis-tered between seventeen and ninety books in the period 1793–1799:

43. BN, Archives Modernes, CXXIX, "Registres du dépôt légal des livres imprimés," reg. 1.

44. The percentage is in fact probably somewhat higher, as Delalain's list extends to 1813, whereas I have limited my survey of the *dépôt* to the years 1793–1799.

Pierre Didot *l'aîné*, Henri Agasse, Pierre Plassan, Louis Rondonneau, the Cercle Social, François Buisson, Honnert, Henri Jansen, Aubry, Pierre-Sebastien Leprieur, Mathieu Migneret, Claude-François Maradan, L. C. Huet, Pierre-Etienne Cholet, and Jean-Nicolas Barba.[45] By number of new editions deposited for copyright protection, these fifteen emerge as the biggest publishers in the capital during the period of the Republic.

Of the fifteen, four were former members of the Paris Book Guild (Didot *l'aîné*, Buisson, Plassan, and Maradan), and one was the direct successor of a guild family (Agasse). Twelve of the fifteen were also printers, and half had dealings in periodical publishing as well. Closer inspection of the record of their deposits offers an extraordinary window into the character of their portfolios and a chance to trace how their literary enterprises evolved over the course of the republican period. Six specialized in theatrical works. Two dealt solely in literature, one of them exclusively in popular novels. Several others had significant concentrations in literary *nouveautés*. Six of the big publishing houses dealt in "arts and sciences"—that is, in works of high literature, history, classical texts, philosophy, and the sciences. One published almost only popular educational books. One alone concentrated entirely on philosophy and politics. By reconstructing the profile of these fifteen publishing enterprises over the years 1793–1799 we can recover something of the literary landscape of the first Republic, together with the processes by which it was forged through the forces of both commercial markets and government patronage.

Philosophy and Politics

Philosophical and political publications are often said to have made the Revolution, but how did they fare under it? On July 25, 1793, a publishing group that called itself the Cercle Social became the first depositor at the newly founded *dépôt légal* of the Bibliothèque Nationale. The group registered thirty-four publications, many dated as far back as 1791. Despite its short-lived publishing career (1790–1793) the Cercle was to be one of the largest literary depositors of the republican period. As Gary Kates has masterfully demonstrated in his recent study of the group, this was no mere commercial publishing house. Rather, it was founded in 1791 by a group of revolutionary intellectuals known as the Confédération des Amis de la Vérité, whose explicit intention was to

---

45. See appendix 5.

regenerate French political and cultural life through the propagation of enlightened and liberal ideas.[46] As one of its most famous participants, the marquis de Condorcet, wrote in a Cercle publication of 1791, "The knowledge of printing makes it possible for modern constitutions to reach a perfection that they could not otherwise achieve. In this way a sparsely populated people in a large territory can now be as free as the residents of a small city. . . . It is through the printing process alone that discussion among a great people can truly be one."[47]

The Cercle printing shop on the rue du Théâtre Français in the radical Cordeliers district was directed principally by Nicolas Bonneville and Louis Reynier, though it enjoyed continuous support from a wide range of well-known politicians and intellectuals, including Jean-Marie Roland de la Platière, François Lanthenas, the marquis de Condorcet, Jacques-Pierre Brissot de Warville, Philippe Fabre d'Eglantine, and Jean-Baptiste Louvet de Couvray.

In its effort to bring all of France into political dialogue with itself, the Cercle Social launched an exceptionally wide and innovative range of publications, addressed to a broad spectrum of audiences. Gary Kates has identified 180 books, newspapers, pamphlets, and ephemeral pieces published by the Cercle between 1791 and 1793, 40 of which ended up in the *dépôt légal.* The lion's share of the works deposited for legal protection were books and pamphlets concerned with politics and political philosophy, including authors such as John Oswald, the marquis de Condorcet, Etienne Clavière, Pierre-Jean-Baptiste Publicola-Chaussard, Nicolas Bonneville, and Joseph Lavallée, as well as the French translation of Thomas Paine's *Rights of Man,* by François Lanthenas. But they also deposited a popular orientalist novel, three plays, a collection of Bonneville's poems, Lavallée's geography of France, an account of travel in the Sahara, a collection of Jean-Baptiste de Monet de Lamarck's writings on natural history and his journal of natural history, and a work on the military fortification of Paris by A.-P. Julienne de Belair.

In 1792 the Cercle also published an extraordinary spectrum of periodical publications, ranging from the *Bulletin de la bouche de fer,* which offered a forum for exchange of ideas open to all citizens; through readers' letters; to Condorcet's more highbrow political journal the *Chro-*

---

46. Kates, *Cercle Social.* The following discussion is based largely on this work, and especially on part three, "The Imprimerie du Cercle Social," 175–270.

47. Marie-Jean-Antoine Caritat, marquis de Condorcet, *Des conventions nationales* (Paris: Imprimerie du Cercle Social, 1791), 18; cited in ibid., 180.

nique du mois, the rural *Feuille villageoise,* and Louvet de Couvray's news broadside the *Sentinelle,* which was intended to reach the sans-culotte reader on the streets of Paris.

The Cercle publishing house reached its apogee in 1792, along with the political group to which it was most closely attached, the Girondists. From the very start, the Cercle Social was generously patronized by Jean-Marie Roland de la Platière, who put up an initial 26,000 *livres* to open the printing shop. As minister of the interior in 1791–1792, Roland continued to lavish subsidies on the publications of the Cercle: first from the secret funds of his ministry, and then, more overtly, from the 100,000 *livres* assigned by the National Assembly to his controversial office of propaganda, the "Bureau de l'Esprit." The *Sentinelle* alone received 11,000 *livres* in 1792.[48] Roland's resignation in January 1793, however, and the exclusion of the Girondists from the National Convention five months later, spelled the end of the Cercle Social. The key leaders and authors for the publishing house were soon under arrest or in hiding. In fact, the deposit of thirty-four works at the *dépôt légal* on July 25, 1793, was probably one of Nicolas Bonneville's last acts before his arrest.

The Cercle made a minor reappearance in the records of the *dépôt* after the fall of the Jacobins, for in 1794 two deposits are recorded in its name, another in 1796, and yet another in 1799.[49] The records of the *dépôt* thus confirm Gary Kates's conclusion that with the end of government patronage and the political persecution of its key members, the group collapsed. The Cercle Social may have been the most innovative cultural experiment of the revolutionary period, but its fate was tied to politics rather than the market. Despite the initial profits of the *Bulletin de la bouche de fer,* as a publishing venture the Cercle was a commercial failure, unable to sustain itself without government favor and subsidies.

Popular Literature

Several publishing enterprises proved that it was possible to make a profit in book publishing, even in the most turbulent moments of the Revolution—but not from serious political and philosophical works. As Villebrune observed in 1794, in the early years of the Revolution it was prose

48. Kates, *Cercle Social,* 228, 235–242, 260–261.

49. Philippe Fabre d'Eglantine's *Intrigue épistolaire* and Pierre Manuel's *Etude de la nature et de l'homme* in 1794, Pierre-Simon de Laplace's *Exposition du système du monde* in 1796, and the *Vie du Capitaine Thurot* (ed. of 1791) in 1799.

fiction that captured what remained of the book market.[50] Not surprisingly, several publishers concentrated almost exclusively on novels.[51] By far the most successful in the early years of the Revolution was Pierre-Sebastien Leprieur, on the rue de Savoie. In 1794, he registered sixteen popular novels in small formats (in 12 and 16) at the *dépôt légal*. Among them were six by François-Guillaume Ducray-Duminil: *Alexis, ou la maisonette dans les bois* (1793, orig. ed. 1789), *Petit-Jacques et Georgette* (1794, orig. ed. 1789), *Lolotte et Fanfan* (1794, orig. ed. 1788), *Le Codicile sentimental et moral* (1794), *Les Cinquantes Francs de Jeannette* (1798), and *Coelina, ou l'enfant du mystère* (1798); two by Joseph-Marie Tréogate de Loaisel: *Dolbreuse, ou l'homme du siècle* (1794, orig. ed. 1783) and *Lucile et Milcourt* (1794); one by Pivert de Senancour: *Aldomen, ou le bonheur dans l'obscurité* (1794); and two, *Félix et Pauline* (1794) and *Félicie de Vilmard* (1798), by Pierre Blanchard. These were exactly the kind of popular novels that the head of the Bibliothèque Nationale, Villebrune, and the director of the Commission on Public Instruction, Ginguené, complained were infecting the minds of citizens with useless fictions and idle pleasures.

Leprieur was in business before 1789, but he had not been a member of the Paris Book Guild. According to records of the Napoleonic administration, Leprieur opened shop in Paris in 1784.[52] Significantly, this date coincides closely with the first edition of Tréogate de Loaisel's *Dolbreuse*, which appeared in Paris in 1783, though with Amsterdam on the title page as the place of publication. With the suppression of the book guild Leprieur surfaced on the Parisian scene, and over the course of the Revolution he built a major publishing house on the commercial demand for prose fiction. He dealt exclusively in popular novels, children's stories, and fairy tales, most notably those by Ducray-Duminil, Tréogate de Loaisel, and Blanchard, and between 1794 and 1799 deposited twenty-six editions (eight in 1794, three in 1795, two in 1796, one in 1797, three in 1798, and nine in 1799). His first edition of Ducray-Duminil's *Victor, ou l'enfant de la forêt* (1797) introduced the French to the *roman noir*. It swept the nation like wildfire, rapidly becoming one of the most widely

50. For more on the prose fiction of the early years of the Revolution, see Malcolm Cook, "Politics in the Fiction of the French Revolution, 1789–1794," *Studies on Voltaire and the Eighteenth Century*, no. 201 (1982): 237–340; and Martin, Milne, and Frautschi, *Bibliographie du genre romanesque français*.

51. Many publishers handled novels, but several handled them almost exclusively, including François Louis, Lavillette, J.-J. Lepetit, and J.-J. Delance.

52. See AN, ser. F18, carton 25, "Registre de MM. les libraires de Paris qui ont déclaré vouloir continuer leur état—ou l'abandonner" (1811).

read French novels of the revolutionary period.⁵³ By 1799 he had moved
his business into the heart of the old publishing world, on the rue St-
Jacques. In 1806, Leprieur's daughter married Léonard-François Belin,
scion of an old eighteenth-century printing family. Their union led to the
creation of the Belin-Leprieur Company, which was to become one of the
important publishing houses in the nineteenth century.

While Leprieur's line of romances and gothic thrillers captured the
imagination of an entire generation of young revolutionary readers, the
editor Aubry answered the government's calls for authors and publishers to woo the minds of future citizens toward a more useful and edifying reading diet.⁵⁴ Aubry, describing himself as an "editor and publisher of works for republican instruction," established his business at 2,
rue Baillet, near the rue de la Monnaie, in 1791.⁵⁵ Three years later he
deposited six educational works for children—*Syllabaire républicain pour
les enfants, Petit Traité de grammaire française, Principes de J. J. Rousseau,
Premières Notions de morale, Rituel républicain, Eléments d'arithmétique décimale*—and a technical pamphlet on dying processes. In 1795 he added a
new French adaptation of Daniel Defoe's *Robinson Crusoe* to his list. In
1798–1799, he brought out a series of works on weights and measures,
several more children's schoolbooks, including a French Petrarch, and
an almanach. In all, between 1794 and 1799 Aubry registered twenty-
two titles at the *dépôt légal*.

Aubry also dealt in commissions and catalogue sales on a large scale.
Giving himself the title of "director of the *cabinet bibliographique*," he
edited the trade journal *Feuille de correspondance du libraire* between 1791
and 1793 and then launched another trade journal, the *Magasin du
bibliophile*, in 1797. Aubry was one of the very few publishers to announce,
by his own reports to the government, that his business was thriving in

---

53. For more on the popular novel during the revolutionary period, and on Tréogate
de Loaisel and Ducray-Duminil in particular, see Cook, "Politics in the Fiction of the
French Revolution"; and Pierre Barbéris and Claude Duchet, eds., *Manuel d'histoire littéraire de la France, Vol. 4: 1789 à 1848* (Paris: Editions Sociales, 1972), esp. 138–147 and
366–377. See also James Smith Allen, *Popular French Romanticism: Authors, Readers, and
Books in the Nineteenth Century* (Syracuse: Syracuse University Press, 1981).

54. For Aubry's solicitations of government patronage and his submissions to the
schoolbook competitions, see Guillaume (ed.), *Procès-verbaux du Comité d'Instruction Publique*
4:41, 466; and AN, ser. F17, carton 1010a, doss. 2403, for Aubry's submissions to the
competitions opened by the Committee on Public Instruction (1794).

55. AN, ser. F18, carton 25, "Registre de MM. les libraires de Paris qui ont déclaré
vouloir continuer leur état—ou l'abandonner" (1811).

the year II.[56] A catalogue of his stock from that year lists seventeen titles in "public instruction" published or in press under his name, and a retail stock of forty-three additional titles from other publishers that was dominated by the works of the major *philosophes* (especially Voltaire and Rousseau), geographies, atlases, and travel literature.[57] Having built a fortune in commissions, Aubry deployed his literary capital to meet the republican demand for a revolutionary pedagogy. By 1798 Aubry, like Leprieur, moved off the back streets to a prominent address in the heart of the old publishing world on the Quai des Augustins.

Arts and Sciences

Six of the top depositers at the *dépôt légal* dealt in serious works of high literature, history, philosophy, and the sciences. The most notable among them was Pierre Didot *l'aîné*, the eldest son in the most distinguished branch of the greatest family in eighteenth-century French typography and printing.[58] In 1789, at least seven members of the Didot family were engaged in publishing. Pierre Didot's establishment was on the rue Pavée St-André des Arts when the Revolution began. Despite a brief flirtation with political periodical publishing in 1789, he concentrated his energies during the revolutionary period on maintaining the tradition of fine arts printing and elite literary culture.[59] Indeed, Didot's main ambition during the Revolution was to eclipse the works of his great rival, the Italian editor and printer of classical texts Giambattista Bodoni.

During the six years of the Republic, Didot registered thirty-one volumes at the *dépôt légal*. Upon its opening in 1793, he immediately deposited his lavish folio edition of *Publii Virgilii Maronis Bucolica, Georgica et Aeneis,* printed with the neoclassical typefaces designed by his younger brother Firmin Didot and including twenty-three plates engraved after drawings by Gérard and Girodet. His beautiful editions of classical texts continued to appear regularly at the *dépôt*. Along with classical works, he also took on a treatise on Islamic monies translated by the great orientalist

56. AN, ser. F17, carton 1010a, doss. 2403.

57. For Aubry's list of stock in the year II (1793–1794), see ibid.

58. For a brief history of the contributions of this family to the art of printing, see Albert J. George, *The Didot Family and the Progress of Printing* (Syracuse: Syracuse University Press, 1961).

59. In 1789, Didot printed the first two issues of the *Véridique*, a weekly political journal of moderate temperament, which covered the proceedings of the National Assembly; see Rétat, *Journaux de 1789*, 265–267.

Isaac-Silvestre de Sacy; a series of classical French authors, including Molière (1795), Jean-Pierre Claris de Florian (1796), Pierre-Joseph Bernard (1797), Jean Racine (1798), and Nicolas Boileau-Despréaux (1799); the stories and fables of Jean de La Fontaine (1795, 1798) and Simon-Pierre Mérard St. Just (1796); as well as an edition of the *Maximes et réflexions morales* of François, duc de La Rochefoucauld (1796), several collections of poetry, a few educational books, and some works on weights and measures.

Despite the vicissitudes of revolutionary print culture, Didot was to see his cultural ambitions realized. His *Oeuvres de Racine* were judged by both the National Exposition of 1806 and the London Universal Exposition of 1851 as "the most perfect typographic production of all countries and all times."[60] Didot's conservative bias toward the classical French literature of the seventeenth and eighteenth centuries did not, it should be noted, prevent him from collaborating with Gide and Gay on the publication of an English novel in translation, the *Vicaire de Wakefield*, in 1797.

Didot did not succeed by his own resources alone. The government of the Directory lent significant support to his enterprise. In 1795 they purchased his edition of the constitution of 1791 with engravings by Helman and Ponce.[61] And in 1797 the minister of the interior invited him to move into the rooms at the Louvre formerly employed by the Imprimerie Royale, there to produce his beautiful editions of French classical authors, which came to be known as his "éditions du Louvre."[62] In 1810, the Napoleonic inspector described Pierre Didot as a man of "merit and literary refinement. It is not possible to have a better equipped printing shop, with the most beautiful characters and every possible advantage. Superbly located. Honest, upright, and respectful; but despite his fame he finds himself reduced to circumstances where he cannot meet his expenses."[63] Still, the Napoleonic regime maintained Didot's license to print, despite his financial instability.

Didot's career illustrates the persistence during the revolutionary period of the elite literary culture and the typographic traditions of Old Regime Paris, with its emphasis on classical literature, fine arts printing,

60. Ibid., 8.
61. Guillaume (ed.), *Procès-verbaux du Comité d'Instruction Publique* 5:429 (January 15, 1795).
62. Edmond Werdet, *De la librairie française* (Paris: Dentu, 1860), 203–205.
63. AN, ser. F18, carton 25, "Notes sur les imprimeurs ci-après désignés" (1810–1811).

and large-format, multivolume luxury editions. But Didot was able to continue his projects only with the help of government subsidies, and even then, as the Napoleonic inspector reported, he was unable to meet his costs. Villebrune, head of the Bibliothèque Nationale in the year II, had been right when he reported that with the Revolution, the elite market in lavish editions was too weak to sustain itself independently.

Three other descendants of the old Paris Book Guild, however, showed greater adaptability to the new cultural demands and possibilities of the revolutionary period: Pierre Plassan, François Buisson, and Henri Agasse. Plassan began his career working for Charles-Joseph Panckoucke on the rue des Poitevins. By 1792 he had his own establishment, nearby on the rue du Cimitière-St-André des Arts. His first *dépôt* submissions were made in 1796: three volumes of an edition of the *Oeuvres de Virgile*, translated by Desfontaines; two volumes of the *Oeuvres de Montesquieu;* and Ladivco Ariosto's *Orlando furioso,* in four volumes. In 1798, though, his business took a new direction with the deposit of the *Histoire naturelle des poissons* by Etienne de la Ville, comte de Lacépède, and the *Voyage de Lapérouse.* In 1799 he deposited several more of Lacépède's works, thus definitively marking his shift toward the natural sciences. In that same year, he also published his first work of contemporary fiction, Joseph Fiévée's novel *Frédéric.* Thus, over the course of the republican period Plassan's ventures evolved from classical and eighteenth-century philosophy toward the natural sciences and then, finally, the novel.

Under Lacépède's protection, Plassan became the printer for the Legion of Honor. When he died in 1810, his son was maintained as a printer by the Napoleonic authorities. But they had this to say about Plassan the elder: "Well kept shop [but] was resistant to police surveillance. He has just died. The emperor has ordered the suppression of his edition of Pagenel's manuscript entitled 'Essai historique et critique de la Révolution française.'"[64] Plassan had thrived under the Directory. Devoting himself to the propagation of republican philosophy and the natural sciences, he easily gained the favor of the intellectual establishment and the republican government. With Napoleon's coup d'état however, both the cultural and the political winds shifted, pushing Plassan toward not only the vogue in the novel but also the political opposition.

François Buisson, on the rue du Hautefeuille, near to the Cordeliers, had been in the publishing business since 1783, when he brought out his

64. Ibid.

women's fashion magazine the *Cabinet des modes*.[65] It was a huge success, and in 1786 he launched an international edition from London entitled the *Magasin des modes nouvelles françaises et anglaises,* which he was to continue during the revolutionary period as the *Journal de la mode et du goût*.[66] Buisson also had a boutique in the Palais Royal. He was thus in a very good position to move into political journals after the declaration of the freedom of the press in 1789—and even a bit before. It was Buisson who first flew in the face of the Old Regime literary police and published Brissot's *Patriote français* in the spring of 1789. If the *Patriote français* was any example, political journals were highly profitable ventures.[67] Within a year he had also taken up the Cercle Social's *Bouche de fer,* as well as the ultrarevolutionary *Annales patriotiques et littéraires de la France,* edited by Jean-Louis Carra and Louis-Sebastien Mercier.[68] He continued with the *Annales* until December 1794, claiming as many as six thousand subscribers.[69] In 1795, after Thermidor, he also submitted three issues of the *Journal de l'opposition* for copyright protection at the *dépôt légal.*

But Buisson was interested in more than periodicals. Between 1794 and 1799 he registered fifty books at the *dépôt.* In 1794 alone he made ten deposits, ranging from a political potboiler he had produced in 1792 entitled the *Vie privée du maréchel de Richelieu,* to French translations of serious philosophical works such as Thomas Gordon's *Discours historique sur Tacite et Salluste,* Jean-George-Adam Forster's *Voyage philosophique sur les bords du Rhin,* Adam Smith's *Recherches sur la nature et les causes de la richesse des nations,* and several other works of political and constitutional thought and political economy, like the multivolume *Bibliothèque physio-économique.* Buisson's London connections, not surprisingly, led him to specialize in translations, especially from the English.

In 1795 and 1796 his interests became increasingly literary. He published several works by Denis Diderot (his *Essai sur la peinture, La Religieuse,* and *Jacques le fataliste*), more *voyages,* and an English novel in translation. From 1797 to 1799 Buisson continued to publish English novels

---

65. For the date of his establishment, see ibid., "Registre de MM. les libraires de Paris qui ont déclaré vouloir continuer leur état—ou l'abandonner" (1811). For the *Cabinet des modes,* see Bellanger (ed.), *Histoire générale de la presse française* 1:319.

66. Bellanger (ed.), *Histoire générale de la presse française* 1:495–496.

67. For the profits made on publishing the *Patriote français,* see ibid., 439.

68. For Buisson's involvement in the *Patriote français* and the *Annales patriotiques et littéraires,* see Rétat, *Journaux de 1789,* 398–399; and for his involvement in printing the *Bulletin de la bouche de fer,* see Kates, *Cercle Social,* 185.

69. Rétat, *Journaux de 1789,* 32–35.

and philosophy (notably Adam Smith's *Théorie des sentiments moraux*), and he added a group of memoirs, correspondences, contemporary histories, and political tracts, such as Benjamin Constant's *Suite de la contre-révolution de 1660 en Angleterre,* to his list. Finally, he also produced a collection of exemplary *Lives,* intended for the schools: a *Vie de Catherine II,* a *Vie de Voltaire,* an *Esprit de Mirabeau,* a *Vie de Général Hoche,* and a *Vie de Benjamin Franklin.*

Although a member of the Paris Book Guild, Buisson in his willingness to put his name on Brissot's *Patriote français* in 1789 revealed a man who cared little for the traditional authorities or their regulations, and who kept his business closely attuned to the pulses of the revolutionary movement. This was as true of his serious books in the years after Thermidor as it was of his revolutionary political journals of the years 1789–1794. Indeed, Buisson's book publications from 1794 to 1799 resonated very closely with the cultural policies espoused by Grégoire, Chénier, Garat, and others in the chambers of the Commission on Public Instruction and on the floor of the National Convention, especially after Thermidor: consider his anglophilia, and especially his interest in English political economy; his timely publication of Diderot's *Essai sur la peinture* just as the convention began to seek theories and examples of an enlightened aesthetics; and his exemplary civic *Lives* intended for the schools. In fact, there is evidence of direct government patronage of at least two of Buisson's editions from this period: Adam Smith's *Théorie des sentiments moraux* and the *Vie de Général Hoche.*[70] Having founded his fortune first in fashion magazines and then in ultrarevolutionary political journals, by Thermidor Buisson was well established as one of the two largest publishers of serious enlightened philosophy and literary culture in the capital. The other was Henri Agasse.

In 1794, at the height of the Terror, Henri Agasse assumed directorship of the Paris publishing business of his father-in-law, Charles-Joseph Panckoucke.[71] Comprising twenty-seven presses and employing over a hundred workers, Agasse's establishment on the rue des Poitevins was

70. For Joseph Garat's proposal that the Commission on Public Instruction pay for the translation of Adam Smith's *Théorie des sentiments moraux,* see Guillaume (ed.), *Procès-verbaux du Comité d'Instruction Publique* 5:169 (1794). On government subsidies and purchases of the first two editions of the *Vie de Général Hoche,* see AN, ser. F17, carton 1215, doss. 5. For diverse purchases of works from Buisson by the Bibliothèque Nationale in 1794, see AN, ser. F4, carton 2554.

71. Tucoo-Chala, *Charles-Joseph Panckoucke,* 495.

the largest privately owned commercial printing and publishing house in France, if not the world.[72] Along with the printing shop, Agasse came into possession of two of the largest publishing ventures of the revolutionary period: Charles-Joseph Panckoucke's monumental stepchild of Denis Diderot's great *Encyclopédie,* the *Encyclopédie méthodique;* and the largest daily newspaper in France, the *Moniteur universel.*[73]

The *Moniteur* was the first large-format national daily political newspaper in France.[74] Like many Parisian publishers and printers, Panckoucke created the *Moniteur* in response to the public demand for "news" after the freeing of the press in 1789. But in contrast to the majority of those new Parisian periodicals, which modeled themselves on Brissot's *Patriote français,* the *Moniteur* prided itself on the accuracy of its political information rather than on its political opinions or the rhetorical skills of its authors. Its meticulous stenographic coverage of National Assembly proceedings immediately established the *Moniteur* as an unrivaled source of daily political information for the country. Its success was immediate, and by 1791 Panckoucke could boast of eighty-five hundred subscribers. The *Moniteur* was the only periodical to survive the political vicissitudes of the revolutionary period. Recognized—even by the government under the Terror—as one of the most accurate sources of political information, by 1794, when Agasse took over, the *Moniteur* was receiving considerable state subsidies to insure its continuance. In 1799 it became the government's official newspaper. By 1810 Henri Agasse was described by the government as "one of the most honest men in the world, who has sacrificed everything for his father-in-law, Panckoucke. He prints the *Moniteur* and other works that are important and full of merit. A superb printing shop that runs day and night. A rich business. . . . He enjoys a comfortable life; on top of his income as the key stockholder, he receives an income of 3,000 *livres* for editing." Indeed, because he left the running of the printing shop to his director, Ruault, Agasse was free to pursue his own interests in publishing.[75]

72. Darnton, "L'Imprimerie de Panckoucke."

73. For more in the *Moniteur,* see Tucoo-Chala, *Charles-Joseph Panckoucke,* 475–490; also Kulstein, "Ideas of Charles Joseph Panckoucke." For a complete history of the *Encyclopédie méthodique,* see also Darnton, *Business of Enlightenment.*

74. The following discussion of the *Moniteur* is based on Tucoo-Chala, *Charles-Joseph Panckoucke,* 475–484; Darnton, *Business of Enlightenment,* 484; Bellanger (ed.), *Histoire générale de la presse française* 1:435, 441, 487–489, 507, 510, 535, 550, 554–558; and Popkin, "Journals," 151–154.

75. AN, ser. F18, carton 25, "Notes sur les imprimeurs ci-après désignés" (1810–1811).

Using his *Moniteur* profits, Agasse was able to sustain a serious publishing house, concentrating, like his father-in-law, on philosophy and natural sciences. Agasse registered twenty-five publications at the *dépôt légal* over the course of the republican period. Not surprisingly, his first deposit was the fifty-second to fifty-sixth installments of the *Encyclopédie méthodique*. Deposits of this work were to appear regularly on the *dépôt* lists during this period. Agasse also inherited a significant list of other books from Panckoucke; many of these, including Charles-François Dupuis's rationalist exposé of the *Origine de tous les cultes, ou religion universelle*, two editions of Jean de La Fontaine's *Fables,* and Montucla's *Histoire des mathématiques*, he successfully published during the Revolution.[76]

In 1795, following a government encouragement of 32,000 *livres*, Agasse registered a new work at the *dépôt:* Condorcet's *Esquisse d'un tableau historique des progrès de l'esprit*.[77] He made no further deposits until 1798, when he suddenly submitted a group of seventeen new titles: several scientific works by Jean-Baptiste de Monet de Lamarck and the chemist Antoine Baumé, as well as several works in political economy, including Adam Smith's *Essais philosophiques*. In 1798–1799 he also published two works intended for public instruction and an English novel by William Godwin.[78] Finally, in 1799, he began publishing LaHarpe's monumental survey of literary history, the *Lycée, ou cours de littérature*.

Despite their obvious differences, the revolutionary careers of all four of the "serious" book publishers—Didot *l'aîné*, Plassan, Buisson, and Agasse—had common characteristics that are worthy of attention. For one thing, all were printers as well as publishers. Although the enterprise Agasse inherited from Panckoucke was unparalleled in scale, it bore some striking resemblances to Buisson's business. First, the fortunes of both were founded in the unprecedented demand for political and commercial periodicals that emerged at the end of the eighteenth century, and especially after the freeing of the press in 1789. Second, each used this wealth derived from printing and publishing newspapers to launch less lucrative publishing ventures in serious works of philosophy, literature, and science. And third, both displayed a special interest in political economy and English works, particularly those of Adam Smith. As for Plassan, the report of the Napoleonic inspector suggests

76. Tucoo-Chala, *Charles-Joseph Panckoucke*, 491–495.

77. AN, ser. F4, carton 2554, doss. 4.

78. The two works for public instruction were a French grammar and François de Neufchâteau's *L'Institution des enfants, ou conseils d'un père*.

that his financial security was also linked to his printing business rather than his book publishing ventures.

All four of these publishers, moreover, relied to some extent on government subsidies to publish their serious books. The one among them who devoted himself exclusively to the fabrication of luxurious fine editions, Pierre Didot, was found to be unable to meet his payments. Serious works of high literature, science, and philosophy, in short, were incapable of sustaining themselves on the market: they required subsidies, whether in the form of profits earned from printing or periodicals, or in the form of government encouragements. If these careers are any indicator, they suggest that Villebrune and Grégoire were right: the revolutionary free market in ideas was incapable of spreading enlightenment, at least by means of printed books.

This is not to suggest that their enterprises did not respond to the demands of both the commercial market and the government's cultural agendas as they evolved throughout the republican period. They did. Indeed, we find an overwhelming interest in travel and political economy during the years just after Thermidor generally, with the evolution in the stocks of Agasse, Buisson, and Plassan more specifically revealing trends from classical and enlightenment philosophy, first toward travel narratives, political economy, and the natural sciences, and then toward the novel, especially the English novel. Even Didot *l'aîné*'s intensely conservative cultural instincts by 1798 could no longer check the irresistible temptation to invest in the publication of *Vicaire de Wakefield*.

Official Culture

The government's cultural policies played no small role in reorienting Paris publishing during the republican period. Government agencies alone deposited fifty-two works for copyright protection during those years. But the impact of official cultural policies extended far beyond government publications. In his speech to the National Convention on the need for "encouragements for men of letters" in 1794, Henri Grégoire noted with special concern the recent commercial failure of an edition of the works of the German archeologist Johann Joachim Winckelmann. The fate of works of great intellectual value such as this, Grégoire insisted, could not simply be left to the vicissitudes of the commercial literary market. They required government support.[79] Whether the Winckel-

---

79. Grégoire, *Rapport sur les encouragements*, 5.

mann edition received a government subsidy remains a mystery, but Grégoire was probably referring to the edition of Winckelmann's *Histoire de l'art chez les anciens,* which was submitted to the *dépôt légal* by the editor Henri Jansen in 1794. There can also be little doubt that the new cultural climate after Thermidor, initiated by Grégoire's call for a republican history and greater awareness of foreign cultures and geography, along with Garat's demand for translations of the important new German and English works, played no small role in reversing Jansen's fortune.

Henri Jansen arrived in Paris from The Hague in 1770 and applied his knowledge of German, English, and Dutch to a career as a translator and editor.[80] By 1791, Jansen had gone into publishing.[81] His business was foundering when it came to Grégoire's attention in 1794, whereupon it suddenly flourished under the Directory. Between 1793 and 1799 Jansen submitted to the *dépôt légal* more than twenty editions of serious works in history, politics, and philosophy, beginning in 1793. In 1794, the edition of Winckelmann's *Histoire de l'art* appeared on the *dépôt* registers, followed in 1795 by a translation of an Italian work of political philosophy. In 1796–1799 he deposited another group of philosophical and political works in translation, notably Joseph Priestley's *Discours sur l'histoire et sur la politique* and Emmanuel Kant's *Projet de paix perpetuelle,* as well as several volumes of voyages in Africa. Whether Jansen owed his brief but important publishing career directly to state patronage or merely to the cultural climate created by the government under the Directory remains obscure, but Jansen's publishing career clearly left him well placed and well regarded within elite political and cultural circles. In 1804, Jansen left the publishing business to become the librarian to Charles-Maurice de Talleyrand-Périgord, and after 1810 he was appointed as one of Napoleon's imperial censors of the book trade.[82]

Although the origins of the printer and publisher Honnert, who appeared on the rue du Colombier near the Abbaye St-Germain in 1795, are even more obscure, his connection to the cultural policies of the Directory cannot be mistaken. In 1796 Honnert's establishment housed the office of the *Nouvelliste littéraire des arts et sciences,* a literary journal edited by Lenoir and Morin, formed after Thermidor with the explicit purpose of wooing readers away from the passions of politics and to-

80. For biographical information on Jansen, see Michaud frères (eds.), *Biographie universelle* 20:550–551.

81. See the entry for H.-J. Jansen, in Delalain, *Imprimerie et la librairie à Paris,* 109.

82. Ibid.

ward useful sciences and the civilities of good literature.[83] Between 1795 and 1799 Honnert deposited sixteen of a total twenty volumes of the *Soirées littéraires ou mélanges de traductions nouvelles des plus beaux morceaux de l'antiquité,* a collection of classical literature in translation edited by the former royal censor and former professor of rhetoric at the Collège de Navarre, Jean-Marie Louis Coupé.[84] The great nineteenth-century bibliographers Joseph-François and Louis-Gabriel Michaud described the *Soirées* as "a kind of journal intended to restore good taste in literature."[85] There can be little doubt about the official character of this effort to soften the spirits and refine the manners of citizens by spreading classical literature: volume two was registered at the *dépôt* directly in the name of the Committee on Public Instruction. Apart from the *Soirées,* Honnert deposited five more volumes of classical literary texts, including Homer, Ovid, and Seneca, translated and edited by Coupé, and a volume of erotic novellas and poems by Eusèbe Salverte. Clearly well connected in the political circles of the Directory, in 1799 Honnert became the publisher of Lucien Bonaparte's novel *La Tribu indienne.* Then suddenly, like Jansen, after 1802 Honnert disappeared from the publishing scene. Nevertheless, however short-lived their enterprises, Jansen and Honnert made no small contribution to the revival and propagation of classical literature, philosophy, and science under the Directory.

Theater

At least six of the great publishing fortunes of the revolutionary period were made—or remade—in the genre of theatrical works. While Didot *l'aîné* cautiously crafted his fine editions of Racine and Molière the streets of republican Paris were being flooded with cheap editions of popular plays, vaudevilles, comic operas, and *faits historiques.*[86] Between 1793 and 1799, the *dépôt légal* registered nearly three hundred theatrical

83. The *Nouvelliste littéraire* was published in Paris from germinal, an IV (April 1796), to germinal, an IX (April 1806). See also above, chapter 4.

84. For more biographical information on Coupé, see Michaud frères (eds.), *Biographie universelle* 9:349–351.

85. Ibid., 351.

86. On the traditions of boulevard theater and vaudeville in the eighteenth century, see Robert Isherwood, *Farce and Fantasy: Popular Entertainment in Eighteenth-Century Paris* (Oxford: Oxford University Press, 1986). And on the explosion of popular theater after the collapse of the Old Regime privileges for theaters, see Root-Bernstein, *Boulevard Theater and Revolution,* esp. 201–229.

works: approximately fifty per year, almost all originating in Paris. Under the Republic, the Paris publishers L.-C. Huet, Pierre-Etienne Cholet, Louis Rondonneau, Claude-François Maradan, Mathieu Migneret, and Jean-Nicolas Barba reoriented the world of dramatic publishing from elite editions of the *Oeuvres de Molière* toward the popular *Souper de Molière* or *Le Quart d'heure de Rabelais*—and made a fortune in the process.

The popularity of comic opera and vaudeville alone was so intense that by the end of the period of the Directory two of these publishers, Huet and Cholet, specialized in these subgenres exclusively, and another, Rondonneau, devoted an entire sideline of his publishing business to it. The three of them alone accounted for 163 (over half) of the plays deposited at the *dépôt* between 1793 and 1799. L.-C. Huet first appeared in the Paris publishing world, according to the Napoleonic inspectors, in 1792.[87] He began submitting works to the *dépôt légal* shortly after it opened in 1794, starting with an operatic version of Henri Bernardin de St. Pierre's popular romance *Paul et Virginie*. Over the course of 1794 he registered nine more theatrical comedies, many with explicitly historical and political themes, such as *Les Vrais Sans-culottes* and *La Prise de Toulon*, as well as operatic romances like *Roméo et Juliette*. He also submitted a vaudeville by Louis-Abel Beffroy de Regny (known as "Cousin Jacques") entitled *Allons, ça va, ou le Quaker en France*, and a *fait historique* in one act, *La Famille indigente*. Huet made few deposits between 1795 and 1798. But his business must have continued to grow, because by 1800 he had opened a second shop.[88] And suddenly, as if in a panic, Huet appeared at the *dépôt légal* in 1799 with fifty-four plays, comic operas, and vaudevilles, ranging from serious tragedies like Baudouin *l'aîné*'s *Démétrius* to light comedies like the *Dupe de soi-même* by François Roger. His panic no doubt had something to do with Pierre-Etienne Cholet and his Théâtre et Imprimerie du Vaudeville.

With the exception of publishers of sheet music, Pierre-Etienne Cholet was the single most frequent depositer at the *dépôt légal*, registering ninety theatrical works between 1794 and 1799 alone. The earliest trace we have of Cholet's publishing activities during the revolutionary period is his first

87. AN, ser. F18, carton 25, "Notes sur les imprimeurs ci-après désignés" (1810–1811).

88. Delalain, *Imprimerie et la librairie*, 101. Delalain first places Huet on the rue Vivienne in 1797; a second shop, at the Palais du Tribunat, galerie du théâtre français, was opened in 1800. Huet is last traced by Delalain in 1804. The widow Huet becomes Mme Masson shortly thereafter and continues in business until her death in 1816. Nicolas-Charles Huet appears on the rue St-Jacques between 1810 and 1812.

deposit, of the play *L'Heureuse Décade, divertissements patriotiques, vaudeville,* in 1794. Cholet soon became the official printer and publisher of the Théâtre du Vaudeville.[89] The exact date of his association with the theater remains unclear, but in 1798 Cholet suddenly registered seventy-one vaudevilles, *faits historiques,* and comedies for copyright protection. By 1799 he had a printing shop on the rue des Droits de l'Homme and a bookshop on the rue de Malthe, at the Théâtre du Vaudeville, and was referring to himself as the "printer and publisher of the Vaudeville Theater."

Cholet's stock, more than that of anyone else, captured the revolutionary culture of working people. He had a line of eight harlequin plays in which traditional characters found new company with figures of a more decidedly revolutionary bent: thus, for example, *Arlequin décorateur, Arlequin cruello, Arlequin pygmalion, Arlequin tailleur,* and *Arlequin tout seul* were joined by those notorious disseminators of popular revolutionary culture *Arlequin afficheur* and *Arlequin journaliste.* It was Cholet, as well, who issued popularized classics like the *Souper de Molière* and *Le Quart d'heure de Rabelais.* He also published a series of new revolutionary plays that recounted historical tales, such as the life of Rousseau in the *Vallée de Montmorency, ou J. J. Rousseau dans son hermitage,* as well as dramatizations of recent news events depicting the little heroes of the Revolution in their everyday struggles to ward off the clergy, save the nation, console a broken family, or nurse the wounded and orphaned, in one-act *faits historiques* like *Encore un curé, Le Divorce, La Fille soldat, Le Canonier convalescent.* Thus the publisher Louis Prudhomme reminisced in 1814, with no small measure of cynicism and tragic insight:

> The Directory, which needed to corrupt the inhabitants of Paris in order to reenslave them more easily, and to make them forget the misery they had suffered and the famine that plagued them, multiplied the number of . . . theaters. There were theaters in shopfronts, and even on the fourth floors of houses in the faubourgs St-Jacques, St-Antoine, St-Martin, St-Denis, etc. . . . We saw at a shoemaker's, at the back of a courtyard, in the faubourg St-Denis, a theater, illuminated by candle stubs stuck onto the walls. This shoemaker was playing the lead roles of theatrical masterpieces.[90]

Where Henri Grégoire had envisaged the regenerative possibilities of "a new theater" infused with republican values, Louis Prudhomme, the

89. The Théâtre du Vaudeville was founded in 1791. It remains unclear exactly when Cholet first became associated with it.

90. Louis Prudhomme, *Voyage descriptif et philosophique de l'ancien et du nouveau Paris. Miroir fidèle* (Paris: Prudhomme, 1814), 1:24.

former publisher of the ultrarevolutionary *Révolutions de Paris,* insisted on a more Rousseauian, and hence more tragic, view of the popular craze for theater. He saw it as a cultural ruse to divert the masses from their political reenslavement by the wealthy ruling oligarchy of the Directory who had repressed the popular political movement in Paris after Thermidor.

Whether inspired by a self-conscious cultural conspiracy on the part of the political elites or by a popular longing for solace and entertainment, the commercial success of popular theater, and especially vaudeville, during the later years of the Directory is a fact. In the same few years, 1797–1799, the printer, law book publisher, and director of the national depository for laws, Louis Rondonneau, could not resist the temptation to get in on the vaudeville mania.[91] He associated with Huet and Thomas Brunet to produce thirty issues of a specialized periodical entitled *Les Diners du vaudeville,* eighteen issues of which ended up in the *dépôt légal.* But with the end of the republican period, the craze for vaudeville waned, and by 1807 the Paris guidebook *Le Pariséum* noted that "vaudeville has been out of fashion for some time."[92] Not surprisingly, however, at least some of the fortunes made in theater were quick to shift to new cultural terrain.

From Theater to the Novel

Three of the major publishers of the revolutionary period, Claude-François Maradan, Mathieu Migneret, and Jean-Nicolas Barba, used fortunes they built producing theatrical works to become key figures in the resurgence of literature, and particularly the novel, toward the end of the Directory period. The most prominent of them was the former Paris

---

91. For more on Louis Rondonneau's career during the Revolution, see Delalain, *Imprimerie et la librairie,* 184. His own biographical statement, written in 1814, can be found in the papers of the Ministry of Justice, AN, ser. BB16, carton 783, doss. 867. He was employed to catalogue manuscripts for the Académie de Belles Lettres from 1780 to 1788, then as manager of the office of accounting for the Assembly of Notables, and finally for the Estates General. In 1791, Rondonneau became "manager of the office of decrees and the archives of the keeper of the seals for the minister of justice," from which post he resigned in 1793. According to his account he founded the *dépôt des lois* with Anisson-Duperron, and then attempted to buy part of Anisson's *biens des condamnés* after his death (see AN, ser. AA, carton 56, doc. 1524). In 1793 he bought out the former guild member Prault's collection of laws, which became the basis of his *dépôt.* Between 1793 and 1799 he registered twenty-one titles at the *dépôt légal.* His first deposit is a law book, but then he went into theater publishing with Thomas Brunet in 1797. Rondonneau continued his business with his son Jacques-Charles until 1813. Over the course of the Revolution, Rondonneau regularly supplied the government with laws. In 1809 he ceded his business to his son-in-law, Dècle, who was not maintained as a printer in 1810. Finally, Rondonneau made a bid to become the official royal *dépôt des lois* in 1814.

92. Blanvillain, *Pariséum,* 322.

Book Guild member Maradan, with premises on the rue St-André des Arts. Maradan had specialized in the theater before the Revolution.[93] He also had extensive dealings in the underground book trade of the Old Regime.[94] In 1789 and 1790, Maradan, like many publishers, ventured briefly into periodical publishing.[95] And like many members of the old guild, he went bankrupt on April 24, 1790.[96] Although he was forced to sell off a large amount of his stock in theater,[97] Maradan rebounded—in no small part by rebuilding that same business in popular theater. In 1794, he registered at the *dépôt légal* nineteen plays (both contemporary and classic), a children's schoolbook, a translation of Edward Gibbon's *Histoire de la décadence et de la chute de l'empire romain,* one book on medicine, and a physics text by Jean-Baptiste de Monet de Lamarck. In 1795, in collaboration with another publisher, Smits, Maradan received the controversial government contract for the new fifth edition (\ the *Dictionnaire de l'Académie.*[98]

Then in 1796, he published a purportedly titillating novel by Mme Jeanne-Félicité Mérard de St. Just and another medical text. The next year, three English novels in translation appeared at the *dépôt* in his name, as well as two works of contemporary political history. In 1798, this trend in Maradan's deposits away from theater and toward science and English novels continued with the deposit of Mary Wollstonecraft's *Maria ou le malheur d'être femme;* another novel, *Frédéric et Jenny;* and two more medical works. In 1800, the newspaper *Amis des lois* reported that Maradan's light literary publications had captured the Parisian literary market. He apparently could not print them fast enough.[99] Maradan sustained a second bankruptcy on November 2, 1803.[100] But he appears to have bounced back yet again, this time not through theater, but through the novel. In 1804

93. See Jean-Yves Mollier, *L'Argent et les lettres. Histoire du capitalisme d'édition, 1880– 1920* (Paris: Fayard, 1988), 325.

94. See Belin, *Commerce des livres prohibés;* and AP, Fond Faillite, ser. D4B6, carton 106, doss. 7773.

95. Between 1789 and 1790 Maradan published the *Journal de la ville,* the *Journal de la ville, par Jean-Pierre-Louis de Luchet,* and finally the *Journal de la ville, par une société des gens de lettres.* See Rétat, *Journaux de 1789,* 134–139, 404.

96. AP, Fond Faillite, ser. D4B6, carton 109, doss. 7773, Declaration of bankruptcy, 1790. Maradan's assets totaled 701,035 *livres,* and his debits amounted to 646,953 *livres.*

97. See Mollier, *Argent et les lettres,* 325.

98. Guillaume (ed.), *Procès-verbaux du Comité d'Instruction Publique* 6:404–405, 443– 444, 501, 621, 680, 683, 688. See also Alphonse Aulard, ed., *Paris sous le Consulat,* (Paris: Le Cerf, 1903–1909), 3:416–417.

99. See Aulard (ed.), *Paris sous le Consulat* 1:330.

100. AP, Fond Faillite, ser. D11U3, carton 23. His assets totaled 584,429 *livres,* and his debits amounted to 391,020 *livres.*

Maradan moved to the rue des Grands Augustins. By 1807 the guidebook *Pariséum* cited Maradan as the premier Paris bookdealer specializing in novels.[101]

A similar pattern can be detected in the career of Mathieu Migneret. Before the Revolution, Migneret was the shop floor supervisor for the guild printer Pierre-François Gueffier. With the declaration of the freedom of the press Migneret opened his own printing shop on the rue Jacob. Migneret did not, however, start registering works at the *dépôt* until 1797, when he brought out six theatrical comedies and vaudevilles. At the same time, he also began depositing a series of Jean-François de La-Harpe's works, including *De l'état des lettres en Europe* (2d ed.), *Du fanatisme dans la langue révolutionnaire* (2d ed.), *La Guerre déclarée par nos derniers tyrans à la raison*, and *Réfutation du livre de l'esprit*, as well as a medical text, Alexis Boyer's *Traité complet d'anatomie*. In 1798, Migneret moved more solidly in the direction of theater, registering three operas and ten dramatic comedies. He also brought out LaHarpe's *Pseautier*.[102] But in 1799 Migneret took a new turn, depositing an English novel, *Le Faux Ami*, by Mary Darby Robinson.[103] During the next few years Migneret really struck gold, with editions of Chateaubriand—first *Le Génie du christianisme*, and then *Atala*—who sold so well and so fast, Migneret could barely keep him in print.[104]

But no career more vividly illustrates the evolution of key publishers from theater to the novel over the revolutionary period than that of Jean-Nicolas Barba. Barba first appeared in the Palais Royal in 1791, where he took over the fledgling establishment of two old members of the Paris Book Guild, Jean-Nicolas Duchesne and Etienne-Théodore Dabo.[105] He also bought the huge stock of theater titles that Maradan was forced to sell after his bankruptcy in 1790.[106] Between 1795 and 1799 Barba registered thirty-eight works at the *dépôt*. His first deposit

101. Blanvillain, *Pariséum*, 205.

102. In 1801 he bought de LaHarpe's entire corpus from the author; see Christopher Todd, *Voltaire's Disciple: Jean-François de LaHarpe* (London: Modern Humanities Research Library, 1972), 73.

103. During the first Empire, Migneret's business took yet another turn. In 1810 he was described by the Napoleonic inspectors as dealing exclusively in medicine and surgery and as attached to the emperor's surgeon, Boyer. He was maintained as a printer in 1810. See AN, ser. F18, carton 25, "Notes sur les imprimeurs ci-après désignés" (1810–1811).

104. See Alphonse Aulard (ed.), *Paris sous le Consulat* 2:229, 282; 4:699.

105. See Nicole Felkay, *Balzac et ses éditeurs, 1822–1837. Essai sur la librairie romantique* (Paris: Promodis, 1987), 31, 34, 89, 106–107; and Mollier, *Argent et les lettres*, 325.

106. Ibid.

was Charles-Pierre Ducancel's Thermidorean drama *L'Intérieur des comités révolutionnaires*. All of his titles were in theater, ranging from serious tragedies like Marie-Joseph Chénier's *Azémire* or the theatrical rendering of Voltaire's great anticlerical cause in *Jean Calas*, to comic operas like Severin's *Le Villageois qui cherche son veau*.

He was also a notorious literary pirate and dealer in pornography. In 1796, he was accused of pirating Philippe Fabre d'Eglantine's *Intrigue épistolaire*, and in 1797, Migneret's edition of de LaHarpe's *Du fanatisme dans la langue révolutionnaire*.[107] By 1802 Barba was, as the prefect of Paris described him, "very well known for this kind of trade."[108] Barba also orchestrated numerous illegal editions of the marquis de Sade's *Justine*, until the police finally discovered his secret warehouse in 1802.[109] Known for driving hard bargains, both legal and illegal, Barba was enormously successful.

By 1795 he had moved to the rue Git-le-coeur, in the heart of the old publishing district, and he maintained a second shop in the Palais Royal. Five years later he also had an outlet nearer to the theater at the Palais du Tribunat. Having founded one of the great publishing fortunes of the revolutionary era through popular theater, pornography, and literary pirating, Barba, too, branched out into the novel, beginning with Guillaume-Charles-Antoine Pigault-Lebrun's libertine romances. By the 1820s Barba had become one of the first editors of Honoré de Balzac.[110] Like Maradan and Migneret, Barba was instrumental in turning Paris publishing from classical theater to the romantic novel, from civic to domestic genres.

The early years of the Revolution witnessed an explosion in the number of newspapers, pamphlets, and other ephemera that poured forth to

107. For the case of Fabre d'Eglantine, see Aristide P. Douarche, *Les Tribunaux civils de Paris pendant la Révolution (1791–1800): documents inédits recueillis avant l'incendie du Palais de Justice de 1871 par Casenave* (Paris: Le Cerf, 1905–1907), 2:305 (5 floréal, an IV [April 24, 1796]). For the case of LaHarpe, see ibid., 2:435 (14 fructidor, an V [August 31, 1797]).

108. See the report of the prefect of Paris to the minister of police of September 11, 1802, in Aulard (ed.), *Paris sous le Consulat*, 3:245.

109. For the history of this case see the reports from the prefect of Paris to the minister of police of July 27 and 29, September 10 and 11, 1802, and September 13, 1803, in ibid., 3:178, 180, 245, 247, and 250.

110. See Nicole Felkay, *Balzac et ses éditeurs*, 31, 34, 89, and 106–107; and Jean-Yves Mollier, *Argent et les lettres*, 200.

meet the public demand for political news and debate after 1789. After being strictly limited to thirty-six for over a century, the number of printing shops in Paris therefore suddenly quadrupled. Yet while the periodical press flourished between 1789 and 1794, book publishing collapsed as a consequence of the ruthless deregulation of the book trade and the diversion of the nation's elites toward political rather than cultural concerns. Even so, political news was not all that thrived after the freeing of the presses: cheap popular romances did as well. After Thermidor, massive government intervention in the publishing world and the reopening of international markets ushered in a new cultural moment marked by a revival of book publishing in all genres, but especially classical literature and history, as well as political economy and the natural sciences. Theatrical and pedagogical works addressed to a broader audience also flourished after 1795. Finally, by 1798, the novel, and particularly the English novel, had begun to capture a significant share of the Parisian literary market.

The printing and publishing fortunes of the French Revolution thus disclose two major cultural consequences of the freeing of the presses in 1789. First, there was a deep yet perceptible shift of the center of gravity in commercial printing, from an elite literary culture centered in the production and consumption of expensive and time-consuming books toward a democratic culture of ephemeral pamphlets, broadsides, song sheets, and especially newspapers and periodicals. Second, the greatest publishing houses of Paris developed their literary portfolios more broadly, moving from classical texts, enlightenment philosophy, and politics in the early years of the Revolution, toward theater, history, and the sciences under the Directory, and finally toward the novel with the coming of the first Empire. If Agasse's *Moniteur,* with its eighty-five hundred subscribers, most embodied the nineteenth-century legacy of Panckoucke's *Encyclopédie* by putting useful information and enlightened opinions into the hands of the people, it was publishers like Maradan and Barba who, through fortunes amassed in popular theater, pornography, and literary piracy, created a bridge spanning the cultural distance between the salons of Voltaire and the literary marketplace of Balzac.

The New Literary World

Taken as a whole, the records of the *dépôt légal* for the years 1793–1799 offer an extraordinary panorama of the literary civilization created by the French Revolution, or at least of those productions to which authors and publishers attributed enduring value and hence sought to insure their legal claim (table 3). Music and literature clearly dominated commercial publishing, despite the bias of official deposits toward works published or supported by, or seeking favor, from the government. Only in 1793 did deposits of political works exceed those in literature, and that almost exclusively because of the deposits of the Cercle Social. Publishers of sheet music and songs were by far the most frequent clients of the *dépôt légal,* and most notably Imbault, Naderman, Vogt, Pleyel, and Boyer, who deposited between 40 and 280 pieces of sheet music each during the six years of the Republic. In the category of literature, the popular literary genres, such as songs, theater pieces, and novels, as opposed to classical literature, poetry, memoirs, and correspondence, dominated the publishing world of the Revolution. On the whole, the record confirms the perception of the head of the Bibliothèque Nationale, Jean-Baptiste Lefebvre de Villebrune, that it was fictions rather than truths, literature rather than history, philosophy, and science, that issued forth from the freed presses and literary markets after 1789. While deposits in all categories of literature, with the exception of songs, increased markedly in 1798, the novel showed a striking upward trend a year earlier, in 1797 (see appendix 5). By 1801, the annalist Pujoulx wondered when the passion for novels would be sated: "First it was a rage, then it became an addiction; now it is nothing short of a mania. . . . They are translated, composed, recopied, old ones are reprinted; and in spite of this, the demand for them can barely be satisfied."[111]

Nor was it just the political elites who expressed suspicions and concern about the corrupting effects of a literary market dominated by popular romances. Outcry against the novel came from members of the old publishing elite as well, who remained wedded to a vision of literary life firmly rooted in classicism, entombed in lengthy and lavish volumes, and sustained by patronage and protectionism rather than market demand. Thus the publisher Louis Ravier wrote that novels

> render those who read them soft and effeminate; the young reader . . . no longer sees anything in a military career but perils and exhaustion, in jurisprudence nothing but the art of negotiation and empty debate, in the duties of a husband nothing but burdens, and in commerce nothing but cold calculation. His thoughts will turn only to repose and pleasure.

111. J.-B. Pujoulx, *Paris à la fin du XVIIIe siècle* (Paris: Mathé, 1801), 26.

Table 3 Works Registered at the *Dépôt Légal*, Bibliothèque Nationale,
July 19, 1793–December 31, 1799, by Genre

	1793[a]	1794	1795	1796	1797	1798	1799	Total
Arts	3	0	2	2	6	10	7	30
Music	0	178	105	132	99	114	203	831
Education	2	18	12	3	7	22	20	84
Geography	3	5	3	3	2	8	9	33
History	0	9	3	3	16	27	24	82
Law	1	1	2	1	6	10	20	41
Literature	13	115	84	87	132	269	297	997
Philosophy	8	7	3	10	15	20	10	73
Politics	22	27	16	14	31	38	37	185
Religion	3	5	0	4	12	8	3	35
Science	4	11	9	19	26	94	71	234
Technical	10	20	12	9	10	37	39	137
Total	69 (6)[b]	396 (1)	251 (5)	287 (9)	362 (13)	657 (31)	740 (38)	2,778[c] (103)

SOURCE: Archives Modernes, CXXIX, "Registres du dépôt légal des livres imprimés" (July 19, 1793–December 31, 1799).
[a]July 19–December 31, 1793, only.
[b]Numbers in parentheses indicate number of books submitted by non-Parisian publishers.
[c]Total includes 16 unidentified works.

. . . Novels pass from the hands of [women and young men] into those of their children, and from there into the servants' quarters, and from there into the kitchen; they bring all the diverse classes of society together, . . . by seeding passion in every heart they seduce them by the same principles of weaknesses or exaltation.[112]

For Ravier, freedom of commerce in publishing seemed to be corroding the most fundamental elements of the natural, social, and civic orders: the distinctions between children and adults, men and women, and servants and mistresses. Jacob *l'aîné*, former syndic of the book guild in Orléans, drew an even broader picture of the evils that had ensued from the revolutionary deregulation of the printing trades and literary commerce. He saw a direct connection between the explosion in the number of journals and ephemeral literature in the early years of the Revolution and the boom in the novel as the republican period closed:

> When France found itself inundated with journals that disappeared almost as quickly as they saw the light of day, each journalist still wanted to keep his own printing shop. One or two presses, a single type character, sufficed to satisfy this ambition. Abandoned by their subscribers, they rebuilt their businesses in *novels,* the graveyard of literature, good taste, or more accurately, the seed of corruption and scandal. . . .
>
> The new book dealers became the *entrepôts* of the novelists, so that they could spread with profusion . . . the poison that is distilled in the majority of their works.[113]

Both Jacob and Ravier explicitly linked the craze in the novel to the freeing of the press and deregulation. Journals, political ephemera, and then the novel, according to Jacob, were the three distinctive cultural contributions of the liberated printing and publishing world of revolutionary Paris. Further, he argued that with the waning (and, he might have added, repression) of political passions after Thermidor, the producers of journals and political ephemera redirected their enterprises toward novels, in order to exploit more private passions—those of the heart.

Moreover, Ravier and Jacob both insisted that the private consumption of novels was not without public and political consequence. Despite their seeming innocence, novels corrupted public morals and weakened

112. Ravier, *Répertoire de la librairie,* xliii–xliv.

113. Louis Jacob, l'aîné, *Idées générales sur les causes de l'anéantissement de l'imprimerie et sur la nécessité de rendre à cette profession, ainsi qu'à celle de la librairie, le rang honorable qu'elles ont toujours tenues l'une et l'autre parmi les arts libéraux* (Orléans: Jacob l'aîné, 1806).

the body politic, tempting young men and women away from the responsibilities and duties of family life and effeminizing the sons of the Republic. Novels celebrated private pleasures over public virtues. Worse still, by passing freely between wives and maids, they eroded class boundaries within the household and threatened to disrupt the social as well as the sexual and civic order.

But if popular literature, and increasingly the novel, dominated the literary markets of the Republic, the copyright records nonetheless reveal a positive impact of intensive government patronage beginning under the Terror and expanding after Thermidor, particularly in scientific and technical publishing, but also in classical literature, history, travel, and political philosophy (see appendix 5). These works clearly contributed in no small part to the revival of book publishing after Thermidor. As Jean Dhombre has shown, scientific publishing not only revived, but it also considerably improved both the quantity and the quality of texts produced in the closing years of the Directory.[114] Publishers like Aubry, Plassan, Honnert, Buisson, Agasse, and Jansen all responded to the government's calls from the year II (1793–1794) on for a new pedagogy, a new literature, a new history, and a new science.

A central cultural tension thus emerged in the publishing world under the Republic: between a commercial literary market dominated by political journals and novels that inflamed the public and private passions of citizens, on the one hand, and a subsidized official culture that sought to inculcate the cool discipline of scientific reason and to propagate the republican virtues of utility, productivity, and the public good, on the other. In the literary world at any rate, the revolutionary tension between capitalism and republicanism came to express itself as a rivalry between *eros* and *philos*.

114. Dhombres, "Books: Reshaping Science."

CHAPTER SIX

Crisis, Again, and Administrative Solutions, 1799–1810

The Crisis

In the last years of the eighteenth century, the government poured millions of *livres* in aid into the book publishing world, and scores of new book publishing and selling establishments opened in the capital. The number of titles registered per year at the *dépôt légal* climbed steadily from 1797 onward, doubling by 1799 (362 to 740) and increasing by another half in 1802 (1,329), where it leveled off before leaping up again in 1806 (1,536).[1] Figures for new novels alone reveal a similar trend, increasing steadily from 1795 onward, surging up in 1799 (from 96 to 174), and reaching a plateau at the turn of the century (151).[2] Yet although the bare numbers indicate a significant revival of the French book trade at the beginning of the nineteenth century, the account books of Parisian publishers offer a more sobering picture.

In 1799, at least three significant bankruptcies, involving outstanding debts (*passifs*) of over 100,000 *livres*, sent a minor tremor through the publishing community (figure 5).[3] A second tremor of similar intensity and

---

1. Estivals, *Statistique bibliographique*, 415. See also Bellos, "Conjoncture de la production," 552–557.

2. Martin, Milne, and Frautschi, *Bibliographie du genre romanesque français*, xxxvii.

3. AP, Fond Faillite, ser. D11U3, carton 8, August 3, 1799, anonymous "printer"; August 30, 1799, Henri Gabriel Nicolle, publisher; and ibid., carton 9, September 3, 1799, Guillaume Denné *le jeune*, publisher. Despite the monetary reforms of the year IX (1800–1801), Paris printers and publishers continued to compute their accounts in *livres* rather than *francs*. According to the expert Guy Thuillier, the use of *livres* was standard practice in the business community until the end of the decade. In any case, the difference in value,

financial impact occurred two years later, in 1802.[4] And in 1803, Paris publishers witnessed a full-scale financial earthquake. Twelve more publishers declared bankruptcy.[5] The crisis not only widened, it deepened, hitting some of the larger and more extended establishments: Nicolas Fauvelle, a printer, with a *passif* of 100,458 *livres;* Jacques-Denis Langlois, publisher-printer, with debts totaling 102,979 *livres;* Nicolas Moutardier, publisher, owing 268,870 *livres;* the publisher Claude-François Maradan, with 378,329 *livres* in outstanding debts; Jean-François Ouvrier, publisher, with a *passif* of 110,534 *livres;* and François Dufart *père*, printer and publisher, defaulting on 254,352 *livres* of debts.[6] In all, the debts disavowed through bankruptcy in 1803 soared to 1,579,099 *livres*, bringing the amount of default for the years 1799–1803 to a grand total of 1,773,562 *livres*.

In the next few years, things only went from bad to worse. Seven more bankruptcies came in 1804, adding another 898,848 *livres* to the total debt.[7] Two publishers, Fuchs and Louis-Edme Gérard, each owed over 200,000 *livres*.[8] Six more members of the community declared themselves

---

for our purposes, is not very significant: in 1799–1800, 5 *francs* equaled approximately 5 *livres*, 1 *sou*, and 3 *deniers*. See Thuillier's *La Monnaie en France au début du XIXe siècle* (Geneva: Droz, 1983), 68–69.

4. AP, Fond Faillite, ser. D11U3, carton 16, August 5, 1802, Mathieu Carvin, publisher; October 22, 1802, Antoine Caillot, publisher; and ibid., carton 17, December 31, 1802, Antoine Lenoir, publisher. The total *passif* for 1802 (with figures available for only two of the three accounts) was 84,060 *livres*.

5. Ibid., carton 18, January 19, 1803, Jacques-Philippe Jacob, publisher-printer; ibid., carton 19, April 14, 1803, Nicolas Fauvelle, printer; April 30, 1803, Jacques-Henri Tardieu, publisher-printer; ibid., carton 20, July 7, 1803, François-Marie Marchand, publisher; July 9, 1803, Louis Cordier and François Legras, publisher-printers; July 19, 1803, Jacques-Denis Langlois, publisher-printer; ibid., carton 21, August 27, 1803, Nicolas Moutardier, publisher; ibid., carton 21, October 12, 1803, Delaplace, publisher; ibid., carton 23, November 2, 1803, Claude-François Maradan, publisher; November 2, 1803, Jean-François Ouvrier, publisher; November 29, 1803, Henri-Joseph-Philogone Meurant, publisher; and December 1, 1803, François Dufart *père*, publisher-printer.

6. See note 5.

7. AP, Fond Faillite, ser. D11U3, carton 24, February 2, 1804, Fuchs, publisher; February 2, 1804, Brochot *père*, publisher; February 10, 1804, Jean-Charles Poncelin and wife Marie-Geneviève-Béatrix Debarle, publishers; February 16, 1804, Louis-Edme Gérard, publisher; March 28, 1804, Claude-Augustin Léger, publisher; ibid., carton 25, April 11, 1804, Pierre-Henri Genest, publisher; and ibid., carton 26, August 14, 1804, Jacques-Henri Tardieu, publisher-printer.

8. See note 7.

in default the following year.[9] This crash brought down some of the oldest, wealthiest, and most reputable members of the Paris community, like Eugène Onfroy, François-Jean Baudouin, and Adrien Leclerc.[10] The losses for 1805 ran to at least 883,669 *livres,* not including Baudouin, whose accounts, unfortunately, no longer exist. And the situation was to get worse still. Yet another thirteen bankruptcies marked 1806 (counting Pierre-François Didot *le jeune,* whose records have been lost).[11] Five of these publishers declared over 100,000 *livres* each in outstanding debts.[12] The bankruptcy of Frédéric Schoell and Company alone broke the one million *livres* mark.[13]

Between 1799 and 1806, then, at least forty-two publishers, printers, or booksellers declared bankruptcy—nearly *one-fifth* of the publishers in the capital, accounting for almost half the total number of publishing and printing bankruptcies for which we have a record between 1770 and 1806. The outstanding debts of the bankrupt Parisian publishers, printers, and booksellers between 1799 and 1806 came in all to over 5.5 million *livres.* It was a crisis of unprecedented proportions.

Of course, printers and book publishers were not the only sector of the Parisian commercial world to go into default in the opening years of the nineteenth century, and especially in 1805–1806. The year 1805 was altogether one of national financial reckoning, with the crisis precipitated by the declaration of default by the directors of the newly founded

9. AP, Fond Faillite, ser. D11U3, carton 27, February 22, 1805, Jean-François Ouvrier, publisher; March 6, 1805, Eugène Onfroy, publisher; March 15, 1805, François-Jean Baudouin, printer-publisher; April 11, 1805, Pierre-Marie-Sebastien Catineau, printer; ibid., carton 29, September 12, 1805, Germain-Aignon Benoist-Dumont, publisher; and October 29, 1805, Adrien Leclerc, publisher.

10. See note 9.

11. AP, Fond Faillite, ser. D11U3, carton 32, January 18, 1806, Laurent-Mathieu Guillaume, publisher; ibid., carton 33, February 14, 1806, J. Pierre Hénée, printer-publisher; February 14, 1806, Frédéric Schoell et Cie., publisher; ibid., carton 34, March 20, 1806, Philippe-Laurent Caillat, printer; March 29, 1806, Hermann Henrichs, publisher; ibid., carton 35, April 16, 1806, Mme Richard (widow of Jean-Georges-Antoine Stoupe), publisher; April 24, 1806, N.-L. Achaintre, publisher; ibid., carton 36, July 2, 1806, François-Marie Marchand, printer; ibid., carton 37, September 4, 1806, Jean-Nicolas Barba, publisher; October 18, 1806, anonymous printer; and ibid., carton 38, December 15, 1806, Charles-Frédéric Perlet, publisher. For the bankruptcy of Didot, see AN, ser. BB16, carton 760, doss. 5723, Complaint of M. Marervaux, creditor of Didot *le jeune,* to the minister of justice, concerning the liability for Didot's debts. He attests that Didot declared bankruptcy on December 2, 1806.

12. See note 11.

13. See note 11. Schoell declared his *passif* (outstanding debts) to be 1,057,584 *livres.*

Banque de France in November 1805 sending shockwaves throughout the Parisian commercial world and, in turn, causing the number of bankruptcies in Paris to skyrocket.[14] The troubles in Paris book publishing were thus part of a larger financial storm.

Indeed, the minister of justice reported to the minister of police in April 1803 that the financial crisis, and specifically the loss of easy credit, was driving under "several major Paris publishing houses."[15] But the crisis also took on specific characteristics within the world of print. According to the prefect of Paris, although the printing industry in that city had long been in a slump, the epicenter of the current crisis was in publishing rather than printing.[16] Of the forty-two businesses that declared bankruptcy, only four were exclusively printers. Nonetheless, the printers were in no condition to meet such a crisis, for they had troubles of their own.

The battle with the Imprimerie de la République continued, but then Napoleon's coup d'état on 18 brumaire, year VIII (November 9, 1799), reawakened their hopes. Within a month of the coup the newly constituted consuls received another petition from twenty-five printers of Paris denouncing the monopoly of the Imprimerie de la République. In contrast with the petitions and pamphlets of the year III (1794–1795), the complainants' tone had become less accusative and more beseeching: "All the printing shops of Paris . . . are languishing in ruinous inaction," they wrote. "It is not upon declamations . . . that we found our demand, but upon equality, which grants each citizen the right to utilize his talents."[17] Their appeals, however, were met with yet another reaffir-

14. For an overview of the banking and credit crisis of 1805–1806, see A. Dauphin-Meunier, *La Banque de France* (Paris: Gallimard, 1936), 46–52; Robert Bigo, *Les Banques françaises au cours du XIXe siècle* (Paris: Sirey, 1947), 89–98, 128–133; and Louis Bergeron, *Banquiers, négociants et manufacturiers parisiens du Directoire à l'Empire* (Paris: Mouton, 1978), 282–292. I would like to thank Tom Luckett for sharing his unpublished research on Parisian bankruptcies during the revolutionary period, to appear shortly as "Credit and Society in Eighteenth-Century France."

15. See the report from the minister of justice to the minister of police of April 28, 1803, in Aulard (ed.), *Paris sous le Consulat* 4:26.

16. See the reports from the prefect of Paris to the minister of police of July 11, 1802, and October 19, 1803, in ibid., 3:149 and 4:440–441.

17. AN, ser. BB4, carton 33, doc. 3, *Pétition présentée aux consuls de la République, par les imprimeurs de Paris soussignés* [signed "frimaire, an VIII, Knapen, Prault, Stoupe, Clousier, Pierres, Couturier, Ballard, Quillaud, Baudouin, Lottin, Didot *l'aîné*, Didot *le jeune*, Agasse, Plassan, Belin, Barbou, Gratoit, Crapelet, Goujon, Migneret, Boiste, Leclerc, Veuve Delaguette, Veuve Panckoucke, Citoyenne Huzard"] (Paris: Stoupe), 1.

mation of the wide purview of the Imprimerie de la République on 19 frimaire, year X (December 10, 1801).[18]

Further, in October 1803, the Consulate created a commission charged with the task of centralizing and standardizing publishing contracts for classical texts to be used in the schools. This initiative brought forth a collective outcry from eighty-seven publishers and printers of Paris against these new affronts to "the friends of letters and sciences, and of the freedom of the press, rightly understood."[19] To make matters worse, in the first year of its rule the Consulate implemented radical measures to limit and control the political press: at the moment of the coup d'état in 1799, there were approximately sixty political journals in Paris; by a decree of 27 nivôse, year VIII (January 17, 1800), the consuls reduced that number to thirteen.[20]

With the losses of government contracts and then the suppression of nearly fifty Parisian periodicals, the financial crisis in the commerical book publishing community hit the printers hard as well. The Napoleonic inspectors therefore compiled a long list of small tragedies to report for the largest and finest printing shops in Paris. In considering the eighty most substantial and reputable printers, for example, the inspector noted that Pierre-Robert-Christophe Ballard "had suffered losses."[21] As for François-Jean Baudouin's troubles, "his plight is well known" and so required no details. Even Pierre Didot *l'aîné*, "despite his fame, found himself unable to meet his payments." The Jacobin printer Charles-Frobert Patris, who lost 40,000 *livres*, and Louis Prudhomme were forced to bankruptcy. The printer Georges-Adrien Crapelet's father, the inspector noted, "died of bitterness, having lost 150,000 francs to publishers." So, too, François Belin and J.-J. Delance "had seen bad times." Jean-Ange Clô had been an associate of Adrien Leclerc "before the latter went bankrupt, causing him a loss of 75 percent," and Jean-Joseph Laurent *l'aîné* "has been under the threat of bankruptcy." Finally, the giant Levrault establishment "had declared a bankruptcy whose total reached 800,000

18. Duprat, *Histoire de l'Imprimerie Impériale*, 403. After yet another round of protests and debates, the purview of the Imprimerie Impériale was again reaffirmed by a decree of March 24, 1809; see ibid., 410.

19. *Les Imprimeurs et libraires de Paris, au Ministre de l'Intérieur* (Paris, an XII [1803–1804]).

20. André Cabanis, *La Presse sous le Consulat et l'Empire (1799–1814)* (Paris: Société des Etudes Robespierristes, 1975), 11–13, 319.

21. All the cases mentioned in this paragraph are in AN, ser. F18, carton 25, "Notes sur les imprimeurs ci-après désignés" (1810–1811).

francs." With little else to hold onto when the commercial publishers went under, the printers went with them. It was not surprising that the struggle over government contracts was so intense and so sustained.

The characteristics of the publishing and printing crisis of 1803–1806 were remarkably different from those of the crisis of the 1790s. That decade saw an explosion of the periodical press that caught book publishers off guard. They witnessed the total collapse of the book market following the declaration of the freedom of the press, as well as the devaluation of their stock in the face of the revolutionary demand for *nouveautés* and *lumières*. Revolution and then war drove their principal clientele to emigrate and closed down their international markets. In contrast, the early nineteenth century saw a forced contraction of the periodical press by government decree. Book publishing, in turn, appeared to be flourishing, and émigré readers of "long-winded works" were beginning to return to France. What, then, caused the crisis in commercial book publishing? Both the publishers and the imperial government wanted answers.

Government Inquiry

The consuls were aware of the crisis in the book trade. Even before the great banking crisis of 1805, recognition of the need to reform publishing was in the air. On 28 nivôse, year XI (January 18, 1803), for example, the consuls received a report from the head of the Bureau of Arts and Manufactures in Paris, detailing the disarray of the book trade and calling for reform of the legislation of July 19, 1793.[22] A year later, the newly formed Council of State began a formal inquiry into the situation. The ministers of justice and the police set out to solicit information and policy recommendations from notable printers and publishers in preparation for a full-scale reform. Thus the former printer for the Crown in Paris, Philippe-Denis Pierres, reported on 15 fructidor, year XII (September 2, 1804), that "six months ago, the Chief Justice charged me to draw up a plan for the reorganization of French printing, publishing,

---

22. AN, ser. F18, carton 10a, plaque 1, doss. 18, "Rapport au gouvernement: exposition des principes qui ont dirigé la rédaction du projet d'une loi relative à la propriété des auteurs," Costaz *le jeune*, director of the Bureau of Arts and Manufactures, 28 nivôse, an XI (January 18, 1803).

and book selling."[23] Over the next six years the government was to receive numerous reports and proposals from the elites of France's post-revolutionary publishing and printing world. These memos offer rare insight into the causes and character of the crisis in the republican book publishing world. The universal call was for re-regulation of the trade. But along what lines, and toward what ends?

There was little doubt about the devastating effect the credit crisis of 1805 had on book publishing. The printer Jean-Georges-Antoine Stoupe issued a pamphlet in 1804 denouncing corrupt "speculators in false bankruptcies" as the main cause of the financial crisis.[24] But in 1807 the publisher Louis Ravier offered greater illumination on the subject. According to Ravier, after nearly a decade of devastation under the Revolution, the book trade had indeed begun to revive in the last years of the eighteenth century, and especially after the March 1802 Treaty of Amiens reopened the British and European markets to Paris book dealers. No sooner had they begun to take advantage of this situation, however, than the peace broke down, leaving publishers in the lurch with their investments.[25] But the real key to the recent financial vicissitudes of the publishing world, in Ravier's estimation, lay in the revival of credit institutions under the Directory, and especially the opening of the Commercial Discount Bank in 1797.

With renewed access to credit, book publishers overplayed their hands. The Commercial Discount Bank, Ravier wrote, although a "fecund source of prosperity for those businessmen who use it with measure, . . . has brought about the ruin of several Parisian publishers because of their abuse of it." Some publishers as much as quintupled their capital through credit in order to invest in huge speculations, he reported, and then found that the market did not respond with adequate sales.[26] Then the crisis hit. They had overextended in anticipation of the recovery of the European market, and then the Commercial Discount Bank was forced to close in April 1803 and to call in its bills at the

23. BN, nouv. acq. fr. 12684, "Documents et correspondance concernant Philippe-Denis Pierres, imprimeur à Versailles (1741–1808)," feuille 63, Petition from Pierres to His Majesty the Emperor.

24. Jean-Georges-Antoine Stoupe, *Réflexions sur les contrefaçons en librairie, suivies d'un mémoire sur le rétablissement de la communauté des imprimeurs de Paris* (Paris, an XII [1803–1804]); reedited in 1806 as *Mémoire sur le rétablissement de la communauté des imprimeurs de Paris, suivi de réflexions sur les contrefaçons en librairie et sur le stéréotypage.*

25. Ravier, *Répertoire de la librairie*, xv–xvi.

26. Ibid., xvi.

very same moment that the newly established peace began to fail. The result was disaster. Here is how Ravier described it:

> When this bank was closed down . . . it was impossible to raise the actual sums from their merchandise in order to settle with the bank. This brought on bankruptcies, and more bankruptcies. They succeeded each other during this period with frightening rapidity. . . . For the first time a single publishing house declared a bankruptcy of over a million, and another of more than eight hundred thousand francs, etc.[27]

Since the renewal of the war with England, Ravier concluded, the French book trade found itself again limited to the borders of the empire.

Beyond the general issue of the credit crisis, publishers and printers blamed factors specific to the state of the industry. Stoupe called for the reestablishment of a printer's guild and a restriction of the number of printing shops as the only remedy to the current moral deterioration, attested to, he asserted, by the large number of literary speculations ending in bankruptcy.[28] He was seconded in this view by Pierre-Marie-Sebastien Catineau-LaRoche, a printer in Versailles.[29] Calls for limits on the number of printing shops came from other corners as well. The former royal printer in Orléans, Louis Jacob *l'aîné*, also demanded new restrictions on the number of printers, but for different reasons than Stoupe. According to Jacob, the problem was not corrupt credit practices, but genuine commercial stagnation, which was driving honest and hard-working printers to the humiliation of bankruptcy.[30] This stagnation, he argued, resulted from overproduction. There were too many printers serving France, and especially Paris; moreover, they were serving poorly. Thus he wrote:

> In the first few years of the Revolution, did the demand for printed matter expand to the point of requiring, in a very short time, the founding of eight hundred printing shops in Paris, in place of thirty-eight, and an equally disproportionate number in the departments? I dare to say no. And I submit that the quantity of *posters,* the mass of *newspapers,* and the

27. Ibid.

28. Stoupe, *Réflexions sur les contrefaçons en librairie.*

29. Pierre-Marie-Sebastien Catineau-LaRoche, *Réflexions sur la librairie, dans lesquelles on traite les propriétés littéraires, des contrefaçons, de la censure, de l'imprimerie et de la librairie* (Versailles: Catineau-LaRoche, 1807).

30. Jacob l'aîné, *Idées générales sur les causes de l'anéantissement de l'imprimerie,* 5.

infinity of other *ephemeral works* did not replace the void suddenly created by the absence of literature. For a few moments, the printers employed by the government or the local administrations truly did augment the number of their presses; but this expansion could never compensate for the loss of the other work, which ceased the moment men of letters could no longer think of anything but saving their own lives. The disappearance of *church books* and works of *jurisprudence* left an equally important lacuna.[31]

The collapse of the book trade had not been compensated for by the explosion in ephemeral matter. To make matters worse, according to Jacob, what was left of the printing business was now being eaten up by a crowd of new, smaller printers:

> *Portable printing presses,* which sold in profusion, were . . . the first blow. . . . In the beginning acquired *merely for a hobby,* these little printing presses ended up inspiring *commercial ideas* and soon started to take over from the old printing shops all *biblioquets,* or small trade jobs, such as *announcements of weddings and deaths, calling cards, posters, leaflets,* and so forth.[32]

Thus, it was not simply the shady financial dealings of a few big Parisian publishers that had brought ruin on the printing and book publishing trades; it was the multitude of new printing shops that had opened as a consequence of the freedom of the press.

These new little printers were responsible not only for driving the larger printers to ruin, Jacob argued; they were also responsible for the moral decline of French literary culture, because they themselves printed the degenerate literary genres that the Revolution had spawned. It was they who had first flooded France with inflammatory political newspapers and then, having exhausted that market, turned to the corruption of youth by propagating romantic novels. And it was not just the number of new printers that plagued the trade and steered it toward less than noble ends; the government, too, had taken its toll on the livelihood of commercial printers: "In the printing business, everything is being centralized in the capital."[33] Even government jobs were no longer subcontracted out to departmental printers. With too many printers and too little worthy material to print, Stoupe and Jacob asserted, the financial and moral crisis in the trade could be resolved only by restricting the

31. Ibid., 18–19.
32. Ibid., 20–21.
33. Ibid., 23.

number of printing shops in Paris to fifty, and to nine hundred for the nation as a whole.

So much for the problems of printers. The responses of publishers to the government's inquiry revealed a clear consensus that the deregulationist policies of the revolutionary period, and in particular the law on literary property of July 19, 1793, were both legally and institutionally inadequate for commercial book publishing. They, too, clamored for re-regulation. Thus Jacob wrote: "Will it be claimed that in demanding a renewal of the old regulations, one is demanding restrictions upon *the freedom of the press?* . . . Do not call liberty what in reality is no more than license and piracy."[34]

After all, Jacob noted, the great eighteenth-century free trade reformer, the minister of finance Anne-Robert-Jacques Turgot, had exempted the printing and publishing trades from his deregulationist edicts of 1776, in the interest of public order and safety. Pierre-Marie Bruysset, publisher in Lyon, equally condemned revolutionary deregulation as the "first and foremost cause of the decline of the book trade":

> At that moment when so many men lost their profession and their resources, the effervescence of thought gave the book trade a momentary allure of prosperity because of the spontaneous explosion in consumption of ephemeral matter. . . . The door to the profession was barely opened to everyone before a crowd rushed in.[35]

The Paris publisher Pierre-Michel Lamy was less vituperative and more specific. It was not simply that too many people were practicing the trades, it was that the laws organizing them were insufficient: "In 1793, the law that came to regulate us struck at the root of literary property. The results were losses for the foremost publishing houses and universal disorder. Immorality eclipsed the good faith of yore."[36] Louis Ravier held similarly negative views of the law,

> whose penalties, as rigorous as they are, discouraged a few of the least dishonest pirates, but never checked the audacity of the most dangerous. Deprived of adequate means of enforcement, this decree, so to speak, is more troublesome than useful to the publishing world, giving rise to shameful speculations on forms of property that are insecure and soon to expire, in order to obtain the right to pursue in the courts another man,

34. Ibid., 42–43.
35. AN, ser. F18, carton 11a, plaque 1, Pierre-Marie Bruysset, Lyon publisher, "Observations," September 29, 1810.
36. Ibid., Pierre-Michel Lamy, Paris publisher, May 8, 1810.

who at least as often through ignorance as intention has found himself an accomplice in the dissemination of a pirate edition.[37]

The duration of literary property claims was too limited. And as there was no definitive public record of property claims, publishers could not even be certain which editions were legitimate and which pirated. Provincial publishers were of like opinion. Catineau-LaRoche, of Versailles, described the legislation of 1793 as "that law which is immoral in principles, and insufficient in its means."[38] A unanimous call was raised for greater regulation of the publishing as well as the printing world.

Two issues lay at the heart of the publishers' complaints: literary piracy and unregulated competition. The law of 1793, publishers explained, was totally ineffectual as protection against "piracy." The head of the Bureau of Arts and Manufactures assessed the law thus: "The lacunae in the law are so numerous that neither the state administration, nor the law courts, are capable of applying the law in a regular and uniform manner." In order to pursue someone for having produced a pirate edition, he continued,

> You must present memoranda and send with the formal grievance a copy of the pirate edition, as well as the original copy of your own certificate of deposit at the Bibliothèque Nationale. . . . That is not all. You must wait for the decision. There are numerous delays, and in consequence the unpunished pirate, who has now been informed that he is being pursued, will not hesitate to get rid of the pirated books.[39]

The fine arts printer Bertrand-Quinquet, in his *Traité de l'imprimerie* of 1799, also gave a vivid picture of the problem of pirating since the beginning of the Revolution:

> Pirating has become so common in recent times that a printer or publisher who undertakes an edition includes an estimate of his losses to pirated editions . . . in his initial calculations. Before the French Revolution, when the number of printers in this part of Europe was limited and the freedom of the press restrained, Rouen and Lyon were practically the only cities inside France where people dared to engage in this sort of piracy, and even then they did so only with moderation, whereas in Brussels and Liège and throughout Switzerland pirating was openly practiced. . . . Today, now that Paris has seen printers (though in name only) open up in every corner of the city, there are few who would blush at engaging in this dishonorable

37. Ravier, *Répertoire de la librairie,* xiv.
38. Catineau-LaRoche, *Réflexions sur la librairie,* 30.
39. AN, ser. F18, carton 10a, plaque 1, doss. 18, "Rapport au gouvernement," Costaz *le jeune,* 28 nivôse, an XI (January 18, 1803).

trade. Most of them do not even reflect on the enormity of the crime they are committing by printing a work that belongs to someone else.[40]

Like many of the printers whose businesses dated back to before 1789, Bertrand-Quinquet blamed the deregulation of the trade and the new printers for the explosion in pirate editions.

To make matters worse, Louis Ravier added, provincial judges treated accusations of pirating by Paris publishers as persecuting local businesses.[41] And pursuit of domestic pirate editions was only half the problem, as Paris printer and publisher Jacques-Denis Langlois pointed out. Equally if not more damaging to the French book trade was the lack of effective means of preventing the importation of pirate editions produced across the border.[42] The Marseille publisher Auguste Mossy voiced a similar complaint about Paris book dealers who were, he claimed, in cahoots with foreign printers.[43] The law of 1793, silent on the question of importing books, was useless in this situation. Louis Jacob *l'aîné* revived the old argument of Diderot and the Old Regime Paris Book Guild, demanding that "literary property be respected in the same manner as all other forms of property."[44]

Behind these observations lay years of harsh experiences, like those of the geriatric author in Sens, Pélée St. Maurice, who discovered in 1795 that the second edition of his work on the cultivation of Italian poplar trees was being pirated in Paris.[45] His appeal for action, first to the Committee on Public Instruction and then to the minister of the interior, was met with the following response: "Your complaint against the pirate edition of your work could not be more just, but it is before the civil tribunals that you must take it. The police no longer deal with matters of piracy."[46] Yet the records of the civil tribunals of Paris show no trace of the aging Pélée St. Maurice. Pursuing such a case in the local courts, especially if it involved travel, was a costly and risky business.

40. Bertrand-Quinquet, *Traité de l'imprimerie* (Paris, an VII [1799]), 257.

41. Ravier, *Répertoire de la librairie*, xv.

42. AN, ser. F18, carton 11a, plaque 1, Letter from Jacques-Denis Langlois to M. le comte de Portalis, in response to his request for information, February 27, 1810.

43. AN, ser. F17, carton 1207, doss. 8, Letter from the publisher Mossy in Marseille to the minister of justice, 22 fructidor, an V (September 8, 1797).

44. Jacob l'aîné, *Idées générales sur les causes de l'anéantissement de l'imprimerie*, 48. See also chapter 3.

45. AN, ser. F18, carton 565, Letter from Pélée St. Maurice to the Committee on Public Instruction, 17 frimaire, an IV (December 8, 1795), and the response of the minister of the interior.

46. Ibid.

Some people, of course, did take their cases to the courts. The widow of Philippe Fabre d'Eglantine, for example, sued the publisher Nicolas Barba for pirating her late husband's work *L'Intrigue épistolaire* in 1796.[47] Barba was sued again in 1797 by Jean-François de LaHarpe and his publisher, Mathieu Migneret, for pirating LaHarpe's *Du fanatisme dans la langue révolutionnaire*.[48] And the publisher Jacques-Simon Merlin took Barba and his associate François Dufart to court in 1798 for yet another pirate edition, this time of Jean-François Marmontel's *Contes moraux*.[49] In 1799, the novelist Anne-Jeanne-Félicité Mérard St.-Just and her husband sued the publisher Claude-François Maradan for publishing a second edition of her *Mémoires de la baronne d'Alvigny* without her consent.[50] Joseph-Gaspar Cuchet's successor, A.-J. Dugour, found himself tied up in the courts in 1799 as well, pursuing the Paris publisher Jean-François-Pierre Deterville for a pirate edition of the *Dictionnaire élémentaire de botanique*.[51]

Not only did no preventative measures exist to combat pirate editions, but, as the head of the Bureau of Arts and Manufactures observed, pursuit of the perpetrators in the courts after the fact could drag on for years. Thus in the case of the widow of Fabre d'Eglantine, a trial, appeal, and retrial lasted three years.[52] And her difficulties were minor compared to those of Dugour, who, at the same time that he was battling Deterville over his *Dictionnaire élémentaire de botanique,* was embroiled in a lengthy suit with the Leroy brothers, printers and publishers in Lyon, over a pirate edition of Rozier's *Dictionnaire, ou Cours complet d'agriculture*.[53] Dugour had purchased the *Cours complet d'agriculture* as part of Cuchet's stock in 1797; Cuchet, in turn, had purchased the privilege from Rozier in 1783. The Leroy brothers now claimed that they had produced this edition of the *Cours* in 1792—that is, in the period *between* the abolition of privileges in August 1789 and the new law on literary property of 1793. As a consequence, they argued, they were perfectly within their rights to have

47. Douarche (ed.), *Tribunaux civils* 2:305, 318, 426, 471 (April 24, 1796–February 23, 1798).
48. Ibid., 435 (August 31, 1797).
49. Ibid., 582–585 (December 3–13, 1798).
50. Ibid., 618 (February 25, 1799).
51. Ibid., 606 (January 26, 1799).
52. Ibid., 305, 318, 426, 471 (April 24, June 10, 1796; August 11, 1797; February 23, 1798).
53. AN, ser. ADVIII, carton 7, "Consultation pour le citoyen A. J. Dugour, propriétaire du *Cours d'agriculture* par Rozier, contre les citoyens Leroy, imprimeur-libraires à Lyon," (1797–1803).

produced the new edition.[54] The case dragged on for at least six years, from 1797 to 1803.

Such arguments were not rare. The comte de Buffon's widow found herself involved in an even more arcane legal dispute with Behemer, printer and publisher in Metz, over her late husband's *Histoire naturelle*.[55] "The former privileges accorded to authors of useful works, were they abolished by the laws of August 1789?" her lawyer queried. "Is it legal for a foreigner who has moved to France to market a pirate edition of a work because it was produced in a foreign country that has since been 're-united' with France?"[56] It took four years, from 1798 to 1802, and an appeal reversing the decision of a lower court to get a firm decision in her favor.

The widow Buffon was not alone in struggling with these international legal disputes. As Langlois had observed, the problem of foreign pirate editions was endemic. Henri Bernardin de St. Pierre and his publisher in Paris, Laurent-Mathieu Guillaume *le jeune*, became locked in a long and bitter battle with the Brussels publisher Lefrancq over Bernardin de St. Pierre's own works, as well as those of Jean-Pierre Claris de Florian; Stanislas-Jean, marquis de Boufflers; and Marguerite Daubenton. [57] Lefrancq's lawyers argued, too, that the abolition of privileges in August 1789 had abrogated Bernardin de St. Pierre's claims on his texts between 1789 and 1793.

Bernardin de St. Pierre was not new to the world of literary piracy. He had fought battles over pirate editions since the beginning of the Revolution, first over *Paul et Virginie, Etudes de la nature,* and the *Chaumière indienne* between 1791 and 1793, then, in 1796, over a second pirate edition of the *Etudes*.[58] That same year, he also declared bankruptcy.[59] In association with Guillaume *le jeune*, he then decided to produce another

54. Ibid., 14.

55. AN, ser. F18, carton 1, *Mémoire* on behalf of the widow Buffon against Behemer, 1802.

56. Ibid., 3.

57. The dossier concerning this dispute is found in AN, ser. AA, carton 56, doc. 1525, Guillaume *le jeune*, Paris publisher [1802–1806]. For a similar dispute, see AN, ser. F18, carton 565, *Mémoire* on behalf of the publishers of Brussels against the publishers of Paris, 1807.

58. See chapter 3 for more on the 1791–1793 battles. For the fight over the 1796 pirated version of the *Etudes*, see Douarche (ed.), *Tribunaux civils* 2:282, 329 (February 8, 1796).

59. AN, ser. AA, carton 56, doc. 1525, doss. "Guillaume *le jeune*," *Aperçu sur les difficultés qui s'élèvent entre les libraires de l'intérieur de la France et les libraires des pays réunis* [n.d., n.p.], 3.

edition of his *Oeuvres* to recover his losses. Shortly thereafter Guillaume, in Brussels on business, discovered that they were yet again victims of pirate editions of the *Etudes* and *Paul et Virginie*.[60] Bernardin de St. Pierre may have been one of the most widely published authors of the revolutionary period, but he was not well remunerated from his writings. In 1806, Guillaume *le jeune* also joined the ranks of bankrupt publishers.[61]

Pirate editions and the ambiguities of the law of 1793 were not the only factors undermining the commercial stability of the Paris book publishing community. Just as damaging, according to reports received by the Napoleonic Council of State, was the problem of unregulated editions of the same works, which after the abolition of privileges had entered the public domain. Among his "causes of the troubles in the book trade," for instance, the Paris printer Théodore Demaison listed "the competition of different editions whose editors cannot come to an understanding with one another and thus contribute to their mutual ruin."[62] Ravier, too, identified "the multiplicity of editions" of the same works as the "second cause [after pirating] for the decline in the business." He explained, "The only reason they produce new editions daily is because the majority of the new printers and book dealers from the revolutionary period are ignorant of the numerous editions that already exist of these works; but they must know that the best book, multiplied too many times, ends up being the worst to sell."[63] And Pierre-Marie Bruysset, the Lyon publisher, added his voice: "Among the books that have come into the public domain, it occurs sometimes that four or five editions of the same book are produced in the same time, in the same city, and these editions create unintended and ruinous competition for one another, harmful to each of the entrepreneurs."[64] The former Paris Book Guild publisher Pierre-César Briand stated the case thus:

> Modern publishing consists of all the books that are reprinted endlessly, which are no one's property, and which anyone can make use of by virtue of the law of 1793. This branch of the book trade [is] the most extensive, [and] the most certain, . . . because it . . . encompasses the best books. It could offer an honorable living to all publishers if they were to know how

60. Ibid., 4, 5.
61. AP, Fond Faillite, ser. D11U3, carton 32, January 18, 1806.
62. AN, ser. F18, carton 11a, plaque 1, Report from Théodore Demaison, Paris printer, October 14, 1810.
63. Ravier, *Répertoire de la librairie*, 3.
64. AN, ser. F18, carton 11a, plaque 1, Pierre-Marie Bruysset, "Observations," September 26, 1810.

to make proper use of it, but instead they bring themselves ruin because they abuse it.

They all print the same works for lack of being able, or willing, to come to terms with one another; they print them out of rivalry with each other and end up remaindering them. But the public does not even profit from the low prices because the editions are abridged, inaccurate, and poorly produced, which harms the art and the honor of French publishing in the eyes of Europe.[65]

Publishers were driving each other under by undermining one another's markets. Unregulated production and over-production, rather than lack of production, lay behind the new crisis in the publishing world.

Bruysset gave several examples of works that had become unprofitable because of unregulated competition: the *Nouveau Dictionnaire d'histoire naturelle,* produced simultaneously by the Bruysset brothers in Lyon, Jean-François-Pierre Deterville in Paris, and the Levrault brothers, also in Paris; the *Dictionnaire historique,* released at the same time in Paris by both the brothers François-Joseph and Louis-Gabriel Michaud and Louis Prudhomme; and the *Dictionnaire, ou Cours complet d'agriculture,* published by both Pierre Buisson and Jean-François-Pierre Deterville, again in Paris.[66] This last text, which had been the victim of piracy as the private property of A.-J. Dugour in 1797–1803, now, having become part of the public domain in 1803, fell prey to the unchecked competition of Parisian publishers.[67]

Publishers like Buisson and Deterville had to fight tooth and nail to emerge afloat. Thus, for example, Buisson wrote to one of his editors:

It is of the highest importance for the success of our enterprise with the *Cours complet d'agriculture* to bring out volume three on the 25th of this month, because our adversaries *will release the three first volumes of their edition on the very same day.* You can count on it. . . . You know that our adversaries will bring heaven and earth together against us.[68]

The sad reality was that there were no winners in these wars to capture the market, even in cases where publishers started out in a spirit of

65. Ibid., Report from Pierre-César Briand, Paris publisher, April 2, 1810.

66. Ibid., Pierre-Marie Bruysset, "Observations," September 29, 1810.

67. The author of the *Dictionnaire ou Cours complet d'agriculture,* François Rozier, died in 1793, leaving his publisher Dugour until 1803 to exploit the text exclusively. See AN, ser. ADVIII, carton 7, "Consultation pour le citoyen A. J. Dugour, propriétaire du *Cours d'agriculture* par Rozier," 5.

68. AN, ser. AA, carton 57, doc. 1526, Letter from Pierre Buisson, Paris publisher, to Dubois, an editor of the *Cours d'agriculture,* March 14, 1809 (emphasis in original).

cooperation. Such was the case with the beautiful Houel edition of the *Oeuvres complètes de Condillac* of the year VII (1798–1799).[69] Six printers and publishers of Paris—Jean Gratoit, Théophile-Etienne Gide, Loret, Laurent-Mathieu Guillaume *le jeune,* Charles Houel, and Louis Prud-homme—formed a business association to produce Condillac's complete works. Upon dividing up the printed copies of the edition, they agreed by written contract to minimum wholesale and retail prices that none of them were to undersell. The association enjoyed the support of the government, which purchased 150 copies of the complete edition. Loret cut in yet another Paris publisher, Denis-Simon Maginel, and the two of them in turn passed on a significant proportion of their share to the Paris retail bookseller Joseph-Philogone Meurant. Everything went smoothly until Guillaume *le jeune* ran into financial trouble, which pre-sumably, forced him to make a fast move. On 18 prairial, year VII (June 6, 1799), Maginel received the following note from Loret:

> I just received this morning, my friend, a visit from Citizen Hue, book dealer in Rouen, who came to buy some Condillacs from me. He proposed a price that made it impossible for me to do business with him. It seems that Guillaume is selling this book through colporteurs at a vile price. I beg a favor of you. Within the next two days, lock up the door to the warehouse.[70]

Maginel no doubt locked the warehouse door, but nonetheless, within the next five years Guillaume, Meurant, and Prudhomme were all in default.[71] Guillaume, cut down first by literary pirates, proceeded to drag others under with his own unprofitable competition. Even more tragically, the Houel edition of Condillac's *Language of Calculation,* still celebrated as one of the greatest monuments of enlightened science and republican typography, ended up in the remainder bins of the revolu-tionary literary market.[72]

---

69. The complete history of this edition is documented in the correspondence and business records of the publisher Denis-Simon Maginel and the printer Loret, both of Paris; see AN, ser. AQ24, carton 6, *Papiers privés,* Maginel, libraire, doss. "C. Loret, im-primeur à Paris, an VII" (1798–1799).

70. Ibid.

71. AP, Fond Faillite, D11U3, cartons 23 and 32 (1803 and 1806).

72. For more on this edition, see Dhombres, "Books," 177–202.

Beneath the financial crisis of 1799–1806 lay a deeper dilemma for the revolutionary publishing world. The law of 1793 had rendered book publishing commercially inviable. The limiting of private copyright claims to ten years after the author's death reduced the commercial value of a copyright to a single edition. Pirating was rampant because there was no effective mechanism to prevent it after the suppression of the royal Administration of the Book Trade. But most serious was the problem of competing editions of works in the public domain, because such editions made up the majority of book commerce. Although the revolutionary government had intended to stimulate commerce by abolishing all exclusive claims to texts whose authors had been dead for over ten years, the lack of a national administration and of a compulsory system for registering editions in print meant that competition could not be regulated, even by the publishing community itself. The fundamental dilemma of commercial publishing under the Republic went beyond the instability of credit institutions and markets; in the final analysis, commerce in the printed word had been rendered "too free" to be capable of fulfilling Jacques-Pierre Brissot de Warville's revolutionary dream of "spreading light in every direction"—at least through the medium of the printed book. Books require protection in order to exist. Faced with this insight, the Revolution's cultural elites were compelled to abandon their laissez-faire idealism of 1789 and to rethink how the ideal of a free *and* enlightened Republic could best be achieved.

The government inquiry into the book publishing community, which lasted from 1803 to 1810, brought forth a clamor for re-regulation. Some, like Théodore Demaison and Jean-Georges-Antoine Stoupe of Paris, Pierre-Marie-Sebastien Catineau-LaRoche of Versailles, Louis Jacob *l'aîné* of Orléans, and Pierre-Marie Bruysset of Lyon, recommended a return to the *Code de la Librairie* of 1723, as interpreted by the old Paris Book Guild: reviving a national Administration of the Book Trade to register and monitor copyrights, legally limiting the number of persons permitted to practice the trades of printing and publishing, reinstituting compulsory prepublication registration of all printed matter with the state, and insuring that texts be treated like any other form of property—inheritable and transmissible in perpetuity.[73] Others, like Langlois, proposed a return only to the *règlements* of 1777: reestablishing the

73. AN, ser. F18, carton 11a, plaque 1, Pierre-Marie Bruysset, "Observations," September 29, 1810; and Théodore Demaison, October 14, 1810.

book guilds and inspectors of the book trade to protect against piracy, and returning to a system of limited privileges on texts as a means of regulating competition in the public domain. He reasoned, "If the law of '93 gives all publishers the right to print all books that belong to the nation . . . , these books belong, above all, to him who represents the nation, and by consequence, to the emperor."[74] Through the sale of privileges, Langlois suggested, the emperor could finance censors, inspectors, and book guilds.

Pierre-César Briand was less quick to request a return to the Old Regime. Instead he suggested appropriation and adaptation of one of the most innovative institutions of eighteenth-century publishing, the system of permissions, introduced by Chrétien-Guillaume Lamoignon de Malesherbes in the 1750s when he had served as director of the Administration of the Book Trade.[75] By requiring publishers to register all *editions* with a government agency and to receive a permission to publish, Briand argued, this system could insure that no two identical editions of the same text circulated simultaneously or cut into each other's markets. It was a simple idea, and easy to administer through a national registry of works in print. Briand was supported in his proposal by the heir to the Panckoucke publishing empire, Henri Agasse. Indeed, it was no coincidence that Agasse chose the year 1809 to bring out the first edition of Malesherbes's *Mémoires sur la librairie et sur la liberté de la presse*.[76] Perhaps Panckoucke had been right in 1790 when he had argued that literary property was fragile, requiring special surveillance and protection to be of value. In the first decade of the nineteenth century the major printing and publishing houses of Paris called almost unanimously for strengthened laws on literary property, the revival of a national administration for surveillance and protection of copyrights, and greater regulation of the commercial exploitation of texts in the public domain. The government was ready to listen.

Remaking the Administration of the Book Trade

The Napoleonic Direction of the Book Trade did not descend *deus ex machina* in 1810 upon an unwitting world of printers and publishers. Rather, it was born out of a series of negotiations between the government

74. Ibid., Jacques-Denis Langlois, Paris printer-publisher, February 27, 1810.
75. Ibid., Report from Pierre-César Briand, April 2, 1810.
76. Malesherbes, *Mémoires sur la librairie*.

and the various constituencies within the publishing and printing world.[77] As in the early 1790s and 1795–1796, in 1800 the initiative to re-regulate and revive the book trade was accompanied by an equally vigorous effort to restrict the political periodical press. In January 1800, the consuls suppressed all but thirteen political journals in Paris and submitted these remaining journals to continuous surveillance and censorship.[78] The administrative reorganization of the nation on February 17, 1800, and especially the installation of the system of prefects a month later, made centralized national surveillance of the press an administrative possibility.[79] The periodical press, however, was not the only form of the printed word to fall under the purview of the prefects.

As early as November 1801, the minister of police, Joseph Fouché, was employing the prefect of police in Paris to confiscate books and pamphlets from printing shops, editors, and booksellers because of their moral, political, or religious content.[80] These repressive measures were soon to be complemented by preventative ones. The Paris prefect of police thus reported:

> By his letter of 20 messidor, year XI [July 9, 1803], the chief minister of justice has charged me to inform all printers and publishers that they must deposit with me two copies of everything that they propose to publish,

77. This chapter was researched and written in 1983–1984, before I became aware of Bernard Vouillot's unpublished 1979 thesis for the Ecole des Chartes entitled "L'Imprimerie et la librairie à Paris sous le Consulat et l'Empire (1799–1814)," which treats some of the same archival material I consider here. I would like to thank him for his permission in 1989 to consult his thesis, from which I profited considerably in revising this portion of the manuscript, and especially for his references to printed pamphlets concerning the re-regulation of the trades between 1806 and 1810. Nonetheless, my own interpretation of the causes and significance of the revival of the national Administration of the Book Trade differs considerably from Vouillot's. While he sees censorship as the most critical motivation behind, and consequence of, re-regulation, I see the commercial viability of printing and publishing, especially of books, as the central concern in shaping the policies of the Napoleonic authorities, and as the key reason for the support for these measures within the printing and publishing world. See also Vouillot, "Révolution et l'Empire."

78. André Cabanis, *Presse sous le Consulat*, 12–13, 319–320.

79. Louis Bergeron, *France Under Napoleon*, trans. R. R. Palmer (Princeton: Princeton University Press, 1981), 23–31, 208–209.

80. For examples, see AN, ser. F18, carton 39, Orders from the minister of police to the prefect of police in Paris to confiscate the following items: *Lettres de M. de Fronsac, fils du duc de Richelieu au chevalier de Dumas*, 2 vols. in 12, chez Michelet (4 frimaire, an X [November 25, 1801]), because of obscenity; *Charles de Tersannes, ou familles rayées de la liste des émigrés*, Imprimerie Raquin (13 frimaire, an X [December 4, 1801]), because of its politically controversial content; *Sur l'émigration* and *Religion de l'état*, chez la fille Durand (14 frimaire, an XI [December 5, 1802]), because of politically and religiously controversial content.

eight days before they release it. He has charged me, as well, to have the works examined during this period and to send him a report containing my judgment, along with a copy of each work.[81]

Thus, by the summer of 1803 an obligatory *dépôt* at the Prefecture of Police had been laid in place. Hundreds of reports from the prefect to the minister of justice concerning individual texts between 1803 and 1804 testify to the execution of these orders. Soon, though, the first consul himself wrote to the minister of justice clarifying that "his intention was not to impose police censorship on works pertaining to the arts and sciences," but only on politically sensitive materials.[82] The minister of justice consequently instructed the prefect not to send him reports on, or copies of, every work deposited; literary and scientific works, he suggested, should only be inspected briefly and returned, "as soon as you are certain that they treat only the subjects indicated by their titles."[83] This procedure was given official sanction several months later by a consular *arrêt* dated 4 vendémiaire, year XII (September 27, 1803), wherein the consuls announced that "in order to assure the freedom of the press, no publisher will be allowed to sell a work before having presented it to a review committee, which will determine whether it requires censorship."[84] Unlike the *dépôt* at the Bibliothèque Nationale, the inspection at the Prefecture of Police was obligatory.

The declaration of the Empire and Fouché's return to the Ministry of Police in July 1804 resulted in a further expansion of the surveillance and censorship system. Fouché ordered the prefect to revive the obligatory *dépôt* of two copies of everything to be published in Paris.[85] Further, he organized a "Division of the Freedom of the Press" within his ministry. To this division he attached an office of consultants—essentially, a corps of censors.[86] From the summer of 1804 through 1810,

81. Ibid., Report from Dubois, prefect of police in Paris, to Fouché, minister of police, 21 vendémiaire, an XIII (October 13, 1804).

82. Ibid.

83. Ibid.

84. Cited in Peignot, *Essai historique sur la liberté d'écrire*, 157.

85. AN, ser. F18, carton 39, Report from Dubois, prefect of police in Paris, to Fouché, minister of police, 21 vendémiaire, an XIII (October 13, 1804); the minister's response is jotted in the margin. Fouché was restored to his post on July 16, 1804.

86. Ibid. Reports from the Division de la Liberté de la Presse from 18 thermidor, an XII (August 6, 1804) and 18 ventôse, an XIII (March 9, 1805).

then, it was the duty of the prefect of police to send a report and copy of every work published in Paris to the minister of police.[87]

Regardless whether Napoleon initially intended to limit surveillance and censorship to explicitly political printed matter, nothing, in fact, escaped Fouché and his Division of the Freedom of the Press. The division, of course, continued to work at regulating the periodical press.[88] They did not, however, restrict their surveillance to political matters alone, as their concern about the harsh reception of Mme de Staël's novel *Corinne* in the Parisian press suggests.[89] Nor did they limit their censorship to explicitly political texts: Mme Mérard St. Just's novel *Six Mois d'exil ou les orphelins par la Révolution*, for example, was prohibited.[90] Travel literature, as well, received close scrutiny,[91] and the cross-references of the *Dictionnaire universel de la langue française* were combed for possible political innuendos.[92] The division also evaluated works such as Boieldieu's *De l'Influence de la chaire, du théâtre et du barreau dans la société civile* to determine whether they were worthy of government patronage.[93] Writings on military subjects were, of course, carefully studied.[94] Even poetry required close attention and interpretation.[95]

The case of the *Portefeuille volé* reveals how sophisticated the functions of the new division had become by 1805. The *Portefeuille volé* was a collection of light libertine poems, which, according to the censor, were, if a little irreverent, by no means obscene. The publisher, Debray, however, had neglected to deposit a copy at the Prefecture of Police before putting it on the market. As punishment, the prefect ordered the work to be confiscated. The authorities were clearly intent on enforcing conformity to the law. Furthermore, having closely inspected the *Portefeuille*

87. Hundreds of these reports remain in AN, ser. F18, carton 39.

88. See, for example, ibid., Request of the widow Nyon for permission to launch a new journal, 9 fructidor, an XIII (August 27, 1805).

89. Ibid., Mme de Staël, December 22, 1808.

90. AN, ser. F18, carton 39, Anne-Jeanne-Félicité Mérard St. Just (née Ormoy), 17 frimaire, an XIII (December 8, 1804).

91. AN, ser. F18, carton 565, Jean-Georges Treuttel and Jean-Godefroy Wurtz, publishers, Paris, September 12, 1806.

92. AN, ser. F18, carton 39, *Dictionnaire universel*, [1807].

93. Ibid., Marie-Jacques-Amand Boieldieu, lawyer, *De l'influence de la chaire, du théâtre et du barreau dans la société civile*, 18 ventôse, an XIII (March 9, 1805).

94. Ibid., Denis-Simon Maginel, Paris publisher, *Histoire de la campagne de 1800 en Allemagne et en Italie*, 18 thermidor, an XII (August 6, 1804), and the *Histoire de la guerre entre la France et l'Espagne* (October 28, 1808).

95. Ibid., *Portefeuille volé* (a collection of poems), 17 floréal, an XIII (May 7, 1805).

volé, the prefect decided that the work, while not dangerous enough to be permanently banned, "should simply be *tolerated,* it should not be permitted to be advertised, either through posters or in the press. Furthermore, in returning the work to the publisher, tell him that he may not put his name on the title page, so that the publication of this work in no manner appears to have been authorized by the government."[96] Thus, by 1805 the imperial police had revived not only inspections of booksellers and printing shops, but also the system of *permissions tacites* and *tolérances,* by which an officially sanctioned literary civilization could be distinguished from independent and unauthorized cultural initiatives.

The expansion of government censorship and surveillance of the printed word, however, posed constant problems for the administration. Because the government formally recognized the principle of freedom of the press, surveillance and censorship of the book trade were difficult to justify, let alone enforce.[97] The magnitude of the task overwhelmed the resources of the prefect of police, who was facing resistance from publishers and authors to the obligatory deposit: "The majority of them submit only with repugnance to these measures. I imposed this harness on them as gently as possible, but in the end they want to be rid of it, and confidentially they admit that few of them are complying. If it is Your Excellency's [Fouché's] intention to continue this policy, how are the publishers and authors to be made to comply with it?"[98] Overextension of the administrative and police resources led to unclear jurisdiction. Enforcement was arbitrary and corrupt. These realities did little to endear the administrative regime to publishers or authors. When Mme Elisabeth Guénard, baronne de Méré, saw her fourth novel confiscated from the publisher even though she had conformed exactly to the dispositions of the law, she appealed directly to the emperor himself for a reform of the laws pertaining to the book trade.[99]

This kind of influential protest, together with administrative complaints, awakened an interest in investigating and reforming the system. On the basis of what laws did the police require the registration, cen-

96. Ibid.
97. See the report from the prefect of Paris to the minister of police to this effect on August 2, 1804, in Aulard (ed.), *Paris sous le Consulat* 2:445.
98. AN, ser. F18, carton 39, Report from the prefect of police, Dubois, to the minister of police, January 30, 1806.
99. For her allegations of corruption, see ibid., Mme Guénard, baronne de Méré (August 1807).

sorship, or confiscation of books? In 1806, the Division of the Freedom of the Press suggested to the minister of police that legal clarification of its activities might make their work easier:

> When Your Excellency desired that all printed matter be known to him at its time of publication, he conceived of an idea that is as simple as it is just and necessary, and that infringes no more upon the freedom of the press than the census of citizens infringes upon individual liberty. . . . But in the absence of a law on the freedom of the press . . . you must anticipate that there will be difficult types who will refuse to comply.[100]

In fact, there had been no formal declaration or definition of the freedom of the press since the constitution of the year III (1795).[101]

Lack of both formal legitimation of its activities and support from the constituency it policed prevented the division from performing its duties effectively. Comparison of the number of works deposited at the *dépôt légal* at the Bibliothèque Nationale between 1801 and 1809 and of those deposited at the Prefecture of Police in Paris reveals how limited the scope of the prefect's surveillance was. Of the average sixteen hundred works per year deposited for copyright protection, remaining archival sources suggest that only about sixty to one hundred were inspected.[102] From the government's point of view, the police surveillance system was as ineffective as it was legally embarrassing. The remedy to this situation lay in identifying the points of convergence between the political interests of the government and the commercial interests of the publishing and printing world.

The Regulation of 1810

As we have seen, in 1804 the ministers of justice and the police were already making formal inquiries among printers and publishers, exploring the possibilities for reorganizing the world of the printed word. The inadequacies of the system of police surveillance exposed in 1806 and 1807 led to action. By 1808 the imperial Council of State began holding

---

100. Ibid., Report to the minister of police from Pierre-Edouard Lemontey, Joseph-Alphonse Esménard, Defauchery, and Charles-Joseph Lacretelle *le jeune:* the members of the "bureau de consultation" of the Division de la Liberté de la Presse (June 26, 1806).

101. Peignot, *Essai historique sur la liberté d'écrire,* 155–158.

102. For the number of works deposited per year at the *dépôt légal* between 1801 and 1809, see Bellos, "Conjoncture de la production," 554. For extant records of books submitted for inspection at the Paris Prefecture of Police, see AN, ser. F18, carton 40.

regular meetings with the emperor to discuss the situation and present proposals for a forthcoming *règlement*.[103] In the same year, a draft of an imperial decree proposing that "a new Administration of the Book Trade be immediately organized" was circulated informally within the publishing world.[104] The Lyon publisher Jean-Marie Bruysset, recalling that he had "always enjoyed the favor of M. Malesherbes and M. Vidaud de La Tour, former directors-general of the Book Trade," made a bid for the directorship.[105] The publisher Henri Agasse used the power of his presses to make Malesherbes's views on the regulation of the book trade widely available to the public. Numerous other Parisian publishers and printers, notably Jules-Gabriel Clousier *fils aîné*, Jean-Georges-Antoine Stoupe, B. Vincard, Louis Ravier, Joseph Fiévée, and François-Jean Baudouin, also circulated their views in print.[106] They were joined by colleagues from the provinces, including Bruysset, Louis Jacob *l'aîné* in Orléans, and Pierre-Marie-Sebastien Catineau-LaRoche in Versailles.[107] In 1810, the ministers of police and the interior received over twenty solicited and unsolicitied reports and proposals from printers and publishers, disclosing the views not only of Paris notables like François-Jean Baudouin, Pierre-César Briand, Jacques-Denis Langlois, François Chaignieau, and François Buisson, but also of their brethren in Lyon, Orléans, Bordeaux, Carcassonne, and even Turin.[108] Three concerns emerge

103. Jean-Guillaume Locre de Roissy, ed., *Discussions sur la liberté de la presse, la censure, la propriété littéraire, l'imprimerie et la librairie qui ont eu lieu dans le conseil d'état pendant les années 1808, 1809, 1810 et 1811* (Paris: Garnery & Nicolle, 1819).

104. AN, ser. F18, carton 565, Letter from Barthélemy, *homme de lettres* in Lyon, to M. Cretel, minister of the interior, proposing that the Lyon publisher Bruysset be made director of the new Administration of the Book Trade, June 10, 1808. See also AN, ser. F18, carton 39, Proposal from a former royal censor, Raupt-Bapstein, for the formation of a new college of censors, September 15, 1808.

105. AN, ser. F18, carton 565, Letter from Barthélemy.

106. Jules-Gabriel Clousier fils aîné, *Notes sur l'imprimerie, la librairie et la fonderie des caractères d'impression* (Paris, [1801]); Stoupe, *Mémoire sur le rétablissement de la communauté des imprimeurs de Paris;* Ravier, *Répertoire de librairie;* B. Vincard, *Projet sur l'organisation de la librairie, discuté par la majeure partie des imprimeurs et des libraires, et par les hommes de lettres, censeurs, etc. . . . soumis aux membres du Conseil d'Etat* (Paris, [1809]); Joseph Fiévée, *Observations et projet de décret sur l'imprimerie et la librairie* (Paris: Imprimerie Impériale, 1809); and François-Jean Baudouin, *Esquisse d'un projet de règlement pour l'imprimerie, la librairie et autres professions relatives, rédigée d'après les lois anciennes et nouvelles* (Paris, 1810).

107. Jean-Marie Bruysset, *Caractères de la propriété littéraire* (Lyon, [1808]); Jacob, *Idées générales sur les causes de l'anéantissement de l'imprimerie;* and Catineau-LaRoche, *Réflexions sur la librairie.*

108. See AN, ser. F18, carton 11a, plaque 1, Reports from Raymond, a printing shop foreman in Paris, from April 26, May 8, 15, and 17, June 5, 12, and 14, July 14, Sep-

repeatedly from these reports: (1) the need for greater surveillance and protection against pirate editions, (2) the need to regulate the commercial exploitation of works in the public domain, and (3) the need to restrict the number of printers in order to insure adequate employment.[109]

The declaration of the rights of genius of July 19, 1793, comprised a single title and a mere seven articles;[110] it was a legislative act, emanating from the committees of the National Convention. In 1810, a new imperial Administration of the Book Trade was laid into place by executive order. On February 5, the emperor's Council of State promulgated a "regulation of the printing and book trades" comprising eight separate titles and forty-eight articles.[111] The genius of the regulation of 1810 lay in its synthesis of the political needs of the imperial state and the commercial interests of the major publishers and printers into one coherent administrative vision. Title one of the regulation established a "General Direction," with a director and six auditors, under the minister of the

---

tember 29, October 14, December 2 and 10, 1810, and January 5, 1811; AN, ser. F18, carton 39, Letter from Jean-Antoine-Guillaume Bailleul, Paris printer-publisher, January 2, 1810; AN, ser. F18, carton 11a, plaque 1, Letters from François Chaignieau, printer in Paris, January 4, 1810; Joseph-Gaspar Gillé, printer in Paris, January 11, 1810; Pierre Plassan, printer-publisher in Paris, January 28, 1810; François Buisson, publisher in Paris, February 24, 1810; Jacques-Denis Langlois, printer-publisher in Paris, February 27, 1810; François-Jean Baudouin, Paris printer, March 19, 1810; Pierre-César Briand, publisher in Paris, April 2, 1810; Anonymous report on printers in the departments, received April 16, 1810; Letters from Antoine Chambon, printer in Paris, April 27, 1810; Joudou, printer for the prefecture of the department of the Aube, Carcassonne, May 7 and 28, 1810; Pierre Michel Lamy, publisher in Paris, May 8 and 24, 1810; Louis Jacob, printer in Orléans, May 22 and June 14 and 22, 1810; Castillon, printer in Bordeaux, June 28, 1810; Toscanelli, publisher in Turin, July 18, 1810; Théodore Demaison, Paris printer, July 27 and October 14, 1810; Pierre-Marie Bruysset, publisher in Lyon, September 26 and October, 1810.

109. For testimony on the need to limit printers, see AN, ser. F18, carton 11a, plaque 1, Reports from Jacques-Denis Langlois, printer-publisher in Paris; Jean-François Baudouin, printer in Paris, and Théodore Demaison, printer in Paris; Anonymous report on departmental printers of April 16, 1810; Reports of Joudou, printer in Carcassonne; Pierre-Michel Lamy, printer in Paris; Louis Jacob, printer in Orléans; Toscanelli, publisher in Turin; and Jean-Marie Bruysset, publisher in Lyon.

110. AN, ser. F18, carton 1, "Décret de la Convention nationale du 19 juillet 1793, l'an 2 de la République Française, relatif au droit c \a propriété des auteurs."

111. Ibid., "Bulletin des Lois, no. 264: Décret impérial contenant le règlement sur l'imprimerie et la librairie . . . , 5 février 1810." The following summary quotes from this seven-page document.

interior. Title two limited the number of printers in Paris to sixty (extended shortly thereafter to eighty), each required to possess a minimum of four presses. Suppressed printers were to receive an indemnity. When a printer died, preference would be given to his or her family in selecting a successor. Title three outlawed the printing or publication of anything that questioned the duty of "subjects toward the sovereign, or the interest of the state." Prepublication censorship was reimposed: publication of any work, whether new or a re-release in either the private or the public domain, required permission of the General Direction. Title four required all publishers and booksellers to be licensed independently of printers. All new publishers and booksellers, furthermore, had to provide proof of their "clean living and good morals, as well as their attachment to the fatherland and the sovereign." Title five concerned the importation of foreign books: it required all imported books to be registered with the prefects in the border departments and approved by the General Direction and a tariff to be imposed on all imported French and Latin books. Title six revised the laws on literary property, extending private claims on a text to the life of the author, his widow, and their children for twenty years after their deaths. Title seven authorized the formation of a corps of inspectors of the book trade and officers of the police and customs to enforce the regulation. Finally, title eight established a *dépôt* at the Prefecture of Police, in Paris and every other department, with publishers required to deposit five copies of any work they intended to publish. It was then the prefect's responsibility to send one copy to the *dépôt* at the Bibliothèque Nationale.

The structure, services, personnel, and finances of the new imperial General Direction of the Printing and Book Trades in 1810 can be diagrammed (figures 8–9, tables 4–5). As these figures make clear, the priorities of the new administration, in terms of the commitment of both money and personnel, lay in surveillance rather than censorship. Whereas censorship was episodic and half-hearted throughout the Napoleonic period,[112] implementation of the decrees of February 5, 1810, mobilized a small army of Napoleonic inspectors and prefects to produce a massive census of every single printer, publisher, bookseller, manufacturer of printing types, colporteur, and keeper of a *cabinet de lecture* in the entire empire. Thus, an announcement in the newly

---

112. See Victor Coffin, "Censorship under Napoleon I," *American Historical Review* 22 (1916–1917): 291.

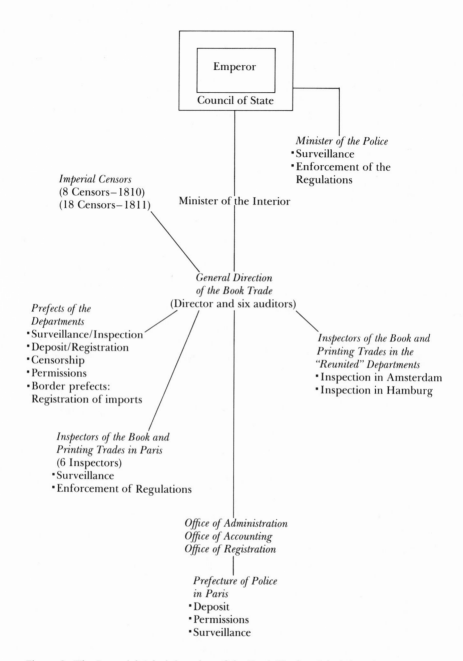

Figure 8. The Imperial Administration of the Book Trade: Administrative Organization, 1810

Source: AN, ser. F4, cartons 2572–2573, doss. 1–2; and BN, nouv. acq. fr. 1362, feuilles 63–64.

Table 4   The Imperial Administration of the Book Trade:
Personnel, 1810

Directors:

Comte de Portalis, 1810
Baron de Pommereul, 1811–1814

*Auditors of the Council of State,
attached to the General Direction (1811):*

Baron de Pommereul
Soumet
Deyeux
Pellene
Guérard
Riquetti-Mirabeau

Imperial Censors:

1810:	*1811:*		
Pellene	Pellene	Johanneau	Vanderburg
Sauvo	Sauvo	Jansen	Malherbe
Lemontey	Lemonty	Salgues	
DelaSalle	DelaSalle	DeManne	
Schiaffino	Schiaffino	LeGraveraut	
Desrenaudet	Desrenaudet	Artaud	
Lacretelle	Lacretelle	Dazigny	
Esménard	Dampmartin	Tabazaud	

Inspectors of the Book and Printing Trades:

Paris: Gaudefroy, Section Sénat
Sardaillon, Section Panthéon
Balzac, Section Hôtel de Ville
Loraux, Section Tuilleries
Delaubepie/Turenne (1811), Section Marchés
Meynard, Section Cité

Secret Foreign Agent: Chauvé

Departments: Prefects

Reunited Departments: Manget, Amsterdam
Johanneau, Hamburg

SOURCE: AN, ser. F4, cartons 2572–2573, doss. 1–2; and BN, nouv. acq. fr. 1362, feuilles
63–64.

Table 5 The Imperial Administration of the Book Trade:
Budget, 1810

BUDGET 1810 (in francs)	
Allocations: —Installation costs	14,000
—Domestic affairs	106,000
—Foreign affairs	80,000
Total	200,000
Expenditures:	
I. Installation costs	14,000
II. Domestic affairs	
—Rental of office space	10,600
—Director's salary	26,500
—Employees' salaries	44,565
—Miscellaneous expenses (12,000 frs. for Chauvé, secret foreign agent)	24,334
III. Foreign affairs	
— Registration expenses in Paris and in the departments (80,000 in credit for foreign services)	11,117
—Censorship: 8 censors and expenses	13,755
—Inspectors' salaries	15,500
—Fees for retainers	5,700
Total	166,071

SOURCE: AN, ser. F4, cartons 2572–2573, doss. 1–2; and BN, nouv. acq. fr. 1362, feuilles 63–64.

founded *Journal de la librairie* informed the publishers and book dealers of Paris on July 2, 1811, that they were to report in person immediately to the secretariat of the Direction of the Book Trade to declare their intention to continue their businesses.[113] The fruits of these censuses are still, in large part, extant in the Archives Nationales.[114] According to the

113. See *Journal de la librairie* 1, no. 31 (July 2, 1811): 256.
114. AN, ser. F18, carton 25, contains the surveys of printers, publishers, and book-sellers in every department and city in France, and some material for the "reunited departments." It also contains specific surveys for Paris. Additional material for Paris may be found in AN, ser. F18, carton 10a, plaque 2, doss. xxv, "Préfecture de Police, Paris: Etat des imprimeurs qui se sont conformés aux dispositions de l'article XI du décret impérial du 5 février 1810 en présentant à la Préfecture de Police un livret pour être côté et paragraphé," April 4, 1810. For the organization of the survey procedure, see AN, ser.

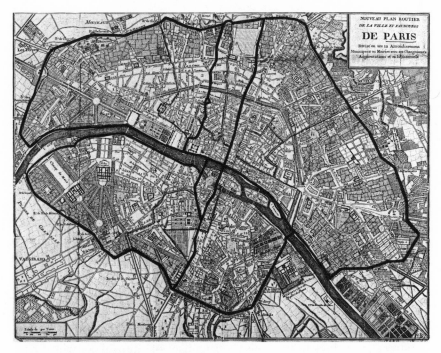

Figure 9. The Six Arrondissements of the Paris Inspectors of the Book Trade, 1810–1811.
Source: AN, ser. F4, cartons 2572–2573, doss. 1–2; and BN, nouv. acq. fr. 1362, feuilles 63–64.

results for Paris, in 1810 there were 157 printers and 588 publishers and booksellers in the capital prior to implementation of the new decrees; thereafter, the number of printers in Paris was halved and every book-seller and publisher in Paris either licensed or suppressed.

Paris was assigned special inspectors of the book and printing trades. The city was divided into six *arrondissements* of inspection, with one man assigned to each.[115] The inspectors were ordered to conduct vigilant

F18, carton 11a, plaque 1, Report from Delaubépie, inspector in Paris, March 26, 1810; and AN, ser. F18, carton 10a, plaque 2, doss. xxxiv, Request for surveys by the Direction, December 6, 1810.

115. AN, ser. F4, carton 2572, doss. 1, "Etat nominatif des inspecteurs de la librairie à Paris . . . , 1810." For the creation of their *arrondissements*, see BN, nouv. acq. fr. 1362, feuilles 63–64, "Lettres et ordres de service de [François-René-Jean] général baron de Pommereul, directeur général de la librairie et imprimerie, adressés à Gaudefroy, inspec-teur de la librairie à Paris, 1810–1814."

surveillance, "not only of the printing, publishing, and bookselling trades, but also of all the professions that service them, such as binders, folders, type founders, press manufacturers, engravers and print dealers, colporteurs, reading rooms, etc.," and every inspector was to keep an exact log of every visit he made and to submit a written report every Monday morning to the director general.[116]

The General Direction of the Book Trade intended to monitor not only every printer, publisher, and bookseller in the entire empire, but also every piece of printed matter. All printed goods in general commerce at the moment of the regulation had to be registered and stamped.[117] Every new publication had to be submitted for a *récipissé* at the Prefecture of Police—a certificate that served as a legal proof of registration and, in effect, a permission to sell the work.[118] Every new edition or reedition, and even new press runs, had to be declared and permissions granted. The Direction of the Book Trade also established a national *Journal de l'imprimerie et de la librairie* to announce all legal works "in print,"[119] with new works to be announced separately from new editions of works in the public domain.[120] The new regime had begun. And it was a new regime based on surveillance rather than censorship as the chief preventative mechanism of cultural control.

The regulation of 1810 reshaped the social as well as the civic dimensions of print culture. On April 27, 1810, the newly formed General Direction received an appeal from the Paris printer Antoine Chambon. Chambon described himself in the following terms:

116. BN, nouv. acq. fr. 1362, feuilles 31–32, "Lettres et ordres de service du général baron de Pommereul."

117. AN, ser. F18, carton 1, "Bulletin des lois, no. 264: Décret impérial contenant le règlement sur l'imprimerie et la librairie . . . , 5 février 1810," 2.

118. AN, ser. F18, carton 40, Instructions from the Director General to "MM. les imprimeurs de Paris," [1810]. He writes, "Some printers are referring to this *récipissé* as a *permission*. This is not an abuse of words."

119. AN, ser. F18, carton 10a, plaque 2, "Copie de la circulaire de monsieur le directeur général, concernant le journal du Sr. Pillet, aux inspecteurs de la librairie aux départements," November 27, 1810.

120. AN, ser. F18, carton 40, Letter from François-René-Jean, baron de Pommereul, director general, to the minister of police, January 19, 1811.

I have been a printer since the age of twelve; I was a printing-shop worker until 1780 when I became a book dealer, with nothing but the fruits of my savings. I continued this trade until 1790 when, following the example of so many others, I took advantage of the declaration of unlimited freedom of the press across France to return to my original profession. . . . I used every resource I had to establish a little printing shop composed of two presses. . . . It has been my source of livelihood to this day.

Chambon was now to be driven from his chosen profession by the new requirement that all printers have at least four presses. And he had a theory as to why these criteria had been imposed:

For a while now a certain number of agitators, among whom there are a few who enjoy a reputation for rectitude, but many of whom are crippled by debts or dishonored by fraudulent bankruptcies . . . , have been knocking at every door soliciting a regulation of this trade. There is no doubt that the decrees of February 5 are the result of the shady dealings and manipulations of this group. . . . Perhaps these greedy men hope to receive jobs in this new administration . . . in order to pay off their debts and restore their honor.[121]

Chambon was an acute observer of his community and its fate. The regulation of 1810 was designed by and for the older and larger printing establishments of Paris and the departments. In exchange for a restricted monopoly, they agreed to surveillance. It was the Baudouins and the Agasses, not the Chambons, who would benefit from the Napoleonic system, as they had from the Old Regime. Indeed, at least one-third of the eighty Paris printers retained in 1810 were from families of the old Paris Book Guild.[122] Lineage counted for something. Yet as the suppression of the Paris printer Demoraine, "printer from father to son for over one hundred years," makes clear, the new regulation did not represent a simple victory of the "old" printers over the "new," but of the bigger and wealthier printers over the smaller ones.[123]

The regulation was intended to have similar consequences for the publishing world. While taking every step to eradicate all but official journals and ephemeral literature, the General Direction did everything

121. AN, ser. F18, carton 11a, plaque 1, Report from Antoine Chambon, printer in Paris, April 27, 1810.

122. See chapter 5.

123. AN, ser. BB16, carton 772, doss. 4543, Letter from Jean-Baptiste Demoraine, printer in Paris, to the minister of justice, February 8, 1811, protesting his suppression after the implementation of the regulation of 1810, which limited the number of printers in the city to eighty.

possible to restore and improve the commercial viability of book publishing. The regulation significantly extended the duration of private
claims on texts, from ten years after the author's death to twenty years
after the death of the author *and* his wife. The commercial value of a
writer's work was thus significantly enhanced. The value of publishers'
portfolios would increase as a consequence, while the rate at which they
would need to replenish their portfolios would diminish. The incessant
quest for *nouveautés* would therefore become less of a commercial imperative. And in exchange for political cooperation with the regime,
publishers enjoyed police surveillance and protection of their property
from literary piracy.

Even more importantly, the General Direction took significant steps
to insure that publishers could fruitfully exploit the public domain, first
by requiring registration of all editions of works and, second, by reserv-
ing the power to grant, deny, or delay permissions to publish; this made
it possible to regulate the number and kinds of editions of a given text
on the market at a given moment. With the publication of the *Journal de
l'imprimerie et de la librairie*, publishers themselves for the first time gained
an effective means to operate strategically in the public domain. In exchange for the services the government provided in regulating the public domain, publishers and printers paid a per-page fee to the General
Direction for all editions they produced of those common works.[124] This
tax single-handedly financed the new administration. The era of the cutthroat free market in common ideas was over.

Assured of sales, works already established as classics now appeared
more commercially attractive to publishers than new books. The regulation of 1810 thus marked a victory for the big printers and publishers
of lengthy works over the little printers and dealers in ephemeral and
periodical literature. The first, but short-lived, head of the Direction of
the Book Trade, the comte de Portalis, announced in an early official
bulletin: "By recovering a more tranquil course . . . and leaving behind
the rebellious, aggressive, and angry tone that it acquired in the past
century, the book trade will change its complexion. It will become a
commerce in books for libraries and instruction, and cease to be one of

124. AN, ser. F18, carton 1, "Bulletin des Lois, no. 366," decree of April 29, 1811. See
also BN, nouv. acq. fr. 1352, feuille 44, Letter from Pommereul, general director of the
book trade, to the Paris inspector Gaudefroy.

seditious pamphlets."[125] The civilization of "the book" re-eclipsed the revolution of "the press(es)."

Significantly, the next director of the book trade, François-René-Jean, baron de Pommereul, referred to the tax on publishers as a "dowry" paid to the administration in exchange for the right to reproduce texts in the common domain.[126] And indeed, the new cultural regime instituted through the decrees of 1810 was a marriage of state regulation and the commercial market, a reshaping through the social metaphor of a family rather than the political metaphor of a republic of citizens. The author, consecrated in 1793 as a civic hero of public enlightenment, now saw the legal lineage of his or her textual property extended not according to political and civic ideals, but along biological and familial lines: a remaining spouse and children replaced the nation as the author's immediate heirs, and authorial legal identity began its course toward reprivatization. Analogically, the relationship between the state and the commerical publishing world was reconfigured within the family metaphor as well: the father/publisher was to offer a "dowry" in the form of a per-page, per-edition tax to the Direction of the Book Trade to insure administrative protection of his daughter/commodity and the reproduction of a national cultural lineage through the printed book. If under the Republic state patronage had advanced *philos* as a cultural ideal in an effort to temper the *eros* of the commercial market, now the paterfamilias would serve as the organizing principle for the public transmission of ideas.

125. Comte de Portalis, *Bulletin*, no. 268, Announcement from the director of the Administration of the Book Trade (1810); cited in Charles Thuriot, "Documents relatifs à l'exécution du décret du 5 février 1810," *Revue critique d'histoire et de littérature*, nos. 43–49 (1871): 340.
126. Ibid.

CONCLUSION

The story of Paris publishing in the French Revolution suggests that literary historians and critics may need a more complex view of the relationship between modern revolutions and cultural change, one that accounts for the political and legal as well as the socio-economic forces that work to reshape the cultural world. There can be little doubt, as socio-cultural historians descending from both the *Annales* and the Frankfurt schools suggest, that the eighteenth-century expansion of commerce in the printed word placed unprecedented pressures on public authorities of the revolutionary period to create a cultural regime grounded in market relations rather than state-controlled corporate monopolies. However, the cultural policies of revolutionary legislators mediated the expression of socio-economic forces through laws, institutions, and political ideals, which reflected their changing conceptions of the public good and which emerged as a result of political negotiation with the private interests of authors and publishers. Indeed, the revolutionaries' economic and cultural values were not always in harmony.

As Jürgen Habermas and Robert Darnton, among others, have stressed, the diffusion of Enlightenment thought accompanied the developing commercialization of the printed word in the eighteenth century.[1] In France, the complicity between black-market booty capitalism working beneath the corporate monopolies of the absolutist state, and the underground cultural movement to "spread enlightenment"

1. See Jürgen Habermas, *The Structural Transformation of the Public Sphere*, trans. Thomas Burger (Cambridge, Mass.: MIT Press, 1989 [orig. German ed. 1962]); and Darnton, *Business of Enlightenment*.

beyond the reach of state censorship was particularly intense. It is not surprising, therefore, that when French cultural revolutionaries seized power in 1789, they turned to the deregulated free market as the ideal mechanism for disseminating Enlightenment thought. Seemingly, the people yearned for underground Enlightenment literature, and the market yearned to deliver it. But once capitalist market relations, as well as the cultural movements they had helped to transmit, were formally legitimated through economic and cultural legislation, the complicity between market capitalism and the cultural program of the Enlightenment collapsed. The reading public demanded amusement rather than education, tales of private passions rather than reasoned discourses on public virtue. And in response to these demands, the liberated commercial presses of the revolutionary period poured forth novels rather than philosophy. Far from representing the commercial triumph of Enlightenment culture, the Revolution represented its undoing. The central dilemma in reshaping the publishing world during the French Revolution became the problem of reconciling the economic ideal of a free market in the world of ideas with the cultural ideal of propagating enlightened science and philosophy.

The process of resolving this dilemma, through negotiation and trial and error, caused the revolutionaries to rethink old ideals. Between 1789 and 1793, the entire infrastructure of licit publishing under the former regime was swept away—the royal Administration of the Book Trade, its censors and inspectors, the system of literary privileges, the academies, and the printers' and booksellers' guilds. As this officially sanctioned literary civilization crumbled, the cultural underground of the Old Regime emerged into the light of day. Enlightenment publishing enterprises moved from the borders of France to its capital. The periodical press boomed. Hundreds of new printing shops and booksellers appeared in the capital "to spread light in every direction."

The revolt against absolutist literary civilization brought anarchy in its wake. Until 1791 there were no national laws limiting what could be said or depicted in print. Only in 1793 were particular claims to authorship or ownership of a published text legally defined. The unlimited freedom to publish remained largely unchecked, except by the sporadic efforts of municipal authorities and the contingent decisions meted out in lower civil and criminal courts. The legal status of the printed word in the period from the abolition of privilege in August 1789 to the laws on sedition and libel of 1791 and literary property of 1793 was never fully resolved.

Following the "October days" of 1789, the National Assembly took its first steps toward founding a new legal regime to regulate the printed word. The Sieyès proposal of 1790 sought at once to define the legal limits of freedom of expression in periodical and ephemeral literature and to protect the claims of authors and publishers on texts as forms of property. In so doing, the proposal politicized the tension in Enlightenment epistemology between the individual/subjective and universal/objective nature of ideas. The conflict over authors' versus public rights gave expression to two competing visions of how the Enlightenment should be translated into a way of life. Horrified by the explosion of seemingly endless quantities of inflammatory pamphlets and newspapers that fueled revolutionary radicalization, the cultural elites within the government sought to restrain public expression by holding authors legally accountable for what they said in print and by encouraging the publication of ideas in less inflammatory forms, such as books rather than newspapers and pamphlets. Sieyès, Condorcet, and Chénier were themselves some of the greatest practitioners of the arts of journalism and pamphleteering, but as they endeavored to consolidate the new regime they came increasingly to promote a conception of Enlightenment culture as, in essence, a culture of "the book"—that is, of lengthy and dispassionate reflection on the world, produced by professional authors who would own and thus be legally accountable for their ideas. This vision of a "republic of letters," forged in reaction to the explosion of ephemera in 1789, stood in sharp contrast to Condorcet's earlier idealistic conception of a cultural world in which public exchange of ideas would be an authorless and classless form of social action, most fully embodied in the model of the periodical press.

Nonetheless, when the National Convention reshaped the political and legal identity of the author, from a privileged creature of the absolutist state into a civic hero of public enlightenment, it did not merely recreate the author as an absolute bourgeois property owner. The declaration of the rights of genius of July 1793 represented an effort to synthesize these two competing visions of Enlightenment cultural practice. Rather than resolving the tension between arguments for the natural rights of authors and instrumentalist notions of the rights of the public, the law gave expression to this tension in the idea of "limited property rights." Individual genius was to be protected and remunerated during an author's lifetime; at death, however, his or her work became part of the public domain, the property of all. Enlightened culture was thus to be transmitted through authored books, but books freely accessible to everyone. With this declaration, in short, the entire literary inheritance of Old Regime France was released from private hands into the public domain.

By the middle of the year II (1794), however, the Commission on Public Instruction of the National Convention and its successors under the Directory and the Consulate became painfully aware that their policies had not resulted in the enlightened literary culture they had envisioned. Liberated from the constraints of Old Regime civilization, citizens did not naturally incline toward reason, science, and utilitarian good. The commercial presses poured forth fictions rather than truths. The cultural policy-makers of the convention thus arrived at the sobering insight that the presses, if left free to respond to the demands of the commercial market, could become agents of passion rather than reason, leisure rather than utility, and conservatism rather than change.

Furthermore, commercial book publishing as a whole was foundering. Ironically, with the severe limitations on private claims upon texts and the abolition of any centralized administration of the book trade, texts that had entered the public domain were rendered commercially inviable. The lack of preventative measures against pirate editions and the exclusive reliance on municipal authorities and civil courts proved wholly inadequate in the face of cutthroat competition over limited literary markets. The duration of exclusive claims on texts was so short that the value of many manuscripts diminished sharply, allowing only one or possibly two editions. For multivolume works, ten years was totally insufficient for the production and distribution of even a single edition. Finally, the works to which the convention had been most concerned to insure public access, that is, the classics of French literary civilization in the public domain, were rendered commercially worthless. Without an exclusive commercial claim, at least on an edition, publishers facing the prospect of being undercut by a second or even third competitive edition of the same work were driven away from the classics into *nouveautés* and ephemera. Texts in the public domain had become "too free" to be spread through the mechanism of the commercial market.

The nation's governments responded to these dilemmas of republican publishing with three successive strategies. The year II witnessed the beginnings of an intensive effort, initiated by the Committee on Public Safety, to centralize the production of printed matter so as to insure dissemination of what they deemed to be enlightened republican culture. Thus the government assembled the Imprimerie de la République, a single printing shop of unprecedented dimensions and productive power. This effort to establish state hegemony over the means of producing printed matter was met with vociferous but ultimately ineffectual opposition from Parisian and provincial printers alike.

The Commission on Public Instruction sponsored a second phase of intervention in the free market in ideas with its policy of "encouragements and rewards." Through massive infusions of capital, it sought at once to bail out French publishing, to subsidize the publication and diffusion of "useful works," and, through saturation, to transform, it hoped, the reading tastes and habits of the nation. Whatever the immediate impact of these two strategies, they proved financially untenable and ultimately failed to resolve the underlying crisis in commercial book publishing.

A third effort to reshape cultural life to match the ideals of the new regime in power occurred at the opening of the nineteenth century. A massive financial crisis in the book trade coincided with a systematic effort by the Napoleonic administration to control the periodical press and trade in political ephemera. As in 1790, the initiative to restrict the press was accompanied by measures to revive book publishing. Political consolidation brought cultural consolidation in its wake. The reforms of the book publishing world during the Napoleonic period were of deeper and more lasting consequence, however, than the limited and brief revival of prepublication censorship. Indeed, the regulation of 1810 did not constitute a restoration of the old cultural regime: control of the world of print was to be principally through surveillance, not censorship.

The regulation of 1810 did not lay a new basis for the commercial exploitation of texts, though it did extend the property claims of the author to his or her immediate family. This revision of the laws on literary property recast the legal notion of authorship in biological rather than political terms: rhetorically, the author was transformed from the civic hero of public enlightenment into the private figure of the *chef de famille*. But the most unprecedented aspect of the 1810 regulation was the creation of institutional and administrative conditions necessary for the commercial exploitation of texts in the public domain, by regulating *editions* of common texts. This legal differentiation encouraged re-editions, rather than first editions—that is, cultural reproduction and consolidation, not innovation.

If the law of 1793 was a "declaration of the rights of genius," the regulation of 1810 marked the institutional consecration of the power of publishers. The idea of private claims on particular editions of public texts allowed the ideal of democratic access to a common cultural inheritance to be reconciled with capitalistic exploitation of that cultural commons. The year 1810 opened the doors to the world of publishers' series like *Pléiade* and *Livre de poche*, with their respective editions of Voltaire, Rousseau, or Diderot. The cultural capital of modern publishing in the public domain would inhere in the paratext rather than in the text itself—that is, in the particularities of the *edition* (its notes, format, paper, preface, and so on). These distinctions now became the crucial elements in the commercial divisions of the literary market.[2] The texts themselves, at least in spirit, were to remain free for all.

The year 1810 also marked the victory of the ideal of enlightened civilization as a civilization of "the book," a civilization existing above the course of events, authored and owned by professional intellectuals. It was here, at these ethereal heights, among these chosen individuals, that progress in human understanding was meant to take its course. Every effort was made to eradicate the cultural populism of the republican period. The indigenous media of the masses, from almanacs and the periodical press to popular song sheets, were vigilantly censored and controlled and would remain so throughout the nineteenth century. In the first year of the Restoration, the Crown released all works over the length of twenty printer's sheets from the tutelage of prepublication censorship.[3] The implications of this oligarchic cultural reaction, this politics of literary genres, did not go unnoticed, or unchallenged, by Benjamin Constant:

> All enlightened men seemed to be convinced that complete freedom and exemption from any form of censorship should be granted to longer works. Because writing them requires time, purchasing them requires affluence, and reading them requires attention, they are not able to produce the reaction in the populace that one fears of works of greater rapidity and violence. But *pamphlets,* and *handbills,* and especially *newspapers,* are produced quickly, you can buy them for little, and because their effect is immediate, they are believed to be more dangerous.[4]

By creating a two-tiered cultural regime that left elite literary culture uncensored while popular literary forms were still rigorously policed,

---

2. For further discussion of the centrality of "paratextuality" to postrevolutionary literary culture, see Genette, *Seuils.*

3. AN, ser. F18, carton 1, "Loi relative à la liberté de la presse sanctionnée et publiée le 21 octobre 1814," title 1, art. 1.

4. Benjamin Constant, *De la liberté des brochures, des pamphlets et des journaux* (Paris, 1814), 1.

the Restoration monarchy remade the "republic of letters" yet again, this time as a *république censitaire:* a cultural oligarchy.

Of course, the victory of "the book" was not a total one. Even among the carefully selected eighty printers of Paris there were individuals, such as Jean-Gabriel Dentu, who resisted the Napoleonic reshaping of revolutionary literary culture. Like Antoine Chambon, Dentu had been a printing-shop worker who took advantage of the declaration of press freedom in 1789 to open his own shop (plate 8). Unlike Chambon, however, Dentu was spectacularly successful. As the survey inspector of 1811 described Dentu, "He has built a first-class printing shop and publishing house, and has just opened a superb boutique in the Palais Royal that is well stocked with books. He does business in all genres."[5] Dentu's was one of the new fortunes of the revolutionary period, and he easily met the material criteria for selection by the new regime. Nonetheless, Dentu did not quite fit into the regime's view of things. Even in the earliest and most glowing accounts of his lavish establishment, the inspector of his district felt obliged to note that "he is suspicious of government surveillance and sees himself as the master of his establishment."[6] It was an inauspicious beginning for relations between Dentu and the new regime.

Louis-François-André Gaudefroy, a Paris inspector of the book trade, took over the *arrondissement* of the Hôtel de Ville by rotation on July 1, 1813.[7] Gaudefroy was a provincial bibliophile from Amiens in his mid-fifties who had taken the inspectorship in Paris better to pursue his passion for books.[8] But he found himself constantly outstripped by the fast pace of the capital and its wily purveyors of the printed word. The move to the *arrondissement* of the Hôtel de Ville brought him into daily contact with the printer Dentu.

Dentu drove Gaudefroy mad.[9] Every time Gaudefroy entered Dentu's

5. AN, ser. F18, carton 25, "Notes sur les imprimeurs ci-après désignés" (1810–1811).
6. Ibid.
7. For biographical information on Gaudefroy, see BN, nouv. acq. fr. 1362, feuille 53. For his assignment to the *arrondissement* of the Hôtel de Ville, see ibid., feuille 120.
8. See ibid., feuilles 53 and 59. Gaudefroy's passion for books earned him a reprimand from the director for conflict of interest in his dealings with booksellers.
9. This concluding account is from ibid., feuilles 173–174, Report from Gaudefroy to the director general of the book trade, Pommereul, concerning the printer Dentu, [1813].

Plate 8. Galeries de bois, Palais Royal, Paris (1825). Jean-Gabriel Dentu's book-shop in the Palais Royal is depicted on the left of this woodblock engraving by the illustrator F. Meaulles. Kubler Collection, Cooper-Hewitt Museum, New York.

printing shop for inspection, the presses were absolutely still and totally empty. Although Gaudefroy was certain that "he always starts printing again . . . the moment I leave his shop," he could not catch Dentu in the act. He was also certain that Dentu printed secretly all night. Still, "at no matter what hour of the day I arrive at his printing shop, I have never seen a single sheet . . . in press." Dentu was too quick for him.

Gaudefroy knew that Dentu was the source of numerous venom-filled pamphlets attacking the regime, such as the *Etat de la France sous la domination de Bonaparte*. But it was less the content of these pamphlets than Dentu's independence that really got under Gaudefroy's skin: "M. Dentu, having founded his business upon the principles of Jacobinism, to which he owes the beginnings of his fortune, behaves as though he is still living in that time of piracy and anarchy. He is the sort who will always be in open rebellion."

It was Dentu's arrogant defiance of state surveillance, his libertarianism, that unnerved the inspector. Dentu wore him down. After several weeks Gaudefroy had to admit defeat to his superior. Telling the director of the book trade that he could no longer face making his regular visits to Dentu's shop, he begged for a reprieve:

> Today I have only one sincere wish to ask of you, Monsieur le Directeur, which is that despite the pains I have suffered for the past five months, and the financial sacrifice that moving from the capital would entail . . . , if in each district of inspection there are no more than four printers as immoral as this one, I would prefer to be transferred immediately to the farthest corner of France.

The nineteenth century was to inherit the revolutionary cultural traditions of Dentu, along with the authoritarianism of Gaudefroy.

APPENDIX 1

An Index of Indebtedness in the Paris Book Guild, 1789–1793 (90 individuals)

Source: AP, Fond Faillite, sers. D4B6 and D11U3.

1. *Debure-d'Houry*
(6,7,8,9,12,13,14,16,17)

Debits	*Credits*
Barbou	*Moutard
Cuchet	*Leroy
*Cailleau	Stoupe
Crapart	Lejay, fils
Didot, fils	Poinçot, fils
l'aîné	
Desroy	**Durand
*Didot (Firmin)	*Didot
	(Firmin)
Despilly	*Cailleau
Fourniers	Maradan
(Dlles)	
Lallemant	Poinçot
	(Claude)
LeClerc	Briand
Laporte	Gobreau
Laurent	Kéralio
	(Lagrange)
*Leroy	Debure
Lamy	Fabre
*Moutard	Guillaume
Mérigot, le	Froullé
jeune	
Morin	
Panckoucke	
Saugrain	
Valleyre	

2. *Prault* (8)

Debits	*Credits*
	Maradan
	**Durand
	Cuchet

3. *Desenne* (8)

Debits	*Credits*
Séguy-Thiboust	
Despilly	
Ballard	
Maradan	
Fournier, le	
jeune	

4. *Gattey*

Debits	*Credits*
Cellot	*Valade
Crapart	
Gueffier	
Laporte	
Plassan	
Saugrain	
*Valade	

(*Continued*)

5. *Savoye* (12)

Debits	Credits
Barrois, je.	(all provincial)
Cellot	
Despilly	
Delalain, l'aîné	
Vve Duplain	
Desprez	
Didot, l'aîné	
Vve Desaint	
Gueffier	
Vve Jombert	
Nyon, je.	
Vve Petit	
Panckoucke	
Delalain, le jeune	
Simon	
Voland	
Barrois, l'aîné	

6. *Briand* (1)

Debits	Credits
	**Durand
	Moutard
	Crapart
	Laporte
	Vve Herissant
	Petit
	Nyon, Imp.
	Cellot
	Demonville
	Plassan
	Despilly
	Knapen

7. *Fabre* (1)

Debits	Credits
Knapen	
Debure-d'Houry	
Bailly	
Onfroy	
Delalain, le jeune	
Leroy	
Cellot	

8. *Maradan* (1,2,3,14)

Debits	Credits
(did not note individuals)	

9. *Lejay, fils* (1)

Debits	Credits
Fournier	(all provincial)
Vve Jombert	
Baudouin	

10. *Duplain*

Debits	Credits
Baudouin	Mérigot, le jeune
Despilly	
Nyon, l'aîné	
Cellot	
Clousier	
Simon	
Petit	
Laporte	
Couturier	

11. *Cussac* (14)

Debits	Credits
(did not note individuals)	

12. *Lagrange/Kéralio* (1,15)

Debits	Credits
Nyon, Imp.	**Durand
Demaisonneuve	Savoye
Debure, le	Bailly
jeune	
Cailleau	Gobreau
Quillau	Legras
Pierres	Royez
Demonville	Monory
Séguy-Thiboust	
Vve Valade	
Vve Herissant	
Ballard	

13. *Poinçot (Claude)* (1,15)

Debits	Credits
Panckoucke	
Valade	

14. *Poinçot, fils* (1,8,11,16)

Debits	Credits
Laporte	**Durand
Maradan	Guillaume
Gueffier, le	
jeune	
Cuchet	
Vve Herissant	
Guillot	
Moutard	
Demaisonneuve	
Cellot	
Bailly	
Cussac	
Périsse	

15. *Lefevre* (12,13,16)

Debits	Credits
Lagrange/	Royer
Kéralio	
Poinçot	Guillaume
(Claude)	

16. *Guillaume* (1,14,15)

Debits	Credits
Nyon	Laurent
Debure-d'Houry	Langlois
Bailly	Pissot
Gueffier	
Onfroy	

17. *Momoro* (1)

Debits	Credits
Bailly	Dubois
Cuchet	**Durand
**Durand	
Servière	
Belin	
Debure-d'Houry	

Numbers in parentheses: individuals on the table who appear in each other's accounts.
*Individuals who appear in both columns of a single account.
**Durand also went bankrupt.

APPENDIX 2

Declarations of Bankruptcy by the Paris Book Guild, 1789–1793 (17 individuals)

Source: AP, Fond Faillite, sers. D4B6 and D11U3.

Capitation Class	Name	Total *Actif* (in *livres*)	Date	Reference
2	*Debure-d'Houry, François-Jean Noël	1,870,247	July 26, 1790	D4B6, carton 110, doss. 7844
7	*Prault, Louis-François	329,935	Nov. 24, 1790	D4B6, carton 111, doss. 7915
9	Desenne, Victor	130,564	Sept. 11, 1792	D11U3, carton 1
11	Gattey, François-Charles	512,099	Oct. 5, 1792	D11U3, carton 1
12	Savoye, Nicolas	213,816	Jan. 26, 1791	D4B6, carton 111, doss. 7944
15	Briand, Pierre-César	172,500	Dec. 24, 1789	D4B6, carton 108, doss. 7657
15	Fabre, Jean	34,821	Apr. 3, 1790	D4B6, carton 109, doss. 7763
15	Maradan, Claude-François	**701,035	Apr. 24, 1790	D4B6, carton 106, doss. 7773
15	Lejay, fils, Louis-Laurent	212,603	Oct. 23, 1790	D4B6, carton 111, doss. 7899
15	Duplain, Pierre-Jacques	114,079	Dec. 2, 1790	D4B6, carton 111, doss. 7924
15	Cussac, Jean	141,503	Apr. 16, 1791	D4B6, carton 112, doss. 7980
16	Lagrange, Jean (Kéralio)	**578,323	Mar. 30, 1789	D4B6, carton 105, doss. 7454
16	Poinçot, Claude	170,410	Mar. 16, 1790	D4B6, carton 109, doss. 7739
16	Poinçot, fils, Claude-François	64,889	Apr. 8, 1790	D4B6, carton 109, doss. 7764
19	Lefevre, Pierre	44,864	Feb. 20, 1790	D4B6, carton 108, doss. 7711

Capi-tation Class	Name	Total *Actif* (in *livres*)	Date	Reference
19	Guillaume, Charles	6,429	Jan. 22, 1793	D11U3, carton 2
20	Momoro, Antoine-François	30,108	June 8, 1790	D4B6, carton 110, doss. 7811

*Printer

**The declarations of Maradan and Lagrange deviate significantly from the pattern of distribution of wealth by capitation class. In the case of Lagrange, this is explained by his covert association with Mlle de Kéralio, whose contribution to the association significantly inflated his financial status. The case of Maradan can be explained by his substantial illicit trade prior to the Revolution.

APPENDIX 3

Signatories of the Petitions of the Printers of Paris, 1795

Sources: AN, ser. C, carton 356, doc. 1888; and AN, ser. AA, carton 56, doc. 1525.

First Petition:

+ 1. Knapen (b,c)
+ 2. Moutard (b,c)
+ 3. Cussac (b,c)
   4. Masson
− 5. Agasse (b,c / Panckoucke)
+ 6. Née de la Rochelle (c)
   7. Demoraine (c)
   8. Deltufo
   9. Hocquet (c)
  10. Pougin (a,b,c)
− 11. Cordier (c / Legras)
  12. Lesquilliers (c)
  13. Casin
  14. Pellier (a,b,c)
+ 15. Laurent, jeune (b,c)
+ 16. Vve Delaguette (b,c)
  17. Galetti (c)
+ 18. Guillaume (a,c)
+ 19. Ballard, fils (a,b,c)
+ 20. Ballard, père (a,b,c)
− 21. Dupont (a,b,c)
  22. Tarin (c)
  23. Migneret (c)
+ 24. Laurent, l'aîné (c)
  25. Renaudière (a,b,c)
  26. Tutot (c)
− 27. Fuchs (Onfroy)
  28. Boiste (b,c)
  29. Sétier (c)

Second Petition:

+ 30. Quillau (b,c)
+ 31. Delormel (b,c)
+ 32. Barbou, frères (b,c)

+ 33. Duchesne (b,c)
+ 34. Clousier (b,c)
+ 35. Guénard Demonville (b,c)
+ 36. Cellot (b,c)
− 37. Eberhart (b,c / Pierres)
+ 38. Belin (b,c)
− 39. Baudelot (b,c / Pierres)
− 40. Delance (b,c / Belin)
  41. Jaquin (b,c)

Addenda:

  42. Arthaud (a)

Third Petition:

+ 43. Lottin (c)
+ 44. Vve Valade (c)
  45. Smith (c)
  46. Chevet (c)
  47. Lefebvre (c)
  48. Millet (c)
  49. Roblot (c)
  50. Cholet (c)
+ 51. Boulard (c)
  52. Lion (c)
  53. Glisau (c)
  54. Pierret (c)
  55. Tiger (c)
  56. Brosselard (c)
  57. Mercier (c)
  58. Lenormand (c)
+ 59. Valade, fils (c)
  60. Forget, A.-Cl. (c)
  61. Vve Gorsas (c)
  62. Lejeune (c)
  63. Charpentier (c)

64. Pallisseaux (c)
65. Devergne (c)
66. Lucas (c)
67. Lepage (c)
68. Vve Potier de Lille
69. Perlet (c)
70. Teulière (c)

71. Gourdin (c)
72. Cretot (c)
73. Aubertin (c)
74. Porte (c)

Individual *Mémoire:*

+75. Baudouin

+ = Former guild member
− = Related to former guild member or direct successor
a = Also signed the "Addenda"
b = Also signed the "Second Petition"
c = Also signed the "Mémoire"

APPENDIX 4

New Printers and Publishers/Booksellers in Paris, 1788–1813 (1,224 establishments)

Source: Paul Delalain, *L'Imprimerie et la librairie à Paris de 1789 à 1813* (Paris: Delalain, [1900]) and AN, ser. F18, cartons 10a and 25.

	(A) P / B-P	(B) P / B-P	(A)+(B) P / B-P
1788, Guild	10 / 51	31 / 82	41 / 133
1788, non-Guild	— / —	6 / 47	6 / 47
1789	— / —	23 / 11	23 / 11
1790	18 / 14	14 / 29	32 / 43
1791	4 / 6	3 / 15	7 / 21
1792	2 / 11	6 / 22	8 / 33
1793	4 / 2	3 / 11	7 / 13
1794	4 / 6	0 / 10	4 / 16
1795	5 / 10	4 / 12	9 / 22
1796	2 / 11	6 / 20	8 / 31
1797	37 / 25	18 / 30	55 / 55
1798	12 / 27	11 / 24	23 / 51
1799	3 / 14	5 / 10	8 / 24
1800	9 / 15	4 / 13	13 / 28
1801	6 / 23	4 / 16	10 / 39
1802	14 / 22	2 / 21	16 / 43
1803	2 / 14	4 / 9	6 / 23
1804	23 / 57	3 / 8	26 / 65
1805	2 / 4	2 / 3	4 / 7
1806	1 / 21	3 / 1	4 / 22
1807	0 / 14	3 / 1	3 / 15
1808	4 / 18	2 / 1	6 / 19
1809	1 / 26	4 / 5	5 / 31
1810	4 / 18	2 / 0	6 / 18
1811	4 / 24	3 / 1	7 / 25
1812	0 / 50	0 / 1	0 / 51
1813	0 / 1	— / —	0 / 1
Total	171 / 484	166 / 403	337 / 887

(A) = Short-term business (under 8 years)
(B) = Long-term business (8-plus years)
P   = Printer
B-P = Bookseller and/or publisher

APPENDIX 5

Publishers, Publications, and the *Dépôt Légal*, 1793–1799

A. Breakdown of publishers depositing works at the *dépôt légal*, Bibliothèque
Nationale, July 19, 1793–December 31, 1799:

Paris book publishers	272
(former guild members = 72)	
Paris sheet music publishers	29
Non-Parisian French publishers	33
Foreign publishers	22
Unidentified individuals	63
Total	419

B. Number of works registered at the *dépôt légal* during the same period, by
depositor class:

Paris publishers	1,201
Paris sheet music publishers	768
Authors	599
Non-Parisian publishers	103
Unidentified depositors	107
Total	2,778

C. The fifteen largest Paris book publishers, by number of works submitted
(where * signifies former guild member, + signifies printer, and −
signifies periodicals):

− + Rondonneau (21): law, theater
− Aubry (22): education, science
− + Honnert (22): literature
+ Jansen (23): literature, history, politics, science
− + Agasse (25): history, philosophy, science
+ * Plassan (25): philosophy, classics, natural sciences, novels
Leprieur (26): novels
+ Migneret (29): theater, literature
− + * Didot *l'aîné* (31): classics, theater, poetry, novels
Barba (38): theater
− + * Maradan (39): theater, science, politics, novels
− + Cercle Social (40): philosophy, politics, science, novels
− + * Buisson (50): literature, science, philosophy, novels
Huet (66): theater
+ Cholet, P.-E. (90): theater

D. Source of works submitted by non-Parisian publishers:

France	*Foreign*
Metz	Constantinople (2)
Beauvais-Oise	Cologne
Nîmes (2)	Venice
Bordeaux	Leipzig (3)
Orléans (2)	Florence
Amiens	Praso
Lyon (3)	Madrid (2)
Narbonne	Cayenne
Meaux	Corsini
Strasbourg (8)	Brussels (2)
Valenciennes	Amsterdam
Montauban	Berlin
Brest	London
Marseille	Philadelphia
Rouen (3)	Padova
Versailles	Warsaw
Perpignan	Geneva
Douai	
Vaucluse	Total foreign deposits: 33
Clermont (3)	
Lille	
Dijon	
Besançon	

Total provincial deposits: 70

Total works submitted by non-Parisians, by year: 1793, 6; 1794, 1; 1795, 5; 1796 (year of first foreign deposit), 9; 1797, 13; 1798, 31; 1799, 38.

E. Works of Literature Registered at the *Dépôt Légal*, Bibliothèque Nationale, July 19, 1793–December 31, 1799, by Genre.

	1793[a]	1794	1795	1796	1797	1798	1799	Total
Literature	1	7	9	15	25	36	48	141
Almanacs	2	4	1	4	6	10	13	40
Classical	1	1	7	15	7	22	14	67
Correspondence and memoirs	1	1	0	2	1	6	4	15
Language	1	4	2	6	9	16	16	54
Novels	1	13	14	17	31	40	44	160
Poetry	2	2	3	6	12	11	14	50

E. Works of Literature Registered at the *Dépôt Légal*, Bibliothèque Nationale, July 19, 1793–December 31, 1799, by Genre. (*Continued*).

	1793[a]	1794	1795	1796	1797	1798	1799	Total
Songs	0	40	29	3	10	3	9	94
Theater	2	40	15	12	17	106	116	308
Travel	2	3	4	7	14	19	19	68
Total	13	115	84	87	132	269	297	997

[a]July 19–December 31, 1793, only.

F. Scientific and Technical Works Registered at the *Dépôt Légal*, Bibliothèque Nationale, July 19, 1793–December 31, 1799, by Genre.

	1793[a]	1794	1795	1796	1797	1798	1799	Total
Scientific Works								
General science	0	0	0	2	1	2	0	5
Botany	0	0	0	1	1	8	3	13
Chemistry, pharmacy, etc.	0	0	1	2	3	8	3	17
Mathematics, astronomy	0	3	1	3	7	18	16	48
Medicine	1	3	5	8	7	21	23	68
Natural history	2	1	0	3	5	18	13	42
Veterinary medicine	1	0	0	0	0	0	1	2
Physics	0	1	2	0	1	5	1	10
Weights and measures	0	3	0	2	1	14	11	31
Total	4	11	9	21	26	94	71	236
Technical Works								
General technical	1	2	2	3	1	6	5	20
Agriculture	1	1	3	2	0	3	2	12
Architecture	5	1	0	0	2	5	13	26
Commerce and Industry	1	10	2	2	5	19	14	53
Military Arts	2	6	5	2	2	4	5	26
Total	10	20	12	9	10	37	39	137

[a]July 19–December 31, 1793, only.

WORKS CITED

Primary Sources

Manuscripts

Archives de la Préfecture de Police de Paris (APP)

Series AA, Procès-verbal de Police, cartons 148, 200.

Archives de Paris (AP), Fond Faillite

Series D4B6, cartons 105, 108–111.
Series D11U3, cartons 2, 8, 9, 16–21, 23–27, 29, 32–38.

Archives Nationales (AN)

Series AA, Collection des lettres et pièces divers, cartons 56–58.
Series ADVIII, Imprimés. Instruction publique, lettres, sciences et arts, cartons
    7, 16, 20, 38.
Series AFI, Procès-verbal des Comités d'Agriculture et de Commerce, meetings
    51, 124, 179, 224.
Series AF*II, Comité de Salut Public, carton 294.
Series AQ24, Archives d'entreprises, carton 6.
Series BB3, Ministère de Justice. Affaires criminelles, carton 81a.
Series BB4, Ministère de Justice. Comptabilité, carton 33.
Series BB16, Ministère de Justice. Correspondance générale de la division civile,
    cartons 703–809.
Series C, Assemblée Nationale, cartons 147, 183, 356.
Series DIV, Comité de Constitution, cartons 30, 50.
Series DIX, Comité Ecclésiastique, carton 81.
Series DXIII, Comités d'Agriculture et de Commerce, carton 1.

Series DXXIX *bis,* Comité de Recherches, carton 16, 32.

Series F4, Ministère de l'Intérieur. Comptabilité générale, cartons 2554, 2572, 2573.

Series F7, Police Générale, cartons 3688, 4637, 4645, 4658, 4722, 4774, 4775.

Series F17, Comité d'Instruction Publique, cartons 1001, 1004a–c, 1005a, 1008a–c, 1009a *bis,* 1009b–c, 1010d, 1199, 1204, 1233, 1258, 1306.

Series F18, Imprimerie, librairie, presse, censure, cartons 1, 10a, 11a, 25, 39, 40, 565.

Series H2, Bureau de la Ville de Paris. Intendance et généralité de Paris, carton 2103.

Series O1, Maison du Roi, carton 611.

Series V1, Grande Chancellerie. Bureau de la Librairie, cartons 549–553.

Series W, Juridictions extraordinaires, cartons 8, 21, 53, 76–78, 332, 339.

Series Y, Procès-verbal du Châtelet, "saisies de libelles par les commissaires de police sous les ordres de M. le lieutenant général de police," nos. 10012, 11441, 11518, 12083, 12085, 13016, 13582, 14353, 14583, 14584, 15021, 15022, 15100, 16008.

Series 144 AP, Archives Privées. Papiers Ormesson, carton 134.

Bibliothèque Nationale (BN)

Archives Modernes, CXXIX, "Registres du dépôt légal des livres imprimés" (July 19, 1793–December 31, 1799).

Fond Français (mss. fr.) 1682, Collection Joly de Fleury, "Librairie, imprimerie et censure des livres: règlements sur la matière, 1607–1789."

6687, Siméon-Prosper Hardy, "Mes loisirs," 1788–1789, vol. 8.

11708, Procès-verbal des délibérations du bureau de Paris, 1790.

21822, 21832, 21861, 21896, 21936, 22004, 22005, 22006, Archives de la chambre syndicale des libraires et imprimeurs de Paris.

22070, 22102, Collection Anisson-Duperron.

Nouvelles Acquisitions Françaises (nouv. acq. fr.) 1362, "Lettres et ordres de service de général baron de Pommereul, directeur général de la librairie et imprimerie, adressés à Gaudefroy, inspecteur de la librairie à Paris, 1810–1814."

1840, Anonymous mss., "Pensées libres sur la liberté de la presse à l'occasion d'un rapport du représentant Chénier à la Convention Nationale," signed A.M., 12 floréal, an III.

2666, Procès-verbal du Comité du district de St-Roch, 1790, fols. 6, 29, 62, 70, 84, 105.

2696, Procès-verbal du district de St-André des Arts, 1789, fol. 109.

2836, Bibliothèques pendant la Révolution (1789–1810).

9192–9193, Instruction Publique. Collection Ginguené.

12684, "Documents et correspondance concernant Ph.-D. Pierres, imprimeur à Versailles (1741–1801)."

Published

Unattributed

Almanach de la librairie. Paris: Moutard, 1781.

Almanach royal. Paris: Debure-d'Houry, 1789.

Amis des lois. Edited by Poultier. Paris, 1800.

Annales patriotiques et littéraires de la France. Edited by Carra and Mercier. Paris: Buisson, 1789–1794.

Annonces de bibliographie moderne ou catalogue raisonné et analytique des livres nouveaux. 2 vols. Paris: Lavillette, 1790.

Annuaire de l'imprimerie et de la librairie de l'Empire français pour l'année 1813. Paris: Pillet, 1813.

Annuaire de la librairie. Paris: Levrault, 1802.

Bibliographie de l'Empire français ou journal de l'imprimerie et de la librairie. Paris: Bossange & Pillet, 1811–1813.

Bouche de fer. Paris: Buisson, 1790–1791.

Bulletin de la bouche de fer. Edited by Bonneville. Paris: Cercle Social, 1790.

Bulletin de l'Ecole de Santé. Paris, [1794–1795].

Bulletin de littérature, des sciences, et des arts. Paris: Lucet, 1796.

Cabinet des modes. Paris: Buisson, 1783–1786.

Charles de Tersannes, ou familles rayées de la liste des émigrés. Paris: Raquin, 1801.

Chronique du mois. Edited by Bonneville. Paris: Cercle Social, 1791–1793.

Chronique de Paris. 1791.

Consultation pour le Citoyen A. J. Dugour, propriétaire du cours d'agriculture par Rozier, contre les citoyens Leroy, imprimeurs-libraires à Lyon. N.p., [1799].

Contre la multiplicité et le danger des brochures, par l'auteur de l'écrit intitulé: Je ne suis point de l'avis de tout le monde. N.p., 1789.

Courrier des 83 départements. Paris: Gorsas, 1789–1793.

Décade philosophique et littéraire. Paris: Say, 1794–1807.

De la liberté de la presse. N.p., 1789.

Dictionnaire universel de la langue française. Paris: Tretteul & Wurtz, 1806.

Dictionnaire de l'Académie. 5th ed. 2 vols. Paris: Maradan & Smits, an VI (1798).

Dictionnaire d'histoire naturelle. Lyon: Bruysset frères, [1803–1804].

Diners du vaudeville. Nos. 1–30. Edited by Barré, Radet & Desfontaines. Paris: Huet, Rondonneau & Brunet, 1797–1802.

Enterrement des feuilles volantes. De profundis des petits auteurs. Agonie des colporteurs. [Paris]: P. de Lormel, [1790].

Esprit de Mirabeau. [Paris: Buisson, 1797].

Feuille de correspondance du libraire. Paris: Aubry, 1791–1792.

Feuille villageoise. Edited by Grouvelle and Ginguené. Paris: Cercle Social, 1792–1793.

Feuille du cultivateur. Edited by Dubois. Paris, an III (1795).

Frédéric et Jenny, ou l'enfant de la sacristie, par J. M. G.**. Paris: Maradan, an VIII (1800).

Imprimeurs et libraires de Paris, au Ministre de l'Intérieur. Paris, an XII (1803–1804).

Intérrogation de Pierre Manuel devant le premier tribunal criminel, 22 mai 1792. N.p., [1792].

Journal de la cour et de la ville. 1791.

Journal de la librairie et des arts. Paris: Ravier, 1797.

Journal de la mode et du goût. Edited by Lebrun. Paris: Buisson, 1790–1792.

Journal de l'opposition. Edited by Réal. Paris: Buisson, 1795.

Journal de physique, de chimie, et d'histoire naturelle, continué de Rozier. Paris: Cuchet, 1794–1798.

Journal des censeurs. Paris, 1795.

Journal des débats et des décrets. 1789– an V (1796–1797).

Journal des hommes libres. Edited by Duval. Paris, 1793–1794.

Journal des mines. 38 vols. Paris, an III (1795)–1815.

Journal général de l'imprimerie et de la librairie. Paris: Pillet, 1810–1811.

Journal typographique et bibliographique. Paris: Roux & Dujardin-Sailly, then De Villevielle & Pillet, 1797–1810.

Lettre d'un libraire de Lyon à un libraire de Paris. [Paris, 1779].

Lettres de M. de Fronsac, fils du duc de Richelieu au chevalier Dumas. Paris: Michelet, 1801.

Magasin des modes nouvelles françaises et anglaises. London: Buisson, 1786–1789.

Magasin du bibliophile. Paris: Aubry, 1797.

Manuel du littérateur. Paris: [Chemin], 1794.

Mémoire présenté à l'Assemblée Nationale au nom des imprimeurs-librairies, propriétaires des privilèges des divers liturgies de France. Paris: N.-H. Nyon, 1790.

Mercure de France. Paris: Panckoucke, 1790.

Modérateur. Paris, 1790.

Moniteur universel. 1789–1790 (Reprint Paris: Panckoucke, an IV [1795–1796]).

Nouveau dictionnaire d'histoire naturelle. 24 vols. Paris: Deterville, 1803–1804.

Nouvelliste littéraire. Paris: Morin & Lenoir, 1796–1806.

Patriote français. Edited by Brissot de Warville. Paris: Buisson, 1789.

Pétition des créanciers-fournisseurs d'Anisson-Duperron. N.p., [1793].

Pétition des membres du ci-devant corps de la librairie et imprimerie de Paris, présentée à l'Assemblée Nationale. Paris: Knapen, June 10, 1791.

Portefeuille volé. Paris: Debray, 1805.

Rapport fait au Corps Municipal par le Département de la Police relatif à M. Manuel. N.p., [1792].

Réflexions sur le premier article additionnel . . . du projet de loi sur les contrefaçons, à présenter par M. Hell. Paris: L. Potier de Lille, [1793].

Religion de l'état. Paris: Durand fille, 1802.

Remerciment des libraires de la rue S. Jacques à M. Necker, suivi de quelques autres pièces relatives aux circonstances. Paris: Desenne, Gattey, Petit, 1789.

Réponse des libraires du Palais Royal au remerciment de leurs confrères de la rue Saint Jacques, à M. Necker. Paris: Desenne, Gattey, Petit, 1789.

Républicain français. Paris, 1792–1798.

Révolutions de Paris. Paris: Prudhomme, 1789–1791.

Sentinelle. Edited by Louvet de Couvray. Paris: Cercle Social, 1792.

Sur l'émigration. Paris: Durand fille, 1802.

Tableau des libraires, imprimeurs et éditeurs des livres des principales villes de l'Europe. Paris: Debray, 1804.

Télégraphe littéraire ou le correspondant de la librairie. Paris: Colas & Vve Panckoucke, 1802–1805.

Véridique. Paris: Didot l'aîné, 1789.

Vie de Général Hoche. Paris: Buisson, [1798].

Vie de Voltaire par T.J.D.V. Paris: Buisson, 1797.

Vie privée du maréchal de Richelieu. [Paris: Buisson, 1792].

Vrais sans-culottes. Paris: Huet, 1798.

Attributed

Année, Antoine, Gersin, and Ferrière. *Arlequin décorateur*. Paris: Cholet, 1798.

Ariosto, Ladivco. *Orlando furioso*. 4 vols. Paris: Plassan, an III (1795).

Aristotle. *Politique d'Aristote*. Translated by Jean-François Champagne. Paris: Bailleul, 1797.

Aubry, ed. *Principes de J. J. Rousseau*. Paris: Aubry, an II (1794).

———, ed. *Rituel républicain*. Paris: Aubry, an II (1794).

———, ed. *Eléments d'arithmétique décimale*. Paris: Aubry, an II (1794).

———, ed. *Syllabaire républicain pour les enfants*. Paris: Aubry, an II (1794).

———, ed. *Premières Notions de morale*. Paris: Aubry, an II (1794).

———, ed. *Petit Traité de grammaire française*. Paris: Aubry, an II (1794).

Barré, Pierre-Yvon, François-Pierre-Auguste Léger, and Rosières. *L'Heureuse Décade*. Paris: Cholet, 1794.

Barré, Pierre-Yvon, Jean-Baptiste Radet, and François-Georges Fouques Deshayes (called Desfontaines). *Arlequin afficheur*. Paris: Cholet, [1798] (orig. ed. 1792).

———. *Arlequin cruello*. Paris: Cholet, [1798] (orig. ed. 1792).

———. *Encore un curé*. Paris: Cholet, [1798] (orig. ed. 1794).

Baudin, P.-C.-L. *Rapport et projet de décret sur la propriété des auteurs dramatiques présentés au nom du Comité d'Instruction Publique par P.C.L. Baudin*. Paris: Imprimerie Nationale, [1793].

Baudouin, François-Jean. *Esquisse d'un projet de règlement pour l'imprimerie, la librairie et autres professions relatives, rédigée d'après les lois anciennes et nouvelles*. Paris, 1810.

Baudouin l'aîné. *Démétrius*. Paris: Huet, 1797.

Beaumarchais, Pierre-Augustin Caron de. *Pétition à l'Assemblée Nationale . . . contre l'usurpation des auteurs*. [Paris]: Dupont, [1791–1792].

Beffroy de Regny, Louis-Abel. *Allons, ça va, ou le Quaker en France*. Paris: Huet, 1793.

Bernardin de St. Pierre, Henri. *Etudes de la nature*. Paris: Didot le jeune, 1788.

———. *Paul et Virginie*. Paris: Didot le jeune, 1788.

———. *Chaumière indienne*. Paris: Didot le jeune, 1791.

———. *Paul et Virginie*. Paris: Libraires Associés, 1798.

———. *Paul et Virginie* (opera). Paris: Huet, [1798].

Bertrand-Quinquet. *Traité de l'imprimerie*. Paris, an VII [1799].

Blanchard, Pierre. *Félix et Pauline*. Paris: Leprieur, an II (1794).

———. *Félicie de Vilmard*. Paris: Leprieur, an VI (1798).

Blanvillain, J.-F.-C. *Le Pariséum, ou tableau actuel de Paris*. Paris: Piranesi, 1807.

Boieldieu, Marie-Jacques-Amand. *De l'influence de la chaire, du théâtre et du barreau dans la société civile*. Paris: Demonville, 1804.

Bonaparte, Lucien. *La Tribu indienne*. Paris: Honnert, an VII (1799).

Boosère, citizeness. *Triomphe de la saine philosophie, ou la vraie politique des femmes*. [Paris, 1795].

Bourdon, Léonard. *Recueil des actions héroiques et civiques des républicains français*. Paris: Imprimerie Nationale, an II (1794).

Boyer, Alexis. *Traité complet d'anatomie*. 4 vols. Paris: Chez l'auteur [and Migneret], 1797–1805.

Briois (called de Belle Roche). *Prise de Toulon*. Paris: Huet, [1798] (orig. ed. 1794).

Bruysset, Jean-Marie. *Caractères de la propriété littéraire*. Lyon, [1808].

Buffon, Georges-Louis LeClerc, comte de, ed. *Histoire naturelle, générale et particulière*. 15 vols. Paris: Imprimerie Royale, 1749–1767.

Bülow, Henri-Guillaume, baron de. *Histoire de la campagne de 1800 en Allemagne et en Italie*. Paris: Maginel, 1804.

Cadet de Gassicourt, Charles-Louis. *Le Souper de Molière*. Paris: Cholet, 1795.

Castéra, Jean-Henri. *Vie de Catherine II*. 3 vols. Paris: Buisson, 1797.

Catineau-La Roche, Pierre-Marie-Sebastien. *Réflexions sur la librairie, dans lesquelles on traite des propriétés littéraires, des contrefaçons, de la censure, de l'imprimerie et de la librairie*. Versailles: Catineau-La Roche, 1807.

Chateaubriand, François-René, vicomte de. *Atala*. Paris: Migneret, 1801.

———. *Le Génie du christianisme*. 5 vols. Paris: Migneret, 1802.

Chénier, Marie-Joseph. *Azémire*. Paris: Barba, 1787.

———. *Dénonciation des inquisiteurs de la pensée*. Paris: Lagrange, 1789.

Clousier, Jules-Gabriel, fils l'aîné. *Notes sur l'imprimerie, la librairie et la fonderie des caractères d'impression*. Paris, [1801].

Condillac, Etienne Bonnet de. *La Logique*. Paris: Esprit & Debure l'aîné, 1789.

———. *Langue des calculs*. Paris: Houel, 1799.

———. *Oeuvres complètes de Condillac*. Paris: Houel, an VII (1798–1799).

Condorcet, Marie-Jean-Antoine Caritat, marquis de. *Fragments sur la liberté de la presse* (1776). In *Oeuvres de Condorcet*, edited by M.-F. Arago, 11:253–314. Paris: Didot, 1847.

———. *Esquisse d'un tableau historique des progrès de l'esprit humain*. Paris: Agasse, 1794.

Constant de Rebecque, Benjamin. *Des suites de la contre-révolution de 1660 en Angleterre*. Paris: Buisson, 1799.

———. *De la liberté des brochures, des pamphlets et des journaux*. Paris, 1814.

Coupé, Jean-Marie, ed. *Les Soirées littéraires ou mélanges de traductions nouvelles des plus beaux morceaux de l'antiquité.* 20 vols. Paris: Honnert, 1795–1800.

Cuchet, Gaspar-Joseph. *Avis.* N.p., [January 11, 1789].

Defoe, Daniel. *Histoire corrigée de Robinson Crusoé.* Adapted by ? Paris: Aubry, an III (1795).

Demoustier, Ch.-A. *Le Divorce.* Paris: Maradan, 1795.

Desfontaines (François-Georges Fouques Deshayes). *La Fille soldat.* Paris: Cholet, [1798].

Diderot, Denis. "Lettre historique et politique adressée à un magistrat sur le commerce de la librairie" (1763). In *Oeuvres complètes,* edited by Roger Lewinter, 5:299–381. Paris: Club Français du Livre, 1970.

———. *Essai sur la peinture.* Paris: Buisson, an V (1797).

———. *La Religieuse.* Paris: Buisson, an V (1796–1797).

———. *Jacques le fataliste.* Paris: Buisson, an V (1796–1797).

Dossion, Etienne-Auguste. *Arlequin pygmalion.* Paris: Cholet, [1798] (orig. ed. 1794).

Ducancel, Charles-Pierre. *Intérieur des comités révolutionnaires.* Paris: Barba, 1795.

Ducray-Duminil, François-Guillaume. *Lolotte et Fanfan.* 4th ed. Paris: Leprieur, 1792 (orig. ed. 1788).

———. *Alexis, ou la maisonette dans les bois.* 4th ed. Paris: Leprieur, 1793 (orig. ed. 1788).

———. *Petit-Jacques et Georgette.* 3d ed. Paris: Leprieur, an II (1794) (orig. ed. 1789).

———. *Codicile sentimental et moral.* Paris: Leprieur, an II (1794).

———. *Victor, ou l'enfant de la forêt.* Paris: Leprieur, an V (1797).

———. *Les Cinquantes Francs de Jeannette.* Paris: Leprieur, an VI (1798).

———. *Coelina, ou l'enfant du mystère.* Paris: Leprieur, an VI (1798).

Dupaty, Louis-Emmanuel-Félicité-Charles. *Arlequin tout seul.* Paris: Cholet, 1798.

Dupuis Charles-François. *Origine de tous les cultes, ou religion universelle.* 7 vols. Paris: Agasse, 1795.

Duverneuil, M., ed. *Almanach du commerce de Paris.* Paris: Vve Valade, an VII [1798–1799].

Fabre d'Eglantine, Philippe. *Intrigue épistolaire.* [Paris: Barba, 1796] (orig. ed. 1791).

Fénélon, François de Salignac de la Mothe. *Aventures de Télémaque.* (orig. ed. 1699).

Fiévée, Joseph. *Frédéric.* 3 vols. Paris: Plassan, an VII (1799).

———. *Observations et projet de décret sur l'imprimerie et la librairie.* Paris: Imprimerie Impériale, 1809.

Forster, Jean-George-Adam. *Voyage philosophique sur les bords du rhin.* Translated by Marie-Charles-Joseph de Pougens. Paris: Buisson, an III (1795).

France. National Constituent Assembly. *Procès-verbal de l'Assemblée Nationale.* 76 vols. Paris: Baudouin, 1789–1791.

————. *Collection générale des décrets rendus par l'Assemblée Nationale*. Paris: Baudouin, 1791.

————. *Constitution française*. Paris: Didot le jeune, 1791.

————. National Convention. *Constitution de la République française*. Paris: Didot l'aîné, an II (1794).

Franklin, Benjamin. *Vie de Benjamin Franklin*. Translated by Jean-Henri Castéra. Paris: Buisson, 1798.

Gerbaux, Fernand, and Charles Schmidt, eds. *Procès-verbal des Comités d'Agriculture et de Commerce*. 4 vols. Paris: Imprimerie Nationale, 1906–1910.

Gibbon, Edward. *Histoire de la décadence et de la chute de l'empire romain*. Adapted from the English by B. Ducos. Paris: Maradan, an II (1794).

Goldsmith, Oliver. *Vicaire de Wakefield*. Translated by Pierre-Louis-Claude Gin. Paris: Gide & Gay, an V (1797).

Gordon, Thomas. *Discours historique sur Tacite et Salluste*. Paris: Buisson, an II (1794).

[Grangé, Jean-Augustin]. *Mémoire présenté à l'Assemblée Nationale pour le corps des libraires et imprimeurs de l'Université*. Paris: Grangé, 1790.

Grégoire, Henri. *Oeuvres de l'abbé Grégoire*. 14 vols. Foreword by Albert Soboul. Reprint Paris: EDHIS, 1977 (orig. ed. Paris, 1788–1832).

————. *Rapport sur les encouragements, récompenses et pensions à accorder aux savants, aux gens de lettres et aux artistes*. Paris: Imprimerie Nationale, an III (1794–1795).

Guillaume, M.-J., ed. *Procès-verbaux du Comité d'Instruction Publique de la Convention Nationale*. 7 vols. Paris: Imprimerie Nationale, 1891–1907.

————. *Procès-verbal du Comité d'Instruction Publique de l'Assemblée Législative*. Paris: Imprimerie Nationale, 1889.

Hell, François. *Rapport fait à l'Assemblée Nationale par M. Hell, député du Bas-Rhin, sur la propriété des productions scientifiques ou littéraires*. Paris: Imprimerie Nationale, 1791.

Jacob, Louis l'aîné. *Idées générales sur les causes de l'anéantissement de l'imprimerie et sur la nécessité de rendre à cette profession, ainsi qu'à celle de la librairie, le rang honorable qu'elles ont toujours tenues l'une et l'autre parmi les arts libéraux*. Orléans: Jacob l'aîné, 1806.

Jourdan, Decrusy, and Isambert, eds. *Recueil général des anciennes lois françaises*. 29 vols. Paris: Belin-Leprieur, 1822–1833.

Kant, Emmanuel. *Projet de paix perpetuelle*. Translated by Henri Jansen. Paris: Jansen, 1796.

Kéralio, Louis-Félix Guynement de. *De la liberté d'énoncer, d'écrire et d'imprimer la pensée*. Paris: Potier de Lille, 1790.

————. *De la liberté de la presse*. Paris: Potier de Lille, 1790.

Lacépède, Etienne de la Ville, comte de. *Histoire naturelle des poissons*. 2 vols. Paris: Plassan, an VI (1798).

La Fontaine, Jean de. *Contes et nouvelles en vers*. 2 vols. Paris: Didot l'aîné, 1795.

————. *Fables de La Fontaine*. Edited by Monger. Paris: Agasse, 1797.

————. *Fables de La Fontaine.* Paris: Didot l'aîné, 1798.

LaHarpe, Jean-François de. *Adresse des auteurs dramatiques à l'Assemblée Nationale, prononcé par M. de LaHarpe dans la séance du mardi soir 24 août.* [Paris, 1790].

————. *La Liberté de la presse défendue par LaHarpe contre Chénier.* Paris: Migneret, an III (1794–1795).

————. *De l'état des lettres en Europe.* 2d ed. Paris: Migneret, 1797.

————. *Du fanatisme dans la langue révolutionnaire.* [Paris: Barba, 1797]. 2d ed. Paris: Migneret, 1797.

————. *La Guerre déclarée par nos derniers tyrans à la raison.* Paris: Migneret, 1797.

————. *Réfutation du livre de l'esprit.* Paris: Migneret, 1797.

————. *Lycée, ou cours de littérature.* 16 vols. Paris: Agasse, ans VII–XIII (1799–1805).

————, trans. *Pseautier.* Paris: Migneret, 1798.

Lakanal, Joseph. *Exposé sommaire des travaux de Joseph Lakanal.* Paris: Didot frères, 1838.

Lambert, L.-T., and Theiry. *Arlequin tailleur.* Paris: Cholet, [1798] (orig. ed. 1793).

Lanthenas, François. *De la liberté indéfinie de la presse.* Paris: Visse, 1791.

Lapérouse, Jean-François de Galaup, comte de. *Voyage de Lapérouse.* 4 vols. Paris: Plassan, an VI (1798).

La Rochefoucauld, François, duc de. *Maximes et réflexions morales.* Paris: Didot l'aîné, 1796.

Laya, Jean-Louis. *Jean Calas.* Paris: Barba, 1791.

Le Chapelier, Issac-René-Guy. *Rapport fait par M. Le Chapelier au nom du Comité de Constitution sur la pétition des auteurs dramatiques, 13 janvier 1791.* Paris: Imprimerie Nationale, 1791.

[LeClerc, Charles-Guillaume]. *Lettre à M*** [sur la propriété littéraire].* [Paris, December 19, 1778].

LePrévost d'Iray, Chrétien-Siméon, vicomte de, and Dieu-LaFoi. *Le Quart d'heure de Rabelais.* Paris: Cholet, 1799.

Linguet, Simon-Nicolas-Henri. *Mémoire signifié pour le sieur Luneau de Boisgermain, défendeur, contre les syndic et adjoints des libraires et imprimeurs de Paris, demandeurs.* Paris, 1769.

Loaisel de Tréogate, Joseph-Marie. *Lucile et Milcourt.* Paris: Leprieur, an II (1794) (orig. ed. 1779).

————. *Dolbreuse, ou l'homme du siècle.* Paris: Leprieur, an II (1794) (orig. ed. 1783).

Locke, John. *Essay on Human Understanding.* (orig. ed. 1690).

Lottin, Augustin-Martin. *Catalogue chronologique des libraires et des libraires-imprimeurs de Paris, 1470–1789.* Paris: Lottin, 1789.

Mably, Gabriel Bonnet de. *Oeuvres.* 15 vols. Paris: Desbrières (Barrois l'aîné), 1794–1795.

Madival, Jérôme, and Emile Laurent, eds. *Archives parlementaires de 1787 à 1860.* 1st ser. 71 vols. Paris: Dupont, 1875–1913.

Malesherbes, Chrétien-Guillaume Lamoignon de. *Mémoires sur la librairie et sur la liberté de la presse.* Edited by Graham E. Rodmell. Chapel Hill: University of North Carolina Press, 1979 (orig. ed. Paris: Agasse, 1809).

Manuel, Pierre. *La Police de Paris dévoilée.* Paris: Desenne, 1791.

Marcillac, Pierre-Louis-Auguste de Crusy, marquis de. *Histoire de la guerre entre la France et l'Espagne.* Paris: Maginel, 1808.

Mardelle, J.-B. *Arlequin journaliste.* Paris: Cholet, 1797.

Marmontel, Jean-François. *Contes moraux.* Paris: Garnery & Maradan, an IX (1801) (orig. ed. 1761).

Mentelle, Edme. *Analyse du cours de géographie.* Paris, an V (1797).

Mérard St. Just, Anne-Jeanne-Félicité. *Six mois d'exil ou les orphelins par la Révolution.* 3 vols. Paris: Volland, an XIII (1805).

———. *Dangers de la passion du jeu.* Paris: Maradan, 1793 (Reedition of *Histoire de la baronne d'Alvigny.* Paris: Maradan, 1788).

Mirabeau, Honoré-Gabriel Riqueti, comte de. *Sur la liberté de la presse.* Paris: Lejay, 1792 (orig. ed. 1788).

Momoro, Antoine-François. *Traité élémentaire de l'imprimerie.* Paris: Momoro, 1793.

Montesquieu, Charles de Secondat, baron de la Brède et de. *Oeuvres de Montesquieu.* 5 vols. Edited by J.-B. Bernard. Paris: Plassan, an IV (1796).

Montucla, Jean-Etienne. *Histoire des mathématiques, nouvelle édition.* 4 vols. Paris: Agasse, an VII (1799)–1802 (orig. ed. 1758).

Neufchâteau, François de. *Institution des enfants, ou conseils d'un père.* Paris: Agasse, [1798].

Paine, Thomas. *Théorie et pratique des droits de l'homme.* Translated by François Lanthenas. Paris: Cercle Social, 1792.

Panckoucke, Charles-Joseph, ed. *Encyclopédie méthodique.* 166 vols. Paris: Panckoucke, then Agasse, 1789–1832.

———. *Mémoire sur les assignats et sur la manière de les considérer dans l'état de la baisse actuelle.* [Paris, 1795].

Parmentier, Antoine-Augustin, and Nicolas Deyeux, eds. *Bibliothèque physico-économique.* 72 vols. Paris: Buisson, 1782–1826.

Piis, Antoine, Jean-Baptiste Radet, Pierre-Yvon Barré, and François-Georges Fouques Deshayes (called Desfontaines). *Vallée de Montmorency, ou J. J. Rousseau dans son hermitage.* Paris: Cholet, 1799.

Planterre, Barthélemy-Ambroise, and Pierre Gaveaux. *La Famille indigente.* Paris: Huet, 1794.

Priestley, Joseph. *Discours sur histoire et sur la politique.* Translated by André-Samuel-Michel Cantwel. Paris: Jansen, an IV (1796).

Prudhomme, Louis. *Voyage descriptif et philosophique de l'ancien et du nouveau Paris. Miroir fidèle.* 2 vols. Paris: Prudhomme, 1814.

Pujoulx, J.-B. *Paris à la fin du XVIIIe siècle.* Paris: Mathé, 1801.

Racine, Jean. *Oeuvres de Racine.* 3 vols. Paris: Didot l'aîné, an VII (1799).

Radet, Jean-Baptiste. *Le Canonier convalescent.* Paris: Cholet, [1798].

Ravier, Louis. *Répertoire de la librairie.* Paris: Crapart, Caille & Ravier, 1807.

Restif de la Bretonne (Nicolas Restif). *Les Nuits révolutionnaires.* Paris: Livre de Poche, 1978 (orig. ed. 1789).

Richard, Louis-Charles, ed. *Dictionnaire élémentaire de botanique.* Paris: Librairie d'Education, des Sciences et des Arts, 1800.

Rivarol, Antoine. *Le Petit Almanach de nos grands hommes.* In *Oeuvres complètes,* 2d ed., vol. 5. Geneva: Slatkine Reprints, 1968 (originally published 1808).

Robinson, Mary Darby. *Le Faux ami.* Paris: Migneret, 1799.

Roger, François. *Dupe de soi-même.* Paris: Huet, 1799.

Roissy, Jean-Guillaume Locré de, ed. *Discussions sur la liberté de la presse, la censure, la propriété littéraire, l'imprimerie et la librairie qui ont eu lieu dans le conseil d'état pendant les années 1808, 1809, 1810 et 1811.* Paris: Garnery & Nicolle, 1819.

Rousseau, Jean-Jacques. *Oeuvres.* 20 vols. Paris: Didot l'aîné, 1801.

———. *Oeuvres.* 37 vols. Paris: Poinçot, 1788–1793.

Roux, Pierre, ed. *Journal typographique et bibliographique.* Paris, 1797–1810.

Royer, Jean-François. *Avis intéressant aux gens de lettres et aux amateurs de bons livres et des bonnes éditions.* N.p., [1789–1790].

Rozier, Jean. *Dictionnaire ou cours complet d'agriculture.* 6 vols. Paris: Cuchet, 1781–1796.

———. *Dictionnaire ou cours complet d'agriculture.* 6 vols. Paris: Marchant, 1805.

———. *Dictionnaire ou cours complet d'agriculture.* 6 vols. Paris: Buisson, 1809.

Sade, Donatien-Alphonse-François, marquis de. *Justine.* The Netherlands, 1800 (orig. ed. 1791).

Schweighäuser, Johannes-Joachim, ed. *Polybii Megalopolitani historiarum.* 9 vols. Leipzig: Weidmann, 1789–1795.

Senancour, Etienne-Jean-Baptiste-Pierre-Ignace Pivert de. *Aldomen ou le bonheur dans l'obscurité.* Paris: Leprieur, an III (1795).

Severin. *Le Villageois qui cherche son veau.* Paris: Barba, [1799].

Sieyès, Emmanuel-Joseph. *Qu'est-ce que le tiers-état?* [Paris, 1789].

Simonin. *Traité d'arithmétique.* Paris: Barbou, an VI (1798).

Smith, Adam. *Recherches sur la nature et les causes de la richesse des nations.* Translated by Rocher. Paris: Buisson, an II (1794) (orig. ed. 1776).

———. *Essais philosophiques.* Translated by Pierre Prévost. Paris: Agasse, an V (1797).

———. *Théorie des sentiments moraux.* Translated by Sophie de Grouchy, marquise de Condorcet. Paris: Buisson, an VI (1798).

Staël-Holstein, Germaine, baronne de. *Corinne.* Paris: Nicolle, 1807.

Steibelt, Daniel, and Alexandre-Joseph-Pierre, vicomte de Ségur. *Roméo et Juliette, opéra en trois actes.* Paris: Huet, [1798] (orig. ed. 1793).

Stoupe, Jean-Georges-Antoine. *Réflexions sur les contrefaçons en librairie, suivies d'un mémoire sur le rétablissement de la communauté des imprimeurs de Paris.* Paris, an XII (1803–1804). Re-edited in 1806 as *Mémoire sur le rétablissement de la communauté des imprimeurs de Paris, suivi de réflexions sur les contrefaçons en librairie et sur le stéréotypage.*

Tardieu-Denesle, Henri, ed. *Almanach typographique*. Paris, an VIII (1799–1800).

Vincard, B. *Projet sur l'organisation de la librairie, discuté par la majeure partie des imprimeurs et des libraires, et par les hommes de lettres, censeurs, etc. . . . soumis aux membres du Conseil d'Etat*. Paris, [1809].

Virgil. *Publii Virgilii Maronis Bucolica, Georgica et Aeneis*. Engravings after Gérard and Girodet. Paris: Didot l'aîné, 1791.

———. *Oeuvres de Virgile*. 4 vols. Translated by Pierre-François Guyot Desfontaines. Paris: Plassan, an IV (1796).

Voltaire (François-Marie Arouet). *Oeuvres de Voltaire. Nouvelle édition avec des notes et observations critiques par M. Palissot*. 55 vols. Edited by Charles Palissot de Montenoy. Paris: Stoupe & Servière, 1792–1797.

Winckelmann, Johann-Joachim. *Histoire de l'art chez les anciens*. 3 vols. Translated by Henri Jansen. Paris: Jansen, then Gide, an II (1794)–1803.

Wollstonecraft, Mary Godwin. *Maria ou le malheur d'être femme*. Adapted from the English by B. Ducos. Paris: Maradan, an V (1797).

Secondary Sources

Allen, James Smith. *Popular French Romanticism: Authors, Readers, and Books in the Nineteenth Century*. Syracuse: Syracuse University Press, 1981.

Aulard, Alphonse. "La Presse officieuse pendant la Terreur." *Etudes et leçons sur la Révolution française*, 1st ser. [n.d.]: 227–240.

———, ed. *Paris sous le Consulat*. 4 vols. Paris: Le Cerf, 1903–1909.

Badinter, Elisabeth, and Robert Badinter. *Condorcet. Un Intellectuel en politique*. Paris: Fayard, 1988.

Baker, Keith Michael. *Condorcet: From Natural Philosophy to Social Mathematics*. Chicago: University of Chicago Press, 1975.

Barbéris, Pierre, and Claude Duchet, eds. *Manuel d'histoire littéraire de la France, Vol. 4: 1789 à 1848*. Paris: Editions Sociales, 1972.

Barbier, Frédéric. *Trois Cent Ans de la librairie et d'imprimerie*. Geneva: Droz, 1979.

Belin, J.-P. *Le Commerce des livres prohibés à Paris de 1750 à 1789*. Paris: Belin frères, 1913.

Bellanger, Claude, ed. *Histoire générale de la presse française*. 5 vols. Paris: PUF, 1969.

Bellos, David. "La Conjoncture de la production." In *Histoire de l'édition française*, edited by Roger Chartier and Henri-Jean Martin, 2:552–557. Paris: Promodis, 1984.

Bergeron, Louis. *Banquiers, négociants et manufacturiers parisiens du Directoire à l'Empire*. Paris: Mouton, 1978.

———. *France Under Napoleon*. Translated by R. R. Palmer. Princeton: Princeton University Press, 1981.

Berkvens-Stevelinck, Ch. "L'Edition française en Hollande." In *Histoire de l'édition française*, edited by Roger Chartier and Henri-Jean Martin, 2:316–325. Paris: Promodis, 1984.

Bigo, Robert. *Les Banques françaises au cours du XIXe siècle*. Paris: Sirey, 1947.

———. *La Caisse d'escompte (1776–1793) et les origines de la Banque de France*. Paris: PUF, 1927.

Bingham, Alfred Jepson. *Marie-Joseph Chénier: Early Political Life and Ideas (1789–1794)*. New York, 1939 (privately printed).

Birn, Raymond. "Le Livre prohibé aux frontières. Bouillon." In *Histoire de l'édition française*, edited by Roger Chartier and Henri-Jean Martin, 2:334–341. Paris: Promodis, 1984.

———. "The Profits in Ideas: 'Privilèges en Librairie' in Eighteenth-Century France." *Eighteenth-Century Studies* 4, no. 2 (Winter 1971): 131–168.

Bollème, Geneviève, Jean Ehrard, François Furet, Daniel Roche, and Jacques Roger. *Livre et société dans la France du XVIIIe siècle*. Paris: Mouton, 1965.

Buchez, P.-J.-B., and P.-C. Roux, eds. *Histoire parlementaire de la Révolution française*. 40 vols. Paris: Paulin, 1834–1838.

Cabanis, André. *La Presse sous le Consulat et l'Empire (1799–1814)*. Paris: Société des Etudes Robespierristes, 1975.

Caron, Pierre. *Paris pendant la Terreur. Rapports des agents secrets du ministre de l'intérieur*. 7 vols. Paris: Picard, 1910–1978.

———. "Les Publications officieuses du Ministère de l'Intérieur en 1793 et 1794." *Revue d'histoire moderne et contemporaine* 14 (1910):5–43.

Carré, Henri. "Quelques Mots sur la presse clandestine à la fin de l'ancien régime." *Révolution française* 25–26 (1893–1894): 102–126.

Carrière, Charles. *Négociants marseillais au XVIIIe siècle*. Marseilles: Institut Historique de Provence, 1973.

Cassirer, Ernst. *The Philosophy of the Enlightenment*. Princeton: Princeton University Press, 1951.

Certeau, Michel de, Dominique Julia, and Jacques Revel. *Une Politique de la langue. La Révolution française et les patois*. Paris: Gallimard, 1975.

Chartier, Roger. "L'Ancien Régime typographique." *Annales E.S.C.*, no. 36 (March 1981): 191–209.

———. "La Géographie de l'imprimerie française au XVIIIe siècle." In *Histoire de l'édition française*, edited by Roger Chartier and Henri-Jean Martin, 2:290–291. Paris: Promodis, 1984.

———. "L'Imprimerie en France à la fin de l'ancien régime. L'Etat général des imprimeurs de 1777." *Revue française d'histoire du livre*, n.s., no. 6 (1973): 253–279.

———. *Lectures et lecteurs dans la France d'ancien régime*. Paris: Seuils, 1987.

———. "Texts, Printings, Readings." In *The New Cultural History*, edited by Lynn Hunt, 154–175. Berkeley and Los Angeles: University of California Press, 1989.

———, ed. *Les Usages de l'imprimé (XVe–XIXe siècle)*. Paris: Fayard, 1987.

Chartier, Roger, and Henri-Jean Martin, eds. *Histoire de l'édition française*. 4 vols. Paris: Promodis, 1983–.

Chartier, Roger, and Daniel Roche. "L'Histoire quantitative du livre." *Revue française d'histoire du livre*, n.s., no. 16 (1977):477–501.

————, eds. *Livre et révolution. Mélanges de la Sorbonne 9.* Paris: Aux Amateurs de Livres, 1989.

Chauvet, Paul. *Les Ouvriers du livre en France.* 2 vols. Paris: Marcel Rivière, 1964.

Chouillet, Jacques. *L'Esthétique des lumières.* Paris: PUF, 1974.

————. *La Formation des idées esthétiques de Diderot.* Paris: Armand Colin, 1973.

Cobban, Alfred. *A History of Modern France.* Vol. 1: *1715–1799.* Middlesex, Eng.: Penguin Books, 1963.

Coffin, Victor. "Censorship Under Napoleon I." *American Historical Review* 22 (1916–1917): 228–308.

Colombet, Claude. *Propriété littéraire et artistique.* Paris: Dalloz, 1980.

Cook, Malcolm. "Politics in the Fiction of the French Revolution, 1789–1794." *Studies on Voltaire and the Eighteenth Century* [Oxford], no. 201 (1982): 237–340.

Dardel, Pierre. *Commerce, industrie et navigation à Rouen et au Havre au XVIIIe siècle.* Rouen: Société Libre d'Emulation de Seine-Maritime, 1966.

Darnton, Robert. *The Business of Enlightenment: A Publishing History of the Encyclopédie, 1775–1800.* Cambridge, Mass.: Harvard University Press, 1979.

————. *The Great Cat Massacre and Other Episodes in French Cultural History.* New York: Basic Books, 1984.

————. "L'Imprimerie de Panckoucke en l'an II." *Revue française d'histoire du livre,* n.s., no. 23 (1979): 359–369.

————. *The Literary Underground of the Old Regime.* Cambridge, Mass.: Harvard University Press, 1982.

————. "Le Livre prohibé aux frontières. Neuchâtel." In *Histoire de l'édition française,* edited by Roger Chartier and Henri-Jean Martin, 2:342–361. Paris: Promodis, 1984.

————. "Philosophy Under the Cloak." In *Revolution in Print: The Press in France, 1775–1800,* edited by Robert Darnton and Daniel Roche, 27–49. Berkeley and Los Angeles: University of California Press, 1989.

Darnton, Robert, and Daniel Roche, eds. *Revolution in Print: The Press in France, 1775–1800.* Berkeley and Los Angeles: University of California Press, 1989.

Daumard, Adeline, and François Furet. *Structures et relations sociales à Paris au XVIIIe siècle.* Paris: Armand Colin, 1981.

Dauphin-Meunier, A. *La Banque de France.* Paris: Gallimard, 1936.

Davis, Natalie Z. "Beyond the Market: Books as Gifts in Sixteenth-Century France." *Transactions of the Royal Historical Society,* 5th ser., 33 (1983): 69–88.

————. "Printing and the People." In *Society and Culture in Early Modern France,* 189–226. Stanford: Stanford University Press, 1975.

Delalain, Paul. *L'Imprimerie et la librairie à Paris de 1789 à 1813.* Paris: Delalain, [1900].

Desbois, Henri. *Le Droit d'auteur en France.* 3d ed. Paris: Dalloz, 1978.

Dhombres, Jean. "Books: Reshaping Science." In *Revolution in Print: The Press in France, 1775–1800,* edited by Robert Darnton and Daniel Roche, 177–202. Berkeley and Los Angeles: University of California Press, 1989.

Didier, Béatrice. *Ecrire la Révolution, 1789–1799.* Paris: PUF, 1989.

Douarche, Aristide P., ed. *Les Tribunaux civils de Paris pendant la Révolution (1791–1800). Documents inédits recueillis avant l'incendie du Palais de Justice de 1871 par Casenave.* 2 vols. Paris: Le Cerf, 1905–1907.

Duprat, François-Antoine-Brutus. *Histoire de l'Imprimerie Impériale de France.* Paris: Imprimerie Impériale, 1861.

Edelstein, Melvin Allen. *"La Feuille villageoise." Communication et modernisation dans les régions rurales pendant la Révolution.* Paris: Bibliothèque Nationale, 1977.

Eisenstein, Elizabeth. *The Printing Press as an Agent of Change.* 2 vols. Cambridge: Cambridge University Press, 1979.

Estivals, Robert. *Le Dépôt légal sous l'ancien régime de 1537–1791.* Paris: Marcel Rivière, 1961.

———. *La Statistique bibliographique de la France sous la monarchie au XVIIIe siècle.* Paris: Mouton, 1965.

Febvre, Lucien, and Henri-Jean Martin. *L'Apparition du livre.* Paris: Albin Michel, 1958.

Felkay, Nicole. *Balzac et ses éditeurs, 1822–1837. Essai sur la librairie romantique.* Paris: Promodis, 1987.

Foucault, Michel. "What Is an Author?" In *Textual Strategies: Perspectives in Post-structuralist Criticism,* edited by Josué V. Harari, 141–160. Ithaca: Cornell University Press, 1979.

Furet, François. *Pensée la Révolution française.* Paris: Gallimard, 1978.

Furet, François, and Denis Richet. *La Révolution française.* Paris: Marabout, 1973.

Gelbart, Nina Ratner. *Feminine and Opposition Journalism in Old Regime France: "Le Journal des Dames."* Berkeley and Los Angeles: University of California Press, 1987.

Genette, Gérard. *Seuils.* Paris: Seuils, 1987.

George, Albert J. *The Didot Family and the Progress of Printing.* Syracuse: Syracuse University Press, 1961.

Godechot, Jacques, ed. *Les Constitutions de la France depuis 1789.* Paris: Flammarion, 1979.

———. "La Presse française sous la Révolution et l'Empire." In *Histoire générale de la presse française,* edited by Claude Bellanger, 1:405–569. Paris: PUF, 1969.

Goubert, Pierre. *L'Ancien Régime.* Vol. 2: *Les Pouvoirs.* Paris: Armand Colin, 1973.

Greenlaw, Ralph. "Pamphlet Literature in France." *Journal of Modern History* 29 (1957): 349–354.

Habermas, Jürgen. *The Structural Transformation of the Public Sphere.* Translated by Thomas Burger. Cambridge, Mass.: MIT Press, 1989 (orig. German ed. 1962).

Hahn, Roger. *The Anatomy of a Scientific Institution: The Paris Academy of Sciences, 1666–1803.* Berkeley and Los Angeles: University of California Press, 1971.

Harari, Josué V., ed. *Textual Strategies: Perspectives in Post-structuralist Criticism.* Ithaca: Cornell University Press, 1979.

Hatin, Louis-Eugène. *Histoire politique et littéraire de la presse en France.* 8 vols. Paris: Poulet-Malassis, 1859–1861.

————. *Manuel théorique et pratique de la liberté de la presse.* Paris: Pagnerre, 1868.

Hermann-Mascard, Nicole. *La Censure des livres à Paris à la fin de l'ancien régime (1750–1789).* Paris: PUF, 1968.

Hesse, Carla. "Economic Upheavals in Publishing." In *Revolution in Print: The Press in France, 1775–1800,* edited by Robert Darnton and Daniel Roche, 69–97. Berkeley and Los Angeles: University of California Press, 1989.

————. "Enlightenment Epistemology and the Laws of Authorship in Revolutionary France, 1777–1793." *Representations* 30 (Spring 1990): 109–137.

————. "Reading Signatures: Female Authorship and Revolutionary Law in France, 1750–1850." *Eighteenth-Century Studies* 22, no. 3 (1989): 469–487.

————. "Le Sort des imprimeurs et libraires parisiens après la chute de la chambre syndicale en 1791." In *Livre et révolution. Mélanges de la Sorbonne 9,* edited by Roger Chartier and Daniel Roche, 21–32. Paris: Aux Amateurs de Livres, 1989.

Hoppit, Julian. *Risk and Failure in English Business, 1700–1800.* Cambridge: Cambridge University Press, 1987.

Hunt, Lynn. *Politics, Culture, and Class in the French Revolution.* Berkeley and Los Angeles: University of California Press, 1984.

————, ed. *The New Cultural History.* Berkeley and Los Angeles: University of California Press, 1989.

Isherwood, Robert. *Farce and Fantasy: Popular Entertainment in Eighteenth-Century Paris.* Oxford: Oxford University Press, 1986.

Kamuf, Peggy. "Criticism." *Diacritics* 12, no. 2 (1982): 42–47.

Kates, Gary. *The Cercle Social, the Girondins, and the French Revolution.* Princeton: Princeton University Press, 1985.

Kennedy, Emmet. *A Cultural History of the French Revolution.* New Haven: Yale University Press, 1989.

Kitchen, Joanna. *Un Journal "philosophique": "La Décade," 1794–1807.* Paris: Minard, 1965.

Kulstein, David I. "The Ideas of Charles Joseph Panckoucke, Publisher of the *Moniteur Universel,* on the French Revolution." *French Historical Studies* 4, no. 3 (Spring 1966): 307–309.

Labrosse, Claude, and Pierre Rétat. *Naissance du journal révolutionnaire.* Lyon: Presses Universitaires de Lyon, 1989.

Lacroix, Sigismond, ed. *Actes de la Commune de Paris (1789–1791).* Series 1 (7 vols.) and 2 (8 vols.). Paris: Le Cerf, 1895.

Lambrichs, Natalie. *La Liberté de la presse en l'an IV. Les Journaux républicains.* Paris: PUF, 1976.

Le Poittevin, Gustave. *La Liberté de la presse depuis la Révolution, 1789–1815.* Geneva: Slatkine Reprints, 1975 (orig. ed. Paris, 1901).

Lescaze, B. "Commerce d'assortissement et livres interdits: Genève." In *Histoire de l'édition française,* edited by Roger Chartier and Henri-Jean Martin, 2:326–333. Paris: Promodis, 1984.

Lough, John. *Writer and Public in France.* Oxford: Clarendon Press, 1978.

Luckett, Tom. "Credit and Society in Eighteenth-Century France." Ph.D. diss., Princeton University, forthcoming.

Lyons, Martyn. *France Under the Directory.* Cambridge: Cambridge University Press, 1975.

McLuhan, Marshall. *The Gutenberg Galaxy.* Toronto: University of Toronto Press, 1962.

Martin, Angus, Vivienne G. Milne, and Richard Frautschi. *Bibliographie du genre romanesque français, 1751–1800.* Paris: France Expansion; London: Mansell, 1977.

Martin, Biddy. "Feminism, Criticism, and Foucault." *New German Critique* 27 (1982): 3–30.

Martin, Henri-Jean. "Conditions politiques: La Librairie et les pouvoirs." In *Histoire de l'édition française,* edited by Roger Chartier and Henri-Jean Martin, 2:64–93. Paris: Promodis, 1984.

———. *Livre, pouvoirs et société à Paris au XVIIe siècle.* 2 vols. Geneva: Droz, 1969.

———. "La Prééminence de la librairie parisienne." In *Histoire de l'édition française,* edited by Roger Chartier and Henri-Jean Martin, 2:262–282. Paris: Promodis, 1984.

———. "Le Voltaire de Kehl." In *Histoire de l'édition française,* edited by Roger Chartier and Henri-Jean Martin, 2:310. Paris: Promodis, 1984.

Martin, Jean-Clément. "Le Commerçant, la faillite et l'historien." *Annales E.S.C.* 35, no. 6 (November–December 1980): 1251–1268.

Martin St. Léon, Etienne. *Histoire des corporations de métiers.* Paris: Alcan, 1909.

Mathiez, Albert. "Mélanges. La Presse subventionnée en l'an II." *Annales révolutionnaires* 10 (1918): 112–113.

Michaud, Louis-Gabriel, and Joseph-François Michaud, eds. *Biographie universelle ancienne et moderne.* 85 vols. Paris: Desplaces, 1811–1862.

Michon, Georges. *Essai sur l'histoire du parti feuillant. Adrien Duport.* Paris: Payot, 1924.

Miller, Nancy K. "A Feminist Critic and Her Fictions." *Diacritics* 12, no. 2 (1982): 48–53.

Minard, Philippe. "Agitation in the Work Force." In *Revolution in Print: The Press in France, 1775–1800,* edited by Robert Darnton and Daniel Roche, 107–123. Berkeley and Los Angeles: University of California Press, 1989.

———. *Typographes des lumières.* Seyssel: Champ Vallon, 1989.

Mollier, Jean-Yves. *L'Argent et les lettres. Histoire du capitalisme d'édition, 1880–1920.* Paris: Fayard, 1988.

Mornet, Daniel. *Les Origines intellectuelles de la Révolution française, 1715–1787.* Paris: Armand Colin, 1967 (orig. ed. 1933).

Mortier, Roland. *L'Originalité. Une Nouvelle Catégorie esthétique au siècle des lumières.* Geneva: Droz, 1982.

Moulinas, René. "La Contrefaçon avignonnaise." In *Histoire de l'édition française,* edited by Roger Chartier and Henri-Jean Martin, 2:294–303. Paris: Promodis, 1984.

Necheles, Ruth F. *The Abbé Grégoire, 1787–1831*. Westport, Conn.: Greenwood Press, 1971.

Nesbitt, Molly. "What Was an Author?" *Yale French Studies* 73 (1987): 229–257.

Omont, Henri, ed. *Catalogue général des manuscrits de la Bibliothèque Nationale, ancien petit fond français*. 3 vols. Paris: Leroux, 1897–1902.

Ozouf, Mona. *La Fête révolutionnaire*. Paris: Gallimard, 1976.

Peignot, Gabriel. *Essai historique sur la liberté d'écrire chez les anciens et au moyen âge, et sur la liberté de la presse depuis le quinzième siècle*. Geneva: Slatkine Reprints, 1970 (orig. ed. Paris, 1832).

Perroud, Claude. "Roland et la presse subventionnée." *Révolution française* 62 (1912): 206–213, 315–332, 396–419.

Plongeron, Bernard. *Abbé Grégoire ou l'arche de la fraternité*. Paris: Letouzey & Ané, 1989.

Popkin, Jeremy D. "Journals: The New Face of the News." In *Revolution in Print: The Press in France, 1775–1800*, edited by Robert Darnton and Daniel Roche, 141–164. Berkeley and Los Angeles: University of California Press, 1989.

———. *Revolutionary News: The Press in France, 1789–1799*. Durham, N.C.: Duke University Press, 1990.

Post, Gaines, Kimon Giocarinis, and Richard Kay. "The Medieval Heritage of a Humanistic Ideal: 'Scientia Donum Dei Est, Unde Vendi Non Potest.'" *Traditio* 11 (1955): 195–234.

Queniart, Jean. "L'Anémie provinciale." In *Histoire de l'édition française*, edited by Roger Chartier and Henri-Jean Martin, 2:283–284. Paris: Promodis, 1984.

Quint, David. *Origin and Originality in Renaissance Literature*. New Haven: Yale University Press, 1983.

Radiguer, Louis. *Maîtres imprimeurs et ouvriers typographes*. Paris: Société Nouvelle de Librairie et d'Edition, 1903.

Rapheal, Paul. "Panckoucke et son programme de journal officiel en 1789." *Révolution française* 64 (1913): 216–219.

Renouard, Augustin-Charles. *Traité des droits d'auteur dans la littérature, les sciences et les beaux arts*. Paris: Renouard, 1838.

Rétat, Pierre. *Les Journaux de 1789. Bibliographie critique*. Paris: CNRS, 1989.

Robiquet, Paul. *Le Personnel municipal de Paris pendant la Révolution*. Paris: Jouaust, 1890.

Roche, Daniel. "Censorship and the Publishing Industry." In *Revolution in Print: The Press in France, 1775–1800*, edited by Robert Darnton and Daniel Roche, 3–26. Berkeley and Los Angeles: University of California Press, 1989.

———. *Le Siècle des lumières en province. Académies et académiciens provinciaux (1680–1789)*. Paris: Mouton, 1978.

Root-Bernstein, Michele Marie. *Boulevard Theater and Revolution in Eighteenth-Century Paris*. Ann Arbor: UMI Research Press, 1984.

Rose, Mark. "The Author as Proprietor: Donaldson v. Beckett and the Genealogy of Modern Authorship." *Representations* 23 (1988): 51–85.

Sewell, William, Jr. *Work and Revolution in France*. London: Cambridge University Press, 1980.

Shaw, E. P. *Problems and Policies of Malesherbes as Directeur de la Librairie in France*. Albany: State University of New York Press, 1966.

Söderhjelm, Alma. *Le Régime de la presse pendant la Révolution française*. 2 vols. Geneva: Slatkine Reprints, 1971 (orig. ed. Paris, 1900–1901).

Thuillier, Guy. *La Monnaie en France au début du XIXe siècle*. Geneva: Droz, 1983.

Thuriot, Charles. "Documents relatifs à l'exécution du décret du 5 février 1810." *Revue critique d'histoire et de littérature*, nos. 43–49 (1871): 339–372.

Tocqueville, Alexis de. *The Old Regime and the Revolution*. Translated by Stuart Gilbert. New York: Doubleday, 1955.

Todd, Christopher. *Voltaire's Disciple: Jean-François de LaHarpe*. London: Modern Humanities Research Library, 1972.

Tourneux, Maurice. *Bibliographie de l'histoire de Paris pendant la Révolution française*. 5 vols. Paris: Imprimerie Nouvelle, 1890–1894.

———. "Le Régime de la presse de 1789 à l'an VIII." *Révolution française* 25 (1893): 193–213.

Tucoo-Chala, Suzanne. *Charles-Joseph Panckoucke et la librairie française, 1736–1798*. Pau: Marrimpouey, 1977.

Vouillot, Bernard. "L'Imprimerie et la librairie à Paris sous le Consulat et l'Empire (1799–1814)." Thesis, Ecole des Chartres, 1979.

———. "La Révolution et l'Empire. Une Nouvelle Réglementation." In *Histoire de l'édition française*, edited by Roger Chartier and Henri-Jean Martin, 2:526–535. Paris: Promodis, 1984.

Waquet, Françoise. "La Bastille académique." In *La Carmagnole des muses. L'Homme de lettres et l'artiste dans la Révolution*, edited by Jean-Claude Bonnet, 19–36. Paris: Armand Colin, 1988.

Werdet, Edmond. *De la librairie française*. Paris: Dentu, 1860.

Woodmansee, Martha. "The Genius and the Copyright: Economic and Legal Conditions of the Emergence of the 'Author.'" *Eighteenth-Century Studies* 17, no. 4 (1984): 425–448.

INDEX